VERMONT
COLLEGE

LIBRARY
MONTPELIER, VERMONT

Please remember that this is a library book,
and that it belongs only temporarily to each
person who uses it. Be considerate. Do
not write in this, or any, library book.

Psychology
and
Educational
Practice

Edited by

Herbert J. Walberg

— and —

Geneva D. Haertel

McCutchan Publishing Corporation

P.O. Box 774, 2940 San Pablo Ave., Berkeley, CA 94702

ISBN 0-8211-0733-X
Library of Congress Catalog Card Number 97-70793

Printed in the United States of America

Preface

N. L. Gage

In recent writings (e.g. Gage, 1990, 1996), I have tried to make it clear that the behavioral sciences, including educational psychology, have yielded results whose nonobviousness, consistency, magnitude, practical significance, and affordable usability compare favorably with those of research in some important fields of medical and physical science. For example, teaching methods and practices identified as promising through psychological research—when communicated to teachers through teacher education programs—have been consistently effective in producing substantial improvements in student achievement and attitude in regular classrooms, using the regular curriculum, over a semester or school year.

Unfortunately, though, too much educational reform is based solely on the charisma and salesmanship of its advocates. Too little has been based on rigorous approaches comparable to those that have paid off in medicine and engineering. Yet, as the authors of this book agree, many techniques and programs derived from such approaches have had beneficial effects on students. Moreover, those educational practices are doable—they can be widely implemented.

But research results alone are not enough. The results can be useful only if they reach teachers, administrators, parent, and legislators in readily understandable ways. Well-written accounts of psychological findings and their educational implications can reduce the faddishness of much educational reform and increase the durability of genuine improvements. This book aims to provide such accounts.

Further, this book focuses on the central processes of education: teaching and learning. Better financing, governance, and organization of education provide the underpinning, of course, but it is what goes on in the classrooms and homes—the focus of this book—that makes the essential difference for students.

As people around the world look forward to the twenty-first century, they appreciate more than ever the importance of education. In the United States, everyone agrees that we need improvement. And that improvement should comprise such changes in teaching, learning, and teacher education as those that could flow from the ideas set forth in this book.

The authors of these chapters are well known and highly regarded as experts on what they have written about. They were asked, and have tried, to write for practical people. Teachers, administrators, and policymakers would do well to pay heed.

References

Gage, N.L. (1990). The obviousness of social and educational research results. *Educational Researcher 20* (1), 10-16.

Gage, N.L. (1996). Confronting counsels of despair for the behavioral sciences. *Educational Researcher 25* (3), 5-15, 22.

Contents

Introduction and Overview

Herbert J. Walberg and Geneva D. Haertel*

Beginning in the 1980s, *A Nation at Risk* (National Commission on Excellence in Education, 1983) and other reports focused educators' and policymakers' concerns about student learning. They increasingly recognized the importance of "human capital," that is, knowledge and skills related to economic development and quality of life in the growing "information economy."

Because of youth unemployment, declining industries, and international competition, leaders of other economically advanced nations also grew concerned about how well their students were doing in school. Beginning in 1987 under the auspices of the Paris-based Organization for Economic Cooperation and Development, Austria, France, Switzerland, and the United States held international invitational conferences to develop indicators of

* Geneva Haertel's work on this book was supported in part by the Temple University Center for Research in Human Development and Education (CRHDE). The opinions expressed do not necessarily reflect the position of the supporting agency and no official endorsement should be inferred.

educational progress that might be useful in determining the effects of educational policies.

By the 1990s, the fifty U.S. governors promulgated national learning goals. Congress added two goals to the six originally formulated by the governors, and required measurement of progress toward these goals. Many states and districts began serious efforts to meet these goals. They were joined by twenty-nine leading education organizations, including teachers' unions and principals' groups with more than three million members, which formed the Alliance for Curriculum Reform to find and promote effective practices. With a diminished threat of nuclear war, American policymakers can turn to domestic problems, and educational practice is high on the short list of priorities.

Educational Psychology's Role

Educational psychology derives problems for study from education and applies psychological insights to education practice to solve these problems. The field, however, hardly occupies the limelight of reform. Rather, policymakers have been concerned about finance and governance issues. Courts in more than twenty-five states, for example, have taken up questions of the amount and equality of funding of schools. Legislatures have experimented with educational governance, creating school governing councils and charter schools that allow greater levels of cooperative decision making by teachers and others within schools. Little evidence, however, indicates that organization, funding, and various school reforms have much effect on learning.

Though educational psychology, which recently celebrated its centennial (Walberg and Haertel, 1992), has many good answers on how learning can be increased, its role has been subordinated. Hundreds of studies have compared one kind of teaching with another, showed the effect of parents' encouragement of their children's academic progress at school, and illuminated other practical matters. On some topics, such as the effect of study time on the amount learned, more than one hundred studies have been made. In many instances, the results are quite consistent in showing what works and what doesn't.

Throughout its history, educational psychology has mediated between the disciplines of psychology and education. Such notable psychologists as William James, Edward L. Thorndike, and Jean Piaget devoted some of their energies to educational practices, human abilities, and other phenomena central to school learning. The discipline has been shaped by positivism, progressive education, the child-study movement, developmental psychology, behaviorism, instructional design, research on teaching and classroom practices, and the cognitive sciences. Analysis of education and psychology journals (Walberg and Haertel, 1992) reveals areas of intense research interest, including motivation, reading comprehension, inclusion of special children in regular education classes, parent involvement, and active instruction. Educational psychology is a field of broad variety and scope—which is represented in this book.

Purpose

During the past two decades, the knowledge base on school learning has begun to be formalized (Reynolds, 1989). Research syntheses and meta-analyses have been conducted on a variety of educational practices (Wang, Haertel, and Walberg, 1993; Lipsey and Wilson, 1993). Results of these syntheses indicate that what influences learning most are psychological practices and features that children are exposed to on a day-to-day basis, such as the home learning environment, instructional practices, teacher behaviors, and peer groups. One goal in developing this book was to exhibit the knowledge base of psychological findings that can inform efforts to improve learning. We felt such findings should be presented clearly and concisely. We hoped to assemble in one place the full range of educationally actionable findings from psychology in prose readable by citizens, policymakers, practitioners, students of education and psychology, and psychologists themselves.

Our idea for this book was not to invite textbook writers or those who write popular accounts. Rather we asked people we and others considered to be at the forefront of psychology as it relates to education, those who investigate frontiers of knowledge.

Though they ordinarily write long, complex, academic sentences for their colleagues, we asked them in our invitation letter for six thousand words of "lively, clear prose on topics to which they had devoted years if not decades of work."

We "hoped they might distill their many books and articles into chapters that would complement those of other distinguished authors." Our further hope was that "they would skim lightly over how the knowledge was obtained. Rather the focus would be on what the knowledge is and what... should be done about it." "Such chapters," we said, would be "written authoritatively (the chapter authors are surely authorities). Thus, five or so references at the end would be for further reading rather than to document points."

Though we had little idea how the proposed authors would respond to this unusual assignment, nearly every author we initially asked responded affirmatively. Perhaps it was our luck that universities are now trying harder than ever to help address practical problems and that the American Psychological Association and the American Psychological Society—psychology's leading professional organizations—have also made recent special efforts in this direction.

Organization

The main body of this book is organized into three parts: Students, Instruction, and Environments and Programs. Part One (Students) explains how students' abilities and motivation affect their learning progress and how schools in turn affect students. Part Two (Instruction) concerns how teachers and classroom organization affect student learning. Part Three (Environments and Programs) illustrates how noninstructional aspects of schools and special programs can constructively advance progress toward learning goals.

To whet the reader's appetite and provide an overview of each part, the next three sections identify several highlights of each chapter. Our Conclusion draws together themes that cut across the chapters in each section.

Part One: Students

This first section of the book focuses on abilities, developmental levels, and dispositions that students bring to learning situations. These are, using the vocabulary of an earlier era, "individual differences," or ways that students differ from each other in learning abilities, motives, preferences, and other psychological characteristics. Over decades of research, differences in students' abilities and other psychological characteristics were linked to school performance and workplace success. The first six chapters portray psychological differences among students and their impact on students' lives. The final two chapters address the assessment of students' knowledge and skills. They explore the consistency and soundness of our measures of student learning in the light of advances in psychology and measurement.

Intelligence: Putting Theory into Practice. Robert Sternberg proposes a tripartite theory of intelligence as the basis for diagnosis, instruction, and assessment of children. Analytic abilities include inferring, evaluating, and critiquing. Creative abilities are exemplified by discovering, innovating, and inventing. Practical abilities involve using, implementing, and applying. Students of all ages use these abilities in mastering the school subjects. Evidence confirms that analytic, creative, and practical abilities can serve as a basis for the differentiated diagnosis, instruction, and assessment of students. Sternberg's theory and its application illustrate how schools can better meet the needs of diverse students and suggest new instructional methods and foci for schooling.

Intelligence, Schools, and Society. Thomas Hatch and Mindy Kornhaber describe the use of culturally relevant, informal, project-based learning activities and formal classroom-based, instructional activities that reflect Howard Gardner's theory of multiple intelligences. Teachers can extend and enhance the curriculum to incorporate activities that represent a broad range of intelligences and tailor their teaching to build upon students' diverse abilities and cultural backgrounds. The authors conclude that school personnel must challenge traditional beliefs about intelligence and learning and attend to the strengths and needs of individual students.

The Advancement of Learning. Ann L. Brown argues that the learning theories that dominated psychology through the mid-1960s, in particular behaviorism, had limited ability to advance educational practice. Their emphases on external influences on learning, such as rewards, and the assumption that learning is simply the accretion of bonds among stimuli and responses, omitted the conscious intentions of learners. New insights, however, reveal that learners are active constructors of knowledge. In her chapter, Brown emphasizes the role of learning communities, composed of students and teachers, that foster the discourse structure, goals, and values of the community. She points out that much learning in academic settings requires active, strategic, and purposeful efforts on the part of self-motivated and self-aware students. Thus, developing children's learning strategies is a crucial activity in the educational process. In addition, classroom learning environments should be designed so that learners can develop at different rates and can employ different types of intelligences and abilities. Brown concludes that cognitive research, which describes how complex systems of knowledge are acquired, is a promising source for reforming educational practice.

Motivation and Cognition. Phyllis Blumenfeld and Ronald Marx show how motivation and cognition, or thought processes, can be enhanced to improve students' school learning. Ability and values influence students' choice, persistence, and intellectual engagement in learning. The cognitive strategies students use to complete academic tasks determine how deeply they will think about their work. The use of strategies that influence self-regulation, learning, and volition distinguish successful from unsuccessful learners. Blumenfeld and Marx describe the complex relationship between motivation and cognitive strategies and the impact of the learning environment upon strategy use.

Developmental Psychology. Martin Ford explains the basic nature of development in terms of its biological, motivational, cognitive, social, and economic foundations. For each foundation, he highlights the key patterns, processes, and conditions that educators must address when designing developmentally facilitative environments. Focusing on the whole child, Ford provides developmentally based rationales for the way early childhood and middle and secondary education are conducted. He calls for effective educational practices and policies that are informed by knowledge of diversity and individuality and the dynamic and organized nature of human development.

Moral Development and Character Formation. Larry Nucci's chapter identifies contributions from developmental psychology to meaningful moral and character education. Morality and social convention are distinct conceptual systems, each of which must be given its due in designing education programs. Nucci shows that the moral self is being formed by individuals on an ongoing basis and is not simply the result of inculcating habits. Nucci draws implications for school and classroom practices that foster moral development and character formation.

Student Performance Portfolios. Lauren Resnick's chapter focuses on performance assessments in U.S. schools and the issues that accompany their use. She describes the New Standards Project's system to train scorers to judge students' performances. She argues that new forms of assessment break down the distinction between learning and measurement. The information gathered using performance assessments is a natural byproduct of a meaningful learning activity and represents what students can do in real-life situations. Resnick advises that the measurement of what students know should not encourage narrowly focused instruction on specific assessment items.

Assessing Student Learning. Robert Mislevy traces the evolution of educational assessment from the purposes, constraints, and beliefs about learning and assessment that were current in the 1930s to recent developments. He points to advances in statistical methods and technology as means of more effectively meeting the familiar purposes of assessment. Mislevy argues that new understandings about the nature of knowledge and learning have created additional purposes for assessment that are best met by the new forms of assessment.

Part Two: Instruction

The chapters in this section summarize research on what teachers and other educators do that directly affects students' learning. Unlike the first section that focuses on what students bring to the learning situation, and unlike the final section that describes programs and less tangible aspects of the learning environment such as school culture, this section addresses teachers, teaching, and technologies that educators employ.

Learning Influences. In this chapter, Margaret Wang, Geneva Haertel, and Herb Walberg set the stage for this section by summarizing many studies of factors within and outside classrooms that affect learning. Though they include research on student aptitude, much of the research concerns classroom instruction that shows far larger influences on learning than do the sociological and organizational features of schools. A plot of twenty-eight influences, moreover, shows that alterable psychological practices have more powerful influences than do the demographics, state-level educational policies, and decision making that have preoccupied many policymakers—at the expense of concentrating effort on the practices that yield the biggest effects.

Effective Teaching. Aiming at research-driven practice, Jere Brophy summarizes three decades of research on the core topic of effective teaching. He emphasizes efficient, active teaching of academic content in a conducive classroom environment. Reflecting, however, new insights of cognitive psychology (treated in the first section of this book), he points to the value of students actively constructing their own knowledge by linking new ideas to their pre-existing knowledge and beliefs—a process facilitated by interactive discourse among students and teachers. He cautions us, however, on the paucity of research on student-centered learning, the sometimes unfounded claims for its efficacy, and the need for cautious experimentation and evaluation.

Teaching in the Content Areas. Suzanne Wilson brings insights about teaching required for particular subjects. She started her teaching career with the common view that content is that which is in textbooks and that teaching is founded on a set of generic tools of instruction. Now, however, she believes that content is incompletely represented in textbooks alone, that each subject presents unique teaching challenges, and that their content and pedagogy are hardly separable. She illustrates these points by examples of curriculum frameworks that set forth prescriptions not only for content but also for teaching practices shown by examples of history, mathematics, reading, science, and social science.

Classroom Management. Enlarging on the traditional definition of classroom management as the control of deviant student behavior, Carolyn Evertson views it as constructive activity aside from teaching itself. For the purposes of this section, management may be considered the most productive organizational framework and set of rules of the classroom for teaching and learning to take place. As Evertson explains, readying the classroom, getting a good start for the school year, planning rules and procedures, developing systems of student accountability, prescribing student behavior, and organizing instruction are vital features of classroom management. Evertson concludes with six policies for formulating such practices.

Learning and Teaching with Educational Technologies. Roy Pea considers research on learning effects of educational technologies. A number of findings are truly impressive, but it remains difficult to install technologies in classrooms because of idiosyncratic personal, social, and institutional factors. In particular, the teacher's role appears decisive. Given such difficulties, Pea offers the metaphor of the School Depot, which would provide needed equipment, expertise, and collegueship for implementing a variety of new technologies. Teachers would arrive (possibly via the Internet) with problems, but leave with well-founded visions, equipment recommendations, and strategies to solve their problems. Pea explains seven steps to bring about this innovation.

Teacher Beliefs. Greta Morine-Dershimer and Stephanie Corrigan corroborate Pea's idea that the teacher is central in improving learning. Their case studies show how teachers willingly changed their work to accommodate a new curriculum policy, but that their changes were limited and shaped by their prior educational beliefs, knowledge, and experiences—which may have originated in their own school experiences and been reinforced by institutional connections and senior colleagues. Morine-Dershimer and Corrigan describe several techniques to foster new views of teaching including changing images, confronting contradictions, and case studies. To make these techniques successful, as they make clear, requires time, dialogue, practice, and support.

Part Three: Environments and Programs

Much research has been conducted on effective learning environments, including the home; classroom; schoolwide culture; and school, district, and federal programs. Extending beyond instruction, the six chapters in this section identify those features of environments and programs that are related to students' learning outcomes. Among the features examined are organizational arrangements, student selection for programs, and teacher preparation.

Classroom Environments. Barry Fraser reviews environment assessments as a means of improving classroom learning. He describes advances in conceptualizing, assessing, and researching the classroom environment using paper and pencil measures of students' impressions. Features of the learning environment are consistently and strongly related to student learning and attitudes toward their teachers, classroom life, and schoolwork. A case study demonstrates that teachers can improve their classroom climate by using these assessments.

School Cultures. Avi Kaplan and Martin Maehr's chapter shows that school culture is linked to student motivation and should be a cornerstone of school reform. Two contrasting goals for schooling are identified: the first is task oriented and stresses student learning and academic growth; the second is ability oriented and emphasizes competition, with some students winning and others losing. Task goals are related to more positive attitudes toward learning and schooling, while ability goals are related to disruptive behavior, alienation, and lower self-esteem. Kaplan and Maehr conclude that changes in school culture increase student motivation and love of learning.

Home Environments for Learning. Herb Walberg and Susan Paik review research on the relationship of home environments to school achievement. Programs that promote academically stimulating conditions in homes are positively associated with learning outcomes. Home reinforcement of schoolwork has a strong effect on learning, and graded homework has three times the effect of socioeconomic status. More comprehensive home-enrichment activities are likely to increase children's achievement given the amount of time that children are under the direct or indirect influence of parents during the first eighteen years of life.

Education of Gifted Students. Gary Davis describes the status of gifted education. Program trends are reviewed that affect the quality of education for gifted students, including "detracking," cooperative learning, and funding for gifted programs. He describes difficulties in identifying gifted students and successful strategies for locating them. Current educational practices for serving gifted students are addressed, including acceleration and enrichment, grouping, program models and rigorous, nontrivial curricula that develop high-level thinking. Davis describes the counseling needs of the gifted and common social and psychological difficulties they experience. The chapter closes with a discussion of the legal and ethical problems that confront the gifted; for example, early admission to school, provision of appropriate instruction, and the social balance in gifted classes.

Linguistically Diverse Students. Tomás Galguera and Kenji Hakuta focus on the educational needs of students with limited English proficiency (L.E.P.). In their view, L.E.P. programs must take into account sources that contribute to students' diversity, including their economic, cultural, and educational backgrounds. They address how instruction is made accessible to these students including current assessment practices to select and evaluate students, instructional methods, bilingual and English as a Second Language programs, and complex instruction to accommodate academic heterogeneity. Galguera and Hakuta argue for an inclusive, rather than a categorical approach in creating effective educational programs. Thus, responding to linguistic diversity becomes a responsibility of not just specialists, but all teachers.

Categorical Programs. Maynard Reynolds, Margaret Wang, and Herbert Walberg focus on children at the margins of the school population who require greater-than-usual instructional support and, traditionally, have been placed in categorical programs. While some of these students have severe limitations, such as blindness or profound retardation, others have milder disabilities, such as learning disabled or poverty. The authors argue that the use of some categories, such as "mentally retarded," are arbitrary and stigmatize students. Research suggests advantages for serving exceptional students in regular classes rather than in separate classrooms.

Thus, the chapters in the three main parts of this book analyze a considerable range of educational problems and propose a set of practical solutions. The Conclusion identifies some of the major themes that extend across the chapters.

References

Lipsey, M. W., and Wilson, D. B. (1993). The efficacy of psychological, educational, and behavioral treatment: Confirmation from meta-analysis. *American Psychologist 48*(12), 1181–1209.

Reynolds, M. C. (1989). *Knowledge base for the beginning teacher.* London: Pergamon Press.

Walberg, H. J. (1990). Educational psychology: Core journals, research fronts, and highly cited papers. *Current Contents 22*(13), 5–14.

Walberg, H. J., and Haertel, G. D. (1992). Educational psychology's first century. *Journal of Educational Psychology 84*(1), 1–14.

Wang, M. C.; Haertel, G. D.; and Walberg, H. J. (1993). Toward a knowledge base for school learning. *Review of Educational Research 63*(3), 249–294.

Part I

Students

Chapter 1

Intelligence: Putting Theory into Practice

Robert J. Sternberg

The diagnosis of children's abilities and the instruction and assessment of those children should be of a piece. Common sense suggests why: Only in this way can the outcomes of an educational program fulfill the program's original promise.

Suppose, for example, that children's abilities are diagnosed by using a broad testing procedure, taking into account, say, memory, analytic, creative, and other abilities. The children are then placed in a program whose curriculum primarily benefits excellent memory-learners, and the assessment matches the curriculum.

Preparation of this chapter was supported under the Javits Act Program (grant No. R206R00001 and grant No. R206R50001) as administered by the Office of Educational Research and Improvement, U.S. Department of Education. Grantees undertaking such projects are encouraged to express freely their professional judgment. This chapter, therefore, does not necessarily represent the positions or policies of the government, and no official endorsement should be inferred.

Although creative students were diagnosed as intelligent, their performance in the program described is likely to be undistinguished or even unsatisfactory. The creative students, as well as their teacher, are likely to conclude that the students were misplaced, and that they are not truly able at all. The first conclusion is correct, but the second is not. In reality, the children were set up for failure by instruction and assessment that did not match their abilities.

The same general principle applies to any mismatching of diagnosis, instruction, and assessment. Unless all three match, there is a good chance that children who were identified as able will appear unmotivated or even stupid, because they do not perform at the level expected. The reason, of course, is that the children genuinely are intelligent, but not in the ways valued in the program of instruction and assessment of achievement.

There are numerous theories of abilities that could serve as the basis for a unified model of diagnosis, instruction, and assessment of children. For example, the theory most traditionally relied on is one of intelligence as a single thing, as measured by IQ. This theory holds that there is a general ability (as well as specific abilities of lesser interest), and students higher in this ability will do better in school (Spearman, 1927). In an alternative theory, Thurstone (1938) proposes seven abilities—verbal comprehension, verbal fluency, numerical ability, spatial ability, perceptual speed, memory, and reasoning. Yet another theory proposes seven multiple intelligences (Gardner, 1983)—linguistic, logical-mathematical, spatial, bodily-kinesthetic, musical, interpersonal, and intrapersonal. Guilford's (1967) model proposes as many as 120 abilities. I will focus in this chapter on my own theory—the triarchic theory of human intelligence—and a construct validation of the usefulness of the theory for diagnosis, instruction, and assessment (Sternberg, 1985, 1988).

The Triarchic Theory of Human Intelligence

The triarchic theory distinguishes among three kinds of intellectual abilities: analytic, creative, and practical. Individuals talented in these different ways excel in different activities, and in answering questions instigated by different kinds of prompts. In a nutshell, the analytically gifted are strong in analyzing, evaluating, and critiquing; the creatively gifted, in discovering, creating, and inventing; and the practically gifted, in using, implementing, and applying.

A person might be talented in none, one, two, or three of these ways. Indeed, the theory specifies that the same mental processes, such as making inferences or applying what one has learned, are involved in all three aspects of intelligence. What differs is the levels of experience (how novel is the task?) and the contexts (how real-worldly is the task?) to which the processes are applied, and within each of the three aspects of intelligence, the form of mental representation.

Thus, analytic thinking typically involves application of the components to abstract and often relatively familiar problems; creative thinking involves application of the components to relatively novel problems; and practical thinking involves application of the information-processing components to concrete and relatively familiar everyday kinds of problems. Although people may be strong in varying numbers of these aspects of intelligence, past data we have collected suggest null to moderate correlations among an individual's abilities in these aspects of intelligence, depending on the form and context of measurement.

It is important to note that strength in all three of these aspects of intelligence is not viewed as corresponding to a high level of psychometric "g," or general ability, of the kind touted by psychologists from Spearman (1927) to Herrnstein and Murray (1994) as the basis of intelligence. Intelligence tests of the kinds used by these investigators measure somewhat varied aspects of analytical ability, but hardly consider creative and practical abilities, which the triarchic theory does.

The three kinds of thinking can be applied in any subject-matter area at any level of instruction. In English, students can compare and contrast two literary characters (analytic), write a short story (creative), or discuss how the personal problems of a literary character apply to their own lives (practical). In history, students can analyze how events led to a war (analytic), imagine what they would do if they were in the place of a great historical figure (creative), or discuss the relevance of historical events for the present (practical). In math, students can solve word problems (analytic), learn or even create new systems of numeration (creative), or apply math to their daily lives, as in budgeting (practical). In science, students can analyze experimental results (analytic), design their own experiments (creative), or apply what they have learned in science to improving the environment (practical). In art, students can compare the styles of two artists (analytic), create an artistic composition of their own choosing (creative), or show how art in advertisements influences people (practical). In physical education, students can analyze another team's strategies (analytic), decide on the best strategies for their own team (creative), or work on a method for self-improvement (practical).

Analytic, creative, and practical thinking are needed in all areas of the curriculum, and, indeed, in all walks of life. According to the triarchic theory, what differs across the subject-matter areas is not the mental processes involved, but rather the mental contents (e.g., words or numbers) and representations used.

Potentially, there are both advantages and disadvantages to theory-based identification, instruction, and assessment. We see as the main advantages (a) bringing theory into practice, (b) suggesting new methods and foci of schooling, (c) meeting psychological needs of students, (d) forging closer ties between researchers and educators in the schools, (e) improving the public image of researchers by their having something concrete to offer, and (f) providing a means for testing theories. Potential disadvantages would be (a) having a theory that is wrong, (b) having a theory that is incomplete with respect to the purposes for which it is used, (c) having a theory that does not apply to the purposes for which it is being used, (d) implementing the theory improperly, (e) focusing on the theory rather than on students, (f) becoming rigid in the application of the theory. The point, of course, is that theory-based work, like any other work, must be done with care so that the advantages will clearly outweigh the disadvantages. A careful construct validation can help bring about this outcome.

The Triarchic Theory as a Model of Diagnosis, Instruction, and Assessment

A construct validation of the triarchic theory as a model for diagnosis, instruction, and assessment would ideally be done across the curriculum, in many subject-matter areas. As a matter of practicality, however, construct validations are expensive and time-consuming, and we have to start somewhere. We started with a subject matter with which we are familiar, that we believe is important, and that we deeply care about—psychology (Sternberg and Clinkenbeard, 1995; Sternberg, Ferrari, Clinkenbeard, and Grigorenko, 1996). Here I report the results of a construct validation that we did in the summer of 1993 with a sample of high school students.

The basic question we addressed is whether the realization of compatibility in diagnosis, instruction, and assessment would enhance learning and performance outcomes. Cronbach and Snow's (1977) review of literature on aptitude-treatment interactions might suggest to some that hope for such compatability is in vain—that the only interactions that will be obtained, if indeed any are obtained, will be with general ability. However, the investigators whose work is summarized by Cronbach and Snow did not generally consider the creative and practical abilities defined by the triarchic theory. I propose that in the 1990s we have reached a higher level of theoretical and methodological sophistication than we had reached in the 1960s and 1970s, when most of the studies reviewed by Cronbach and Snow were done.

Thus, our design will call for our measuring analytical, creative, and practical abilities as the context of diagnosis; teaching to each of these three abilities as the context of instruction; and evaluating achievement in terms of these three abilities as the context of assessment. In particular, we predict that students will learn and perform better if the instruction and assessment they receive are at least partially matched to their pattern of abilities than if they are mismatched.

In practice, diagnosis, instruction, and assessment are often done with no theoretical model at all. More often, there is a model, but it is applied only to one or two of the three aspects. When a model is applied only to diagnosis, we end up with tracking. When it is applied only to instruction, we end up with theory-based instruction that may or may not meet students' needs, and that is not followed through in assessment. When we apply a model only to assessment of achievement, we end up with assessments that may not correspond to what was taught. When we apply a model to diagnosis and instruction, students may learn well, but their good learning is not reflected in the assessments of their achievement. If we apply a model only to diagnosis and assessment, it leaves us with instruction that may be a poor fit to the testing procedures. And applying a model only to instruction and assessment may result in use of a model that does not adequately reflect students' patterns of abilities. Ideally, a theoretical model should be applied to all three components—diagnosis, instruction, and assessment.

How the Construct Validation Was Done

Diagnosis. We used a modified research form of the *Sternberg Triarchic Abilities Test (STAT)* to diagnose the high school students. Our goal was to get a representation of different patterns of abilities, using a level of the *STAT* appropriate for advanced high school students and for college students. We sought to measure the three aspects of ability—analytic, creative, and practical—in four content domains—verbal, quantitative, figural, and performance (essay). This use of a variety of content domains would ensure that students who worked well in one particular form of representation but not another would be given the chance to show their capabilities.

The *STAT* included nine multiple-choice subtests, each consisting of two sample items and four test items, for a total of thirty-six test items. Because we were interested in distinguishing only two categories—participants and nonparticipants in our study—a relatively small number of test items was deemed acceptable. The nine subtests were:

1. *Analytic-verbal*: Figuring out meanings of neologisms (artificial words) from natural contexts. Students would see a novel word embedded in a paragraph, and would have to infer its meaning from the context.

2. *Analytic-quantitative*: Number series. Students were asked what number should come next in a series of numbers.
3. *Analytic-figural*: Matrices. Students saw a figural matrix with the lower-right entry missing. They were to choose which option fit into the missing space.
4. *Practical-verbal*: Everyday reasoning. Students were presented with a set of everyday problems in the lives of adolescents (who might be themselves or others), and were asked to solve the problems (e.g., what to do about a friend who seems to have a substance-abuse problem).
5. *Practical-quantitative*: Everyday math. Students were presented with scenarios requiring the use of math in everyday life (e.g., buying tickets for a ballgame or making chocolate chip cookies), and were to solve math problems based on the scenarios.
6. *Practical-figural*: Route planning. Students were presented with a map of an area (e.g., an entertainment park), and were asked to answer questions about navigating effectively through the area depicted by the map.
7. *Creative-verbal*: Novel analogies. Students were presented with verbal analogies preceded by counterfactual premises (e.g., money falls off trees). They were to solve the analogies as though the counterfactual premises were true.
8. *Creative-quantitative*: Novel number operations. Students were presented with rules for novel number operations, for example, *flix*, which involve numerical manipulations that differed as a function of whether the first of two operands was greater than, equal to, or less than the second. Students used the novel number operations to solve math problems.
9. *Creative-figural*: In each item, students were presented first with a figural series that involved one or more transformations; they then had to apply the rule of the series to a new figure with a different appearance, and complete the new series.

The students were also given three essay items, one each stressing analytical, creative, and practical thinking. The analytical problem required students to analyze the advantages and disadvantages of having police or security guards in a school building. The creative problem required students to describe how they would reform their school system to produce an ideal one. The practical problem required students to specify a problem in their life, and to state three practical solutions for solving it.

Preliminary validation of the *STAT* (Sternberg and Clinkenbeard, 1995) has shown it to be appropriate for the intended purpose, and related to other tests. For example, we have found substantial correlations (all significant unless otherwise noted) between the *STAT* and the *Watson-Glaser Critical Thinking Appraisal* (.50 for analytic, .53 for creative, .32 for practical), the *Concept Mastery Test* (.49 for analytic, .43 for creative, .21 for practical—nonsignificant), the *Cattell Culture-Fair Test of g* (.50 analytic, .55 for creative, .36 for practical), and a homemade test of creative-insight problems (.47 for analytic, .59 for creative, .21 for practical).

Instruction. Students were given an intensive, four-week Advanced Placement psychology course. The course met five days a week from 9 A.M. to 5 P.M., with breaks and time for lunch. The course consisted of three main components—text, lecture, and afternoon activity. The first two were common to all groups, whereas the last constituted the treatment, and diverged across groups.

The first component was the text, which was a preliminary version of Sternberg, *In Search of the Human Mind* (1995). It covered an entire introductory psychology course, including the topics of the nature of psychology, history and systems, psychobiology, sensation, perception, consciousness, learning, memory, language, thinking and creativity, intelligence, cognitive development, social development, social psychology of the individual, social psychology of the group, motivation and emotion, personality, psychopathology, psychotherapy, and health psychology.

The second component was the lecture series. Mornings were spent in lecture, which was given by an Associate Professor of Psychology at Yale with considerable experience teaching the introductory course. Attendance at lectures was compulsory.

The third component was the afternoon sections, of which there were four types: memory emphasis (traditional), analytic emphasis, creative emphasis, and practical emphasis. Students were randomly assigned to sections with the constraint that there be comparable numbers of each classification of students (by ability patterns) in each instructional group. Thus, some students were placed in a section that matched their ability pattern, others in a section that mismatched it. Although an ideal psychology course (or any other course) would consist of a balance of these four kinds of activities, instructional treatments were varied for this experiment.

The memory section consisted of discussions emphasizing issues such as "Who said?"; "Summarize . . ."; "Who did?"; "When did?"; "What did?"; "How did?"; "Repeat back . . ."; and "Describe. . . ." The analytical section consisted of discussions emphasizing issues such as "Compare and contrast . . ."; "Evaluate . . ."; "Critique . . ."; "Say why in your judgment . . ."; "Explain why . . ."; "Explain what caused . . ."; and "Evaluate what is assumed by. . . ." The creative section consisted of discussion emphasizing issues such as "Create . . ."; "Invent . . ."; "Imagine what you would do if you were . . ."; "Imagine . . ."; "Design . . ."; "Show how you would . . .," "Suppose that . . .," and "Say what would happen if. . . ." The practical section consisted of discussions emphasizing issues such as "Apply . . ."; "Show how you can use . . ."; "Implement . . ."; "Utilize . . ."; and "Demonstrate how in the real world. . . ."

For example, in the memory section, students might be asked to recount the details of Crick's theory of dreaming. In the analytical section, students might be asked to compare Freud's theory of dreaming to Crick's. In the creative section, students might be asked to design an experiment to test a theory of dreaming. And in the practical section, students might be asked to describe the implications of Freud's theory of dreaming for their lives. The same methods could be applied equally well to any subject-matter area (see Sternberg, 1994).

Assessments. All students received the same assessments of their mastery of the course. The assessments were of four kinds: homework assignments (two), a midterm examination, a final examination, and an independent project. Each of the assessments involved memory use as well as analytic, creative, and practical thinking. For example, one homework assignment asked students to (a) compare and contrast two theories of depression (analytic), (b) present their own theory of depression (creative), and (c) show how their theory of depression could be applied to understand and help people who are suffering from depression (practical). The midterm consisted of a multiple-choice portion measuring primarily recall, and six essays: two analytic, two creative, and two practical. Like the midterm, the final consisted of multiple-choice and essay sections, with a longer multiple-choice section than the midterm and more essays than the midterm (three per type rather than two). The independent project required students to come up with their own investigation and to pursue it analytically, creatively, and practically.

The Participants

The Yale Summer Psychology Program (YSSP) was widely advertised through brochures and advertisements, and schools were welcome to submit nominations of students to us. We then sent the STAT to those schools who sent us nominations so that they could administer the test to the nominated students. Tests were sent around the United States and to some other countries.

We identified five groups of students: high analytic, high creative, high practical, high balanced, and low balanced. Subjects were identified as "high" in an aspect of ability on the basis of their strongest showing. We also identified a "balanced" high group that showed generally high scores overall, but no one particularly high score, as well as a low control group with students who did not reach the cutoffs for selection for our program. For students to be identified as "high" in analytic, creative, or practical ability, their total score for that ability was required to be at least a half standard deviation above their own total score for each of the other two abilities measured by the test (e.g., analytic higher than creative or practical). For students to be classified as balanced, they had to score above the group average for all three abilities; students who scored at or below the group average for all three abilities were classified as being in the low group. Note that the labels "high" and "low" are for purposes of the study; our main concern was with patterns of abilities.

A total of 225 high school students participated originally, but two dropouts left us with 223 students (164 females and 59 males). Of these students, 3 were entering grade nine, 26 entering grade ten, 85 entering grade eleven, and 109 entering grade twelve. The students were fairly widely distributed ethnically (according to their own classifications): 60 percent were European American; 11 percent, African American; 6 percent, Hispanic American; 17 percent, American who did not classify themselves in any of these categories; 4 percent, European African; and 2 percent, African. All African students were from South Africa. Of all students, some were students who were able to pay and thus serve as bases for resources to pay for scholarship students. A total of 199 students were part of the actual design. The fairly diverse ethnic composition of the groups was in part a reflection of the breadth of the diagnostic procedure. We had no special quotas or diagnostic procedures for any one group. The students classified as high in analytic ability were those who were most likely to have been previously identified as gifted by conventional ability tests.

Psychometric Properties of the Identification and Assessment Instruments

Identification. A first question that must be addressed is whether the identification procedure (i.e., the *STAT*) was psychometrically sound, and thus suitable for identifying the various groups that participated in the study.

The KR-20 internal-consistency reliabilities of the identification instruments were computed for the multiple-choice items. These reliabilities assess whether single tests are homogeneous in what they measure. These reliabilities were .63 for the analytic items, .62 for the creative items, and .48 for the practical items. Given the three different kinds of contents and hence of mental representations (verbal, quantitative, figural), very high levels of internal consistency would not be expected. Given that our only requirement was to separate students into groups, we viewed these internal-consistency reliabilities as satisfactory.

Reliabilities for the essay portions of the *STAT* were measured by assessing interrater reliabilities for two raters. The reliabilities were .69 for the analytic essay, .58 for the creative essay, and .68 for the practical essay. Again, we deemed these reliabilities satisfactory for our purposes.

We assessed the intercorrelations of the various subtests of the *STAT*, for multiple-choice and essay portions separately as well as combined. The overall correlations ranged from .38 to .49, which we thought showed that the three aspects of abilities are correlated, although only moderately. Of course, the multiple-choice items were more highly correlated, although part of this correlation can almost certainly be attributed to shared method rather than construct variance.

Assessment of Achievement. We also investigated the basic psychometric properties of the assessments of achievement in the course.

The interrater reliabilities for the four raters used the quality ratings of assignments (analytical quality, creative quality, practical quality) for each of the assignments, final project, and examinations (midterm and final, which were parallel in form). The median reliabilities were .87 for the analytical tasks, .80 for the creative tasks, and .88 for the practical tasks. These reliabilities are good, and suggest that it is possible to achieve reliability in the assessment of creative and especially practical as well as the more conventional analytic measures of achievement.

We examined the intercorrelations of the analytic, creative, and practical tasks for the assignments, final project, and exams. These correlations were generally in the .6 to .8 range, and suggest a good deal of common variation across measurements.

Finally, and perhaps most interestingly, we looked at the pattern of correlations between *STAT* analytic, creative, and practical scores, and analytic, creative, and practical scores on the assessments of achievement on the assignments, final project, and examinations. One would expect the highest correlations to be the on-diagonal ones, where the same abilities coincide (matching of abilities diagnosed by *STAT* with abilities assessed through evaluations of achievement). At the same time, because the triarchic theory specifies that the same mental processes are involved in all three kinds of abilities, and because the assessments did not share the verbal, quantitative, figural, and essay configuration of the *STAT*, one would not expect only on-diagonal correlations to be significant. The results were generally along the lines predicted, especially for the exams.

Testing the Hypothesis of Compatibility

Finally, we turn to the most important analyses of all, namely, those testing the original hypothesis that compatibility in identified ability pattern, instruction, and assessment would lead to better performance than incompatibility.

We tested this hypothesis via contrast analysis. A number of different contrasts could be used that, in general, would be consistent with this hypothesis. We present here the results for a contrast analysis. We used contrast weights of 2 for ability match in people identified as strong in a particular area; 1 for ability mismatch in people identified as strong in a particular area; 3 for balanced people, regardless of section, because these students could draw on their generally high abilities in any section and could combine them in order to perform at a high level in any such section; and -7 for those not identified as strong in any of the abilities assessed by the *STAT*. Small differences in contrast weights (e.g., 2 for balanced gifted and -6 for nongifted) resulted in essentially the same results.

The contrast analyses yielded highly significant results for each of the analytic, creative, and practical tasks. In other words, levels and patterns of results on the *STAT* were predictive of performance in the Advanced Placement psychology course. The results suggest the utility of the *STAT* for predicting differentiated performance in the course according to the triarchic model. Other forms of data analysis (e.g., odds-ratio analysis) supported the same conclusion.

Conclusion

We believe that the results of this study suggest the utility of broadening our procedures for the diagnosis, instruction, and assessment of children in school. In particular, the results suggest the utility of a theory-based differentiation of abilities, namely, along the lines of analytic, creative, and practical ones (Sternberg, 1985). Of course, other theories of intelligence might have served equally well as a basis for differentiated treatments. But to us it is more apparent how the triarchic model could be applied in differentiation across subject-matter areas than other theories. For example, it is not as clear to us how the theory of multiple intelligences (Gardner, 1983) would be applied to identification, instruction, and assessment in a high school Advanced Placement psychology course. This is not to say that intelligences such as the musical or the bodily-kinesthetic could not be injected into the curriculum; but we think their relevance is less obvious.

We are cognizant of the large literature that has failed to show substantial aptitude-treatment interactions (ATIs) (Cronbach and Snow, 1977). We have obtained such interactions via contrast analysis, and believe that our use of a single, targeted, specific, and relevant theory of intelligence for all parts of the study—identification, instruction, and assessment—may have contributed to our results.

At the same time, we are cognizant of the limitations of this single study. Further work will be needed for other levels of schooling, other subject-matter areas, and other course implementations. Moreover, the results, although supportive of our model, were certainly far from perfect.

Education has at times suffered from a lack of theory, and when there has been theory, connection between such theory and actual programs has been weak. We hope that our study has shown a possible way in which one theory, the triarchic one, can be applied to diagnosis of abilities, instruction, and assessment.

References

Cronbach, L. J., and Snow, R. E. (1977). *Aptitudes and instructional methods.* New York: Irvington.

Gardner, H. (1983). *Frames of mind.* New York: Basic Books.

Guilford, J. P. (1967). *The nature of intelligence.* New York: McGraw-Hill.

Herrnstein, R., and Murray, C. (1994). *The bell curve.* New York: Free Press.

Spearman, C. (1927). *The abilities of man.* New York: Macmillan.

Sternberg, R. J. (1985). *Beyond IQ.* New York: Cambridge University Press.

Sternberg, R. J. (1986). *Intelligence applied.* Orlando: Harcourt Brace College Publishers.

Sternberg, R. J. (1988). *The triarchic mind.* New York: Viking-Penguin.

Sternberg, R. J. (1994). Diversifying instruction and assessment. *The Educational Forum, 59* (1), 47–53.

Sternberg, R. J. (1995). *In search of the human mind.* Orlando: Harcourt Brace College Publishers.

Sternberg, R. J., and Clinkenbeard, P. (1995). A triarchic view of identifying, teaching, and assessing gifted children. *Roeper Review, 17,* 255–260.

Sternberg, R. J.; Ferrari, M.; Clinkenbeard, P.; and Grigorenko, E. (1996). A triarchic model for identifying, instructing, and assessing gifted children. *Gifted Child Quarterly, 40,* 129–137.

Thurstone, L. L. (1938). *Primary mental abilities.* Chicago: University of Chicago Press.

Chapter 2

Intelligence, Schools, and Society

Thomas Hatch
and
Mindy Kornhaber

Several years ago, one of us observed the following scene in a kindergarten:

> A number of children are working on their math books at the center table. Rosie and Jenny have kindergarten math books. Maggie, Jane, Kenny and Terry all have first-grade math books. Maggie and Terry talk about how far they are in their books. Jenny complains that she is not very far. She looks up from her book, and points at Maggie's first-grade book. "Anybody that has this kind of book has real homework and that means that all the people that has that kind are smarter than me."

Some of the work described in this chapter was supported by grants from the MacArthur Foundation, the Pew Charitable Trusts, and the Spencer Foundation. The conclusions are solely those of the authors.

I'm a little surprised. "What makes it the real kind of homework?" I wonder.

"Cause it has plus."

"Oh, 'cause it has plus. Are you sure you don't have any plus in yours?" I ask, hoping to defeat her logic.

Jenny flips through her book and demonstrates that she does not.

Later, when Maggie and Kenny are sitting at the snack table, they continue talking about their math books. Maggie reports that Jenny "has a problem" because she doesn't have "any kind of homework stuff." The next day I learn that Rosie, who was listening to the proceedings all day long, went home to tell her mother that she had been given one of the "easy math books" because she is not smart.

Rosie's conclusion reflects her belief that she is the problem in this situation. She does not have a first-grade math book because she is not intelligent enough to have one. If she were only smarter, she would have received a first-grade math book. Rosie's is a common reaction rooted in basic beliefs about intelligence and its development. These beliefs are held not only by young students but also by many adults in our society.

In a traditional, Western view, intelligence is seen as a single, general ability that is reflected in performance in all manner of tasks. Paper-and-pencil exercises involving linguistic and logical-mathematical ability are presumed to be adequate measures of this general capacity. Further, a person's level of intelligence is seen as being determined largely by genetic factors and fixed for life. Thus, how one performs on IQ tests and other linguistic and mathematical exercises at a young age is assumed to predict how one will perform as an adult. From this standpoint, it makes sense for schools to concentrate on teaching basic skills in basic subjects, to assess educational potential and progress by measuring performance on standardized multiple-choice tests, and to sort students into particular tracks with relatively little movement of students from one track to another throughout the students' career. In this view, if Rosie's conclusion is correct, her future does not look so bright. She is likely to be consigned forever to a slower track and is unlikely to achieve the same results as her classmates who toted first-grade math books.

Fortunately for Rosie, there are other possibilities. One theory that offers a different interpretation of Rosie's situation is the theory of multiple intelligence (MI) put forward by Howard Gardner (Gardner, 1983). While traditional theorists often argue that intelligence is a capacity for abstract problem-solving measurable by performances on paper-and-pencil tests, Gardner argues that "an intelligence" is an ability that allows people "to solve problems, or create products, that are valued in one or more cultures." The theory argues that all normal individuals possess seven relatively autonomous problem-solving abilities or "intelligences": linguistic and logical-mathematical (the two traditionally emphasized in school), as well as musical, spatial, bodily-kinesthetic, interpersonal, and intrapersonal.[1] Each individual is distinguished by a different profile of relative strengths and weaknesses among the intelligences; and individuals draw on combinations of intelligences depending on their own unique profiles and the problem or issue at hand. This profile has its roots in the organization of the nervous system, but it is not fixed from birth. The development of the intelligences depends on a rich interplay between biological and neurological factors and the physical, social, and cultural conditions in which human beings live and work.

Gardner's argument for seven intelligences draws on evidence from diverse disciplines, including cross-cultural anthropology, developmental and experimental psychology, neuropsychology, evolutionary biology, as well as psychometrics. This evidence shows that these abilities develop relatively independently, can be damaged or impaired selectively, and contribute to the achievement of important adult roles in different cultures.

Since its publication, this theory has gained considerable attention in educational circles, particularly because it resonates with philosophies and practices that depart from the traditional focus on basic linguistic and mathematical skills to emphasize the unique strengths and needs of the individual. However, the theory and its implications for education go far beyond a change in the number of intelligences that an individual possesses or the number of subjects that should be emphasized in schools. The theory presents an entirely different view of intelligence and how it develops, a view that challenges the premises of tradi-

---

[1] Recently, Gardner (1995) posited an eighth intelligence, that of "the naturalist." This intelligence enables people to draw on materials and features of the natural environment to solve problems or fashion products. It is exemplified by, for instance, E. O. Wilson, Charles Darwin, or traditional herbalists.

tional curricula and conventional assessment practices.

In this view, abilities develop and are assessed most effectively in the context of meaningful activities. Typically, these are activities carried out in life and work outside of school and that contribute to important accomplishments in different disciplines and professions. How one does on the traditional scholastic activities favored in most schools will not necessarily prepare one for performing well or predict how well one will perform in other contexts. For example, several investigators, including Geofrey Saxe and Stephen Ceci, have shown that young vendors in South America who have had little formal schooling—and could not solve math problems in a workbook like Rosie's—can make complicated and quick calculations of prices. Similarly, Andrea DiSessa has shown that students at prestigious universities who can apply the laws of physics in conventional tests and classroom exercises make the same kinds of mistakes as twelve-year-olds when trying to apply those same laws in activities outside of the classroom (see Gardner, 1991, for discussions of these and other studies).

From an MI perspective, Rosie possesses a number of intelligences that are relatively unrelated to how she does in language or math. Regardless of her performance in math, the brilliant spatial skills she displays in colorful paintings could enable her to become a successful architect, engineer, illustrator, or artist. But the theory also suggests that there are other routes to mathematical understanding than those Rosie encounters in her kindergarten math book. Shopping with her parents, selling lemonade, and making measurements and maps for a new playground or classroom layout are all motivating and meaningful activities in which Rosie can develop and display her mathematical abilities. Thus, how Rosie does with math will not necessarily predict how well she writes, draws, or gets along with others in kindergarten. Nor will how Rosie does with "plus" in a workbook necessarily predict how well she will do in other kinds of mathematical activities outside of school or in later life. From this standpoint, describing Rosie as "dumb" is not an intelligent thing to do.

Unfortunately, instituting programs that engage students in the kinds of activities that are valued outside of school and that allow them to use and develop a wide range of abilities is not a simple matter. The traditional view of intelligence is intertwined with a host of expectations and practices at all levels of the educational system. We cannot suddenly change our minds about the nature of intelligence and expect students, teachers, schools, and other educational institutions to follow suit.

In order to create and support successful educational practices and programs that build on an alternative view of intelligence, we have to take into account the expectations, skills, and backgrounds of the individuals involved in the classroom or local setting, the resources and opportunities available to them in that setting, and the societal influences on that setting. Thus, at the individual level, in order for an educational program to respond to Rosie's strengths and needs, Rosie and her teacher cannot equate Rosie's math skills with her overall abilities. Both need to be able to recognize Rosie's strengths, and they need to know how to build on Rosie's strengths in order to help her succeed inside and outside of school. Further, Rosie (and her teacher) cannot equate mathematics with "doing plus." She needs to be able to recognize and participate in a wide variety of mathematical activities, whether they involve using manipulatives, making measurements, or comparing prices.

In order for that to happen, at the local level, Rosie and her teacher need access to the kinds of materials and people that will enable Rosie to exercise and develop a range of abilities. Further, there is a need to address the restrictive curriculum requirements, outdated textbooks, and standardized tests employed in that setting that encourage Rosie and her teacher to spend most of their time in conventional classroom exercises.

Finally, at the societal level, even if Rosie participates in a program that responds to the range of her abilities, thanks to the societal influences, she probably will not feel "smart." The societal expectations about what a "good education" looks like have to be discussed, and members of the broader community need to be introduced to an alternative conception of intelligence.

Only by tackling expectations and practices at all three of these levels—individual, local, and societal—can we create and sustain an effective educational program that supports the range of students' abilities and expands our understanding of their potential.

In this chapter, we begin by providing examples of the kinds of practices and programs that reflect this contextual and pluralistic view of intelligences. First, we describe project-based approaches that engage students in the kinds of meaningful work they are likely to encounter outside of school. While many of these efforts are not based explicitly on an alternative conception of intelligence, they offer students an opportunity to use a range of capacities in culturally valued activities. Second, we describe schools that have developed curricula and assessments based specifically on MI theory. We go on to discuss many of the influences that tend to reinforce conventional educational practices and the traditional view of intelligence and that need to be taken into account in order to create such programs. We conclude by describing some of the different ways that such practices can be supported and discuss their implications for all of those interested in basing education on an alternative view of intelligence.

Learning in the Context of Culturally Valued Activities

Before the advent of formal schooling, "learning in context" was a natural means for the development of a host of skills and abilities. Building on the potential of such "informal" learning experiences, John Dewey and others argued that engaging students in projects like the construction of a building or the management of a farm should be an important part of formal schooling. Since that time, projects and other "authentic activities" have been a hallmark of many progressive educational movements.

In general, projects are ways to involve students in culturally valued pursuits they would otherwise normally encounter only after they leave school. Projects are goal-directed activities in which students tackle problems or fashion products over relatively long periods of time. They include efforts to build a playground, to determine the quality of the town water supply, or to produce a documentary on the history of a school.

Three characteristics distinguish projects from conventional classroom exercises based on traditional notions of intelligence. First, projects provide students with a meaningful and engaging context in which they can develop a number of culturally valued skills. In many classrooms, students read, write, and calculate because they are required to by their teachers. Students have to do some exercises to show they understand the parts of a sentence or have mastered the multiplication tables so that they will perform well on upcoming tests. In projects, there are clear and compelling reasons for students to use their skills and to use them well.

For example, in a public elementary school in Shutesbury, Massachusetts, the entire school participated in a series of projects to investigate the properties of water and to survey and test the quality of the water resources in the community. As Ron Berger, a sixth-grade teacher in the school, suggested when he described the project, the students had many reasons to carry out their work and to do it well:

> I think of first-graders digging channels in the sand, struggling with giant buckets of water to begin the life of a stream. I think of third- and fourth-grade students on a rowboat out in the middle of a town lake, carefully lowering into the water a clever homemade water-sampling contraption built of rope, hardware, duct tape, cork, rocks, a wine jug, and thermometer. More than anything, I think of the excitement and fear in the classroom as my students compiled and posted data from town well samples. The children, teachers, town families, the town board of health and the local newspapers were awaiting these results with impatience and apprehension. But everything was in the children's hands, and there was no way to rush these students. With real lives and health at stake, the students refused to post [any results] until they had been checked and rechecked. They were as terrified of making a mistake as we were of uncovering a crisis. This was serious business! [Berger, 1994, p. 7]

The students were motivated to do these things, and to do them well, because their work mattered.

Second, projects give students an opportunity to use a range of intelligences. In contrast to many conventional classroom exercises that focus on one or two skills in isolation, like reading comprehension or mathematical calculations, projects require students to develop a number of different skills and provide students a chance to build on their intellectual strengths. Thus, in the Shutesbury projects, students had to use and develop their logical-mathematical skills in collecting and analyzing data. They had to use and develop their interpersonal skills as they worked in teams to collect and analyze data. They had to use their linguistic skills as they wrote reports and made presentations to convey their results. They had to use bodily-kinesthetic skills as they built their streams and water-sampling contraptions. They used spatial skills as they illustrated their investigations with drawings, paintings, maps, and graphs. And they had to use their intrapersonal skills as they wrestled with difficult ethical issues about how to handle data that revealed cases and places where the water quality was not as high at it should have been.

Third, projects enable students to develop productive habits and dispositions. The assignment of many classroom exercises, and the short lengths of time in which students are often expected to complete them, leave little opportunity to develop the kinds of habits or dispositions that are needed when people work on their own or with others outside of school. In contrast, in projects, students have to be persistent, cooperative, and reflective in order to find and resolve unanticipated problems, to pursue activities over time, and to work effectively with others. In the Shutesbury projects, the students had to take the initiative in designing the experiments and surveys. They had to develop the persistence and ingenuity to find different ways to collect data even if they did not have the needed equipment or expertise. They had to conquer the impulse to complete the exciting work as quickly as possible and develop the patience and thoughtfulness to ensure that their work was of the highest quality.

Approaches to projects are currently being pursued by several of the nine design teams funded in 1992 by the New American Schools Development Corporation to redesign a number of schools across the country. In the ATLAS Communities Project—a collaboration between the Coalition of Essential Schools, the Education Development Center, Harvard Project Zero, and the School Development Program—students are involved in projects that culminate in exhibitions in which the students present and discuss their work with their classmates and community members. For example, one group of sixth-graders in Norfolk, Virginia, found out that a nearby zoo was redesigning the enclosures for several animals. The students then became participants in the redesign by studying the animals' natural habitats, designing new enclosures, and offering feedback and advice on the presentation of information to onlookers. They presented their work to the staff at the zoo as well as to other members of their school community.

In the Mather Afterschool Project—a collaboration between Brown University, Harvard Project Zero, and the Mather Elementary School in Dorchester, Massachusetts—these same kinds of ideas about projects were applied to an afterschool setting (Goodrich, Hatch, Wiatrowski, and Unger, 1995). The program was intended to give third-, fourth-, and fifth-grade students an opportunity to participate in the kinds of engaging projects they would not normally encounter in school. Thus, the students were expected to carry out projects like publishing a newspaper, developing a recycling campaign, and putting on a play. In the course of these projects, students were given an opportunity both to exercise a variety of abilities and to develop important literacy and thinking skills that could help them in the regular classroom. For example, in one project, students worked in groups to plan and carry out field trips. In order to go on a trip, they had to evaluate a number of potential sites (ranging from the John F. Kennedy Library to a local bowling alley), write a proposal to their teacher explaining where they wanted to go, why they wanted to go, and how much it would cost, and then make the practical arrangements.

Using Multiple Intelligences

Most project approaches give students an opportunity to use and develop a variety of different intelligences, but do not guarantee that they will do so. In contrast, approaches based on MI explicitly incorporate a range of intelligences into the curriculum and the assessments they use. A study of a small number of MI schools suggests that beyond supporting the development of learning in meaningful activities, MI is valuable to these efforts because it provides a framework for reflecting on classroom practice and, thereby, for extending and enhancing curriculum and teaching (Kornhaber and Krechevsky, 1995).

Thus, MI can lead educators to develop means to build on students' diverse strengths and to create activities that involve a much broader range of intelligences. As one teacher who worked in an MI school explained, he drew on students' strengths before, but "I was doing it in a hazy fashion. . . . Gardner gave it a construct, context." Or, as another teacher commented, "unless you put things into terms [words], you aren't necessarily going to be able to do as much effective work on it." Gardner's work helped him in "considering the areas [intelligences] that I don't emphasize . . . " and to find ways to incorporate those intelligences into his classroom practice.

Similarly, MI leads to a rethinking of assessment practices by providing a vocabulary that makes it possible to identify and talk about different learners' strengths and needs. MI enables those teachers, parents, and students who believe that they or their children have strengths that do not show up on traditional tests to name and discuss those strengths. Further, it encourages educators to develop new assessments that will help to bring those diverse strengths to light.

Two different means of incorporating MI into the curriculum are highlighting the individual intelligences and integrating the intelligences. Often, some combination of these two approaches is in evidence in MI schools. To highlight individual intelligences, teachers do such things as organize their rooms into intelligence-based learning centers. For example, some classes might have a variety of centers, such as a reading/linguistic center, a logical-mathematical area in which children work with tangrams or other kinds of puzzles, and a spatial center in which children make constructions from wood and other materials.

Intelligence-specific lessons also support the development of individual intelligences. For instance, one district hired specialists to conduct a series of activities to help develop particular intelligences. Thus, in one classroom, a professional choreographer staged a group of first-graders in a remarkably polished scene from *Oklahoma*! In another, a mathematician carried out a discussion with kindergartners about the meaning and mathematical relevance of terms like "big."

To integrate the intelligences, teachers use a variety of somewhat overlapping strategies. Projects that cut across a number of subject areas are one means that many teachers in MI schools use to integrate the intelligences. Instead of using projects, some teachers integrate the intelligences by incorporating them in traditional subject matter. Thus, one teacher taught fractions by having students works on tasks (such as gardening, woodworking, and architectural drawing) that required grappling with different intelligences in some fashion. A number of MI schools also use the arts as a vehicle for integrating the intelligences into the curriculum. For example, one middle school in the Northeast has thoroughly integrated its art teachers into the regular curriculum in courses such as "Art and Language Arts," "Art and Technology," "Art and Culture." In "Art and Language Arts," students use various art forms—not just writing—to demonstrate their understandings. In addition, the project-based curricula used in many of the courses in MI schools readily calls on, or at least allows for, children to write and perform songs, draw, paint, or model. In all of these examples, simply exercising a broader range of intelligences is not enough. These activities provide students with ways to use their intelligences to address meaningful and authentic problems within valued domains.

In order to assess a range of abilities and to collect and assess the wide range of performances and products students produce in an MI environment, MI schools have devised several creative approaches. These include those that involve diagnosing the strengths of individual students and those that involve the collection of student work in portfolios.

In order to understand the intelligences of individual students, seventh- and eighth-grade teachers and the principal in the middle school discussed above gather information from the incoming sixth-graders. They visit the sixth-grade classrooms, talk about MI, and explore with the youngsters "how would you know if you had a strength in an area?" Then they leave journals in which students can write about areas in which they feel they are strong. The teachers also let the students know they will return in a few weeks' time in order to have the students demonstrate their strengths in any way they would like. At these follow-up meetings, students bring in their collections, play musical instruments, perform karate, and "report" in a variety of other formats on the diverse abilities that teachers may rarely see in schools. The middle-school teachers then use this information in part to design each student's schedule individually for seventh grade.

MI has also been used as a basis for assessments of individuals who are experiencing difficulties in school. In a pre-K through first-grade school, a team of teachers decided to get a more complete picture of one student who seemed to be developmentally delayed and whose two other siblings had already been diagnosed with learning difficulties. The team included the student's regular classroom teacher, the music teacher, the school psychologist, the special education teacher, and the speech pathologist. The members reasoned that rather than seek deficiencies, as traditional assessments of such students reveal, they should organize themselves to look for this student's strengths. They found that alongside his language difficulties, "the little guy was very musical, and his interpersonal skills were absolutely dynamic. He was [also] self-reflective. We discovered a lot of extra things about this child. . . ." They also noticed that an activity "clicked . . . he would practice so hard." The teachers used what they had learned to engage the child in activities that helped him to develop some skills in art and sports. This rendered him both more confident and more capable than an educational program based solely on traditional assessments might have left him.

Portfolios are another way that MI schools assess students' performances in areas and activities not normally reflected on standardized tests. These may include sketches or drafts in various media collected at different stages of the work; a student's own or others' notes on the problem or project; photographs, videos, or cassette tapes of performances of various kinds; or some other final product.

Portfolios have at least two strengths as assessment vehicles for MI-oriented schools. First, portfolios can capture diverse kinds of problem-solving abilities. For example, a teacher working with students who were not skilled writers had his students draw images to illustrate their understanding of a story. Some students spontaneously drew a "pagoda"—a word they claimed not to know. Others exhibited an understanding of the narrator's perspective by drawing what the narrator would see in the harbor as he stood on the ship's deck.

Second, portfolios help demonstrate to parents and other concerned parties what students in MI schools are doing and how they are developing. As opposed to a traditional number or letter grade or a report from a standardized test battery, portfolios provide parents with concrete examples of their children's work in an area. They therefore provide the basis for a richer discussion among teachers, parents, and students about the strengths and weaknesses in students' work and the ways the work has developed over time.

Along with portfolios, teachers in some schools have explored alternative report cards and grading policies as a way to evaluate student work and convey this information to parents. As one principal explains, "What you measure is what you value." Therefore, at his school, where inter- and intrapersonal intelligences are regarded as a vital component to student growth, the whole first page of the report card was revamped to emphasize students' development in these areas. Another teacher reports how he now bases students' grades not only on written reports, but on students' use of charts, tables, and other visual materials, as well as their class presentation.

The Challenges of Developing Alternative Practices

Given their common connection to alternative conceptions of intelligence, MI- and project-based approaches in schools and classrooms also face a number of common challenges. We next describe our development of a project-based approach in the Mather Afterschool Program to provide a good example of how individual, local, and societal influences that affect classroom activity and student learning need to be taken into account in order to deal with the pressures of conventional views of intelligence.

In the Mather Afterschool Program (co-directed by William Damon of Brown University, and Howard Gardner and David Perkins of Harvard University), we chose to develop projects in an afterschool setting in order to escape the traditional constraints of tests and curriculum coverage requirements—some of the local influences—that discourage teachers from trying to develop new curricula like projects. We expected that minimizing these local influences that were rooted in traditional notions of intelligence would make it easier for teachers to develop practices consistent with an alternative view of intelligence.

We found, however, a host of other influences that continued to reinforce conventional practices and made the development of projects difficult even in an afterschool setting. Within just the first few weeks of the program, the difficulties became apparent. It was extremely hard to get the students engaged in any focused activity. When we did get the students started on an activity, they claimed they were finished almost before they had begun. They were very impulsive; if they ran into a problem, they were more likely to tear up their work and quit than they were to try to fix it. In short, the students seemed to lack any interest in or any skills for initiating and carrying through long-term projects.

If we had taken a traditional view of intelligence, we might have simply concluded that these students were incapable of carrying out this kind of self-directed activity. But by taking a more contextual perspective, we were able to identify some of the individual, local, and societal influences that worked together to create this situation and make it difficult—if not impossible— for the students to engage in projects. First of all, students did not come to the program with an interest in doing projects. A further complication was that although the students were not required to attend the program, many thought this was a remedial program because they were told by their teachers that they had been "picked" and that it would be a good thing for them to go. As one student said, he thought he was coming to the program because he got F's. Even if they had been expecting to carry out projects, the students' previous school experiences in no way prepared them to be involved in meaningful projects or self-directed work. In addition, while the teachers who joined the program had an interest in project-based learning, they had not had much experience with such student-directed or authentic projects either. In fact, this was also the researchers' first opportunity to develop projects in a collaborative manner for an afterschool setting. As a result, none of the individuals involved had all the background or the skills they needed to participate in or lead afterschool projects.

At the local level, this was the first year of the afterschool program, so we had no examples of what students had done in previous years. There were no experienced students who could serve as models or provide assistance to their peers. In addition, the afterschool program was carried out in regular classrooms with teachers from the school. As a result, the setting was really designed for conventional classroom exercises, with students seated in rows at desks, and not for students who were involved in self-directed activities or small-group work.

On a societal level, the program had to contend with the

expectations that "real schoolwork" does not involve students in getting up out of their seats to work on their own. While many community members were happy to have a safe and healthy place for students to go after school, they did not look on the program as a place where learning would occur. Or, if they felt that students needed to be learning, they wanted the students to be doing their homework. As a consequence, although many community members supported the program, it was not viewed as a critical part of the students' educational experience.

Addressing the Individual, Local, and Societal Influences on Project-Based Learning

In order to make this program successful and to get students engaged in meaningful projects, we made a number of changes over the next three years. First of all, on an individual level, we addressed the expectations that the students brought to the program. In the second year, instead of telling students to come to the afterschool program, we described the program and the projects and then asked them to apply. In addition, through our experience together, students, teachers, and researchers all began to develop a common understanding about what projects were. In fact, the researchers and teachers worked to identify the characteristics of their most successful projects and were able to use this growing knowledge to support students' activity.

At the local level, we created a supportive environment for self-directed learning. We tried to find classrooms with layouts we could rearrange so that students could move around freely or work together in groups. We collected examples of student work that helped new students and new teachers to understand what was expected. Teachers gathered materials and resources that were needed for different projects. Finally, the teachers and researchers modeled the kinds of behaviors in which we expected the students to engage. In other words, since we expected the students to give each other supportive feedback, the teachers and researchers tried to demonstrate over and over in their interactions with each other and with students what supportive feedback looked like.

These efforts contributed to a significant increase in students' engagement and helped to create opportunities for the students to display and develop skills that neither they nor their teachers thought they had. As one teacher who was with the program for four years commented:

> I've learned over the years how much kids can accomplish and how not to, I try not to expect them not to do anything . . . [A]t first I didn't expect a lot of kids to get, to complete a lot of the things I set out for them to do, but I found that with time, and especially with the last group, that a lot of the kids were able to complete the entire [project].

The impact of these program changes on the students was clearly revealed in increases in students' attendance and the amount, variety, and quality of their work (particularly in writing). Whereas students resisted many focused activities in the first year, in later years students sustained engagement in such activities as writing books, proposals, and letters; organizing drives to promote school spirit; and designing and producing jewelry.

Despite these accomplishments, the societal expectations about learning were never really addressed. While we invited teachers, parents, and others to open houses, those events were not sufficient to demonstrate to the other teachers in the school, the parents, or the members of the community how much the students were able to learn in this afterschool setting or how important it was to those students. As a result, when the funding for our research ended, we were unable to find other sources of funding to continue the program. In the face of competing demands, members of the school community decided to spend their money on other priorities. Thus, although we had created a place where real learning could go on after school, we did not create the support in the wider community for afterschool projects that were an integral part of the students' education and development.

This experience reinforces the belief that change takes time, and it also demonstrates that to develop programs that reflect an alternative view of intelligence, many changes have to take place. The expectations and skills of the students, teachers, and other participants (even the researcher's) may have to change. The materials, requirements, and opportunities have to change. And the attitudes and expectations of the society and the wider community about what "real learning" looks like have to be addressed.

Conclusion

While it is important to attend to these individual, local, and
societal influences when developing new educational practices
and programs, no simple formula describes exactly which factors need to be attended to. But those who wish to try to develop or support such programs can find guidance by looking at
a variety of such different efforts.

Individuals and Intelligence

On an individual level, many of the people who participate in
MI or project-based classrooms do so because these programs
are consistent with their beliefs about education. But even for
those who embrace an alternative conception of intelligence, it
is difficult to break away from old patterns of behavior and conventional routines and practices.

In fact, there may be some common tendencies in developing
MI- and project-based programs that reflect the pervasive influence of traditional notions and need to be overcome (Gardner,
1995). For one thing, there may be an initial inclination to re-
place the "old" curriculum in which everyone is required to develop two intelligences with a "new" curriculum in which everyone
has to develop seven. Alternatively, efforts may be made to teach
the same old subject matter in seven different ways—by having
students listen to music while they calculate or by having them
act out or dance a passage from their reading about history.

Such efforts are inconsistent with an alternative conception of
intelligence that emphasizes that each person develops a unique
combination of strengths. Everyone does not need to develop
every intelligence to a high level nor does every person need to
have every subject or skill introduced in seven ways. Rather, students need opportunities to find and develop their intellectual
strengths, and teachers need to use their knowledge of the
strengths of individual students so that those students can solve
the important problems they are likely to encounter outside of
school. Similarly, there is a danger when putting in place an MI
program that early efforts to identify a student's strengths may

be assumed to predict the student's strengths in high school and beyond. Such examples ignore the rich interplay between genetic predispositions and cultural experiences at the heart of contextual and pluralistic conceptions of intelligence.

Similarly, there may be initial tendencies for teachers to lead projects in much the same way they have directed more traditional classroom activities. If students are to take advantage of their strengths and to develop habits like persistence and perseverance, then those students have to have the opportunity to contribute to the shape and direction of the projects. Another tendency may be to try to teach all the same "basic" mathematical and linguistic skills from the conventional curriculum through projects. Engaging in projects that require students to multiply may help them to understand why they need to multiply and may motivate them to do so, but projects do not have to be the only vehicle or strategy used to help students develop their mathematical skills.

In order to avoid these pitfalls, several steps can be taken to support the development of beliefs and behaviors that are consistent with an alternative view of intelligence. In particular, efforts have to be made to ensure that the new practices and programs actually meet the needs and interests of the students and teachers. There are many teachers and students who have been successful in traditional classrooms. Requiring every school to use a nontraditional or MI approach would be just as destructive and limiting as requiring everyone to submit to the conventional curriculum. In order to ensure that programs and practices actually do meet students' and teachers' needs, they should have some choice in the kinds of activities, classrooms, and schools in which they participate. Regardless of whether or not students and teachers have a choice about participating in a new program, however, it can be helpful for both students and teachers to get a sense of the different expectations they are likely to encounter. Descriptions of classrooms, examples of activities, and samples of student work all serve as useful preparations even before efforts are made to develop a new approach. Such preparations can help even those who are initially resistant to see the need or value of the new approach and help those who are neutral or eager to see where they are headed.

Of course, there are many who are not sympathetic to an alternative conception of intelligence. While it is unlikely that those who believe in a traditional perspective can be forced to change their minds about intelligence, there is no more powerful way to demonstrate the limitations of a traditional perspective than to experience the success of students who exceed conventional expectations. In one school in Somerville, Massachusetts, it was not until a teacher watched a first-grader eagerly engaged in taking apart and putting back together a food mill that she saw him experience any success in the classroom. Upon discovering his spatial intelligence and his interest in mechanical objects, she designated him as the mechanical expert in the class and involved him in writing a dictionary of tools—the first successful writing activity in which he engaged. As she described it, she began to see him as an entirely different person.

Supporting Intelligence in Local Settings

On a local classroom and school level, changes in a number of policies that govern who works and studies in which classrooms at what time, the kinds of materials and resources available in those classrooms, and what students and teachers are required to do can support the changes in activity, roles, and beliefs that need to accompany the development of multiple-intelligence and project-based approaches. Theodore Sizer, of the Coalition of Essential Schools, argues passionately that one cannot teach students one does not know well (Sizer, 1984). Knowing students well, identifying their strengths, and building on their interests are critical to making alternative approaches work. Thus, reducing the student-teacher ratio in high school to 80–1 as the Coalition recommends and keeping it considerably lower in middle and elementary school removes one critical barrier to implementing alternative approaches.

In addition to having to be responsible for large numbers of students, many teachers are often faced with long lists of curriculum requirements that constrain their efforts to devise authentic learning experiences and respond to students' needs. Despite efforts to create new standards that articulate the abilities needed in work beyond school, many curriculum requirements continue to reflect the kinds of decontextualized skills and isolated facts that are consistent with traditional tests of intelligence. As Sizer points out, these requirements also fail to take into account that a focus on a few subjects may lead to deeper and more robust learning than does superficial coverage of many different facts and subjects. These requirements are buttressed by the use of textbooks, tests and assessment procedures, and other classroom resources that often reinforce a conventional view. Replacing old requirements with new requirements will not suffice. Demanding that teachers cover more intelligences or requiring them to carry out a certain number or kind of projects provides little advance. Instead, limiting the demands on what teachers and students need to cover, providing for more options in classroom materials, and allowing for the use of alternative assessments can all help to provide the flexibility needed to build on students' strengths and interests.

At the same time, how to provide such flexibility and still maintain high standards for all remains a vexing question. Thus, efforts to loosen the bonds of classroom requirements need to be accompanied by a commitment to regular reflection and discussion of successful implementation and student performance among the participants. The development by teachers and students of portfolios and shared criteria can support such discussions. Similarly, the more authentic the activity—the more closely connected students' work is to real outcomes that matter to them and to the surrounding community—the more difficult it is to get away with doing work of low quality. It is easier to get by on a test than it is to fool those who are depending on you for high-quality work.

Finding the needed expertise to carry out a project or an MI approach and making it available to students and teachers is another critical consideration. Even those teachers who are enthusiastic about addressing students' strengths and developing authentic activities quickly find themselves struggling to acquire expertise in a host of areas. To implement projects, teachers have to be ready to pursue learning opportunities that they may not anticipate and for which advance planning is extremely difficult. In order to deal with these kinds of demands, teachers often draw on the support of colleagues inside and outside the school. Thus, the projects in Shutesbury benefited from visits from a local naturalist, employees of the town dam and campground, and a professor from a nearby college.

To support MI, teachers in MI schools often work in teams, since few teachers (or other individuals) are strong across all intelligences. Thus, in several MI schools, staff specialists—such as the art, music, and physical education teachers, and the school librarian—take on more central roles in the regular classroom. In another school, three kindergarten teachers team up, each taking responsibility for devising ways to provide rich linguistic opportunities and each "specializing" in two other intelligences. The kindergartners then rotate through the teachers' three adjoining classrooms a few times a week in order to participate in activities highlighting thoughtful uses of each intelligence.

Intelligence and Society

There is no simple way to address, on a societal level, the pervasive influence of the traditional view of intelligence. To be truly effective, such an initiative has to address the broad and powerful economic and political forces that continue to favor a conventional view of intelligence. While recognizing the enormity of such an effort, the most useful initial steps may be those that change the tenor of the current debates and discussions about education. Put simply, debates about increases and decreases in students' test scores need to be replaced by significant discussions of what students actually do: what a good performance is, and how a better performance could be achieved.

A number of things can be done to enable much larger numbers of people to learn about what happens in schools, to participate in the educational process, and to contribute to discussions about what students are actually doing. The School Development Program at Yale University established by Dr. James Comer has had considerable success in getting parents and community members involved in schools by enabling them to participate meaningfully in the decision making at the school and in the support of individual students (Comer, 1980). In the ATLAS project, these efforts are joined with initiatives that enable parents and community members to see and reflect on what students are doing in the classroom. For example, many ATLAS schools hold public exhibitions of student work. In an exhibition in an ATLAS school in Norfolk, Virginia, a shy, quiet, eighth-grader could barely be heard as he turned on a videotape; but as soon as it began, the audience of parents, teachers, administrators, and others was mesmerized as a documentary he made about the Los Angeles riots unfolded. In another ATLAS school in Gorham, Maine, students and their parents and teachers sit together in conferences as the students share a portfolio of their work that documents the progress they have made over the course of the year. These activities give all the stakeholders in schools a chance to express and develop their views and understandings of intelligence and education and a chance to see students exceeding conventional expectations.

Ideally, applying an alternative conception of intelligence to education will involve all aspects of education and all the members of a school community: those inside the classroom and the school, those in the surrounding community, and those establishing the policies that affect us all. While no simple formula, set of instructions, or package of materials can dictate how any of us should apply such a conception, a willingness to question our traditional assumptions and to pay attention to the strengths and needs of each individual is an important first step. In order to take that first step, we have to find a way as a society to show as much concern about students as we do about their test scores. Instead of arguing about how to design programs that will raise achievement levels in general, we need to devote our time and energy to learning how to respond to the unique strengths and needs of each individual.

References

Berger, R. (1994). Water: A whole school expedition. In *Learning expeditions: Studies from the field*. Cambridge, Mass.: Expeditionary Learning Outward Bound.

Comer, J. (1980). *School power*. New York: Free Press.

Gardner, H. (1983). *Frames of Mind*. New York: Basic Books.

Gardner, H. (1991). *The unschooled mind*. New York: Basic Books.

Gardner, H. (1995). Reflections on multiple intelligences: Myths and messages. *Phi Delta Kappan* 77(3): 200–209.

Goodrich, H.; Hatch, T.; Wiatrowski, G.; and Unger, C. (1995). *Teaching through projects*. San Francisco: Addison-Wesley.

Kornhaber, M., and Krechevsky, M. (1995). Expanding definitions of teaching and learning: Notes from the MI underground. In P. Cookson and B. Schneider (eds.), *Transforming schools*. New York: Garland.

Sizer, T. (1984). *Horace's compromise*. New York: Houghton-Mifflin.

Chapter 3

The Advancement of Learning

Ann L. Brown

Neither the hand nor the mind alone would amount to much without aids and tools to perfect them.

Bacon, *Novum Organum*, 1623

This loosely translated quotation is taken from Francis Bacon's *Novum Organum*, not from Vygotsky, as one might well imagine.

Reprinted by permission of the publisher from *Educational Researcher 23*, 8 (1994): 4–12. Copyright © 1994 by the American Educational Research Association.

The work reported in this chapter was supported by grants from the James S. McDonnell Foundation, the Andrew W. Mellon Foundation, the Evelyn Lois Corey Research Fund, and Grant HD-06864 from the National Institute of Child Health and Human Development. But the preparation of the article was supported principally by the Spencer Foundation, whom I would like to thank for giving me time to think. I would like to thank my many colleagues and friends who contributed to the research agenda in this article, but notably I thank my husband and colleague, Joseph C. Campione, for contributions too deep for telling.

In this chapter, I argue that designing aids and tools to perfect the mind is one of the primary goals of educational research. In this spirit, the major themes of the chapter are that

- Instruction is a major class of aids and tools to enhance the mind.
- To design instruction, we need appropriate theories of learning and development.
- Enormous advances have been made in this century in our understanding of learning and development.
- School practices in the main have not changed to reflect these advances.
- The question posed is, Why?

My title, *The Advancement of Learning,* is also taken from Bacon (1605). The title is a metaphor, as I will view the advancement of learning particularly during the thirty years or so since the cognitive revolution. Contemporary theories, unlike those of the past, concentrate on the learning of complex ideas as it occurs in authentic situations including, but not limited to, schools. In keeping with Bacon, I will paint a general picture of progress but at the same time add a cautionary note concerning the infanticide rate of our profession. We repeatedly throw out babies along with bathwater, when we should build cumulatively. No community can afford to lose so many valuable offspring in the service of progress.

I will begin with a personal odyssey. In rereading the Presidential Addresses from the past ten years or so, I realized that this genre, the odyssey, is a popular one. Indeed, the metaphor of an odyssey was the leitmotif of Eliot Eisner's 1993 address. Pivotal to this narrative genre is the retelling of the myriad interesting life experiences of those who subsequently went on to become President of AERA. Now here's my problem. I am a psychologist. I have always been a psychologist of sorts. I started my academic career as an undergraduate studying learning, and I am still doing that today, in my fashion. But what I did then and what I do now are as distinct as night and day.

I was well prepared for my career as a learning theorist. In high school, I specialized in eighteenth-century literature and nineteenth-century history, and was on my way to study history in college. Why switch? I saw a television program on animal learning, on how animals learn naturally in their environments, an introduction to ethology. The heroes of this piece were Huxley, Lorenz, Thorpe, and Tinbergen. Fascinated, I looked up animal learning in my handy guide to universities and found that to study learning you needed a degree in psychology.

Thus prepared I set out for an interview, having seen one television program on ethology and having read Freud's *Psychopathology of Everyday Life* on the train getting there. By chance the head of department was an expert in eighteenth-century literature. We discussed poetry for two hours. I got a scholarship to study psychology!

So in the early sixties I started out for London to study animal learning. I arrived in Iowa, or maybe it was Kansas, feeling a little like Dorothy in *The Wizard of Oz*. The cognitive revolution had not yet come to London. What followed was three years of exposure to behaviorist learning theory. Rather than learning about animals adapting to their natural habitats, I learned about rats and pigeons learning things that rats and pigeons were never intended to learn.

Pan-Associationism

Experimental psychologists in England (and Iowa) at that time were enthralled with a certain form of behaviorism. Dominating the field were the all-encompassing learning theories of Hull/ Spence, Tolman, and Skinner.[1] These theories shared certain features that limited to a greater or lesser extent their ability to inform educational practice. All derived their primary data from rats and pigeons learning arbitrary things in restricted situations. They shared a belief that laws of learning of considerable generality and precision could be found. These basic principles of learning were thought to apply uniformly and universally across all kinds of learning and all kinds of situations. The principles were intended to be *species- age-, domain-,* and *context-independent.*

---

[1] For descriptions and retrospectives on the major psychological learning theories of the mid century, see Koch (1959).

Pure learning was tested in impoverished environments where the skills to be learned had little adaptive value for the species in question. Paul Rozin argued that by studying the behavior of pigeons in arbitrary situations, we learned nothing about the behavior of pigeons in nature, but a great deal about the behavior of people in arbitrary situations.

I will illustrate with a surely apocryphal tale related by Mary Catherine Bateson (1984). Her father Gregory Bateson's favorite tongue-in-check psychologist anecdote was the following:

> It occurred to a throughtful rat-runner after many years of running rats that as rats do not usually live in mazes, mazes were perhaps less than optimal testing grounds for learning. Therefore, he bought a ferret, a species that in nature does hunt in mazes—rabbit warrens. He baited a maze with fresh rabbit meat and set the ferret to find it. On the first day, the ferret systematically searched the maze and found the rabbit quicker than a rat. But what happened on the second day? The rat, as expected, searched the maze and found the bait more quickly than on the original trial. Learning was said to have occurred. But not so for the ferret. It searched the maze and came to the route that had previously led to the reward, but didn't go down it. Why? He'd eaten that rabbit yesterday. What the ferret had learned was colored by its expectation of how the world works—for ferrets. [Anecdote adapted from pp. 170–171]

How did this dominance of certain forms of behaviorism come about? Psychology as a nascent science didn't start out that way. One of the few female pioneers in the early part of the century, Mary Calkins (1915), criticized the overwhelmingly male establishment by arguing that psychology started out as the study of consciousness and then set about to explain it away, even to deny its existence. Throughout her career she argued, in the wilderness, that psychology should be the study of "conscious interacting social selves in relation to other selves and objects." Vygotsky, perhaps, but a far cry from Thorndike, Watson, and Hull.

Animal Learning

The dominance of behaviorism in the mid part of the century has often been blamed on the increasing dependence on animals as experimental subjects. Animals are not known for their introspection, and few investigators were concerned whether animal throught was imageless or not, or whether they entertained theories of mind. This argument does not follow through, however, as early work with animals had a distinctly mentalistic flavor. Leonard Hobhouse, in his delightful book, *Mind in Evolution* (1901), studied a variety of animals, albeit somewhat informally: One reads that the subject were: "a dog, a cat, an otter, and an elephant" or "a rhesus monkey called Jimmy and a chimpanzee named Professor." Using a variety of puzzle-like, meaningful situations (a dog opening a gate to escape its own yard, rather than playing in a Thorndikian puzzle box), Hobhouse found evidence for such mental-sounding entities as purpose, planning, cunning, and deceit, mental entities again being studied today (Griffin, 1992). So too, during the first world war, Kohler's chimpanzees, such as the famous Sultan, were also seen to be insightful as they set about building towers of boxes to reach fruit hanging out of reach, or combining short sticks into long ones to reach outside cage bars.

This mentalism was almost stamped out, but with notable exceptions, such as Lashley's rats on the jumping stand experiencing vicarious (mental) trial and error, or Tolman's rats buried in thought at the start box of a maze, troubled by ideas, hypotheses, and mental maps. Lashley and Tolman were atypical, however; Lashley was trained as an ethologist, and Tolman was always a closet cognitivist, and a self-proclaimed cryptomentalist (see Koch, 1959). But to the dyed-in-the-wool behaviorist, learning did not imply conscious intent but rather was seen as the autonomous outcome of the formation of S-R bonds stamped in or out by reinforcement contingencies with no need for conscious intent. This position had powerful implications for education, whose residual clings today.

Developmental Psychology

Child psychology underwent a similar history. Although at the beginning of the century we saw ingenious studies of children's thought (witness those of Binet, Baldwin, Piaget, and Darwin for that matter), they were forgotten, and a large part of the field become imprinted on behaviorism. The Zeitgeist affected not only the *theories* of learning that were tested but also the *methods* by which they were examined. What were children asked to learn?

Some were asked to stack boxes or use sticks to obtain objects out of reach, just like Sultan the chimp (Sobel, 1939). It did not seem to occur to anyone that a set of boxes more readily affords climbing to an ape than to a less agile human toddler.

Others were asked to run mazes! They were "run" through a child-size maze of darkened runways where they had to complete routes to reach goal boxes in a similar inferential pattern to that shown by rats. It was not until well into the school years that children performed as well at this as did rats (Maier, 1936)! Again, the fact that running in a darkened maze may be a task suitable to no organism, but better suited to rats than preschoolers, did not seem to be open to debate.

Children were tested in cages—well, almost—specifically, a Wisconsin General Test Apparatus designed by Harlow for use with monkeys that bit (see Koch, 1959). I assume children in the 1960s were not rabid, and, therefore, the physical protection of the experimenter could not have been a prime motivation for this odd practice, engaged in, I might add, by myself and many of my closest friends. The prime motivation was in fact to minimize social or verbal interactions with the child. Deliberately, the child could not see the experimenter's facial expressions behind a one-way mirror, and hence could not be influenced by them. The fact that a great deal of learning is inherently social was not a topic of discussion; indeed, we explicitly controlled for such undesirable influences.

The point of this little walk down memory lane is not only to amuse you, but also to make the point that it was on the basis of studies like these that children below age seven or so were deemed incapable of inferential reasoning, insightful learning, and all kinds of logical operations, a position later reinforced by simplistic interpretations of Piaget.

Impact on Education

These developments in psychology impacted educational practice. The dominant learning theories for many years encouraged educational psychologists to concentrate on such external factors as reward schedules and transfer gradients. Transfer could be expected only if identical elements of external situations were held constant, thereby capturing the mind willy-nilly. Even though Thorndike, the originator of much of this, gave up on his position concerning learning and transfer in the late 1920s (Thorndike and Gates, 1929), the theories, albeit somewhat disguised, are still alive today.

Equally important was the model of the child that emerged. It was received wisdom that young children had limited attention spans. They got bored easily in those boxes, mazes, and cages. So it was assumed that the young bore easily in any learning situation. Similarly, young children performed abysmally in settings designed to exploit animal wit. As a result, they were deemed incapable of inferential reasoning, of performing certain types of classification, of insightful learning and transfer in general. Because of these assumed problems of immaturity, it was believed that children in school should work to mastery on simple decontextualized skills for short periods of time under appropriate reinforcement schedules.

Despite this pessimistic legacy, behaviorist theories of learning of the mid century had their clear value. They were in fact remarkably successful at explaining the range of phenomena they set out to explain. For example, Skinnerian theory gave us token economies, fading, scaffolding, and today, valuable clinical methods, such as those used to control nausea during chemotherapy. Tolman was a clear forerunner of cognitive psychology, lending a legitimacy to mental models and states. And Hullian theory has much to say to contemporary connectionism. And in defense of psychologists, those concerned with educational practice were only too ready to adopt these theories in the absence of viable alternatives that did include concerns for context, content, and developmental status.

Behaviorist conceptions of learning and development postulated thirty years ago had important implications for instruction, both positive and negative. The theories permeated the language of schooling—and are still in evidence. Lauren and Dan Resnick (1991) have made this point forcibly regarding the state of the art in standardized testing, where the design of tests still reflects behaviorist theories of the past. Cognitive learning theory is only now beginning to have an effect on classroom practice and the testing industry. The vocabulary is slowly changing. The practices lag behind. Where we once had behavioral objectives, we now have cognitive objectives, although it is sometimes a challenge to find the differences.

New Learning Theory

So what's new in learning theory? Slowly, the cognitive revolution did come to town and upset many accepted beliefs. A dramatic change occurred in what "subjects" were required to learn, even in laboratory settings, accompanied by a dawning awareness that real-life learning is intrinsically entangled with situations. One cluster of such situations is the classroom.

The model of the human learner, including the child, was transformed. Learners came to be viewed as *active constructors* rather than passive recipients of knowledge. Learners were imbued with powers of introspection, once verboten. One of the most interesting things about human learning is that we have knowledge and feelings about it, sometimes even control of it, *metacognition* if you will. And, although people are excellent all-purpose learning machines—equipped to learn just about anything by brute force—like all biologically evolved creatures, humans come *predisposed to learn certain things* more readily than others.

We know now that small children understand a great deal about basic principles of biological and physical causality. They learn rapidly about number, narrative, and personal intent. They entertain theories of mind. All are relevant to concepts of readiness for school, and for early school practices.

Those interested in older learners began to study the acquisition of disciplined bodies of knowledge characteristic of academic subject areas (e.g., mathematics, science, computer programming, social studies, and history). Higher-order thinking returned as a subject of inquiry. Mind was rehabilitated.

Psychologists also began considering input from other branches of cognitive science: anthropology, sociology, linguistics; and they began to consider learning settings outside the laboratory, or even the classroom walls. Clearly a strictly laboratory-based psychological theory of learning is, and always was, a chimera.

Community of Learners

I now turn to my current work in urban classrooms, where my colleagues and I are attempting to orchestrate environments to foster meaningful and lasting learning in collaboration with inner-city grade school students and teachers. We refer to this as the *Community of Learners* (COL) project (Brown and Campione, 1990, 1994).

How did I get here from there? How did I make the journey from testing kids in cages to designing learning communities? To me the journey felt seamless. From studying rote memory for words and pictures, and strategies to enhance it, I progressed to studying memory for stories, narrative, and expository text. As the human mind does not resemble a tape recorder, memory for texts involves seductive simplification and inadvertent elaboration well documented by Bartlett (1932) at the early part of the century. Inferences and strategies abound, and their development in the young interested me.

Texts are understood and re-created in the telling. Understanding admits of degree; monitoring one's understanding of texts requires far more subtle judgment than monitoring if one can recall lists of words or sentences. It was this move away from rote learning of discrete stimuli to understanding text that led me down the slippery slope toward an area of research with obvious educational implications: reading comprehension and comprehension monitoring.

Children have difficulty in recruiting strategies to help them understand lengthy texts. So too the subjective judgment required to monitor whether or not one has understood presents the developmentally young with difficulty, not surprising given the problems college students have with calibrating their attention to avoid the illusion of comprehension. So, my colleagues and I began a series of studies to help children learn from texts, training individual strategies such as questioning, clarifying, and summarizing to help them monitor their progress (Brown, Bransford, Ferrara, and Campione, 1983). This was the precursor to the next step, the design of a reading comprehension instructional intervention that would combine these activities in an effort after meaning. Reciprocal teaching, designed by Annemarie Palincsar and me (Palincsar and Brown, 1984), became that intervention, and, as we will see, it is still a central part of the COL.

Reciprocal teaching involved the development of a minilearning community, intent not only on understanding and interpreting texts as given, but also on establishing an interpretive community (Fish, 1980) whose interaction with texts was as much a matter of community understanding and shared experience as it was strictly textual interpretation. It was to capture this influence of common knowledge, beliefs, and expectations that the notion of a community of learners was developed. For the past ten years or so, my colleagues and I have been gradually evolving learning environments that would deliberately foster interpretive communities of grade-school learners.

Engineering of a Community of Learners

The fundamental engineering principle behind the design of a COL is to lure students into enacting roles typical of a research community. I take this metaphor seriously. The COL classrooms feature a variety of activities that are essentially dialogic in nature, modeled after research seminars, that when working well facilitate interchange, reciprocity, and community.

Theoretically, I imagine such classrooms as enculturating *multiple zones of proximal development*, to use the now popular Vygotskian (1978) term. A zone of proximal development defines the distance between a child's current level of learning and the level she can reach with the help of people, tools, and powerful artifacts—tools and aids to perfect mind, in Bacon's terms. Within these multiple overlapping zones, students navigate by different routes and at different rates. But the push is toward upper, rather than lower, levels of competence. These levels are not immutable, but rather constantly changing as participants become increasingly independent at successively more advanced levels.

Practically I imagine classrooms as learning communities that have extensions beyond the classroom walls. I will share with you a few essential components (for fuller details, see Brown and Campione, 1990, 1994). One is that we feature students as researchers and teachers, partially responsible for designing their own curriculum. A variety of collaborative activities encourage this. I will discuss just two of them: reciprocal teaching learning seminars and jigsaw teaching sessions.

Reciprocal Teaching

Reciprocal teaching began as a method of conducting "reading group," once an established ritual of the grade-school class. Reciprocal teaching seminars can be led by teachers, parents, peers, or other students. Six or so participants form a group with each member taking a turn leading a discussion about an article, a video, or other materials they need to understand for research purposes. The leader begins the discussion by *asking a question* and ends by *summarizing* the gist of the argument to date. Attempts to *clarify* any problems of understanding take place when needed, and a leader can ask for *predictions* about future content if this seems appropriate. These four activities were chosen because they are excellent comprehension-monitoring devices. Quite simply, if you cannot summarize what you have just read, you do not understand, and you had better do something about it (for more details, see Palincsar and Brown, 1984).

Reciprocal teaching was designed to provoke zones of proximal development within which readers of varying abilities could find support. Group cooperation, where everyone is trying to arrive at consensus concerning meaning, relevance, and importance, helps ensure that understanding occurs, even if some members of the group are not yet capable of full participation. Because thinking is externalized in the form of discussion, beginners can learn from the contributions of those more expert than they.

So, unlike many decontextualized skills approaches to reading, skills here are practiced in the context of actually reading. Collaboratively, the group, with its variety of expertise, engagement, and goals, gets the job done; usually the text gets understood. The integrity of the task, *reading for meaning*, is maintained throughout.

Jigsaw

This idea of learning with a clear purpose in mind is a mainstay of all the components of the Community of Learners. In particular it carries over to our version of Aronson's (1978) jigsaw classroom. Students are asked to undertake independent and collaborative research. As researchers, they divide up units of study and share responsibility for learning and teaching their piece of the puzzle to each other.

How does this work? Classroom teachers and domain area specialists together decide on central abiding themes visited at a developmentally sensitive level. Each theme (e.g., changing populations) is then divided into five or six subtopics (endangered species, rebounding populations, introduced species, etc.), dependent in part upon student age and interest. Each group of students conducts research on one subtopic, and then shares its knowledge by teaching it to others.

As a concrete example, recent classes of *second graders* chose to study animal/habitat interdependence. Some children studied how animals protect themselves from the elements or from predators. Others became experts on animal communication or reproductive strategies. Still others studied predator/prey relations. Design teams were then formed that created habitats for an adopted animal or invented an animal of the future. These design teams were configured so that each member had conducted research on part of the knowledge. In each group someone knew about predator/prey relations, someone could talk wisely on the strengths and weaknesses of possible methods of communication, and so forth. All pieces are needed to complete the puzzle, to design the habitat, hence jigsaw. By these methods, expertise is distributed deliberately.

Majoring

Expertise is also distributed by happenstance. Variability in expertise arises naturally because of the different research paths followed by groups and individuals. We refer to this phenomenon as *majoring*. Children are free to major in a variety of ways, free to learn and teach whatever they like within the confines of their subtopic. Some become experts on disease and contagion, some concentrate on bizarre reproductive strategies; others major in pesticides or pollution. All contribute their specific knowledge, thereby enriching the intellectual resources of the community.

Let us consider just one example of majoring: *delayed implantation*. This is a reproductive strategy whereby fertilized eggs lay dormant inside the female until environmental conditions are suitable for the survival of offspring, at which point the eggs begin to develop. This principle was discovered by some fifth graders last year, but not by previous cohorts. At least nine months after their discovery, a group of now sixth graders told me about another example of the principle, the Minnesota Mink, that they had seen in a television program. According to my informants (my commentary in brackets):

- Minks breed aggressively in late winter because their thick coats will protect them from bites and scratching. [This was an inference. On the program, we learned only that mink shed their valuable heavy winter coats for light summer ones. And the mating minks did look like they were engaged in strenuous activity. The inference was actually an example of transfer of prior knowledge from an animal these students had previously studied, the sea otter, with a heavy coat and notably rough mating habits.]
- The females mate with as many males as possible, and subsequent litters consist of pups that are fathered by more than one male. The students argued that this increased the variability of the gene pool [a biologically appropriate inference].
- The last male to mate has more pups, because, the students argued, if he could still mate at the end of the season, he must be pretty strong [inference based on a Spencerian/Darwinian notion of survival of the fittest].
- The fertilized eggs just sit there, another child corrects, lie dormant, until it is spring, and then start to develop.
- Pups are partly "acquarian." [I think they meant aquatic.]

The point about my story is not the demonstration of long-term retention of facts, or the assimilation of new facts about a complex biological mechanism, or even the inferential powers the students displayed. It is their excitement about what they are learning sustained over considerable time, and at their own expense (they were no longer accountable for this topic). I was impressed by their confidence in their own developing knowledge and their belief that this is something that the community will respect and value. And by way of metaphorical extension, delayed implantation is what we do with ideas—plant them in the community and hope they come to fruition when the time is ripe.

The Role of Performance

In telling their story, these students were putting on a performance, for my benefit. Everyone in the community is at some stage an actor and an audience. Regular exhibitions to a variety of audiences are an important component of the community. The sense of audience for one's research efforts is not imaginary, but palpable and real. Audiences demand coherence, push for higher levels of understanding, require satisfactory explanations, request clarification of obscure points, and so on. Students do not have to deal only with a single audience, the teacher, as they often do in school.

These opportunities to display provide an element of reality testing, also an important feature of many of the school activities such as dramatic plays put on by boys' and girls' clubs (Heath and McLaughlin, in press). Such groups typically engage in seasonal cycles of planning, preparing, rehearsing, and finally performing. There are deadlines, discipline, and most important, reflection on performance. So, too, in the COL we have cycles of planning, preparing, practicing, and teaching others. Deadlines and performance demand the setting of priorities—what is important to know? What is important to teach? What of our newfound knowledge do we display?

The Classroom Teacher

The classroom teacher is not absent from these proceedings. She learns along with the children as well as assists their efforts. In addition, she periodically calls the whole class into conference to consider the main theme and the relation among the research activities. The aim is to lead the students to higher levels of thinking and to help them set goals for future research. These whole-class discussions provide a reflection period in which to take stock of where they are and where they want to be.

Extending the Learning Community

Inside the School

For the program to run optimally, adults other than the classroom teacher are needed to guide the learning activities. But we have to live with the feasible. How many extra bodies can there be? Parenthetically, I note that at its peak, Dewey's (1936) Laboratory School had a 4:1 child to adult ratio, not counting adult experts. Because this is unrealistic, the COL relies heavily on the expertise of the children themselves. We use cross-age teaching, both face-to-face and via electronic mail. We use older students as discussion leaders guiding the reciprocal teaching or jigsaw activities of younger students. Such tutoring extends the teaching "capital" available to our students, but it is also a formative aspect of community building.

Outside the School

Any learning community is limited by the combined knowledge of its members. Within traditional schools, members draw on a limited knowledge capital if the faculty and students are relatively static. Or they face jarring discontinuity if there is rapid turnover, as is the case in many inner-city schools. In addition, both teachers' and students' expectations concerning excellence, or what it means to learn and understand, may be limited if the only standards are local.

Schools are not islands. They exist in wider communities, and we rely on them. For example, experts coaching via electronic mail provide us with an essential resource, freeing teachers from the sole burden of knowledge guardian and allowing the community to extend in ever-widening circles of expertise.

Principles of Learning

A major part of my personal effort in the design experiment (Brown, 1992) of creating community is to contribute to a theory of learning that can capture and convey the core essential features. The development of theory is critical for two reasons, conceptual understanding and practical dissemination. The development of theory has always been necessary as a guide to research, a lens through which one interprets, that sets things apart and pulls things together. But theory development is essential for practical implementation as well.

It is for these reasons that we have been concerned with the development of a set of first principles of learning to guide research and practice. But in this light, it is a sobering thought that for decades the Progressive Education Association of America produced sets of principles (usually nine) every few years, prin-√ ciples that were so vague that they could not lead to a conver-√ gence in practice of any kind (Graham, 1967). They included: freedom to develop naturally; work guided by interest; cooperation between home and school; community building; teacher as guide, not taskmaster. All these are principles that I would agree with and will probably reiterate. But what does developing naturally mean? How does one follow interest and guide learning while at the same time helping chart legitimate pathways of intellectual inquiry? Without more specificity, more models, more documentation, more evaluation, these principles become part of a common vocabulary, but influence practice little. Descriptions of current "innovative" programs also share a family resemblance in rhetoric, but again one might ask, do they result in any consensual practice? My own rhetoric in describing principles of learning is far from safe from these criticisms.

And the problem of dissemination is a real one. As a cautionary tale, consider the fate of reciprocal teaching. The program has enjoyed widespread dissemination. It has been picked up by researchers, teachers, and textbook publishers, and has become part of the discourse of the educational community. But too often something called reciprocal teaching is practiced in such a way that the principles of learning it was meant to foster are lost, or at best relegated to a minor position. The surface rituals of questioning, summarizing, and so forth are engaged in, divorced from the goal of reading for understanding that they were designed to serve. These "strategies" are sometimes practiced out of the context of reading texts. Quite simply, if one wants to disseminate a program on the basis of principles of learning rather than surface procedures, one must be able to specify what those principles are in such a way that they can inform practice.

Adaptation and modification are an organic part of any implementation process. When working with new teachers, we encourage *implementation as evolution* (Majone and Wildavsky, 1978) *constrained by first principles.* Here, by way of illustration, we will discuss a few of these first principles of learning. A more complete list is given in Brown and Campione (1994).

Steps Toward Learning Principles of the COL Program

1. *A great deal of academic learning, though not everyday learning, is active, strategic, self-conscious, self-motivated,* and *purposeful.* Effective learners operate best when they have insight into their own strengths and weaknesses and access to their own repertoires of strategies for learning. For the past twenty years or so, this type of knowledge and control over thinking has been termed *metacognition* (Brown, 1978).

Interest in things metacognitive is, of course, not new; it is just that a concentrated period of research has reaffirmed what was already known but not established very well. And that *is* progress. A little recognized progenitor of this position was actually Binet, known in this country primarily for the introduction of intelligence testing. Binet was also interested in the education of the childlike mind. True to the newfound confidence in testing, Binet designed tests of what he called *autocriticism* to root out metacognitive lacunae. For example, what is wrong with these sentences?

- An unfortunate cyclist fractured his skull and died at once; he has been taken to the hospital and we are afraid he won't be able to recover.
- Yesterday we found a woman's body sliced in 18 pieces; we believe she killed herself.

Gruesome Victoriana indeed, but as Binet pointed out, "You would be surprised at how many of the thoughtless young are quite happy with this nonsense."

"Apres le mal, le remede." Binet believed diagnosis to be of little use if it were not followed by remediation. "If it is not possible to change intelligence, why measure it in the first place?" Given this philosophy, not shared by many in the early part of the century who began to believe in the immutability of IQ, Binet developed a remedial curriculum for the "thoughtless young." The curriculum, called *Mental Orthopedics*, was intended to strengthen the child's "unreflective and inconsistent mind." As the thoughtless child "does not know that he does not understand," he needs help "to observe, to listen and to judge better." The curriculum was specifically designed to train, in Binet's terms, "habits of work, effort, attention, reasoning and self-criticism," leading to the "pleasures of intellectual self-confidence" (all quotations from Binet, 1909). Unfortunately for us, he was more than a little vague about how we might do this. Actual descriptions of the training or its outcomes do not survive, a problem in general for past innovative programs.

One might argue that all this talk of strategies and metacognition is silly. Who indeed would want passive, unmotivated, purposeless, indeed mindless, learning? There is certainly a place for mindlessness in human learning; a great deal of learning does occur incidentally, and humans have reasoning biases that allow them to get by on this most of the time (Bartlett, 1958; Tversky and Kahneman, 1974). But scholarship, the domain of schools, demands intentional learning (Bereiter and Scardamalia, 1989). In this context, who could possibly argue against mindful learning? My point is not that peopled argued *against* mindful learning; rather, that they did not campaign actively *for* it. Remember, a belief that rote learning trains the mind has been around for a long time. Advocates of fact acquisition, in and of itself and by whatever means, still stalk the land. One legacy of behaviorism was a concern with capturing the mind in spite of itself. Understanding and reflection were not prominent features of the psychological learning theories of the mid century. The need for a resurgence of interest in mind and its uses was overdue.

2. *Classrooms as settings for multiple zones of proximal development.* I take it as given that learners develop at different rates. At any

time they are ripe for new learning more readily in some arenas than others. They do not come "ready for school" in some cookie-cutter fashion.

The central Vygotskian notion of zones of proximal development is one of learning flowering between lower and upper bounds of potential, depending on environmental support. Bacon's aids, tools, and guides to perfect mind serve to push as much as possible toward the upper bounds of competence. This is also a position that needed to be reinvented. The set of influential contrasting theories that has influenced American schools include errorless learning, mastery learning, skill building, and so on: All attempt to aim instruction at the child's existing level of competence, often interpreted as lower levels of performance. Indeed, many interpret Dewey as suggesting emphasis on lower bounds when he argued in favor of teaching to the child's level. I argue that an essential role for teachers is to guide the discovery process toward forms of disciplined inquiry that would not be reached without expert guidance, to push for the upper bounds.

3. *Legitimization of differences.* A central principle of COL is that individual differences be recognized and valued. I borrowed the term from studies of out-of-school learning (Heath, 1991), but I also see reflections in Howard Gardner's (1983) concern for fostering multiple intelligences in school and Lave and Wenger's (1991) description of multiple ways into communities of practice.

Can we do this in schools; can we rejoice in diversity? What if classrooms were designed explicitly to capitalize on varieties of talent to provide multiple "ways in"—through art, drama, technological skills, content knowledge, reading, writing, teaching, social facilitation, and so forth? Indeed, it is very much our intention to *increase diversity* in COL classrooms.

Traditionally, school agendas have aimed at just the opposite, decreasing diversity. This tradition is based on the false assumption that there exist prototypical, normal students who, at a certain age, can do a certain amount of work, or grasp a certain amount of material, in the same amount of time (Becker, 1972). In our program, although we assuredly aim at *conformity on the basics* (everyone must read, write, think, reason, etc.), we also aim at nonconformity in the distribution of expertise and interests so that everyone can benefit from the subsequent richness of available knowledge. The essence of teamwork is pooling expertise. Teams composed of members with homogeneous ideas and skills are denied access to such richness.

4. *A community of discourse.* It is a common belief that higher thought is an internalized dialogue. To foster this we create the active exchange and reciprocity of a dialogue in our classrooms, which are intentionally designed to foster interpretive communities (Fish, 1980). The sociologist Wurthnow (1989) argued that changes in communities of discourse led the way to powerful movements in society—the Reformation, the Enlightenment, and European Socialism. At a less grandiose level, our baby COLs foster change by encouraging newcomers to adopt the discourse structure, goals, values, and belief systems of the community. Ideas are seeded (or implanted) in discussion. Sometimes these ideas migrate throughout the community via mutual appropriation and negotiated meaning, sometimes they lie fallow, and sometimes they bloom. These interpretive communities (Fish, 1980) give place to multiple voices in Bakhtin's (1986) sense of voice as the speaking personality.

5. *Community of practice.* Learning and teaching depend heavily on creating, sustaining, and expanding a community of research practice. Members of the community are critically dependent on each other. No one is an island; no one knows it all; collaborative learning is not just nice, but necessary for survival. This interdependence promotes an atmosphere of joint responsibility, mutual respect, and a sense of personal and group identity.

These five principles are closely intertwined, forming as they do a *system.* Multiple zones of proximal development presuppose distributed expertise, distributed expertise presupposes legitimization of differences, and so on. Two final pairs of principles form systemic clusters: (a) the need for *deep conceptual content* that is sensitive to the *developmental level* of the students; and (b) the need for assessment procedures that are authentic, transparent, and aligned with the curriculum (Frederiksen and Collins, 1989). I have space to discuss just the first set.

Need for a Theory of Development

I am reminded of a story told by Jerry Bruner in his book *Actual Minds, Possible Worlds* (1986). After he had given a presentation, a member of the audience stood up and said she had a question about his claim that any subject could be taught to a child at any age in some intellectually honest way. Bruner was expecting the usual question about calculus in the first grade. But no, the question was much more thoughtful: "How do you know what's honest?" Now that really is the pivotal question.

It is not an easy question to answer. Most contemporary school reform projects finesse the problem by adopting a "one-size-fits-all" philosophy. The principles and structure of the program are the same, independent of age. The developmental model is missing. Of course, from some theoretical stances, learning and development are synonymous: learning = development; development is simply the outcome of learning, a truly Skinnerian argument.

Implicit developmental assumptions are governing school practices nonetheless. We teach the young social studies in reference to their own neighborhood. Why? Because someone decided this was developmentally appropriate? A unit on boats was thought suitable for third graders at the Lincoln School, and six-year-olds in the Chicago Lab School studied "occupations serving the household." Why do we teach fractions (American history, biology) when we do?

It is traditional in educational circles to make up developmental theory. My favorite example is that of G. Stanley Hall, sometimes called the father of developmental psychology. Brushing aside the need for empirical validation, Hall (1881) championed a developmental-stage theory made up of cultural epochs, a notion subsequently picked up by Dewey. Hall argued that a curriculum should mimic the history of mental evolution. Young children at the "savage" stage should study material from the corresponding historical epoch, that is, ancient myths and fables. High school boys should study the knights of the feudal period because, developmentally, they were in the period of chivalry and honor. Young women were not accorded a corresponding period! There existed no scientific justification for these developmental stages whatsoever.

This story is not just one of historical curiosity. In contemporary curriculum design, in both science and history, a simplistic interpretation of Piagetian theory has led to the consistent underestimation of young students' capabilities. This slant on Piagetian theory encourages sensitivity to what children of a certain age *cannot* do because they have not yet reached a certain stage of cognitive operations. The "theory" still prevails in the face of thirty years of ingenious work by developmental psychologists emphasizing the impressive cognitive abilities that children *do* possess. Especially relevant to the design of, for example, science curricula is the painstaking documentation of children's evolving knowledge about biological and physical causality. Similarly, we know a great deal about children's impressive *reasoning* processes within contexts that they do understand. Again my point is that the design of school practice is influenced by theories of development more typical of the 1950s than the 1990s.

It is essential to the philosophy of the COL that the students be engaged in research in an area of inquiry that is based on deep disciplinary understanding, and that follows a developmental trajectory based on research about children's developing understanding within a domain.

Deep Disciplinary Understanding

Although it is surely romantic to think of young children entering the community of practice of adult academic disciplines, awareness of the deep principles underlying disciplinary understanding enables us to design academic practice for the young that are stepping stones to mature understanding, or at least are not glaringly inconsistent with the end goal. For example, in the domain of ecology and environmental science, a contemporary understanding of the underlying biology would necessitate a ready familiarity with biochemistry and genetics, not within the grasp of the young. Instead of watering down such content, we invite young students into the world of the nineteenth-century naturalist, scientists who also lacked modern knowledge of biochemistry and genetics. Ideally, by the time students are introduced to contemporary disciplinary knowledge, they will have developed a thirst for that knowledge, as indeed has been the case historically.

Developing Understanding Within a Domain

I take seriously the fact that a scientific understanding of the growth of children's thinking in a domain should serve as the basis for setting age-appropriate goals. As we learn more about children's knowledge and theories about the biological and physical world (Carey and Gelman, 1991), we are better able to design a spiraling curriculum such as that intended by Bruner (1969). Topics are not just revisited willy-nilly at various ages at some unspecified level of sophistication, as is the case in many curricula that are self-described as spiraling, but each revisit is based on a deepening knowledge of that topic, critically dependent on past experience and on the developing knowledge base of the child. It should matter what the underlying theme is at, say kindergarten and Grade 2; it should matter that the sixth-grade students have experienced the second-grade curriculum, and so on.

In designing the ecology/environmental science/biology strand, we seek guidance from developmental psychology concerning students' evolving biological understanding (Carey, 1985; Hatano and Inagaki, 1987). We know that by age six, children can fruitfully investigate the concept of a living thing, a topic of great interest that they refine over a period of years, gradually assimilating plants into this category. Second graders concentrate on design criteria for animal/habitat mutuality and interdependence. Sixth graders study the effect of broad versus narrow niches, and by eighth grade the effect of variation in the gene pool on adaptation and survival is not too complex a research topic. Whereas second graders begin to consider adaptation and habitats in a simple way, sixth through eighth graders come to distinguish among structural, functional, and behavioral adaptations, biotic and abiotic interdependence, and so forth.

Similarly, a consideration of extant research governs our approach to reasoning within a domain. Again in biology, we permit teleological reasoning (Keil, 1992) and an overreliance on causality, but then we press for an increasingly sophisticated consideration of chance, probability, and necessity that underlies mature disciplinary thinking.

Let us not forget domain-general scientific reasoning (Brown, 1990) if such exists. Do children understand the difference between hypothesis and evidence? What is their understanding of "the scientific method"? Indeed, what should it be? Francis Bacon's or Karl Popper's? Dare we share with them the insights of Peter Medawar that scientists as human beings do what everyday people do? They are *not* omniscient. They tell good stories, they create imaginary worlds. Indeed, the scientific method itself

> like any other explanatory process is a dialogue between fact and fancy, the actual and the possible, between what could be true and what is in fact the case—it is story of justifiable beliefs about a possible world. [Medawar, 1982, p. 111]

And then there is the age-old problem for a developmental psychologist—transition mechanisms. What triggers conceptual change? In short, the amount of work involved in mapping a spiraling curriculum that is truly developmentally sensitive is quite overwhelming. But it would be more so if we fail to capitalize on the impressive amount we already know by throwing out the bathwater *and* the babies.

Conclusion

There is a conundrum running throughout this chapter. I have argued that

- School practices are influenced by outmoded theories of learning and development that are relics of psychology's behaviorist past;
- Contemporary theories are better suited to inform the design of schooling because they take as their data base the learning of complex systems of knowledge characteristic of what we want schools to enculturate; and
- The new theories are making little headway at influencing school practices.

To quote Bacon again, "All things change, but nothing perishes." Why? I argue that this is because what the new theories ask is *so hard*. It is easier to organize drill and practice in decontextualized skills to mastery, or to manage 164 behavioral objectives, than it is to create and sustain environments that foster thought, thought about powerful ideas. We are asking a great deal from everyone in the learning community. But we know a great deal more about how to do it now than a century ago. Advancement in our understanding of learning is slow but real.

So, I conclude with a paraphrase of quotations from John F. Kennedy, Lee Shulman, and Jerry Bruner, to show my catholic tastes:

"We choose to do this, not because it is easy, but because it is hard." (Kennedy, 1962)

"Those that understand, teach honestly." (Shulman, 1986, p. 14)

Those that teach honestly teach ideas that are "lithe and beautiful and immensely generative." (Bruner, 1969, p. 21)

I believe that a century of research has helped us know what these ideas are and better prepared us to design instruction in the form of aids and tools to perfect hand and mind.

References

Aronson, E. (1978). *The jigsaw classroom.* Beverly Hills, Calif: Sage.

Bacon, F. (1605). *The advancement of learning.* Oxford: The Clarendon Press.

Bacon, F. (1623). *Novum organum.* Oxford: The Clarendon Press.

Bakhtin, M. M. (1986). *Speech genres and other late essays* (C. Emerson & M. Holquist, Eds., V. W. McGee, Trans.). Austin: University of Texas Press.

Bartlett, F. C. (1932). *Remembering: A study in experimental and social psychology.* Cambridge: Cambridge University Press.

Bartlett, F. C. (1958). *Thinking: An experimental and social study.* New York: Basic Books.

Bateson, M. C. (1984). *With a daughter's eye: A memoir of Margaret Mead and Gregory Bateson.* New York: Morrow.

Becker, H. (1972). A school is a lousy place to learn anything in. *American Behavioral Scientist 16,* 85–105.

Bereiter, C., and Scardamalia, M. (1989). Intentional learning as a goal of instruction. In L. B. Resnick (ed.), *Knowing, learning, and instruction: Essays in honor of Robert Glaser,* pp. 361–392. Hillsdale, N.J.: Erlbaum.

Binet, A. (1909). *Les idees modernes sur les infants.* Paris: Ernest Flammarion.

Brown, A. L. (1978). Knowing when, where, and how to remember: A problem of metacognition. In R. Glaser (ed.), *Advances in instructional Psychology 1*, pp. 77–165. Hillsdale, N.J.: Erlbaum.

Brown, A. L. (1990). Domain-specific principles affect learning and transfer in children. *Cognitive Science 14*, 107–133.

Brown, A. L. (1992). Design experiments: Theoretical and methodological challenges in creating complex interventions in classroom settings. *The Journal of the Learning Sciences 2*(2), 141–178.

Brown, A. L.; Bransford, J. D.; Ferrara, R. A.; and Campione, J. C. (1983). Learning, remembering, and understanding. In P. H. Mussen (series ed.) and J. H. Flavell and E. M. Markman (vol. eds.), *Handbook of child psychology: Vol. 3. Child development* (4th ed., pp. 77–166). New York: Wiley.

Brown, A. L., and Campione, J. C. (1990). Communities of learning and thinking, or A context by any other name. In D. Kuhn (ed.), *Contributions to Human Development 21*, 108–125.

Brown, A. L. and Campione, J. C. (1994). Guided discovery in a community of learners. In K. McGilly (ed.), *Classroom lessons: Integrating cognitive theory and classroom practice*, pp. 229–270. Cambridge, Mass.: MIT Press/Bradford Books.

Bruner, J. S. (1969). *On knowing: Essays for the left hand.* Cambridge, Mass.: Harvard University Press.

Bruner, J. S. (1986). *Actual minds, possible worlds.* Cambridge, Mass.: Harvard University Press.

Calkins, M. W. (1915). The self in scientific psychology. *American Journal of Psychology 26*, 495–524.

Carey, S. (1985). *Conceptual change in childhood.* Cambridge, Mass.: Bradford Books, MIT Press.

Carey, S., and Gelman, R. (1991). *The epigenesis of mind.* Hillsdale, N.J.: Erlbaum.

Dewey, J. (1936). The theory of the Chicago experiment. In K. C. Mayhew and A. C. Edwards (eds.), *The Dewey School: The laboratory school of the University of Chicago, 1896–1903*, pp. 463–477. New York: Appleton-Century.

Fish, S. (1980). *Is there a text in this class? The authority of interpretive communities.* Cambridge, Mass.: Harvard University Press.

Frederiksen, J., and Collins, A. (1989). A systems approach to educational testing. *Educational Researcher 18*(9), 27–32.

Gardner, H. (1983). *Frames of mind: The theory of multiple intelligences.* New York: Basic Books.

Graham, P. S. (1967). *Progressive education, from Arcady to Academe: A history of the Progressive Education Association, 1919–1955.* New York: Columbia University, Teachers College.

Griffin, D. R. (1992). *Animal minds.* Chicago: University of Chicago Press.

Hall, G. S. (1881). The contents of children's minds. *Princeton Review 11*, 249–272.

Hatano, G., and Inagaki, K. (1987). Everyday biology and school biology: How do they interact? *The Newsletter of the Laboratory of Comparative Human Cognition 9*, 120–128.

Heath, S. B. (1991). "It's about winning!" The language of knowledge in baseball. In L. B. Resnick, J. M. Levine, and S. D. Teasley (eds.), *Perspectives on socially shared cognition*, pp. 101–126. Washington, DC: American Psychological Association.

Heath, S. B., and McLaughlin, M. W. (in press). Learning for anything every day. *Journal of Curriculum Studies*.

Hobhouse, L. T. (1901). *Mind in evolution*. London: Macmillan.

Keil, F. C. (1992). The origins of autonomous biology. In M. R. Gunnan and M. Maratsos (eds.), *Minnesota symposium on child psychology: Modularity and constraints on language and cognition*, pp. 103–137. Hillsdale, N.J.: Erlbaum.

Kennedy, J. F. (1962). Televised address from Rice University, September 12.

Koch, S. (ed.) (1959). *Psychology: A study of a science: General systematic formulations, learning, and special processes. Vol. 2*. New York: McGraw-Hill.

Lave, J., and Wenger, E. (1991). *Situated learning: Legitimate peripheral participation*. New York: Cambridge University Press.

Maier, N. R. F. (1936). Reasoning in children. *Journal of Comparative Psychology 21*, 357–66.

Majone, G., and Wildavsky, A. (1978). Implementation as evolution. In H. E. Freeman (ed.), *Policy studies review annual. Vol. 2*, pp. 103–117. Beverly Hills: Sage Publications.

Medawar, P. (1982). *Pluto's republic*. Oxford: Oxford University Press.

Palincsar, A. S., and Brown, A. L. (1984). Reciprocal teaching of compre-hension-fostering and monitoring activities. *Cognition and Instruction 1*(2), 117–175.

Resnick, L. B., and Resnick, D. P. (1991). Assessing the thinking curriculum: New tools for educational reform. In B. R. Gifford and M. C. O'Connor (eds.), *Future assessment: Changing views of aptitude, achievement and instruction*. Boston: Academic Press.

Shulman L. S. (1986). Those who understand teach: Knowledge growth in teaching. *Educational Researcher 15*(2), 4–14.

Sobel, B. (1939). The study of the development of insight in preschool children. *Journal of Genetic Psychology 55*, 381–385.

Thorndike, E. L., and Gates, A. I. (1929). *Elementary principles of education*. New York: Macmillan.

Tversky, A., and Kahneman, D. (1974). Judgment under uncertainty: Heuristics and biases. *Science 185*, 1124–1131.

Vygotsky, L. S. (1978). *Mind in society: The development of higher psychological processes*. (M. Cole, V. John-Steiner, S. Scribner, and E. Souberman, eds. and trans.). Cambridge, Mass.: Harvard University Press.

Wurthnow, R. (1989). *Communities of discourse: Ideology and social structure in the Reformation, the Enlightenment, and European socialism*. Cambridge, Mass.: Harvard University Press.

Chapter 4

Motivation and Cognition

Phyllis C. Blumenfeld and
Ronald W. Marx

Since the advent of public education, debates have ebbed and flowed about the best way to achieve valued educational goals. The past fifteen years have witnessed a renewal of this debate, one noteworthy focus of which concerns the goals of education themselves. Whereas past goals for school learning were largely that students cover substantial amounts of information and develop basic skills, new goals require that students develop a deep understanding of content and critical thinking skills. This shift has been driven at least partially by the work of educational psychologists who have shown that even when students master the basics and pass tests, many demonstrate an alarming lack of ability to apply what they know to new and different situations. That is, their learning is inert; it is not dynamic. At the same time, there has been a corresponding change in basic and applied research in learning and motivation undertaken by educational psychologists that can help inform the dramatic changes that are taking place in curriculum and instruction as educators address the new goals.

In this chapter we examine current ideas about motivation and cognition, and about how to enhance each to improve students' learning in school. Through this examination, we answer two essential concerns of teachers, school administrators, and educational policymakers: How can we help students choose to work on school learning tasks and to persist at these tasks, and how can we engage students thoughtfully as they work in order to increase their learning and understanding?

First, we discuss current views of motivation. These views of motivation are organized around two issues—ability and values—that influence students' choice, effort, persistence, and cognitive engagement in school learning. We then look at cognitive engagement in terms of the learning strategies that students use to complete academic tasks. These strategies determine the quality of the students' engagement. For example, simple strategies that aid memorization tend to engage learners on the surface and do not support the deep and thoughtful learning that requires more complex strategies aimed at information comprehension and organization. Learners must also be strategic about how they control their work—they use self-regulation strategies to plan, keep track of progress, evaluate results, and determine what strategies to use. And to maintain concentration, they use volitional strategies. The way students orchestrate their learning, the way they use strategies, ultimately influences their achievement.

After examining motivation and cognition and their links, we discuss factors in classrooms that affect each, considering teacher behavior and instruction, academic tasks, classroom organization, and assessment. We emphasize that environments have profound effects on motivation and thoughtfulness; the same learner will behave quite differently in different situations.

Motivation

If you ask parents what comes to mind when they hear the word *motivation*, they usually say that it has something to do with interest and with what their youngsters choose to spend time on. They might even say that it is influenced by incentives, like rewards and punishments. Psychologists include these meanings for motivation, but they have a much more complex understanding of the term as composed of sets of perceptions and reactions around two issues, ability and values. Also fundamental to an understanding of motivation is the idea of perception. It is not so much the objective reality of experience that affects motivation, but the perceived reality. One thing that strongly influences choice of activities and the quality of engagement in them is whether people believe they can be successful and whether the success is desirable. People make this judgment based on a variety of factors, including their overall perceptions of whether they can do a particular task (efficacy) and of whether that success will lead to desirable goals (values).

Perceptions of Ability

So how do students form perceptions of their abilities? They use different sources of information, decide on causes for their successes and failures, and make expectancy judgments based on whether they know what to do to complete a task successfully, and whether they think they can actually do it.

Sources of Information about Ability. One aspect of life in schools that influences beliefs about abilities is actual outcome or feedback about performance. Students primarily use grades and teacher feedback to judge ability. But doing well is not the only influence. A second influence is comparison. Children compare their performance with others to decide how able they are, and they are likely to feel more capable in situations where they do better than others. Success when many others succeed tells one relatively little about one's capabilities—everyone is smart. On the other hand, to fail when others do well is more telling, and can lead students to perceive themselves as less able.

This story is still more complicated. Successful students do not necessarily think they are smart, and those who fail do not necessarily think they are incapable. The attributions students make to explain their successes and failures is a third influence on ability perceptions (Weiner, 1985). Students who believe their successes are caused by their abilities or their effort, and their failure is caused by lack of effort, are more likely to judge themselves as capable. They presume they will do well subsequently on similar tasks, and therefore persist after a poor performance. In contrast, students who think their successes are the result of factors they cannot influence (like luck or easy tasks) but their failures are caused by a stable factor (like lack of ability) are less likely to persist with renewed effort after doing poorly. They do not assume they will do well on similar work in the future. In other words, students who think the causes of success and failure are under their control are more likely to adopt approaches like exerting effort or trying new strategies that ultimately will result in success. They see themselves as the cause of success, take pride in their accomplishments, and are resilient in the face of failure. Thus, even if two children are equally successful at an academic task, their attributions for this success might lead one to conclude that she is able, experience positive emotions, and presume she will do well in the future; the other might feel unable, experience debilitating emotions, and be less sure that she will succeed again.

Moreover, perceptions of ability are related to feelings of self-worth. Students want to believe they are academically competent. To maintain that belief, students may engage in protective strategies that have deleterious effects on their learning but do not make them appear unable. Under these circumstances, effort is a double-edged sword—trying hard can lead to success, but trying and failing leads to the conclusion that one is unable. Thus, students might procrastinate or not try so that they do not look dumb. They might take on tasks that are too easy, thus insuring success, or they might try tasks that are too difficult, thereby allowing them to conclude that they failed because the task was very hard, not because they are unable. In any case, such students are not motivated to engage productively in learning.

As students grow up, their judgments of their abilities become more realistic—they become better able to interpret feedback, compare their performance with that of others, and draw conclusions about their ability. Ironically, at about the fourth grade, as they become more capable of making these comparisons, they begin to perceive themselves as less able, and they continue to perceive themselves as less and less able as they progress through middle and high school. One reason, as we discuss later, is due to instruction and evaluation practices. Also, there is mixed evidence that the genders differ in ability perceptions. While many studies indicate that girls and boys who do equally well see themselves as equally capable, others suggest that even when they are performing similarly, boys think of themselves as more able and have higher expectancies than do girls.

Groups differ in their perceptions of ability also. There is some evidence that African-American children have higher expectancies and that these are less related to their performance than are expectancies of European Americans. But these studies often do not distinguish student social class in making the comparisons. Several studies suggest that Japanese students attribute success and failure to effort whereas Americans focus more on ability. Also, beliefs about ability differ. Japanese are more likely to see ability as incremental; one can get better with effort. Americans see ability or talent as fixed or stable; trying harder does not make you smarter.

Efficacy. Efficacy concerns children's confidence in their ability to organize and accomplish courses of action to solve a problem or complete a task. It includes beliefs about what actions are necessary to do the task, and beliefs about capability to do the actions required (Bandura, 1994). Perceived efficacy is related to perceived ability, but it is more situation-specific; that is, students might think of themselves as generally capable ("I am a good writer"), but when faced with a particular task, like writing a movie critique, be uncertain about what to do to produce a good critique. Efficacy is influenced by previous performance ("I've done well on this type of task before. I know how to do it"), by vicarious learning ("I saw how other kids are doing the task. I can do it the same way"), by encouragement ("My teacher told me that I can do it"), and by physiological reactions ("I'm really nervous; I probably can't do it").

Value

In addition to asking, "Can I do this work?" students ask, "Do I want to do this work?" Decisions to undertake tasks and the quality of engagement in them are affected not only by perceptions of ability and expectations for success but by personal judgments of the value of the task. Students might decide to undertake a task and engage fully or moderately, or they might decide to avoid it altogether depending on whether they perceive that accomplishing the task is useful, is intrinsically rewarding, and leads to their goals.

Utility. Children may see a task as useful or important if it helps them learn something or achieve something that leads to other desirable ends. In school, this may lead to taking math because it is a prerequisite for college entry, for a career as an engineer, or for eligibility to play sports, not because the student values math per se. Similarly, students may want to learn about computers because they believe such skills are important for job opportunities or to be able to do college-level work, or because they want access to information or games on the Internet. The computer may not be interesting for its own sake, but for what it affords.

Attainment. Tasks also have different attainment values, which are related to students' self-concept or identity. Attainment value relates to what students consider important to their lives. Often, attainment value is related to gender roles, because self-concept is often wrapped up with a learner's perceptions of male or female identity. Although gender roles are changing rapidly, it is still the case that some girls might devalue achievement in mathematics because they see success in math to be more important for boys than girls. Similarly, even though students might not find a subject intrinsically interesting, they might value achievement in that subject because academic success is central to their identity. For example, a student might not find physics intrinsically interesting, but might strive for success in physics because lack of mastery of school subjects is contrary to his or her identity as a successful student.

Intrinsic Value. Intrinsic value is often thought of as enduring and as resulting in high levels of engagement (Deci and Ryan, 1985). Students are intrinsically motivated when they see the task as interesting, challenging, or exciting. Students may derive pleasure from simply participating in activities or from improving their skills, not from external rewards or grades that might result. The term *flow* has been used to characterize experience during intrinsically motivating activities (Csikszentmihaly, 1988). Flow is a feeling of being immersed as action and awareness merge. It is total concentration and involvement; self-consciousness recedes as the learner gets lost in the task. Flow often occurs during participation in sports (athletes and coaches talk of "being in the zone") and music, dance, or dramatic performances. Writers also experience flow, as do students who are totally engrossed as they try to solve a problem or master something new. Flow tends to occur when people are employing, adapting, and honing their skills to meet a challenge. Obviously, individuals can be intrinsically motivated when working on something, but not always experience flow. Practicing a new piece of music, working on a hook shot, or writing a paper can be difficult and not always result in the pleasurable feelings associated with flow. However, people find endeavors more attractive if they sometimes experience such feelings.

It is important to note that interest need not be enduring; it can be transitory, affected by particular situations. Students might be interested in a task because of novelty, discrepancy, or humor. This interest is situational and does not necessarily result in concentration or thoughtful engagement in the task. Many attempts in school to make things interesting or fun often backfire because the interest created is temporary; students are willing to attend, but this attention is not likely to result in sustained commitment to understanding. In fact, too many "bells and whistles" can detract from learning by directing students' focus to irrelevant aspects of schoolwork.

Goals. Two types of goals characterize students' orientations to schoolwork. In learning or task goals, students focus on mastering or understanding the material. In performance or ego goals, students try to look smart, gain teacher or parent approval, or get good grades. Students who adopt learning goals exert more effort, use more complex learning strategies to gain understanding, and persist longer in the face of difficulty. They use strategies that help them summarize and organize material, and relate it to what they already know. Students with performance goals often stop at simply memorizing without trying to elaborate ideas or connect them to previously encountered material. They direct their energies to what is needed to get a good grade rather than to what is needed to learn the material. Most of us have heard a student say to a friend, "Do I have to know that? Will it be on the test?"

It is important to note that students can hold both learning and performance goals at the same time. Classrooms, like work settings, and unlike leisure-time activities, are not free-choice situations. Tasks need to be done, deadlines must be met, papers need to be written, and exams must be taken. These realities and students' concern about successful outcomes may propel learners to get started on a task, but it is the strength of a student's learning goals that seems to determine the quality of engagement as the student works.

Also, students hold many goals besides those most closely related to achievement. While learning and performance goals are central to the academic missions of schools, students have social goals as well. As they get older, youngsters become increasingly concerned with peer acceptance. Some also are concerned with being socially responsible, that is, doing the right thing, being a good citizen, and meeting the expectations of others. Both types of goals can affect how students approach schoolwork. Yet, despite popular wisdom, it is important to note that learning and social goals need not compete. Academically oriented students often choose friends with similar goals; thus, doing well in school and gaining peer acceptance are compatible. However, if a youngster's peer group does not endorse doing well in school, she will either sacrifice achievement or else try to hide the achievement efforts from friends. This dilemma is especially problematic for minority students, who often do not receive support from peers for academic pursuits.

Students may want to learn material in school and improve their skills, but besides social goals they may have other responsibilities, obligations, and interests that affect whether they adopt learning goals. If they decide the material is very difficult, might take more time and effort than they are able or willing to devote, or will detract from other pursuits, they may decide to not try hard. Or if they have the option, they might forgo the activity altogether. Many high school students have part-time jobs and engage in extracurricular activities in addition to their schoolwork. In an attempt to balance, for example, playing in the jazz band, working at the library, and doing a complex assignment, a student might adopt performance goals rather than learning goals to avoid the more deep involvement and investment of time and effort that trying to learn the material well would entail.

Summary

In summary, students who are motivated tend to select activities when they have a choice, try harder when they are working on them, and persist longer at them, even in the face of distractions. As we have already suggested and as we discuss below, motivation is related to the quality of students' thinking. Whether students are motivated to work in school depends on their perceptions of themselves and the tasks on which they are asked to work. Self-perceptions are concerned with ability, attributions about what caused previous successes and failure, and judgments of efficacy to carry out particular tasks. They are influenced by the student's knowledge about what to do to accomplish the task and beliefs about being able to do it. The second set of issues concerning students' motivation relates to their judgments about value; namely, whether the activity leads to something useful or desirable, or is interesting or pleasurable. In addition, what students want to accomplish—to learn something or to perform well (e.g., get a good grade)—also affects motivation.

It is important to note that while students differ from one another in their general motivational orientations, there are also variations within an individual. A person who feels very capable under some circumstances or who is interested in an activity will feel less able and less interested in other situations or tasks. In other words, an individual's motivation is situational and change-able; it depends on his or her perceptions of ability and value. Thus, in academic settings, the classroom environment strongly influences student motivation. We will discuss this environmental influence later.

Cognition

Motivation itself does not lead inevitably to achievement. Its influence comes from what tasks students select and how they apply themselves. As students complete schoolwork, their actual performance results from their persistence and how they think while they work. Put simply, greater learning and understanding result from more cognitive effort and deeper thinking. Psychologists categorize ways of thinking into three types of cognitive strategies: *self-regulation* strategies refer to how students allocate and control their cognitive resources; *learning* strategies are organized, mental activities students use to recall and comprehend information; and *volitional* strategies refer to how students maintain effort while working. Below we provide a brief overview of these strategies, how motivation influences their use, and how their use influences motivation.

Self-Regulation

Self-regulation involves planning, monitoring, evaluating, and modifying; it is essential for success at schoolwork. As students attempt schoolwork, they need to decide on a course of action, track their progress, assess their success, and modify their efforts. For instance, consider what is necessary to write a paper. The student must decide on the topic (or if it is determined, how to address it), the types of resources and research required to gather information, and a work schedule so that the paper can be completed on time. If students are collaborating on the paper, then they must also divide up tasks and decide how to coordinate their efforts. As the student engages in the planning, researching, and writing, she needs to monitor the work—Do I have enough library references to address the topic? Is it the right information? Do I understand what these references are saying? As she begins her draft of the paper, the student needs to evaluate her work— Am I addressing the key issues? Is my writing clear? Is it appropriate for the audience? If the answer to any of these is no, the student must ask, "What will it take to revise my writing to make it clearer?" If the student fails to regulate her thinking at any of these places (and more!), the quality of the final paper will suffer, as will the learning that the teacher intends from the writing assignment.

Learning

As students read books and articles for writing papers or preparing for exams, they engage in a number of learning strategies designed to help them remember, comprehend, and understand the material. They might use strategies like underlining, rehearsing, or creating a rhyme, image, or mnemonic (e.g., every good boy does fine) to help them recall terms or facts. Learning strategies like these are surface or rote. They help insure that learners remember information—that they can simply reproduce what they have read or heard. But, such strategies are less likely to lead to comprehension or understanding. More advanced learning at any age requires deeper thought in order for students to uncover the meaning of the material they are learning. To aid comprehension, they might elaborate the material by paraphrasing or summarizing it, or they might write short sentences about the main ideas in the reading. To understand the material, that is, to see relationships among ideas and between what they are reading and what they already know, students might create concept maps or outlines.

Self-regulation and learning strategies are related but function differently. Indeed, cognitive-strategy use without self-regulation may not effectively help performance. That is, students must be thoughtful about what strategies might work best to accomplish their goals. Thus it is not just a matter of using strategies, it is a matter of considering when, where, and how to best use strategies. This interaction can easily be seen in the question commonly asked by students even as early as the upper elementary grades— Will the test be multiple choice or essay? Students who employ both self-regulation and learning strategies know that the answer to this question will inform them about how to prepare for the exam. Multiple-choice tests will more likely call for use of surface-level strategies, while essay tests are more likely to require deep learning strategies.

Volition

Finally, students must exercise volition in order to manage and control their efforts, maintain their concentration, and keep themselves from succumbing to competing intentions. Learners block out distractors and maintain concentration in a variety of ways. For instance, they might sustain focus by creating a quiet place to work (away from the television), selecting a study time when they feel most alert, or telling a noisy peer, "Be quiet so I can concentrate." To maintain concentration, learners also must find ways to control distracting emotions like boredom or anxiety about performance ("If I fail this test, I will get a low grade in the class. If I get a low grade, I will not get into a good college. If I don't get into a good college, I will be a financial failure. My life is ruined!"). They might engage in self-assurance when facing difficulty ("I can do this." "This isn't so hard"), adjust the task in some way to make it more palatable ("Let's see if I can make this a game"), or reward themselves for persistence ("I will go get a soft drink after I finish those last ten quadratic equations.").

Motivation and Cognition: The Relationship

Strategy use distinguishes high achievers from the low. Successful learners employ self-regulation and learning and volitional strategies. Research suggests that students make use of strategies because they are motivated and know how to use them. Alternatively, lack of knowledge about strategies or lack of motivation is the reason why some students do not use them. That is, they lack the skill, the will, or both. What is clear is that there is a complex relationship between motivation and strategy use. We consider these connections in this section.

The Motivation-to-Cognition Link

Students who hold expectations that they can complete schoolwork because they perceive themselves to be skilled or able demonstrate higher cognitive engagement with the work. Interestingly, the effects of these perceptions are independent of the students' actual level of skill. Competent students who perceive that they cannot succeed at work that they really can perform are less likely to engage in it at deep levels than equally competent students who have more favorable perceptions of themselves. In simple terms, this work confirms the "power of positive thinking." Students who believe they are able report using self-regulation strategies like setting goals and monitoring progress, and deep-level learning and volitional strategies. Recall that self-regulation and learning strategies play somewhat different roles; one thing students do when they self-regulate is to decide what learning strategies best meet the needs of the task. They also evaluate whether what they are doing is working or whether other strategies might be more productive. Thus, self-regulation contributes to effective strategy use.

It is important to note, however, that there is a limit to the powerful role of self-perceptions. High motivation will not translate into high levels of learning in the absence of the cognitive skill needed to succeed. Obviously, strategy use will not lead to equal outcomes for all students. The motivated use of cognitive strategies will not necessarily erase differences in the performance of low and high achievers, but it will enhance the achievement of both groups.

Values also influence performance through their impact on cognitive-strategy use. Students who are interested in the material or who think it is important will be more cognitively engaged than their less interested friends. Values and goals may be an important component to consider in determining how students come to use different strategies and how they become effective, self-regulated learners. The important link here is through cognitive engagement. A child who is interested in a topic in school will not simply learn more about it due to interest. But the interest can influence learning by leading to more thoughtful engagement. While teachers may help students see the value in the work, doing so will not necessarily lead directly to improved performance; it will do so indirectly through students' greater willingness to be cognitively engaged.

These findings indicate that motivation alone is not sufficient for doing well. It is important for students to be motivated, but to do well they must also be proficient at using self-regulation, learning, and volitional strategies. It is possible that students who are motivated but do not necessarily do well do not know how to use useful strategies. If so, they may eventually decide they are unable, with subsequent decline in motivation and ultimately reduced achievement. Psychologists have addressed this important issue, and in the next section we consider the work on teaching cognitive strategies and how they contribute to motivation.

The Cognition–Motivation Link

It is common sense that all other things being equal, successful students know more than their less successful peers. They know more about the subject matter. They also use self-regulatory, learning, and volitional strategies more than do low achievers. Several reasons have been posited for why low achievers do not use strategies or use them inconsistently: a student might be unaware of the strategy, might know about the strategy but not know how to use it, or might know about the strategy and how to use it but not know when to use it.

Based on this reasoning, a number of interventions have been designed to teach students about strategies, especially in reading (Pressley and El-Dinary, 1993). The logic behind this work is that if students learn appropriate strategies for comprehending and understanding, their motivation will increase because they will perform better and feel more efficacious. When faced with a difficult learning task, students who know what strategies to use and how to use them will feel they are able to do the work, will expect to succeed, and thus will be more likely to apply themselves. As a result, they will do better and, in a cyclical fashion, will perceive themselves as more able. In other words, success will beget success. But, unfortunately, although students do learn strategies, they do not always use them.

It turns out that a more complex set of relationships holds among all of these factors. Teaching learning strategies outside of the context in which they will be used and without close attention to the motivational issues at stake when they are used is not highly effective. Students can acquire the skill to use the strategies, but not the will. For example, students might have mastered the what, when, and how of strategy use, but not employ strategies because of expectancies—they do not think they have the ability to use the strategies effectively. Or values and goals might be at issue; they do not believe that strategy use will improve performance. Alternatively, they might see the potential benefits but not care enough about or be interested in understanding the material to exert the effort that strategy use requires. Finally, students might be trying to protect their feelings of competence. Consider a student who is doing poorly. He learns to use strategies, tries to use them to comprehend difficult material, but is not successful. The outcome may reinforce his perceptions of his low ability. To protect his self-worth, it might be better for him to avoid using the new strategy and attribute poor performance to a disinterest in the material or to a hostile and unsupportive teacher. In light of these concerns, intervention programs now incorporate elements that address both teaching cognitive strategies and motivational beliefs about their use.

How Classrooms Influence Motivation and Cognition

Students differ in their general motivational and cognitive orientations, but an individual's motivation and thinking can also differ markedly depending on circumstances. People who are motivated in one context may not be motivated in another. Youngsters might like science one year and not the next, or like to work on computers at home but dislike computer instruction in school. Or they might enjoy learning in one class but work only for grades in another. Moreover, they might be inconsistently motivated even within the same context, depending on what is occurring at the time. Some of the variability in motivation and thoughtfulness in school is affected by classroom experiences. Teacher behavior and instruction, the nature of schoolwork, classroom organization, and evaluation methods all influence student motivation and cognition. We address ways each can be used to enhance motivation and thoughtfulness as well as problems that merit attention. Finally, we must emphasize that for the purpose of our discussion we treat each of the issues separately, yet they are intertwined. Instruction must be coherent and serve to provide opportunities for meaningful learning.

Teacher Behavior and Instruction

Teachers play an important role in the classroom as they structure the setting for learning and design learning activities. They influence motivation and cognition in many ways—through the climate they create, by modeling motivation to learn, and by their instructional practices (Blumenfeld, Puro, and Mergendoller, 1992).

Learning Environment. Teachers create the learning environment as they interpret curriculum guidelines by selecting and designing tasks and activities, evaluating student learning, and managing the classroom by exercising authority and granting students autonomy. Students' perceptions of their teacher influence their motivation; students' attitudes and achievement are enhanced when they view their teacher as enthusiastic, nurturing, respectful, and trustworthy. Students try to please teachers whom they like and perceive as nice and who make things interesting. These teacher characteristics need not mean that the teacher holds low standards. Teachers can hold high expectations and help students meet them. Giving students easy work and praising them for success can backfire—students interpret this as indicating that the teacher thinks they have low ability.

Teachers communicate their expectations for learning and thoughtfulness through the types of material they present. Teachers who give easy work so that students can succeed with little effort actually communicate low expectations about the class's ability. Teachers also communicate expectations for individual students by how they treat them (Good, 1987). Students are sensitive to what teachers communicate to them about their ability through powerful nuances in interaction. For example, teachers can create high expectations for success by presenting challenging questions to students and then giving them time to think through their answers and formulate a response. On the other hand, when teachers direct hard questions to only a few students or quickly move to another student to answer, the message to the faltering student is, "You cannot answer this question, someone else is more capable than you."

Teachers can model motivation to learn by showing their enthusiasm, interest, and personal investment. They can personalize topics by describing how they use information and how it relates to what they have read or experienced, and by posing questions about what they would like to know and how they pursue answers to these questions. Teachers can communicate expectations that students should be thoughtful by avoiding the message, "Getting work done regardless of its quality is more important than the thinking that the task requires."

Instructional Practices. Students can be motivated yet not be thoughtful, either because the tasks or evaluations themselves do not require it or because they are not effective strategy users. Here we focus specifically on how teachers promote thoughtfulness.

Several approaches from research focus on enhancing students' self-regulation and learning strategies. Strategy instruction can be more effective when teachers integrate strategy use into the day-to-day routine of the class rather than simply give lessons on strategies isolated from other academic work. For example, showing students how to elaborate or organize material, but then not reminding, prompting, or requiring students to use what they have learned is not effective. It also is important for students to consider what strategies might be effective for a task and to evaluate their application as work progresses. Rather than simply assigning work, teachers should take time to ensure that students engage in self-regulation and are mindful of their thinking, not just their answers. Such an approach to the use of cognitive strategies will improve the chances that students will be able to apply them to a wider range of learning situations both in and out of school.

Teachers must support students in their efforts to use learning strategies to integrate, synthesize, and analyze information. If students are planning an investigation, teachers can help students break tasks into smaller parts and provide checkpoints so that students can monitor their own progress and obtain feedback. Teachers can also demonstrate procedures and alert students to possible problems they might encounter. Teachers can model their own use of self-regulation, learning, and volitional strategies by thinking aloud as they work through a problem and anticipate difficulties. Rather than immediately providing right answers to students' questions, teachers can solve the problem with students. They also can allow time for students to make plans and to discourage students who jump into work without reflection. Moreover, teachers can use assistants, including other adults or older, more experienced peers so that students need not be dependent on a single instructor.

Students must be held responsible for actually trying to understand the material; they cannot be passive participants. Teachers create expectations that students must be thoughtful by making sure that many students participate, asking students to indicate their agreement or disagreement with responses, and having students debate the merits of different answers. Teachers also can require explanations and justifications for responses and encourage students to make connections among ideas.

Schoolwork

The type of schoolwork students are assigned affects their expectancies, values, and goals. Schoolwork also influences the quality of student engagement through the types of cognitive strategies it requires. Meaning, challenge, variety, and choice are important dimensions of tasks on which students work. While they are important at all grade levels, there is some evidence that it is exactly these dimensions that change for the worse from elementary to middle school. Moreover, the change is more prevalent in some subjects, like math, and results in declines in student motivation.

Meaning. Teachers can create meaning in two ways. The first is by presenting content that is coherent and has intellectual integrity. The second is by highlighting the relation of the material to be learned to the world beyond the classroom. Doing both increases interest and value; moreover, by its very nature, such work necessitates thoughtfulness.

Presenting coherent content entails covering a few key ideas in depth rather than touching quickly on many, assigning learning activities that are closely related to the main ideas, focusing on application of the ideas, and having students create complex products that represent their understanding of these ideas, not just the recall of facts. Merely relying on textbooks that typically contain many facts rather than highlighting connections among key ideas is not likely to result in meaningful learning. For example, having students learn about water quality by investigating their local water supply is likely to engender meaning more than would memorizing a list of scientific terms from hydrology and applying them to an abstract situation. When students are taught facts about hydrology and the chemistry of water in this disconnected manner, they often cannot apply their knowledge to help understand phenomena in the real world.

Even if classwork is intellectually meaningful, students may not be willing to use deep cognitive strategies if they do not perceive the material to be learned as having personal meaning. Students find schoolwork meaningful when they draw on their prior knowledge or experience, acquire skills that can be applied out of school, develop self-understanding, or experience opportunities for future course selection or career options. Attempts to enhance meaning can be overdone, misdirected, or simply trite. Stressing that math or science are instrumental so that students can get to college may detract from intrinsic interest in the subject and focus students on performance or grades. However, attempts to enhance meaningfulness should focus on demonstrating that what is being studied is useful for life outside the classroom. Tasks and assessments must help to illustrate this point. Worksheets or short-answer tests do not demonstrate to students the real-life value of material to be learned.

It is important to note that the often-used technique of having students engage in a series of hands-on activities as a way to involve students can be shortsighted. If activities are merely opportunities for learners to be active, without requiring focused and intense concentration on learning important ideas, then little educational value will result. Teachers need to be aware that involvement does not necessarily equate with thoughtfulness and that completion does not mean students understand the ideas.

Besides cautioning against activity for activity's sake, some researchers argue that trying to create meaningfulness through exhortation is of little value. An alternative is to create curriculum and instructional activities that relate directly to problems in the world beyond the schoolroom. These researchers propose a more coherent educational approach that incorporates many of the elements described in this section and above (for example, in science, a number of developers have created programs such as Computer as Lab Partner, Communities of Learners, Project-Based

Science, and Scientists in Action [Blumenfeld, Marx, Patrick, Krajcik, and Soloway, forthcoming]).

Challenge. Tasks that are challenging but can be accomplished with reasonable effort are likely to evoke student interest. Unfortunately, there is a great deal of evidence that much classroom work requiring simple recall and reproduction of information is not intellectually challenging. Completing such work does not require students to do more than use memory strategies and engage in superficial learning. Challenging activities require deeper thought and more mental effort, where students must organize and elaborate information to create meaning and understanding.

The question remains unanswered about how to optimize challenge so that students will respond with reasonable effort to learn. Students may resist difficult work, where what is required is often ambiguous (e.g., what must be done to memorize the definitions of scientific terms is clearer than what the student must do to design and conduct a study to determine the effect of acid rain on plants). This issue is complicated because students are concerned about grades and may be unsure about what they need to do to succeed on challenging tasks. In addition, students may not be willing to exert effort because they may not value what they will gain from the endeavors. Moreover, if the task is time-consuming or complex, students need to exercise considerable self-regulation and volition as they create goals, monitor progress, and evaluate their approach. In the absence of good self-regulation and volitional strategies, students may simply complete work by using surface-level strategies rather than trying to construct meaning. Finally, there is often an implicit norm in classrooms about what constitutes reasonable effort. These norms, however, are influenced by the nature of the work that is typically assigned. Students who are used to difficult work are less likely to be put off by challenge than are those used to easier fare. Thus, assigning easy work in an effort to motivate students is counterproductive; students are not likely to see the work as valuable and also become more resistant to doing anything that requires thought.

So, challenge poses a dilemma; work that is too easy is not likely to be interesting or result in improved skills or perceptions of efficacy. That which is too difficult may "cost too much" time, emotional energy, or cognitive effort; it may engender feelings of anxiety and low efficacy, or result in a focus on performance rather than on learning. All of this is complicated because challenging work is more likely to result in errors and false starts, which might be interpreted by teachers and learners as failure. Thus, teachers need to know how to help students learn from mistakes and not perceive the mistakes as representing students' low ability.

Choice. Providing opportunities for choice and control over work enhances interest and adoption of learning goals. Students can exercise choice regarding what, when, and how to work and what products to create to show understanding. For instance, students can be given options for the problems or activities on which they will work. Or given a problem or project, they might decide their approach to the problem, what resources to use, and how to organize themselves to complete the work. Obviously, highly structured and predefined tasks leave little room for student choice. For example, higher motivation and cognitive engagement are more likely to result from a science curriculum that allows students to design and conduct research on problems that interest them than from defined laboratory activities that have a predetermined answer. Yet it is important to note that providing choices between tasks that lack meaning, variety, and challenge is not likely to result in enhanced interest.

Striking a balance between students' need for choice and control with the need for students to address and learn curriculum content is not easy. Optimal allocation of student choice and teacher control will depend on student expertise and maturity. Ensuring that students make wise choices that can expand their knowledge but are not too demanding requires careful negotiation and guidance as well as skillful support as students work.

Variety. Students who work on a variety of tasks besides filling out worksheets or answering questions from the textbook are likely to be more interested in learning. Variety results from adding gamelike, fantasy, or novelty elements to tasks and from using different ways for students to learn information (e.g., doing investigations, collaborating with community members, or using the World Wide Web), demonstrate their understanding, and organize themselves for work. However, if not used wisely, variety itself can actually be detrimental to both motivation and performance. It can detract from a focus on the real content and may not sustain motivation to learn over the long haul; variety may incur short-term interest but little prolonged effort. For instance, students may get hooked by dramatic but extraneous fantasy rather than focusing on the problem to be solved.

Similarly, new educational technologies in which students can use different types of software and produce multimedia documents offer the possibility of variety—but caution is necessary. Creating learning products that include a combination of text, video, audio, or graphic material can help students better understand the material, but without proper guidance these projects can simply occupy students' time with extraneous work without enhancing their thinking. For example, students might spend more time shooting video or creating a graphic image than thinking about what they should actually depict and how it contributes to the overall representation of information. Thus, when introducing variety, it is critical to be concerned about the content of the material more than its form. Otherwise, it is possible to create tasks that are appealing but have little educational benefit.

Classroom Organization

Grouping practices can make ability differences more or less prominent in classrooms. When differences are obvious, they invite students to make comparisons about smartness. Students who draw negative conclusions about their ability perceive themselves as less competent and have lower expectancies for success—which in turn will adversely affect their motivation. Although grouping students for short periods for help or enrichment is sometimes necessary, the practice of using fixed-ability groups over time is especially problematic. For instance, ability grouping for reading has been justified as providing appropriate instruction for students at different skill levels; often, however, the result is that youngsters in even the very early grades label themselves as good or bad readers, with a serious drop in the "bad" readers' expectations that they can learn to read. Grouping can also result in lowered teacher expectations and different opportunities for students to learn. For instance, as compared to students in lower reading groups, students in higher groups are likely to spend more time on discussions about the content of stories and less time on the mechanics of reading, such as phonics. Thus, their comprehension skills as well as their liking of reading itself are affected. And at some point, unfortunately, students in the low group cannot advance to other groups, because they are too far behind in what they have been taught and mastered.

Ability grouping is also detrimental when the students stay in the same groups for instruction in other subjects, such as reading groups staying together for math and social studies. Such grouping not only labels students, but can also reduce efficacy by limiting poorer performers' contact with more competent students, from whom they might learn. Grouping also limits student contact within classrooms, restricting the range of friendships formed and also appreciation for the different talents children may have. For elementary school students, status hierarchies based on ability that develop when students are in fixed groups influence peer interactions on the playground and in other areas of classroom life. Recent research has shown that eliminating tracking in high school English classes so that low achievers can enroll in Advanced Placement classes improves the motivation and achievement of the low-achieving students.

Another aspect of classroom organization that can affect motivation is whether students work on the same thing at the same time. When everyone works on the same task at the same time, students can readily determine who is doing well and poorly, making it easy to place themselves in an ability hierarchy. Students who judge themselves to be low in these hierarchies suffer reduced motivation for and engagement in learning, which ultimately diminishes their success at school.

Another organizational practice—use of cooperative groups—can improve motivation (Slavin, 1983). Cooperative learning groups can enhance interest and improve attitudes because students are more involved in work and also feel a greater sense of belonging to the group. If done well, such grouping can also help students meet social goals by satisfying their desire to be with friends. In one model of cooperative learning, students receive rewards for the group's success. When they work with peers to achieve a group reward based on individual improvement, students try harder and their attitudes improve. In another model of cooperative learning, individual group members are given responsibility for learning important information that is essential for completing the group's work. This arrangement gives youngsters of different talents the opportunity to demonstrate competence and results in wider friendship patterns and better attitudes.

However, cooperative learning arrangements are not simple to apply. Unless they are implemented carefully, it is possible that children will like working with others, but the liking might not translate into greater thoughtfulness. Assignments must require students to be interdependent, to actually work together to solve problems or create products. Also, students must be accountable for contributing to the group effort rather than just relying on others to do the work. Group composition needs to be considered and should be based on the purpose of the endeavor. If enhancing skills is the purpose, then a combination of high and low achievers is appropriate; if the purpose is to improve students' attitudes toward each other, then combining students to insure a range of talents in each group is more crucial. Moreover, preparation for group work is essential for success. Collaboration requires that students be able to offer suggestions or opinions without ridicule or rejection from others, which means that students must respect each others' ideas. Collaborating also requires that students communicate clearly, consider alternatives systematically, compare their points of view with those of others, and decide on the best course of action or the most reasonable explanation. Thus, cooperative learning can have considerable benefits for students' motivation and thoughtfulness, but it requires considerable preparation.

Assessment and Evaluation Practices

One of the most central jobs of teachers is to assess learning, provide feedback about learning to students and parents, recognize commendable performance, and identify failure. Because of its central role in all school learning, careful attention to assessment and evaluation is necessary in order to capitalize on its power to motivate and enhance thoughtfulness and to avoid many of the deleterious effects of poor practice in using rewards and using forms of assessment that neither require thoughtfulness nor tap understanding.

Interest and mastery motivation are reduced when teachers use rewards, especially when the rewards are not tied to quality performance or progress. The likelihood of receiving rewards or punishments provides students with external justifications rather than personal reasons for engaging in schoolwork. As a consequence, students tend to lose interest and work to minimum standards rather than for their own enjoyment or improvement. Eventually, they might cease to choose a previously enjoyable activity unless rewards are offered. For instance, active readers who are promised prizes for the number of books they read, continue to read. But rather than choose interesting books, or ones that challenge their skills or add to their knowledge, they select easy books with simpler language or with ideas with which they are familiar. In a sense, their energies are diverted from enjoying or trying to understand the book to finishing as many books as possible. Obviously, school is not entirely or even largely a free-choice situation. Nevertheless, teachers need to balance the benefits of using incentives to get students to work, with the adverse effects of such practices on students' interests and thought.

In addition to rewards, other practices that focus students on performance outcomes can decrease their thoughtfulness. Deadlines may have the effect of getting students started, but too much time pressure can detract from meaningful engagement with the work as students struggle to finish. Moreover, practices that promote comparison with others, such as publicly listing test grades or giving prizes for best performance, increase students' concern about being smart and detract from attempts to master the material. To encourage effort, students need to be given opportunities to improve if their performance is not up to standard, and improvement needs to be recognized.

Recently, concern has been raised that typical forms of assessment detract from motivation and from thoughtfulness and do not give an accurate picture of what students know. The claim is that standardized tests are divorced from the students' experience of learning, stress recall of decontextualized facts rather than understanding, and do not result in helpful diagnostic feedback for students. Moreover, students who perform well on tests often cannot use what they learn in school outside the classroom. These characteristics of assessments do not contribute to students' intrinsic motivation or the use of deep-level thinking strategies.

In response to these problems, many attempts, including using performances and portfolios, are underway to make assessment more authentic. Authentic assessments provide opportunities for students to demonstrate mastery of subject matter, integrate prior knowledge with new learning, and receive meaningful feedback about their performance. These kinds of assessments are often embedded in the stream of instructional activities instead of being separate from them. Thus, they have value to the student beyond grades, and consequently are more likely to evoke learning goals and associated sophisticated thought. For instance, rather than take a test in order to illustrate what they have learned, students might give a presentation or prepare a report for a local agency, write an article for others to read, or prepare a demonstration for others to see. Preparing artifacts of this type represents what has been called "understanding performances"; they occupy a central and meaningful role in student learning. Similarly, use of portfolios can enhance motivation, because the pieces included are unique to each student and students have some control in deciding what to include. Moreover, the work is selected to show change and highlight improvement. Finally, in contrast to standardized tests, students are more likely to see creation of the portfolio and feedback about its contents as more meaningfully tied to what they actually do in classrooms and to reflect their actual competence.

Conclusion

In simplest terms, students' motivation in school is a combination of expectancies for success and values. Expectancies are influenced by students' perceptions of their ability and efficacy for specific tasks. Students' value of the task and their engagement in it are influenced by their interest in the topic, beliefs about its usefulness for both personal attainment and utility for future goals, and experiences while engaged in tasks. However, motivation does not translate directly into learning. Instead, answers to the questions, "Can I?" and "Do I want to?" influence student choice, persistence, and quality of thought. Students who answer "yes" to these questions are more likely to work meaningfully in school. They use learning strategies to help them remember, comprehend, and understand, and they regulate themselves by planning, monitoring progress, and evaluating their approaches in order to determine whether to adhere to their course of action. Students who answer "no" become less thoughtful. They are likely to exert less effort to understand the material—they simply do what is necessary to get by. Of course, for motivation to translate into thoughtfulness, it is important that students know these learning and metacognitive strategies and how and when to use them. Expectancies and values are relevant here too—students need to think that they are capable of using the strategies and that their use will be helpful.

Classroom factors shape how students answer the "Can I?" and "Do I want to?" questions. Students are more likely to believe they can succeed when teachers themselves model learning by demonstrating their own thought. Teachers can promote motivated engagement in tasks by helping students use strategies and by giving feedback about and by coaching thinking processes. Merely providing correct answers is insufficient. Students are also more likely to believe they can succeed when assessments are closely tied to classroom learning and require demonstration of competence, not just memorized answers to isolated questions, and when evaluation is focused on improvement, not merely the number of right answers. Finally, students are likely to say "I can" when they work on different tasks and when classrooms are organized to minimize comparisons about performance and competence, such as by using flexible grouping rather than fixed grouping based on ability.

Students are more likely to respond "I want to" when they perceive tasks to be useful or interesting. It is desirable for students to have a personal interest in the topic under study, but even in the absence of intrinsic interest, student motivation can be enhanced though variety, novelty, or humor, or by using different work organizations, like cooperative grouping. Moreover, choices about what to do, how to do it, and when to do it induce students to want to do the work. However, while these practices increase student motivation, such motivation does not automatically translate into thoughtfulness while doing schoolwork unless there is actually something to think about.

Teachers must act in ways that promote cognitive engagement— they must press for thinking by giving their students authentic learning activities that have meaning beyond the confines of the school door. Curriculum needs to be structured around concepts and ideas, not facts, with activities, discussion, and presentations designed to make the ideas and their interrelationships apparent to students. If lessons and assignments emphasize memorization or simply hunting for answers in a textbook, students will rely on superficial thought rather than try to understand the work. In addition, teachers must hold students accountable, and evaluation must be based on demonstrating real understanding.

In sum, learning in school needs to be coherent and sensible. The content needs to emphasize ideas and be meaningful; work needs to be presented so that students want to do it; the class should be organized to focus on learning rather than invidious comparison; the teacher needs to encourage and support students' efforts; and evaluation needs to assess students' thoughtful engagement and resulting understanding. In classrooms designed around these ideas, motivation and cognitive engagement are likely to be high and learning for understanding a more reliable result.

References

Bandura, A. (1994). *Self-efficacy: The exercise of control.* New York: W. H. Freeman.

Blumenfeld, P. C.; Marx, R. W.; Patrick, H.; Krajcik, J.; and Soloway, E. (Forthcoming). Teaching for understanding. In B. J. Biddle, T. L. Good, and I. F. Goodson (eds.), *The international handbook of teachers and teaching.* Dordrecht, The Netherlands: Kluwer.

Blumenfeld, P.; Puro, P.; and Mergendoller, J. (1992). Translating motivation into thoughtfulness. In H. Marshall (ed.), *Redefining student learning* (pp. 207–240). Norwood, NJ: Ablex.

Csikszentmihalyi, M. (1988). The flow experience and its significance for human psychology. In M. Csikszentmihalyi and I. S. Csikszentmihalyi (eds.), *Optimal experience* (pp. 15–35). Cambridge, Mass.: Cambridge University Press.

Deci, E., and Ryan, R. (1985). *Intrinsic motivation and self-determination in human behavior.* New York: Plenum Press.

Good, T. (1987). Teacher expectations. In D. Berliner and B. Rosenshine (eds.), *Talks to Teachers* (pp. 159–200). New York: Random House.

Pressley, M., and El-Dinary, P. B. (eds). (1993). Strategies instruction (Special issue). *Elementary School Journal* 94(2).

Slavin, R. (1983). *Cooperative learning.* New York: Longman.

Weiner, B. (1985). An attributional theory of achievement motivation and emotion. *Psychological Review* 71, 3–25.

Chapter 5

Developmental Psychology

Martin E. Ford

Psychological development is fascinating, and much more complex and multifaceted than was originally imagined. To deal with this complexity, a growing number of developmental researchers are using increasingly sophisticated conceptual and methodological tools to address an ever-widening array of basic and applied problems. The field no longer routinely frames developmental questions in terms of superficial age difference descriptions and oversimplified theoretical dichotomies (e.g., nature vs. nurture, stability vs. plasticity, stage-like vs. continuous change). Instead, it is now commonplace for research in this field to be conducted within interdisciplinary frameworks in which development is considered the product of a web of interacting influences operating within complexly organized systems at multiple levels (Berger and Thompson, 1995; D. Ford, 1994; Ford and Lerner, 1992; Horowitz, 1989).

As a result of these advances, the task of summarizing what we know about development and its implications for education is far more difficult than it was a decade or two ago. There is much more information available about virtually every aspect of development, but also a much greater appreciation for the difficulty of integrating all that information. As Damon (1989) explains:

> The study of child development is by nature an expansive enterprise, long ago having burst the boundaries of anything that reasonably could be called a unified scientific discipline. In recent years, child development has incorporated new approaches and expanded into new areas at a rapid rate. . . . Previously unexplored territories in children's emotional, intellectual, and social lives have been opened up for scientific analysis. As a consequence, this field-in-motion has generated far-reaching new insights into children's behavioral and mental processes. [P. xiii]

It is far beyond the scope of this chapter to attempt to enumerate all of these insights. Instead, my focus will be on explaining the basic nature of development and highlighting the key patterns, processes, and parameters that must be addressed in educational policies and practices designed to facilitate positive developmental outcomes. Consistent with this focus, primary emphasis is placed on research and interventions oriented toward the whole child rather than on information about particular domains of development.

The Nature of Development

Development is like a game of Scrabble (Ford and Lerner, 1992). Each player (child) begins with a set of tiles (biological, psychological, and behavioral capabilities) that define the player's initial developmental options. The game then proceeds in a rule-governed but open-ended manner, with progress determined by the interaction between what the player can do and what the game board (developmental contexts) will support. Progress is facilitated by the acquisition of new tiles and the emergence of new opportunities on the game board. Conversely, developmental options can be thwarted or inhibited by the absence of key tiles on the game board or in the player's possession, or by sudden changes in the context that force the player to adjust to new circumstances. Sometimes, players can overcome these limitations and obstacles through creative use of their existing capabilities or by identifying new opportunities on the game board.

In other cases, players fail to capitalize on options because they prematurely give up trying to identify new opportunities. Players may also simply be unable to make progress because of the poor "fit" between their capabilities and the opportunities available at a particular point in the game.

Just as success in the game of Scrabble requires good tiles, a strong vocabulary, and a great deal of mental effort, developmental progress involves a combination of luck, skill, and persistence. Factors associated with the "luck of the draw"—the child's genetic makeup, family and neighborhood context, and socioeconomic circumstances—define the initial developmental parameters and have a pervasive influence throughout childhood and adolescence. But developmental outcomes cannot be fully predicted from knowledge of a young child's talents, personality, and social background. Motivation plays an enormous role in human development, as do learned capabilities that enable children to meet social and academic expectations, make wise decisions, and deal with the challenges and stresses of everyday life.

Of course, developmental progress is not solely a function of a child's own effort and ability. Like the game of Scrabble, development is a collaborative process that requires a responsive environment capable of creating and supporting opportunities for learning and achievement. Internal resources can help a child overcome problems and obstacles up to a point, but these are not sufficient conditions for developmental progress. Ultimately there must be a reliable and continuing flow of learning opportunities and material, social-emotional, and informational resources available to the child. If these opportunities and resources are missing in the child's primary developmental contexts (school, home, church, etc.), then efforts to identify "pockets" of environmental responsiveness—caring adults, committed mentors, positive role models, and the like—will be needed. Moreover, the minimum level (and kind) of assistance needed will vary depending on the child's personal resources. In cases where significant motivational and skill deficits are impeding developmental progress (e.g., neglected or abused children; children with physical or learning disabilities), substantial environmental support and assistance may be needed. This is analogous to the Scrabble player with a tray full of consonants who is depending on other players to create the conditions needed for progress (e.g., by placing vowels in strategic places on the game board).

Although developmental pathways usually manifest considerable coherence and continuity, the diversity of personal and environmental factors influencing a child's progress makes development somewhat unpredictable and probabilistic (Berger and Thompson, 1995; Ford and Lerner, 1992). The difficulty of predicting specific developmental outcomes is illustrated in the game of Scrabble by the fact that different players with exactly the same set of tiles can end up with very different results. The initial words provide a foundation for the game and can create either a good "head start" or a deficit that the player must try to overcome later in the game. However, the initial outcomes do not fully determine the future course of the game. As more words are played, new possibilities will emerge that can significantly alter the course of the game. Some of these opportunities may be vigorously pursued, with extensive elaboration of a portion of the playing surface. Other opportunities may be only briefly explored and then left dormant while attention is directed elsewhere. Still other opportunities may go unrecognized and eventually become lost as the game board is filled up.

As more and more tiles are played, the developmental possibilities can seem virtually limitless. Developmental pathways can continue to emerge and grow indefinitely in one new direction after another. Players can also return to familiar territory and further extend their development in that arena. Even when a player is "stuck," there is always hope for the future, as both the game board and the player's tiles are always changing, at least sometimes for the better.

Although it is exciting to consider the developmental pathways that may become available to young people as they develop new capabilities and are given new learning opportunities, this open-ended process does involve numerous constraints. Many options require unique talents or special training that may be difficult to acquire (analogous to the Scrabble player who needs specific, hard-to-find letters to make significant progress). Unalterable choices must often be made that not only facilitate growth in one area, but also foreclose other possibilities. Bad luck (e.g., disabling accidents; neglectful caregivers) or poor choices (e.g., risky behavior; dropping out of school) can make further progress virtually impossible, at least temporarily—much like the Scrabble player who is trapped into a small area of the board with few options.

In most cases, it is difficult to change in rapid fashion the capabilities and life circumstances contributing to or impeding a child's developmental progress. Just as Scrabble players must anchor their tiles to existing words on the board, development can occur only by building in some manner on what already exists (Ford and Lerner, 1992). It is simply not possible to magically wipe out prior learning or to transform someone into a whole new person. Similarly, learning complex skills cannot occur in the absence of a foundation of basic skills. Children develop by modifying, elaborating, and reorganizing concepts and capabilities they already have rather than by erasing old ideas and behavior patterns and tacking on new ones. Thus, efforts to facilitate development require patience and a clear understanding of the history and personality that the child brings to the learning situation or intervention setting.

This does not mean that transformational change is impossible. Discontinuities can and do occur in biological, social, and cognitive development. Some of these changes (e.g., pubertal development; the "5-to-7 shift" in children's cognitive capabilities) are characteristic of humans in general; others (e.g., the development of intense interests; the discovery of new strategies or insights) are idiosyncratic to a particular child or group of children. However, such changes are still solidly anchored to prior learning. In fact, there is usually much more developmental activity below the surface than is visually apparent in the time period immediately preceding transformational change, with the emergence of new patterns or capabilities representing the culmination of a lengthy process rather than a brand new development. Such changes are analogous to the Scrabble player's dramatic use of all seven tiles on a triple-word square after carefully cultivating a particular area of the board for a number of turns to "set up" this game-transforming play.

In sum, *development is a complex, open-ended, collaborative process* that is facilitated and constrained by the person's biological, psychological, and behavioral capabilities and by current life circumstances and opportunities (D. Ford, 1994; Ford and Lerner, 1992). Just as in the game of Scrabble, young people generally try to do the best they can with what they have in their current circumstances. Sometimes, progress seems almost effortless as the opportunities for growth are plentiful and the person's capabilities are just right for the circumstances. Other times, it takes a great deal of creativity and effort to make even modest progress. And sometimes, there are truly few options, with little progress possible until either the person or the context has new resources. In such situations, efforts to promote development may focus on strengthening *the child's resources* (e.g., through health care, education, or social service interventions), *the resources available in the environment* (e.g., through family, school, or community interventions), or *the fit between the child and environment* (e.g., by seeking out goals and learning contexts that are optimal for a particular child). Such efforts can create new developmental options and pathways, but only to the extent that the existing biological, motivational, cognitive, social, and economic foundations of development can support these efforts.

Biological Foundations of Development

It has become increasingly clear that genetic factors play an important and pervasive role in virtually every aspect of development (Berger and Thompson, 1995; Horowitz, 1989). They do so in part by defining the boundaries within which changes in intellectual and personality functioning may occur. Although these boundaries may be influenced by experience, and are generally fairly broad, there are significant limits on the extent to which educational interventions can influence basic personality traits (activity level, sociability, emotionality, psychopathology) and cognitive abilities (academic intelligence, learning disabilities, mental retardation). Consequently, *policies and practices that do not recognize the need to define optimal progress in different terms for different individuals are developmentally inappropriate.* Just as the Scrabble player's scoring aspirations must vary according to the situation, standards for developmental progress must be flexible both across individuals and over time.

Competence development is also influenced by a variety of environmental hazards and conditions, including several associated with school settings. Indeed, the greater prevalence of health hazards in communities of lower socioeconomic status households is one of the factors contributing to the strong association between poverty and deficits in intellectual and social development. Policies and practices designed to prevent or control these educationally relevant health threats are important facilitators of child and adolescent development. These include childhood immunizations; accident-prevention interventions; adherence to developmentally sound nutritional standards; removal of asbestos, lead, or hazardous arts and crafts materials; education regarding the hazards of drug, alcohol, and tobacco use; and information on how to prevent sexually transmitted diseases.

Motivational Foundations of Development

Motivation is the central organizing force in personality development and a crucial prerequisite for learning and behavior change (M. Ford, 1992). It is also the secret to overcoming personal and environmental limitations that might otherwise lead to some kind of developmental casualty. And yet, motivation is almost never mentioned in textbooks on child and adolescent development, even as an index term. This is a major gap in the developmental literature, and almost certainly a major factor contributing to the historical acceptance of a number of developmentally inappropriate educational practices, such as those associated with labeling, tracking, standardization, and competitive grading practices.

Children are born motivated; the trick is not to demotivate them. Just as they begin life with certain perceptual and motor capabilities, children have built-in goal systems that direct and organize their behavior toward a variety of positive developmental outcomes. For example, children are strongly motivated to maintain a sense of security, and to do so they seek proximity with their caregivers from time to time, especially when the children are under duress. Children are also naturally motivated to explore their environment and to seek out challenges that can provide them with a sense of self-determination and personal accomplishment. These motivational systems provide the initial foundation for social and intellectual development.

In developmental settings rich in resources and learning opportunities, most children will actively engage these settings in ways that facilitate personal growth. However, when the environment is lacking in responsiveness or variety, children may become more focused on self-protective motives than on growth motives, like a Scrabble player who is more concerned with completing his turn than with making a good play. Needless to say, the long-term developmental consequences of these different motivational patterns can be very dramatic. That is why it is crucial for parents and teachers to routinely expose children to new experiences and opportunities, and to provide support and encouragement for those experiences that will help provide a strong motivational foundation for children's future development.

Goal-directed action is regulated by two different kinds of motivational processes: emotions and personal agency beliefs (M. Ford, 1992). Emotions evolved to help people alter and augment ongoing behavior patterns based on changing circumstances (e.g., fear can help people avoid dangerous circumstances; anger can help people overcome obstacles to goal attainment; interest can help people sustain productive patterns of activity) (D. Ford, 1994). In addition to this immediate regulatory impact, emotions play a very significant role in human development by suggesting possible new interests and by providing the central ingredient in avoidant behavior patterns.

Personal agency beliefs (PABs) also play a central role in determining which goals will be pursued, and with what level of effort and persistence. PABs are thoughts about whether one can accomplish a particular goal, such as completing a task or getting someone to respond to a bid for assistance. Because goal attainment requires both a skillful person and a responsive environment, there are two types of PABs: capability beliefs (beliefs about personal skills) and context beliefs (beliefs about whether the environment will facilitate or impede progress) (M. Ford, 1992). In general, people are disinclined to pursue goals when they do not believe they are capable of success or do not believe the context will give them an opportunity to succeed. These beliefs can become even more demotivating if they trigger inhibiting emotions such as anxiety and depression.

The literature on infant attachment illustrates the developmental importance of a strong motivational foundation in early life. Infants in a secure attachment relationship with their caregivers appear to develop the view, through both their exploration of their environment and their interpersonal relationships with caregivers, that the world is a caring and responsive place (positive context beliefs) and that they are personally capable of producing effects on it (positive capability beliefs). This world view in turn empowers children as they encounter new developmental tasks. For example, in subsequent years, these children, compared with their insecurely attached peers, are more curious, outgoing, and independent, and are more likely to be seen as potential friends and leaders by their classmates.

Fortunately, young children tend to hold optimistic personal agency beliefs. Like a Scrabble player who continues to believe she can succeed despite a run of bad luck, most children seem capable of "bouncing back" from demotivating relationships and experiences as long as they are not traumatized in the process. However, after about third grade, children become better able to appreciate the broader implications of environmental unresponsiveness, and are better able to integrate information about their personal limitations into their PABs. As a result, older children are less likely to be able to ignore failure feedback and negative social-comparison information, and are more likely to amplify the meaning and significance of negative experiences through cognitive rehearsal and rumination. The implications for educational practice are enormous, as it is precisely at this point that many schools begin to reframe the child's educational experience in ways that focus more on limitations than on improvement—that is, by emphasizing competition over cooperation, social comparison over individual mastery, and performance over exploration and understanding.

Cognitive Foundations of Development

Over the past fifty years, developmental psychologists have made steady progress in resolving the debate over whether cognitive development is a unified, universal, and internally regulated phenomenon, or more of a task-specific, context-specific, and externally regulated enterprise. The emerging resolution is a balance between these two views (Case, 1992; Damon, 1989).

The cognitive foundations of development include built-in capabilities for perceiving, remembering, and organizing information, with semi-autonomous information-processing systems for different kinds of content (e.g., linguistic, numerical, spatial, musical, and social information). Biologically based, systemwide changes in encoding and representational processes, the size and efficiency of working memory, and self-regulatory capabilities potentiate qualitative changes in the upper limits of cognitive functioning, but they do not automatically produce these changes. For individuals to perform at or near the upper limits of what the cognitive system can support requires that they have a continuing motivation to learn the content being presented and extensive exposure to developmentally appropriate information by skillful teachers and mentors (Case, 1992).

As a result of systemic, age-related changes in a variety of children's cognitive capabilities, there is a general advance associated with virtually every aspect of cognitive functioning. Cognitive development is particularly dramatic in the second year of life and around the age of five or six, although systemwide changes continue to raise the upper limits of cognitive development throughout the school-age years. However, cognitive development is not nearly as unified as was once believed. Although children generally exhibit predictable developmental progressions within a given content domain, there is very little relationship between progress in one domain and progress in other domains. Cognitive development is clearly not a monolithic process. Rather, it is more like a game of Scrabble where different areas of the game board are elaborated at different times and in different amounts depending on available personal and environmental resources and opportunities. Although it is possible to summarize this progress with a single number (as is often the practice in educational assessments), such numbers are not very informative about either a child's current developmental status or her future developmental potential.

Education represents an intentional effort to facilitate the elaboration of conceptual structures in different content domains. Unfortunately, many well-intentioned educational efforts are less effective than anticipated because they implicitly assume that extensive exposure to relevant information will be sufficient to produce enduring change. But exposure alone will generally produce little more than superficial, temporary change. Like a Scrabble player who is unable to recognize new options because of a limited vocabulary, a child cannot automatically translate information into understanding. Children must actively construct that understanding with the help of skilled teachers and mentors who can diagnosis the child's current developmental status and guide the child's progress within an optimal instructional and motivational "zone" (Case, 1992; Damon, 1989; M. Ford, 1992).

Another barrier to the development of a strong cognitive foundation is the failure of many educators to recognize that a great deal of practice is often required to consolidate learning. It is easy to assume that correct usage of a concept or strategy in one or two instances means that a reliable change has taken place. However, because development always builds on what already exists, the potential for falling back on old, less adequate concepts and strategies may remain for some time, especially if the new acquisitions have been learned in a narrow set of contexts (Ford and Lerner, 1992). Enduring changes in conceptual structures require continued use of the concept or strategy in a diversity of personally meaningful contexts (Case, 1992; M. Ford, 1992).

Social Foundations of Development

As noted earlier, secure attachment relationships can facilitate the development of a strong motivational foundation for social and cognitive development. This is just an example, however, of what appears to be a more general phenomenon. Specifically, it appears that children's development is facilitated when adults in their life (1) impart a sense of trust, personal engagement, and emotional warmth; (2) communicate clear, developmentally appropriate ideas, values, and behavior patterns; (3) hold high standards and expectations for achievement and mature behavior; and (4) provide informative feedback about developmental progress. This combination of social elements facilitates goal clarity and salience, positive emotions, and robust personal agency beliefs—the three elements comprising strong motivational patterns (M. Ford, 1992). It also provides the basic interpersonal and informational parameters needed for effective instruction.

Children whose parents fit the above pattern of behavior are likely to be more mature and more competent on a wide variety of dimensions compared to those whose parents do not fit this profile. For example, these children are more self-confident, have more friends, are more generous with others, do better in school, and are less likely to engage in problem drug use and other delinquent behaviors (Berger and Thompson, 1995).

Conversely, parents who are uninvolved with their children, or whose involvement is erratic and expedient, provide a very inadequate foundation for development. Like a Scrabble player missing half of her letters, a child who is deprived of parental involvement (as evidenced by physical neglect or emotional detachment) will almost inevitably have significant cognitive and personality deficits. Moreover, these deficits are likely to become more severe over time without extraordinary corrective action (Berger and Thompson, 1995).

Similarly, parenting relationships characterized by harsh and inconsistent discipline, poor monitoring and supervision of the child's activities, and a lack of emotional warmth are fertile grounds for the development of antisocial behavior patterns (Horowitz, 1989). Children socialized within these relationships tend to be aggressive, rejected by their peers, unable or unwilling to conform to classroom rules and expectations, and at great risk for academic failure. The relentlessness of this developmental trajectory is illustrated by the fact that efforts to intervene with these children in their adolescent years rarely produce more than limited success. Moreover, because these behavior patterns are socially disruptive, alternative educational settings are required in many of these cases. Unfortunately, little is currently known about how to make these settings educationally effective, although it seems evident that meaningful progress will often require transformational change rather than "business-as-usual" intervention strategies. In Scrabble terms, significant change may require the players to go outside the normal rules of the game by, for example, tearing apart a set of words and reconstructing that portion of the game board in the hope of discovering new possibilities (Ford and Lerner, 1992).

Research on the social factors associated with effective instruction and effective schools reveals a profile very similar to that identified for effective parenting (Berger and Thompson, 1995; Horowitz, 1989). Developmentally powerful educational settings are characterized by (1) energetic leadership, personal involvement, and a sense of emotional safety; (2) clear communication of instructional objectives and desired outcomes; (3) high expectations for achievement and proper conduct for all children; and (4) frequent monitoring of students' performance, with ample opportunities for personally meaningful feedback. These features of the social context of education strengthen both the motivational and cognitive foundations of development—especially when they are amplified by parental support and involvement—and provide children with an opportunity to learn under developmentally optimal conditions.

Economic Foundations of Development

Children who chronically experience the conditions associated with poverty are particularly likely to develop health problems (injuries, contagious diseases, and premature death), delays in intellectual development and academic achievement, and emotional and conduct difficulties (e.g., anxiety and depression, aggression and juvenile crime, premature sexual activity, and school dropout). Like a Scrabble player who is unable to draw new tiles, children who grow up in impoverished circumstances face many developmental constraints and have few resources to draw upon. Such children find it increasingly difficult to "catch up" intellectually and socially as these circumstances persist over time.

To increase the developmental options of children living in poverty, multifaceted interventions are needed that directly combat the mechanisms by which poverty has its deleterious developmental effects. Such interventions may include efforts to provide children with needed material resources (e.g., food, housing, toys, books). They may also focus on enhancing the quality of children's home experience through training, child care, and social-support activities designed to protect children from neglect, excessive television viewing, harsh discipline, and caregiver conflict. Economic interventions may also involve, however, school policies and practices designed to insure that learning opportunities are not compromised by poverty-related deficits in social and material resources. For example, schools often participate in programs designed to meet children's basic nutritional, child care, and transportation needs. Efforts to provide extended learning opportunities before and after school may also be provided to directly address developmental delays.

In these cases, the potential for developmental harm is unusually high—far greater than in cases where one is trying to move from an adequate to an enriched level of resources. Consequently, policies and practices designed to insure a sound economic foundation for development are an essential prerequisite for educational success.

Early Childhood Education: New Resources, New Developmental Opportunities

Although development is always open-ended and probabilistic (Ford and Lerner, 1992), it is clearly better to intervene early rather than later if there are chronic biological, motivational, cognitive, social, or economic problems present that are likely to have a continuing impact on development. Whereas by adolescence it is very difficult to "go back and play the game over again," one can generally expect to be able to make up much (if not most) of a child's early losses by improving his developmental circumstances in infancy or early childhood. That is the rationale for many early education programs, especially those targeted toward disadvantaged populations.

Evidence is rapidly accumulating to show that quality early education programs are indeed able to help create more promising developmental trajectories for children whose early lives have been impacted by neurological or cognitive deficits, inadequate parenting, poverty, or other developmental problems (Berger and Thompson, 1995). Compared to disadvantaged children without access to the resources and opportunities afforded by high-quality early education programs, children who attend such programs are less likely to be retained or placed in special education classes, and are more likely to graduate from high school. They are also less likely to become pregnant or to engage in drug use or delinquent behavior in adolescence. Preliminary evidence also suggests that children who participate in early education programs will have greater earning power and family stability in adulthood, will be less likely to engage in criminal activity, and will require fewer social services.

Given the Scrabble-like nature of development, it is perhaps not surprising that the benefits of early education are cumulative—benefits increase as the child spends more time in this developmentally enriching setting. Also consistent with this metaphor is the fact that the benefits are less pronounced for children whose home environments already have ample resources and learning opportunities. In other words, early education works by creating more options for future development.

The message for educational practitioners and policymakers is clear: Target at-risk children and begin addressing their unmet developmental needs as early as possible. Because many cases involve multiple risk factors, early education programs must simultaneously address a broad range of cognitive, social, economic, and health needs if they hope to have significant and enduring effects. Moreover, these programs must be adequately staffed by well-trained and well-supervised personnel who are able to provide the motivational and instructional resources needed to help build a strong, secure developmental foundation.

Middle and Secondary Education: A Developmental Mismatch?

For most young people, the preadolescent and adolescent years are no more stressful or chaotic than other developmental periods. The exciting and empowering changes associated with puberty and the emergence of new capabilities for abstract thought, self-awareness, and intimate relationships do of course create some confusion and new problems, just as a tray full of new letters does for a Scrabble player. However, most young people are able to handle these challenges sufficiently well that their educational progress and personal well being remain basically "on track" throughout their teenage years.

Nevertheless, there is an increasingly urgent sense that those who enter this phase of life with significant developmental deficits need prompt assistance. During the late-elementary and secondary school years, the academic stakes are higher and less forgiving, the social and personal costs of antisocial behavior are steeper and less reversible, and the consequences of poor decision making are more damaging, in some cases even life threatening. The cumulative loss of human potential that is possible and perhaps even likely without effective educational intervention is staggering. It is estimated that as many as one in four adolescents are extremely vulnerable to failure in school and involvement in high-risk behaviors, with others at a lower but still significant level of risk (Carnegie Council on Adolescent Development, 1989).

For many of these at-risk youth, the resources and learning opportunities available in their middle and secondary schools are their best hope of overcoming major developmental obstacles. At the very least, these educational settings should not contribute to the cognitive, social, and motivational problems of vulnerable adolescents. And yet it is the consensus of developmental scholars that this is precisely what many schools do. For example, a recent evaluation of the potential of middle schools to positively affect development concluded that

> Middle grade schools . . . are potentially society's most powerful force to recapture millions of youth adrift. . . . Yet all too often these schools exacerbate the problems of young adolescents. A volatile mismatch exists between the organization and curriculum of middle-grade schools and the intellectual and emotional needs of young adolescents. Caught in a vortex of changing demands, the engagement of many youth in learning diminishes, and their rates of alienation, substance abuse, absenteeism, and dropping out of school begin to rise. As the number of youth left behind grows, and opportunities in the economy for poorly educated workers diminish, we face the specter of a divided society: one affluent and well-educated, the other poorer and ill-educated. We face an America at odds with itself. [Carnegie Council on Adolescent Development, 1989, pp. 8–9]

Precisely what is the nature of this "volatile mismatch" between what young people need and what most middle (and secondary) schools do? It is essentially a failure to conform to the four elements of developmentally optimal social contexts noted earlier. One factor contributing to this mismatch is the sheer size of most middle and secondary schools. Large schools afford fewer opportunities for warm relationships, personal mentoring, and meaningful participation in school activities. Consequently, these schools create a sense of alienation in many students rather than a sense of involvement and personal responsibility. Alienated youth are in turn at greater risk for school failure and dropout, teen pregnancy, drug and alcohol abuse, and suicide and depression.

The antidote to these unintended effects is to create "schools within schools"—small learning communities where close, stable relationships with adults and peers can develop and thrive (Carnegie Council on Adolescent Development, 1989). As part of this restructuring, each student should be assigned at least one adult advisor who is responsible for understanding the student's overall life circumstances and for closely monitoring the student's progress at school in partnership with the student's parents or caregivers. These arrangements can facilitate at least two of the four elements of developmentally optimal social contexts, namely, a sense of personal involvement and emotional safety, and ample opportunities for meaningful feedback on the child's progress at school.

The other major factor contributing to the developmental mismatch between adolescents and the schools that serve them is an overreliance on competitive sorting and grading practices. In general, development is advanced by inclusive practices such as cooperative learning and mainstreaming, and thwarted by practices that segregate students into groups or pit students against one another in competitive goal structures (e.g., tracking, high-stakes testing, grading on a curve). Such arrangements are motivationally debilitating for those who fail, and contribute to a sense of alienation from the school context. Moreover, these practices are developmentally inhibiting for those who succeed because they tend to focus students' attention on goals such as winning and social approval rather than on learning and mastery goals. Competitive practices also make it impossible to maintain high expectations for achievement for all students, since competition, by definition, sorts students into winners and losers. In contrast, cooperative goal structures, when effectively implemented, reliably increase achievement for both low- and high-achieving students, and contribute to children's social understanding and ability to work effectively in teams and in diverse social settings (M. Ford, 1992). The result is analogous to a Scrabble game in which players can increase their own score by helping others achieve their highest potential.

Conclusion

Development is like a game of Scrabble. The fundamental rules of the game and strategies for maximizing progress are essentially the same for all players. However, because everyone starts with a different set of tiles and plays a different pattern of words, each player faces unique challenges and opportunities throughout the course of the game. That is why effective educational policies and practices must be based on notions of diversity and individuality, not on norms and group averages. Although education often occurs in group settings, development always proceeds one child at a time.

Just as a variety of factors influence progress in the game of Scrabble, many factors influence the course of development in children and adolescents. Biological, motivational, cognitive, social, and economic factors were highlighted in this chapter, and there are many others that could have been noted (e.g., perceptual capabilities, language proficiency, motor skills, communicative competencies, religious training, etc.). Adding to this complexity is the fact that each of these factors and the ways in which they interact with each other are constantly changing. Effective educational policies and practices must therefore be based on a recognition of the dynamic, complexly organized nature of human functioning and development. There are no simple solutions to most developmental problems.

People who offer advice about how to enhance development in children and adolescents often convey the impression that there is only one right way to proceed and only one pathway that can be considered normal or optimal. But the *equifinality principle*—that is, that there are usually many different pathways to the same goal—is just as valid in human development as it is in the game of Scrabble. In other words, effective educational policies and practices must be based on the premise that positive developmental outcomes can usually be achieved in a variety of ways. If a commonly used educational program or procedure does not work with a particular child (e.g., because of language deficiencies, handicapping conditions, learning-style differences, or variations in family circumstances), there will almost certainly be other programs and procedures that will work for that child.

It is the responsibility of educators to keep searching until a pathway to success has been identified.

The concept of development is often associated with dramatic, inevitable changes that are outside the educator's control. But this is, for the most part, a misconception. Developmental progress is rarely sudden or automatic. As in a game of Scrabble, progress generally proceeds in a gradual, albeit uneven fashion, with much more time and energy spent on consolidating, integrating, and automatizing developmental achievements than on the initial acquisition process. That is why effective educational policies and practices require a proactive orientation to change and a great deal of persistence and patience. In most cases, good things will *not* happen to those who simply wait. Educators need to invest time, effort, and expertise to produce positive developmental outcomes.

Finally, although educators can have a tremendous impact on the lives of children and adolescents, it is unrealistic to expect this group of professionals to routinely work developmental miracles with troubled or disadvantaged students. Contemporary developmental psychologists recognize that people shape their own development in many different ways—for example, by choosing particular interests and activities, by affiliating with particular friends and social groups, by seeking out particular learning opportunities, and by actively constructing self-concepts and personal agency beliefs. Teachers, counselors, and other education professionals can influence these processes, but they cannot control a student's thoughts and behavior patterns. That is why effective educational policies and practices must insist that students take personal responsibility for their learning and achievement, while also recognizing that education practitioners and policymakers have a profound and unique professional responsibility to help young people construct the strongest possible foundation for future development.

References

Berger, K. S., and Thompson, R. A. (1995). *The developing person through childhood and adolescence* (4th ed.). New York: Worth.

Carnegie Council on Adolescent Development (1989). *Turning points: Preparing American youth for the 21st century.* New York: Carnegie Corporation.

Case, R. (1992). *The mind's staircase.* Hillsdale, N.J.: Erlbaum.

Damon, W. (ed.) (1989). *Child development: Today and tomorrow.* San Francisco: Jossey-Bass.

Ford, D. H. (1994). *Humans as self-constructing living systems: A developmental perspective on behavior and personality* (2d ed.). State College, Penn.: Ideals.

Ford, D. H., and Lerner, R. M. (1992). *Developmental systems theory: An integrative approach.* Newbury Park, Calif.: Sage.

Ford, M. E. (1992). *Motivating humans: Goals, emotions, and personal agency beliefs.* Newbury Park, Calif.: Sage.

Horowitz, F. D. (ed.) (1989). Children and their development: Knowledge base, research agenda, and social policy applications. *American Psychologist* 44, 95–445.

Chapter 6

Moral Development and Character Formation

Larry Nucci

As in many areas of educational research, the field of moral education is rife with controversy. These disputes are not limited to psychological accounts of the nature of moral development or character formation, but extend to the very definition of educational aims in this area. Arguments about the aims of values education capture the essential quandary for any pluralist democracy attempting to construct a shared civil society without privileging the particular values of any one group. At the heart of the matter is whether we can point to a set of moral values that would form the basis of an overlapping consensus that would permit approaches to moral education that appeal to more than local or particularistic values. Without such consensus, the incommensurable qualities of local values would render shared notions of a moral community impossible. A related issue is whether there are features of individual psychology that can be appealed to in fostering the development of children who would act in accordance with such common or transcendent moral values.

The contribution that educational psychology can make with regard to these issues is to clarify how moral and social values are formed, and to address the social and psychological factors that contribute to the tendency of individuals to act in ways that are concordant with their own well-being and the welfare of others. Controversies notwithstanding, the past several decades have witnessed a great deal of progress in our understanding of these issues. This chapter will address those aspects of what has been learned in the areas of developmental and educational psychology that can help educators engage in meaningful moral and character education.

Historically, these issues have been approached from two perspectives with divergent, though overlapping, interests and differing sets of assumptions about the nature of social development and socialization. On the one hand have been traditional character educators (Ryan and McLean, 1987) whose emphasis has been on processes of internalization and self-control that would ostensibly result in virtuous conduct. On the other hand have been cognitive developmentalists (Power, Higgins, and Kohlberg, 1989) whose emphasis has been on the development of structures of moral reasoning that ostensibly underlie action choices. These two points of view, one (character education) emphasizing nonrational mechanisms of self-control and behavioral follow-through, and the other (cognitive developmental) emphasizing rationality in the form of moral decision making, have irreconcilable underlying philosophies. Moreover, at the level of educational policy, these two perspectives have tended to take turns over the past thirty years in dominating the attention of educators interested in fostering children's social as well as academic growth. Yet, neither point of view, in their traditional form, provides a sufficient basis for guiding educational policy. There can be no meaningful moral action in the absence of moral judgment, since morality by definition requires choice and intent. Thus, proponents of educational policies that ignore the development of moral decision making have generally absented themselves from offering suggestions in the area of moral education. Conversely, the development of moral judgment, though necessary, is not a sufficient aim of moral education (Power, Higgins, and Kohlberg, 1989). For moral judgment in and of itself does not lead to a particular course of action. It would appear, then, that the divergent aims of these two points of view for the development of moral reasoning and the development of characterological propensities for moral followthrough are both desirable and necessary components of any educational contribution to children's moral growth. In this chapter, therefore, I will pull information from diverse areas of research to construct a coherent picture integrating both sets of concerns. In order to reconcile these points of view, I will need to appeal to contemporary cognitive theories of personality formation (Sarbin, 1986) and to recent work on the development of the moral "self" (Noam and Wren, 1993), rather than restrict discussion to the behavioral and social learning perspectives that have traditionally been used in support of character education. We begin this discussion by looking at the issue of moral judgment.

The Development of Moral and Social Understandings

What Do We Mean by Morality?

A large part of the controversy surrounding moral or character education has to do with how morality is defined. In everyday discourse, morality refers simply to the norms of right and wrong conduct. At issue, however, is what is meant by moral right and wrong, and whose criteria shall be used to judge the wrongness of actions. As it turns out, this diversity at the level of public opinion has a corollary in the underlying heterogeneity of the structures of the individual's social concepts. Within the individual, concepts of social right and wrong are not all of one type, but are organized within distinct conceptual and developmental frameworks. In research conducted over the past twenty years, it has been discovered that individuals treat some forms of social behavior as moral universals, other forms of social conduct as subject to determination by local cultural or social norms, and still others as matters of personal choice (Turiel, 1983). More specifically, these conceptual differences emerge when formal criteria for morality are employed that define morality as those interpersonal behaviors that are held to be right or wrong independent of governing social rules, and are maintained as universally binding (Turiel, 1983). Prescriptions that meet these criteria refer to actions, such as hitting and hurting, stealing, and slander, that have an impact on the welfare of others. Accordingly, concepts of morality are structured by underlying conceptions of justice and welfare (Turiel, 1983). Morality, then, may be defined as one's concepts, reasoning, and actions that pertain to the welfare, rights, and fair treatment of persons.

Morality (defined in terms of justice, welfare, rights) can be distinguished from concepts of social conventions, which are the consensually determined standards of conduct particular to a given social group. Conventions established by social systems—such as norms or standards of dress, how people should address one another, table manners, and so forth—derive their status as correct or incorrect forms of conduct from their embeddedness within a particular shared system of meaning and social interaction. The particular acts in and of themselves have no prescriptive force in that different or even opposite norms (e.g., dresses for men, pants for women) could be established to achieve the same symbolic or regulatory function (e.g., distinguishing men from women). The importance of conventions lies in the function they serve to coordinate social interaction and discourse within social systems. In keeping with this definition, research has found that concepts of social convention are structured by underlying conceptions of social organization (Turiel, 1983).

The distinctions that have been drawn between morality and social convention have been sustained by findings from over fifty studies conducted since 1975. This research has indicated that children, adolescents, and adults treat violations of morality, such as harming another, as wrong whether or not there is a governing rule in effect, and generalize these judgments of wrongness to members of other cultures or groups that may not have norms regarding such actions. Conventions, on the other hand, are viewed as binding only within the context of an existing social norm, and only for participating members within a given social group. While there is some controversy over whether the distinction between morality and convention is made by members of all cultural groups, a number of studies have demonstrated that subjects from a wide variety of the world's cultures do differentiate between matters of morality and convention. Evidence in support of the morality/convention distinction has been obtained from subjects in Brazil, India, Israel (Arab and Israeli subjects), Korea, Nigeria, the Virgin Islands, and Zambia. Moreover, recent research has demonstrated that something parallel to the distinction between morality and social convention operates within the moral and normative conceptions of religious children and adolescents with respect to their conceptions of religious rules. It has been found (Nucci, 1989) that children and adolescents from observant religious groups (Amish-Mennonite and Orthodox Jews) judged certain religious norms (e.g., day of worship, work on the Sabbath, baptism, circumcision, wearing of head coverings, women leading worship services, premarital sex between consenting adults, keeping Kosher) in conventional terms in that they regarded these as contingent on religious authority or the word of God, and as particular to their religion. In contrast, these children regarded moral issues (e.g., stealing, hitting, slander) as prescriptive (wrong to do), independent of the existence of a rule established by religious authority or by God's word and as obligatory for members of all other religious groups.

The discovery of these psychological distinctions between moral and conventional forms of social right and wrong provides an empirical basis for beginning to address some of the definitional issues vexing moral education (Nucci, 1989). In differentiating what is moral from what is socially "proper," these findings can allow educators to focus the discussion of moral education on questions of how best to develop children's moral understandings (i.e., concepts of welfare and fairness) and their tendencies to act in accord with such moral principles; educators need not be captured by heated arguments over which set of local conventions or religious norms ought to be included within the collection of values to be addressed by the curriculum. In keeping with the broad cross-cultural generalizability of this research, the identification of morality as centered around issues of justice and human welfare is consistent with the commonsense goal of values education—to foster the development of people who don't lie, cheat, steal, or hurt others. At the same time, by grounding these definitions of the content of morality in basic developmental research, we avoid falling into the trap of what Lawrence Kohlberg so aptly and perjoratively labeled the "bag-of-virtues" approach to establishing the aims of moral education. These core moral concerns for fairness and welfare are not virtues in the usual sense, but constitute the central issues for moral judgments and consequent actions.

The distinction between morality and convention also allows the educator to give convention its due. Earlier analyses of children's moral development, such as Kohlberg's stage theory (see Power, Higgins, and Kohlberg, 1989), interpreted attention to convention as characteristic of the reasoning of persons at the lower stages of moral development, and therefore as something to be overcome through moral education. As stated above, concepts of conventions are now understood as distinct from moral understandings and as structured by children's and adolescents' emerging conceptualizations of social systems and social organization. Conventions are constituent elements of social systems. Just as morality is fundamental to interpersonal interaction, conventions are essential to the operation of society. The development of children's and adolescents' understandings of the functions and purposes of social convention, therefore, have educational worth in their own right (Nucci, 1989). In sum, current research on the structure of children's social concepts provides an empirical basis for differentially addressing development within each of these conceptual systems rather than reducing either morality or conventional norms to a single framework.

Context, and the Inevitability of Controversy

The discovery of distinct domains of social knowledge can help to focus the aims of moral education by identifying the core content of morality (Nucci, 1989). But the heterogeneity in people's social understandings and the contextual overlap of moral and nonmoral normative components in everyday life means that an honest approach to moral education will always need to contend with contradiction and controversy. Such overlap is inevitable given that all social interactions take place within societal systems framed by conventions. Thus, although many everyday issues are straightforward instances of either morality or convention, many others contain aspects from each domain. In such cases, people may differ from one another in the information they may bring to a situation, or the weight they may give to one or another feature of a given issue. Two basic forms of overlap occur between morality and convention. In one form, called domain mixture, conventional norms sustaining a particular organizational structure are in harmony or conflict with what would objectively be seen as concerns for fairness or rights. Examples of such overlap would be conventions for lining up to purchase tickets, or gender-role conventions that proscribe areas in which men or women may participate. In the former case, the convention (lining up), while a morally neutral and arbitrary way to arrange people, could be used to serve a distributive justice function (turn taking), and cutting in line would, therefore, become unfair. In the latter case, the convention (gender role) may be in conflict with fairness if the convention prevents members of one gender from obtaining opportunities afforded the other. The second type of moral/convention overlap, labeled second-order moral events, occurs when the violation of a strongly held convention is seen as causing psychological harm (insult, distress) to persons maintaining the convention. In our culture, for example, attending a funeral in a bathing suit would generally be seen as insensitive toward the deceased and the grieving family, and not merely an instance of unconventional conduct.

In responding to issues that involve elements from more than one domain, individuals may either subordinate the issue to a single dimension and reduce an issue of overlap to one that is primarily either moral or conventional, or engage in an effort to coordinate the multifaceted nature of the issue, taking the moral as well as nonmoral aspects of a given situation or event into account. These responses to overlap at an individual level help to account for the inconsistencies we observe within people as they respond to events in different contexts (a subject I will take up later). They also help to explain how cultural groups or subgroups arrive at different readings of social issues they consider to be morally neutral or charged with moral meaning. Within Western society, those instances of overlap in which convention and morality are in harmony account for the moral component of what is generally viewed as mannerly and respectful conduct, and for the moral aspect of norms and procedures that sustain participatory forms of government. For the most part, within democratic societies, these areas of overlap are noncontroversial inasmuch as they represent values concordant with morality and the conventional status quo. Consequently, values-education programs purporting to foster such conventional values enjoy wide public support. Controversies are likely to emerge, however, whenever the relations between moral and nonmoral components of issues are not in accord and, therefore, are likely to be viewed differently by the affected parties. In the case of second-order issues such as disputes over what constitutes modesty in forms of dress (e.g., women's skirt length), the essentially conventional nature of such issues generally allows for local consensus to settle the matter. While some civil libertarians might protest any constraint on student choice with respect to personal conduct, and some conservative religious people might protest as immoral any alteration in the norms of public conduct, such second-order issues are generally resolved by elected school boards or by school policy. More problematic for curriculum designers and educational policymakers are potential conflicts between morality and convention embedded within the norms that sustain the existing social order, and by implication benefit members of the privileged social classes.

An illustrative example of this type of issue is captured in the following incident described by Maya Angelou in her novel, *I Know Why the Caged Bird Sings*. The passage recalls an incident in which a local judge mistakenly refers to Angelou's grandmother by the title "Mrs." The use of the title was a mistake, because the depression-era conventions of the South decreed that whites, but not blacks, be referred to by titles. Through the discriminatory use of titles, whites symbolically maintained their social supremacy over blacks. In the situation described by Angelou, her grandmother was subpoenaed to give testimony before the judge. Angelou writes:

> The judge asked that Mrs. Henderson be subpoenaed, and when Momma arrived and said she was Mrs. Henderson, the judge, the bailiff and other whites in the audience laughed. The judge had really made a gaffe calling a Negro woman Mrs., but then he was from Pine Bluff and couldn't have been expected to know that a woman who owned a store in that village would also turn out to be colored. The whites tickled their funny bones with the incident for a long time, and the Negroes thought it proved the worth and majesty of my grandmother. [1971, p. 39]

From the vantage point of our current understanding of racial prejudice and segregation within American society, the treatment accorded to Maya Angelou's grandmother was clearly unjust and immoral. That is, despite the arbitrary and conventional nature of titles, we now generally acknowledge that their discriminatory use as depicted in this particular context served the immoral purpose of symbolically subjugating and consequently humiliating African Americans. What is interesting in this example is how the parties at that time viewed the employment of the titles "Mr." and "Mrs." In general situations, these titles serve to convey hierarchical relations between adults and children, and in formal situations, establish respect between adults of equal status. In the situation described by Angelou, they were used to establish the socially inferior position of African Americans in relation to whites. From the white position of power, the judge's "gaffe" was a source of humor, because the judge could not have intended to elevate a Negro woman to the same status as a white. For those whites who viewed the use of first names in addressing adult African Americans as sustaining the social system, and for those African Americans who might have accepted the status quo, the issue was one of conventionality, and the judge's gaffe was simply a humorous error. From that vantage point, the judge as a white man would have been correct, and had the right to refer to Maya Angelou's grandmother by her first name. On the other hand, for those African Americans in Maya Angelou's community who viewed it as unjust to employ titles to symbolically maintain them in an inferior social position, the issue was one of morality, an understanding that could be arrived at only by coordinating concerns for fairness with concepts of conventions as constitutive elements of the social order. From that vantage point, the judge's implicit acknowledgment of Angelou's grandmother's social accomplishments (being a store owner) put her on an even footing with whites, and served as a source of pride and confirmation that the discriminatory social practices African Americans endured were artificial and unsustainable in the light of an objective view of the situation. From the point of view of the African-American community, the judge's gaffe inadvertently correctly captured the right of Maya Angelou's grandmother to be called "Mrs."

While this incident from America's past is easy to look at in the cool light of history, such issues are not easily dealt with when they concern contemporary practices. Two of the elements

that lend to the difficulty in dealing with these issues are captured in the above example. First, the conventionalized practices (e.g., forms of address, modes of dress) in and of themselves
are morally neutral and play themselves out in the course of
everyday life. Thus, people steeped in a particular way of life
may not be cognizant of the moral implications of their particular social system. The problem here, of course, is that inequita-
ble systems may simply perpetuate themselves, and educational
curricula based on transmitting the values of the community may
become the handmaidens of immorality. Second, because such
issues are multifaceted, they lend themselves to more than one
interpretation, raising the specter of controversy for the educational system. This is particularly problematic for public schools,
since such controversies tend to have political ramifications.
Generally, people in positions of relative power and privilege
are more likely to view such issues in conventional terms and
favor maintenance of the status quo, since the conventional system serves their personal interests. People on the receiving end
of such conventionalized inequities, on the other hand, are less
likely to subordinate such overlapping issues to convention, and
are more likely to be cognizant of their moral status. The moral
dilemma these overlapping issues pose for educators is how to
allow students to address the moral contradictions posed by some
of society's conventions in areas such as gender and race relations without themselves becoming subject to the positions held
by political groups that inevitably align themselves with one or
another side of such issues.

Moral Diversity and Informational Assumptions

Variations in the moral meanings people attribute to particular actions not only stem from the areas of overlap between morality
and the conventions of social systems, but also arise as a result
of the differences in factual assumptions people make about given
acts. Within our own culture, for example, people hold different
views about whether it is morally wrong or right to engage in
the physical punishment of children. In her research on this
issue, Wainryb (1991) found that parents in favor of corporal
punishment held the view that this behavior was all right be-

cause it was a highly effective, educative act rather than one of unprovoked harm or abuse of the child. When such parents were presented with information that spanking is no more effective than other methods of disciplining children, significant numbers of parents shifted their view of corporal punishment, stating that it was not all right for parents to engage in the behavior. Likewise, when parents who maintained that it was wrong to engage in corporal punishment were presented with information that experts had found spanking to be the most efficient method to teach young children, there was a tendency for such parents to shift toward a view that corporal punishment would be all right.

In the above example, the morality of an action shifted as a function of the informational assumptions people had regarding the effect of the act. In other cases, informational assumptions can alter people's views of the moral culpability of the actor. Many people in our culture, for example, view homosexuality as an immoral lifestyle choice (Turiel, Hildebrandt, and Wainryb, 1991). In their view, being a homosexual entails a conscious decision to engage in behavior that they consider offensive and indecent. Leaving aside such questions as to whether homosexuality should be viewed in such normative terms or as a matter of private, personal conduct, the issue of choice is central to whether the individual may be held accountable for his or her sexual orientation. Information that would bear on that issue (e.g., findings of a substantial genetic component in determining sexual orientation) would undoubtedly impact the moral evaluation many people would make of homosexuals, even if it had no impact on their view of homosexual acts.

In sum, the moral worlds within which people act out their lives are affected by informational as well as contextual variables that enter into their evaluations about particular courses of action. As with issues of domain overlap, the impact of new information regarding the causes or effects of social behaviors both complicates and enriches the role of education in preparing students to deal with social and moral issues. From a policy standpoint, we are once again confronted with the need to recognize that values education within a pluralistic, information rich, democratic society means preparing students to coordinate fundamental moral understandings of fairness and human welfare with potentially changing conventions and informational assumptions.

Understanding Inconsistencies in Individual Conduct

Domain overlap and differences in informational assumptions help not only to account for disagreements between people about the moral meaning of social issues, but also to explain some of the inconsistencies we observe within individuals. Just as different groups of people may disagree over the moral meaning of contextualized social issues, individuals may differ in their attribution of moral meaning of actions within different contexts. In relatively unambiguous cases, deciding on the moral or conventionally correct course of action is fairly straightforward. However, in cases where moral and conventional expectations are in conflict, where the information regarding the meaning of the action is ambiguous, or when moral concerns run counter to highly salient pragmatic or personal desires of the actor, individuals display inconsistency in their social judgments and subsequent actions. Domain theory explains such inconsistencies as the inevitable consequence of applications of a multifaceted conceptual framework to heterogeneous social contexts. This is not a case of situational ethics. People do not make up their morality on the spot. The place of morality within a given context, however, will vary as a function of the person's application of the totality of his or her social understandings and concerns to a given situation.

Reconceptualizing the Developmental Aims of Moral Education

Given what we currently know about moral cognition, it is sensible to propose that the core focus of moral education be on students' conceptions of fairness and human welfare and rights, and the application of those moral understandings to issues of everyday life (Nucci, 1989). Research on the development of children's moral understandings has shown that morality begins in early childhood with a focus on issues of harm to the self and others. Preschool-aged children are very concerned with their own safety, and understand that it is objectively wrong to hurt others. Children as young as three years, understand, for example, that it is wrong to hit and hurt someone even in the absence of a rule against hitting because, "When you get hit, it hurts, and you start to cry." Young children's morality, however, is not yet structured by understandings of fairness as reciprocity (treating others as one would wish to be treated). Young children will often express fairness in terms of personal needs and the sense that they are not getting their just desserts. "It's not fair," often means, "I didn't get what I want," or that someone's actions caused the child to experience harm. By age ten, nearly all children have constructed an understanding of fairness as reciprocity, but have difficulty in coordinating their sense of fairness as equality with notions of equity. Expanding the sense of fairness to include compassion, and not raw justice, and to tie that sense of compassionate justice to a conceptually compelling (logically necessary) obligation to all people and not just the members of one's community, is the developmental task of adolescence and adulthood.

Similar research on the development of children's understandings of social convention (Turiel, 1983) indicates that constructing an understanding of why conventions matter is a long process. Unlike morality, there is nothing intuitively obvious about the functions of convention. Even though most children have learned the content of their society's conventions by early elementary school, the purpose of such rules is not easily understood. In fact, it is not until middle to late adolescence that children develop a coordinated understanding of conventions as constituents of social systems. It is little wonder, then, that children so often seem disconnected from society's rules even when their normative content (e.g., "Don't talk with your mouth full") has been repeatedly presented to them.

This developmental research can be of enormous value to educators interested in developing "good" children. It provides curriculum designers and classroom teachers a framework from which to direct educational efforts at moral education that are appropriate for students at different points in development, and provides a basis from which to differentially address both the moral and conventional dimensions of social values. In doing so, educators will contribute to the development of a fair and compassionate moral citizenry that also understands and respects the need for convention. As we have just seen, however, contextualized moral judgments may often call on the person's ability to weigh or coordinate moral and nonmoral considerations.

Defining the aims of moral education in such circumstances becomes more complex. Put simply, the moral educator is not only interested in developing the students' moral and conventional understandings in such contexts, but is also interested in whether or not the student will be aware of and prioritize the moral elements of such issues when deciding on a course of action.

In the past, this issue was dealt with rather neatly by Kohlberg's six-stage sequence of moral development (see Power, Higgins, and Kohlberg, 1989). According to Kohlberg's standard account, moral development moves from early stages in which moral understandings of fairness are intertwined with prudential self-interest and concrete concerns for social authority, to conventional moral understandings in which morality (fairness) is intertwined with concerns for maintaining social organization defined by normative regulation. Finally, at the highest, principled stages of morality—attained by a minority of the general population—morality as fairness is fully differentiated from nonmoral prudential or conventional considerations, and morality serves as the basis from which the individual not only guides personal actions but is able to evaluate the morality of the conventional normative system of society. This progression has been appealing to moral educators for several reasons. First, because the sequence was empirically based and purportedly described a universal developmental progression, this description of development offered educators an "objective" nonpolitical basis from which to engage in moral education. Second, because the stages were presumably "content free" in that they do not pertain to particular issues, but instead refer to structures of reasoning, educators did not need to be concerned about the specific positions students take with respect to given issues. Finally, the sequence moved ultimately to a principled moral resolution of the kinds of complex issues of overlap discussed above. In other words, from the teacher's point of view, philosophical and political conundrums were resolved by the natural logic of the developmental process.

What we have now come to understand is that the progression identified through Kohlberg's paradigmatic research program does not adequately capture the ways in which people make sociomoral judgments and cannot, therefore, serve as the sole guide to moral education. Kohlberg described the sequence of age-related changes in the ways in which moral and nonmoral (especially conventional) concerns are typically integrated in overlapping contexts. For example, Stage 4 (conventional) moral reasoning as described in the Kohlberg system reflects the emergence in middle to late adolescence of understandings in the *conventional* domain that social norms are constituent elements of social systems (Turiel, 1983). Although these age-typical integrations are captured by Kohlberg's stage descriptions, they do not represent the full range of sociomoral decision-making patterns that individuals present. For example, in the process of conducting their careful and extensive research aimed at standardizing moral-stage scoring, the Kohlberg group discovered that individuals at all points in development may respond to Kohlberg's moral dilemmas by reasoning from a perspective of either rules and authority or justice and human welfare. From the vantage point of our current understanding of the domain-related heterogeneity in people's social cognition, such within-stage variation can be accounted for by recognizing that the Kohlberg tasks generate reasoning employing knowledge from more than one conceptual system.

In moving beyond Kohlberg's landmark research on children's moral development, not only are educators liberated in how they might conceptualize the opportunities they have to engage students in moral reflection and behavior, but they are also vested with greater responsibility for stimulating students to think and act in such moral terms. If, in fact, children at all points in development are capable of considering moral issues from a moral perspective of justice and welfare, then it becomes important that educators increase the likelihood that children will "read" and prioritize the moral component of contextualized social issues, rather than simply attempting to move their students toward a distal "principled" stage of moral judgment where such moral prioritization becomes a matter of course. This is not say that development does not matter. Achieving principled moral understandings, in the full sense of Kohlberg's theory, presupposes a fully developed understanding of societies as social systems—an understanding that is arrived at in only middle to late adolescence (Turiel, 1983). In addition, the ability of children to "see" the morality of certain actions requires a similar level of sophistication, also attained in late adolescence, in the area of convention. For example, when we presented the issue of a person wearing shorts and a tee shirt to a formal wedding, many young adolescents (twelve to fourteen years of age) failed to see any problem other than the possible disapproval of adults. In their minds, since conventions (such as those regarding dress) were nothing other than the arbitrary dictates of authority, and since the important issue in this case was attendance at the wedding, there was nothing wrong with going to a wedding in informal clothes. To be sure, some of the young adolescents we interviewed were aware that the wedding party might find such casual dress offensive. A number of those adolescents indicated that it would therefore be wrong to wear casual clothes, since it would be wrong in their minds to upset the wedding party over so minor an issue. When questioned further regarding the reason why casual dress would be considered offensive, they were at a loss, and simply chalked it up to ancient history and habit. Older adolescents, however, who had constructed an understanding of conventions as constituent elements of social systems, recognized that form of dress was an integral element defining the wedding as an important and distinctive social event. From their vantage point, they were able to clearly appreciate the second-order moral implications that might arise from violating this social convention. They reasoned that a failure to conform to the dress conventions of a formal wedding would be wrong, since within the societal framework of the wedding, dress conveyed a sense of respect and support for the wedding party (Nucci and Weber, 1991).

The point being made here is that attention to development within moral education needs to be accompanied by attention to students' reading of overlapping social issues. In focusing on development within each of these conceptual (moral and conventional) frameworks, educators contribute to students' capacity to understand and function within their social and moral worlds. However, because these systems interact in context, strictly developmental aims as set forth in the traditional Kohlbergian position need to be reconsidered. Since it has been found that students' reasoning about such complex issues is not the result of reasoning structures within a single system, the weight that students give to moral and nonmoral considerations—and not just their reasoning within the moral domain—becomes of interest. For example, whether students viewed the Maya Angelou story described above in moral or conventional terms might well be as significant as whether the students were at early or advanced points in their social development. As was illustrated in the Maya Angelou excerpt, there is no guarantee that individual development alone will lead to such a reading of overlapping social issues. Unfortunately, even individuals at Kohlberg's postconventional stages of reasoning are subject to social pressures and situational cues in their reading of the moral meaning of actions (see the discussion of the Milgram study in Turiel, 1983).

Some research demonstrates that teachers can impact the ways in which students read social issues, and the tendencies of students to attempt to address both the moral and conventional aspects of complex social issues. In their study, Nucci and Weber (1991) divided students into three discussion groups that met for four weeks. During these groups, students discussed issues that were primarily moral, primarily conventional, or overlapping both morality and convention. Throughout the course of these weekly discussions, one group was directed to treat all issues in terms of moral concerns for fairness and human welfare; a second group was directed to treat all issues as matters of social convention and social order; and the third group was directed to treat moral issues from a moral perspective, conventional issues from a conventional perspective, and to coordinate moral and conventional components of multifaceted issues. Following this intervention, students' levels of moral and conventional reasoning were assessed through interviews. Students in all three groups were able to clearly respond to unambiguous moral or conventional issues. However, when asked to write their views about the values contained in an incident that had both moral and conventional features, subjects in the moral-only group subordinated complex issues to moral concerns, and subjects in the convention-only group subordinated complex issues to matters of norms and social organization. Only the third group spontaneously looked at both features of issues and attempted to coordinate them. As this relatively benign and short-term treatment illustrates, education can be influential in framing the meaning individuals will give to complex social situations.

Given that many of the moral issues of everyday life are enmeshed within conventionalized norms and contexts, it seems imperative that children be given the intellectual and attitudinal tools necessary to deal with these realities. What this means in practice is that students not only be given opportunities to develop their understandings and ways of reasoning about morality and convention, but also be engaged in the more complex task of evaluating and coordinating the moral and social organizational elements of multifaceted social issues. These processes will necessarily be different at differing points in development. Adolescents with complex understandings of societies as systems will address such issues in ways that are more integrative and complex than will children. Nonetheless, meaningful discourse about the moral component of multifaceted social standards can be addressed across a broad age range. Furthermore, the contexts in which morality and convention may overlap are not confined to the distal world of adult society, but also arise in contexts structured by the norms of children and adolescents. For example, engaging children in "seeing" the moral implications of group norms of exclusion that might arise within cliques that don't want "geeks" as members, or helping them to deal with masculine norms of toughness in the context of playground disputes, can help them to formulate ways of constructing "societies" that are nondiscriminatory, just, and safe. Thus, helping students come to terms with the difficult task of integrating what is moral with the need for social order and organization need not be seen as far afield from the straightforward business of raising "good" children who do not lie, cheat, steal, or hurt others.

If we have learned anything over the past thirty years, it is that moral education cannot be isolated to one part of the school day or to one context, but must be integrated within the total school experience. Bringing the approach described here to the curriculum as a whole, however, may prove unsettling for some. Engaging children in critical moral reflection about issues raised in literature, or about existing or historical social standards contained within social studies or history texts, may seem threatening to those who maintain the recapitulation view of the mission of public schools to foster citizenship. From that point of view (see Ryan in Nucci, 1989), values education serves the purpose of bringing the young into the existing social order so that society may be preserved and perpetuated. But at odds with that perspective is that pluralist democracies are dynamic, and efforts to stifle critique run counter to the very nature of the democratic society such people hope to preserve. Whether we wish to engage the resources of our schools to develop the ability of our citizenry to engage in thoughtful moral critique of our culture is a political and moral decision. As I have laid out, the knowledge base from which to construct such an approach to moral and social education is available.

Character Formation: The Moral Self

The preceding discussion has highlighted the basic reasons why moral education must attend to issues of social cognition and moral reasoning. Knowing right from wrong is more than a simple process of being aware of specific social rules, and doing the right thing is not a simple matter of putting those rules into practice. Social contexts are not fixed and, therefore, do not always lend themselves to habitual or formulaic ways of responding. Moreover, extant social rules may themselves require changes to bring them in line with morality. Reading and evaluating what is morally right, therefore, entails judgment. Being a good person, however, is more than a matter of understanding what is morally right. In philosophy, a distinction is made between deontic judgments of what is morally right and aretaic judgments of responsibility, which involve a commitment to act on one's deontic judgment. In everyday language, the term "character" refers to the tendency to act in ways that are consistent with what one understands to be morally right. A person of good character is someone who attends to the moral implications of actions and acts in accordance with what is moral in all but the most extreme of circumstances. This everyday usage of the term "character" captures an important feature of what is ordinarily meant by a good person. The question for us as educators becomes one of understanding how these commonsense notions of character map onto actual human psychology, and what aspects of the educative process can contribute to character formation. Unfortunately, most of the current rhetoric about character education has little to do with what people are actually like, and more to do with a political agenda that would return us to mistaken practices of the past. It is important to remember as we move forward in our efforts to engage schools in meaningful

moral and character education just why character education fell
out of favor in the first place.

Limitations of Traditional Forms of Character Education

Traditional character education, which had its heyday in the
early part of this century, had as its central aim fostering formation of elements of the individual's personality and value structure that would constitute socially desirable qualities or virtues.
In the late 1920s, a major research effort was undertaken by Hugh
Hartshorne and Mark May to identify the factors that contributed to the formation of character. The design of their research
was based on the reasonable premise that the first step should
be to identify those individuals who possessed moral virtues. What
they had expected to find was that the population of eight thousand students they studied would divide up into those who displayed virtuous conduct nearly all of the time, and those who
did not. To their surprise and disappointment, the researchers
discovered that few students were virtuous, and that, instead, most
children cheated, behaved selfishly, and lacked "self-control" most
of the time. Virtue, according to their data, seemed context
dependent, as students cheated, lied, or were selfish in some
situations and not in others. As Clark Power noted, Hartshorne
and May concluded that there were no character traits *per se* but
"specific habits learned in relationship to specific situations which
have made one or another response successful" (Power, Higgins,
and Kohlberg, 1989, p. 127).

The reference to habit by Hartshorne and May is concordant
with traditional views of character formation. Since Aristotle, the
development of virtue has been thought to emerge out of the
progressive accumulation of habits. Contemporary character educators (Ryan and McLean, 1987; Wynne in Nucci, 1989) likewise
rely heavily on psychological theories that emphasize punishment
and reward systems to reinforce desired behavior, and systems
of inculcation that are presumed to instill values and virtues in
the young. It is worth remembering that in response to their
findings, Hartshorne and May concluded that such traditional
approaches to character education—didactic teaching, exhortation, and example—probably do more harm than good, since

such practices do not take into account the practical demands of social contexts. In other words, such rigid instruction runs counter to the evaluative and contextualized nature of moral life. By focusing solely on efforts to instill proper values and habits, such approaches fail to develop students' capacities to make the social and moral judgments that contextualized actions require. Moreover, these rigid approaches run counter to the multifaceted and complex nature of human personality. Research on personality conducted over the past thirty years (Sarbin, 1986) has served to confirm the view of character offered by Hartshorne and May by demonstrating that people cannot be accurately described in terms of stable and general personality traits, since people tend to exhibit different and seemingly contradictory aspects of themselves in different contexts.

The Moral Self

Findings that individual personality and character are multifaceted, complex, and responsive to contextual cues seems to comport with such common experiences as knowing people who are shy in some contexts and gregarious in others, and fits our general commonsense understanding that people are not always consistent in their moral positions or actions. On the other hand, our awareness of such inconsistencies also runs counter to our shared experiences that people are more or less shy than others, kinder and more trustworthy than others, and so forth. In other words, we seem to sense that human personality or character is consistent. Resolving this apparent contradiction in our nature has been the task of contemporary personality and social psychology. Resolution with respect to issues of morality and character seems to rest on a recognition that judgments and not just habits are operating when people respond to social contexts. In this light, observed consistencies within individuals across contexts may be accounted for with reference to the ways in which individuals address moral consistencies or inconsistencies within themselves. In other words, if individual moral actions are guided by choices and not simply the result of unreflective habit, then the issue for character education rests not with inculcation and habit formation, but in understanding how it is that people judge the worth of their own actions in relation to their world view and sense of themselves as moral beings. We need to move away from the notion of character as a set of externally provided traits and habits to a view of the moral self as constructed rather than absorbed and as being updated and reconstructed continuously (Sarbin, 1986).

Self in this view is not so much an entity as it is a story or a narrative we tell ourselves in which we are the featured character. Who we are emerges as we engage the social world and attempt to provide ourselves an account of how we initiate actions (a sense of agency), of who that agent is (a sense of identity), and of who we wish that agent to be (a combination of agency and identity). What we call the self is a psychological construction that we form in social contexts. Before we are born, aspects of the content of who we will become are already set. We live in a particular time period, cultural and historical context, and family situation. We are given a name, assigned a gender, and live in a society in which race matters or does not matter. All of this comes without our asking, and none comes with prepackaged understandings. Our personal development, then, is in part a function of how we interpret the hand we are dealt at birth, and the meanings and ways in which we enact the different roles (e.g., boy, girl, athlete, scholar, gang member, professor, someone named Larry or Maria) that we assume in context. In a sense, such social roles imply scripts, and some social learning theorists have mistakenly reduced social conduct to knowledge of social scripts. Social life, however, is not rigidly scripted, and to the extent that one can use this metaphor, it would be more in the sense of a broad outline in which persons present an interpretation of a given role (e.g., mother) that they enact and modify in social context. In addition, social roles are not simply accepted by individuals, but are evaluated and modified to comport with individuals' constructions of what a social role should be as it relates to themselves. Finally, personhood and a sense of agency require personal choice, and individuals engage in choices that would establish their uniqueness (see Nucci and Lee in Noam and Wren, 1993).

The connection between this dramaturgical or narrative view of self and the present discussion of character has to do with how individuals construct a view of themselves as moral beings, or what some have called the moral self (Noam and Wren, 1993), and the relation between this moral self and the more general narrative we construct, which constitutes our personal identity. Self as singular—that is, the "I" we refer to when we speak about ourselves, we see when we look at our own baby pictures, and who experiences the sense of agency when we engage in actions— is, in fact, multifaceted. The salience or importance of those facets of who we are vary both as a function of the general narrative we have constructed about ourselves and the particular situation we find ourselves in. Our "moral selves," what some have been calling "character," is only a part of who we are and functions in relation to our totality (see Blasi in Noam and Wren, 1993). When we act in context, our reading of the social situation may or may not engage our moral understandings. And when our moral understandings are involved, it may or may not be the case that the moral part of who we are is the most salient. Richard Nixon, for example, argued that being president was different from being an ordinary citizen—the president is required to act in extralegal and amoral ways when the pragmatic interests of the United States are at stake. In essence, Nixon's understanding of the role of president meant that morality was secondary to political pragmatics. Implicit in his argument was the notion that Nixon's moral self remained intact, but on hold, while he was acting from pragmatics. We see similar forms of argument in the self-reports of adolescents who engage in aggressive acts to steal from others (Guerra, Nucci, and Huesmann, 1994). Often, these adolescents explain their actions (e.g., hitting a woman to steal her purse) in means-end terms in which the moral consequences of their actions (hurting another person) are placed well below the pragmatic goal of obtaining goods. While these adolescents will describe themselves in moral terms (e.g., fair, respectful) in relation to general dealings with people, especially family members, they use very "business" like terms (e.g., taking care of business) when describing their actions on the street.

Character and the Moral Self

In his work on the moral self, Blasi makes the point that morality may or may not be a central element of the general narrative we construct about who we are (in Noam and Wren, 1993). In other words, morality may or may not be a salient issue in constructing our personal identity. The fact that virtually all children construct basic moral understandings about fairness and human welfare does not mean that being a person who acts on that knowledge in relation to others is necessarily an important part of children's self-definition. For the adolescents described above, or for some businessmen for that matter, being moral may not be as integral to their self-definition as are other facets of their personal identities (e.g., gang member, successful businessman). According to Blasi, *only* those of us for whom morality is an integral part of our personal identity will experience "guilt" or moral responsibility in situations in which we act counter to what we know is morally right. In other words, a central feature of moral character is the degree to which being a moral person is a part of our self-definition. For individuals of "good" character, acting in consonance with their own deontic moral judgments is important for a sense of intrapersonal coherence in the vast majority of contexts.

From an educational standpoint, this means that character formation is not a curricular issue in the usual sense of a course or program designed to teach a particular content. Character emerges from the more general interactions between individuals and their environment, from which students construct their sense of themselves. There is no simplistic model or formula for "building" character. And, as much as those of us who each year brave Chicago's character-building winters would like to believe, no specific set of experiences leads to good or strong character. Schools contribute to character to the degree to which they constitute environments conducive to more general social and emotional development. More specifically, schools should be moral environments where students are treated fairly and with respect and where teacher behavior and school policy convey a general climate in which morality (as opposed to arbitrary adult authority) is valued. Having said that, I will end this chapter with a brief summary of some of the policies and practices that schools can engage in to raise the likelihood that schooling will contribute to students' moral development and character. Before doing so, however, I think it is important to recognize the limitations for public policy of any attempt to address larger social issues of crime or violence solely through educational efforts designed to alter the morality and character of individuals.

The Limitations of Reliance on Individual Responsibility

Much of the criminal activity, and juvenile crime in particular, that we see in today's society needs to be understood as a rational response to objective social conditions rather than simply a lack of morality or character in individuals. A study that we (Sapiro and Nucci, 1991) conducted in Brazil of adolescents' and young adults' conceptions of everyday forms of corruption is highly instructive. Nearly all of our young subjects across social classes and economic levels engaged in what they considered to be corrupt social practices (e.g., paying a police officer to avoid a ticket; paying for physician services without asking for a receipt, to enable the physician to avoid taxes and charge a lower fee) at least some of the time. When asked to evaluate these practices, nearly all of our subjects agreed that they were wrong. However, irrespective of their educational level, lower-class subjects were five times as likely as upper-middle-class young people to state that engaging in such practices was justified in the face of an overwhelmingly corrupt social system. In contrast, upper-middle-class university students were more than twice as likely as lower-class subjects (irrespective of their educational level) to argue that it was important to not engage in such practices in order to offer individual resistance to the corrupt social system and thereby change it. What is instructive for us at the policy level is to recognize that these observed class and educational differences in perceptions of the immorality of corrupt public behavior did *not* reflect a difference in the morality of individuals (nearly all subjects saw the acts as objectively wrong), but rather social-class differences in the sense of an individual's political and social empowerment to effect change in the objective social situation, and the belief on the part of the poor and uneducated that such actions constituted a rational form of self-protection from victimization by the general system. While the United States is not Brazil, the lesson to be drawn is that we should not expect school approaches to moral and character education aimed at individual responsibility to completely compensate for the broader changes in social policy that need to take place to improve life for America's poor and disenfranchised.

Conclusion

In conclusion, let me summarize some of the main points of this chapter and indicate some of the implications of recent research for educational practices and policies with respect to moral development and character formation. These practices divide more or less into those that concern academic or intellectual content and reflection, and school policies or practices that affect general school climate or student activities. I begin first with academic practices.

Academic Practices

- *The focus of moral education should be on students' concerns for and conceptions of fairness and the welfare of others.* These moral issues are treated by children and adults as universalizable, and as independent of the specific norms and rules of their particular culture. Morality is distinct from social conventions, which are the agreed upon social norms particular to social or cultural groups. This definition of morality is consistent with individual psychology and may serve as the basis for a common and shared values focus for moral education.
- *Educational practices should be coordinated with student development.* While young children have an intuitive sense of morality, they do not have fully developed understandings of fairness. Nor do they have an understanding of the function of conventions in organizing social systems. For educators to be effective in fostering students' moral and social growth, they need to match educational practices with students' developmental level.
- *Educational practices should take into account the fact that morality and convention develop out of qualitatively different types of social experiences.* Morality deals with justice and human wel-

fare. Thus, children's moral concepts are fostered by school experiences that focus on such issues, engage children in reflection on such concerns, and ask them to resolve genuine moral problems in ways that are the most fair and compassionate for all parties. Issues of convention, on the other hand, deal with concerns for social organization. Thus, children's understandings of the meaning and importance of convention emerge out of efforts to come to agreed upon norms for coordinating the actions of members of a group. In daily school experience, this emerges in the context of discourse over dress codes, rules for hand raising, and the like. In the curriculum, these issues emerge as children attempt to understand the meaning or function of different conventional norms throughout history, or within different cultural groups. Specific suggestions for what is termed "domain-appropriate education" are provided in Nucci and Weber (1991).

- *Moral development is fostered by moral discussion and moral problem solving.* Moral reasoning develops when students recognize inconsistencies and inadequacies in their moral positions. One of the most effective ways to bring this about is through small-group discussions that are characterized by transactive discourse. In such discussions, students are asked to arrive at a resolution of a moral problem in such a way that it would be most fair to all parties. In the process, students must listen carefully to what group members are saying and come to terms with positions at variance from their own. Discussions can be stimulated by readings as well as by actual events, and are not limited to a particular educational subject matter.

- *Moral discussion may also make use of moral exemplars.* Traditional character education has generally included reading literature about morally exemplary figures as an important way to provide students with moral role models. While overreliance on this approach is unjustified, there is a place for providing students with opportunities to consider the thoughts and actions of exemplary figures such as Martin Luther King. Teachers can also expose students to literature that contains morally charged situations as a way to allow students to consider how they might construct their own sense of self with respect to morality. What is critical is that students be actively engaged in constructing a connection between themselves and the role model or the situation in a book. Otherwise, such exercises are a waste of everyone's time.

- *Opportunities for self-reflection can be used to foster moral character.* Stimulating students to raise the salience of their "moral self" and integrate it within their overall identity can often be accomplished through classroom activities and assignments that ask students to reflect on who they are and wish to become. While this can be misused in futile attempts to generate student guilt, it can be productive when students view the activity as serving their own intrinsic interest in learning about themselves. Teachers can encourage students to address inconsistencies and lacunae within their views of self, which can help focus the students' attention on the moral content of their character. This has been successfully used not only as a vehicle for self-examination, but also as a context within which students can develop literacy and communication skills.

- *Moral discussion is most effective when it concerns actual student behavior or issues.* Student motivation and attention is heightened when the moral problems they are asked to address concern real-life issues, and when the consequences of their decisions have a real impact on subsequent policies or actions. This approach also engages students in role enactment related to their construction of a sense of self. Thus, this approach touches not only on deontic judgments, but also on aretaic judgments of moral responsibility and character. A widely studied approach that makes use of this technique is the "Just Community" (Power, Higgins, and Kohlberg, 1989).

- *Moral concerns are often embedded within conventionalized practices.* Since moral actions take place within cultural contexts, many moral issues are embedded within, or overlap with, morality. This has the following educational ramifications.

    (1) *Concerns for fostering moral development should include concerns for fostering moral sensitivity.* Because issues of morality are often embedded within existing conventional practices, the moral meaning of such practices

may be overlooked. If schools are committed to moral education, then one function of such education should be to heighten the likelihood that students will attend to the moral consequences of conforming to the norms of the existing social order. One way to do this is to present students with issues that involve an overlap between morality and convention, and ask them to consider both the moral and conventional aspects of such issues. Examples of this type of approach are provided in Nucci and Weber (1991).

(2) *Moral educators need to be prepared to deal with controversy.* Because issues of overlap often involve established conventional practices, the potential unfairness or harm caused by such practices may be overlooked by the majority of society, or may be important to the interests of particular social groups. A moral dilemma faced by educators and policymakers is whether and to what extent to engage students in consideration of such controversial matters. Engaging in discussion of such issues prepares students to contribute to the moral growth of society. However, schools that take on such issues risk alienating their members of the outside community. The educator's moral duty to enable students to deal with the contradictions inherent in any complex value system, balanced with the educator's role as an agent of that very society, defines the core moral dilemma faced by any teacher.

School Climate and Student Activity

- *General school climate should foster fairness and respect for others.* Moral development and character education are not limited to discrete academic subject areas, but are infused throughout school life. The school climate should be one characterized by mutual respect for all persons. School rules should be ones that protect student safety and promote respect for others. Enforcement of school policies should be characterized by firmness, fairness, and flexibility. School authority should not be characterized by harshness or intolerance.

- *Provide students with opportunities to develop social problem-solving skills.* While not a component of moral development per se, knowledge of conflict resolution and social problem solving allows students greater ability to engage in nonconfrontational peer interactions that allow for dialogue and construction of moral orientations toward others. This works best when students are encouraged to use these skills in resolving actual conflicts while at school (e.g., on the playground).
- *Students should be given opportunities to assume roles that entail moral responsibility.* Much of school life requires little more of students than passive obedience. Opportunities for students to build a sense of themselves as moral beings, such as by actively participating in meeting the needs of their own school and local community, if coupled with opportunities for meaningful reflection can provide content for students to construct a moral sense of self.

References

Angelou, M. (1971). *I know why the caged bird sings.* New York: Bantam Books.

Guerra, N., Nucci, L., and Huesmann, L. R. (1994). Moral cognition and childhood aggression. In L. Rowell Huesmann (ed.), *Aggressive behavior: Current perspectives* (pp. 13–33). New York: Plenum.

Noam, G., and Wren, T. E. (eds.). (1993). *The moral self.* Cambridge, Mass.: MIT Press.

Nucci, L. (ed.). (1989). *Moral development and character education: A dialogue.* Berkeley: McCutchan.

Nucci, L., and Weber, E. (1991). The domain approach to values education: From theory to practice. In W. Kurtines and J. L. Gewirtz (eds.), *Handbook of moral behavior and development (Vol. 3: Applications)* (pp. 251–266). Hillsdale, N.J.: Erlbaum.

Power, C., Higgins, A., and Kohlberg, L. (1989). *Lawrence Kohlberg's approach to moral education.* New York: Columbia University Press.

Ryan, K., and McLean, G. F. (eds.). (1987). *Character development in schools and beyond.* New York: Praeger.

Sapiro, C., and Nucci, L. (April 1991). *Brazilian adolescent and young adults' conceptions of corrupt social practices.* Paper presented at the biennial meetings of the Society for Research in Child Development, Seattle, Washington.

Sarbin, T. (1986). *Narrative psychology: The storied nature of human conduct.* New York: Praeger.

Turiel, E. (1983). *The development of social knowledge: Morality and convention.* Cambridge, Mass.: Cambridge University Press.

Turiel, E.; Hildebrandt, C.; and Wainryb, C. (1991). Judging social issues. *Monographs for the Society for Research in Child Development 56,* 1–103.

Wainryb, C. (1991). Understanding differences in moral judgments: The role of informational assumptions. *Child Development* 62, 840–851.

Chapter 7

Student Performance Portfolios

Lauren B. Resnick

Performance assessment is on the rise. What was, just a few years ago, an esoteric "alternative" promoted by critics of mainstream education and not taken seriously as a potential competitor for standard American forms of testing may soon become a dominant feature of the American educational landscape. Not surprisingly, as states and school districts begin to consider performance assessments as potential official measures of achievement, questions are being raised about the extent to which the new technology of assessment will really be able to deliver reliable, valid, and fair measures of student achievement.

In most discussions of performance assessment, it is tacitly assumed that the new forms of performance assessment are in-

Reprinted with permission from Lauren B. Resnick, "Performance Puzzles," *American Journal of Education* (August 1994), pp. 511-525. Copyright © 1994 by the University of Chicago Press.

Preparation of this paper was supported by grants from the U.S. Department of Education for research on the New Standards Project. I want to thank Robert Mislevy for his helpful comments on an earlier draft of this article. Errors of fact or interpretation, however, are my own.

tended to function just as traditional tests do and so can be judged without complication against traditional psychometric criteria. In one sense, this assumption is correct. Assessments used in officially evaluating students or schools need to deliver information that educators and the public can trust. We must, therefore, have reasonable confidence that the scores offered do not depend unduly on personal biases of judges, special features of the performance tasks that are set for students, or accidents of the conditions under which the assessments are administered. In another sense, however, performance assessment represents such a significant departure from traditional American testing practice that we may never come to grips with either its possibilities or genuine problems unless we address it on its own terms.

There are at least two important ways in which performance assessment as it is developing today differs in fundamental aims and assumptions from our current standardized tests. The first difference, which has been widely acknowledged in general educational discussions but only infrequently discussed when matters of technical adequacy are on the table, is that the new performance assessments are intended to function as integral elements within the education system, rather than as external monitors of the system. The new performance assessments are meant to set standards to which students and teachers can direct their efforts. They must maintain their validity even when they are "taught to." And they must be capable of exemplifying standards, setting clear targets for instruction and learning efforts.

By contrast, our traditional tests are designed mostly to monitor the system. They are not expected to reflect directly curriculum or instructional content. They work as indirect measures—dipsticks or thermometers—of how a student or an institution is doing, and their validity lies substantially in their ability to predict future performances or correlate with more directly observed capabilities. They work best when no one is "teaching the test," for they tend to lost predictive validity when students are drilled on items closely matched to test forms.

The second difference between performance assessment and traditional testing is that they emerge from rather different assumptions about the nature of human knowledge and competence. Traditional testing is rooted in assumptions of associationism, expressed perhaps most elegantly in the psychological writings of one of the founders of American testing, Edward L. Thorndike. Performance assessment, by contrast, is more consonant with the epistemological assumptions of pragmatism, as expressed by John Dewey, George Herbert Mead, and, more recently, by theorists of situated cognition.

Associationist epistemology assumes that knowledge and skill can be fully characterized in terms of collections of separate bits of mental associations or stimulus-response pairs. It further supposes—along with information-processing and structuralist theories of human knowing—that competence is fundamentally a function of internally represented knowledge. Associationist theories of testing seek to identify "traits" or abilities that are, in their essence, unrelated to particular contexts of performance. Traditional testing treats context effects as "noise" or "error." This is true even when the language of traits and general cognitive abilities is avoided in favor of defining domains of competence in academic terms (for example, in the ACT tests or in most standardized achievement tests).

Pragmatic epistemology, by contrast, assumes that competence is being able to perform well *in particular environments.* The tools, people, and institutional demands of a situation interact with an individual's state of preparedness to produce a particular performance. Consonant with pragmatic epistemology and theories of situated cognition, performance assessment is focused more on *certifying accomplishments* than on identifying enduring traits of individuals.

Too much can be made of the differences between performance assessment and traditional testing. The two must serve some of the same functions in society: assessing how well students are doing in meeting the educational goals set for them, evaluating how well educational institutions are doing at helping students meet these goals, estimating how well a person is likely to perform in a new environment of study or work. We must develop a robust technology of performance assessment that will allow it to serve these functions. That job is now barely begun. We cannot expect to succeed at this task, however, if we apply unreflectively the technical tools of a measurement technology different in intent and epistemological underpinnings. Performance assessment will require its own tools and technical standards. I hope to begin here a conversation about those tools and standards that I anticipate will need to continue for many years.

Portfolio and Performance: A Social Design Problem

To get started, it will help to build up our image of performance assessment in its own terms, not as a substitute or alternative to current forms of testing, but as a set of procedures designed to serve certain social and institutional functions. To do this, let us imagine that no formal tests or examinations of any kind exist and that schooling as we know it today has not yet been invented. Imagine instead an apprenticeship system in which young people learn their specialties by working in the production shops of local craftsmen and then go into a broader world seeking employment or commissions or further study and training opportunities. These young people, of course, would need to carry with them some evidence of their capabilities, or bona fides, as it were, of the likelihood of their producing good work in the future or of learning well and becoming a credit to the institution of advanced study that they joined.

To give our problem some personal reality, imagine that the person under consideration is a young woman who has apprenticed as a weaver in her home village and has heard of new and advanced techniques to be learned in the workshop of a famous weaver in the central town of her region. She goes to that town hoping to gain a place as a senior apprentice in that workshop. What questions might the master weaver in the new town workshop ask?

First, we can imagine, would come the question, "Do you know how to do the kind of work required here?" To this, our young woman might say, "Let me show you some examples of work I have done." She would open her satchel and arrange the cloth she has brought in a display designed to show it to best advantage. Examining the weavings, the master weaver would decide whether the quality and kind of work displayed was up to the standards she hoped for and contained the range and variety of styles expected of successful entrants to the workshop. This is *portfolio assessment* in its simplest, purest form!

Is that all that is needed? Well, not quite. For how is the master weaver, faced with an unknown young aspirant, to be sure that the work displayed in the young woman's portfolio is really her own? It is not hard to imagine a system of assurances arising in the region. The young woman's portfolio would, then, include a letter, written in the hand of the craftsman in whose shop she did her initial apprentice work and stamped with the establishment's known seal, certifying that the pieces of work in her portfolio (which might be named and cataloged) were her own. The village craftsman might even add a few words about the reliability and willingness to work—in short, the character—of the aspirant. We now have a portfolio that carries a more trustworthy record than just the work itself. We have, in effect, a certification of accomplishments.

Of course, this system depends on personal connections or at least personal reputation. Suppose, however, that the master weaver had become so famous that applicants for apprentice places in her workshop came not just from a local region but from distant places. Then she might never have heard of the local weaver in whose shop the applicant's portfolio was presumably assembled. The master weaver might be satisfied with another layer of certification, perhaps from the Regional Association of Weavers from which the applicant came, attesting to the honesty and reliability of the craftsman certifying the young person's work. But if the applicant came from very far away, and if there were applicants from many regions, even that certification might not seem trustworthy. The master weaver might then check applicants' ability to produce work of the kind seen in their portfolios by watching them produce a similar piece of work. Then there could be no question of authenticity of the work. If the quality matched that of the portfolio work, the applicant could be accepted with confidence.

We have arrived at the idea of an *on-demand performance assessment*. Presumably the on-demand performances would be as much like the portfolio items as possible, but there would be some compromises necessary: the on-demand performances would need to be shorter and manageable under controlled conditions. As a result, they would be less likely to indicate originality and flexibility than the full portfolio items. And there might be some forms of weaving whose complexity could not be assessed under the constraints of the on-demand performance. Nevertheless, on-demand performances are a welcome, perhaps even necessary, complement to the portfolio, for besides being practical as a check on portfolio work, the on-demand performances would offer another advantage: a reliable basis for comparing a number of applicants on a common set of tasks.

No doubt the master weaver would not want to base admissions solely on these prescribed performances. They would not, after all, be able to indicate originality, flexibility, or design skill as well as the full portfolio items. But as an "anchor" for interpreting the very varied work likely to show up in a set of individual portfolios, on-demand performances would be very useful. In addition, the director might decide to give applicants an on-demand learning test, perhaps presenting them with a new style of craftsmanship not contained in their portfolios and observing how they did at mastering this new mode of work. Or she might pose an invention task, asking the applicants to design and create a weaving that was deliberately different from any included in their portfolios.

Over time, we can imagine, the master weaver would probably become good at judging invented work, as well as the portfolio items and performances on the other on-demand tasks. But if the workload became too great, she might assemble a jury to examine portfolios and evaluate performances. Disagreements among members of the jury would be resolved by discussion among the members and, when necessary, intervention by the master.

We have now designed an assessment system that seems to contain all the elements necessary for a reliable and valid, geographically portable credential. With just a bit more elaboration, we can imagine a system that also functioned to increase weaving ability throughout the land. It is likely that, in local workshops everywhere, trainers of young weavers would try to communicate to their apprentices the criteria for the kind of work they should put in their portfolios when applying to work with the master weaver. They probably would also give their apprentices some practice in the kinds of on-demand learning and invention tasks they knew the master weaver would ask of her applicants. The portfolio criteria and the known kinds of on-demand tasks would, in effect, establish standards for weaving education, clear goals toward which aspiring weavers could work.

Notice what is *not* in this system. There are no tests of "general weaving ability" or of component abilities in the craft. Apprentices might spend some time learning how to do the component skills of weaving—selecting fibers, dying them, and the like. But there is no need for any kind of separate demonstration of competence on these components in the portfolio, because it is understood that weavings in a portfolio were done "from scratch." This understanding is carried in the certification and authentication of portfolios of work. Similarly, there may be some "exercise" or "practice" weavings in the course of weaving education; but these need not enter the portfolio, because they are not considered major accomplishments.

What are the limitations in the picture I have just sketched? "Well," you might say, "your story is nice enough for the very special case you have sketched: a small and elite training workshop, a field of work in which the products can be carried in a small satchel. What about a world in which hundreds of thousands of young people need to be educated in a wide variety of fields and where a master in a field cannot count on personally knowing the certifiers or jurors of another region? Where reliability and fairness in judgment are paramount concerns? Where, unlike crafts or the visual and performing arts, we are not used to defining competence in terms of visible products or performances? And where there is no catalog of established genres of work that can be used as a guideline in setting criteria for portfolio entries?"

These are all legitimate questions, and each deserves a thoughtful response. The responses, which are developed in the remainder of this article, will engage us in a consideration of many of the classical issues of measurement technology: reliability of scoring, generalizability of observed performance, and content and construct validity.

Customized Education on a Large Scale

Let me begin with the issue of a small and elite system versus a mass system. In my story, the young woman had the advantages of small institutions and personalized education both in her initial, local apprentice preparation and in the process of applying for a place in the master weaver's workshop. Her apprenticeship teacher worked with her, coached her, evaluated her work, and helped her choose the weaving products she selected for her portfolio. The master weaver's workshop was also small and personalized enough that the master herself, or a small committee, could evaluate the portfolio of work and judge the necessary on-demand performances.

In American education today, very nearly the opposite situation holds. The schools are serving huge numbers of young people, and they are often large, impersonal places. No one coaches students through the process of preparing a portfolio of accomplishments. Furthermore, the universities and companies students want to join after finishing school often process thousands of applications every year. No single jury could possibly study every portfolio or judge every on-demand performance. But, if multiple juries were used, there would be no chance to compare judgments and talk through disagreements. The juries might each go off in a different direction, and there would be no way to ensure common standards of judgment. On the face of it, it does not look as though we could adapt the apprenticeship and portfolio model to our mass education system.

Yet we cannot afford *not* to do so. Everything points to the fact that the mass education system as we know it has to be reworked rather than accepted as a fact of life. Just about every current program of education reform calls for personalized education and small, face-to-face education communities. Everywhere, educators aiming for superior performance are trying to figure out how to break large institutions into smaller units of personal relationship and human accountability. Small schools, schools within schools, vertical teaching teams, and the like are often our beacon lights of reform.

These beacons of hope have, for the most part, been created by working *against* the existing education system. One of the most important challenges in education reform is to create a system that supports, instead of suppresses, personalized and customized education. One feature of such a changed system will have to be a very different method of assessment than the one we use now. The portfolio-cum-on-demand-checkups approach in my story is a good starting place. Can we make it work on a large—but not a mass—scale? Can we make it work for many people, without losing its essential personal elements?

Assuring Reliability and Fairness of Judgment

The first problem to be solved is the need for hundreds, probably thousands, of juries. How can common standards of judgment be established and monitored? Suppose a "master jury" is established: a set of people whom everyone respects and who are practiced at reaching agreement with each other. We know a good deal about attaining agreement among judges who are in continuous interaction with one another. But we should anticipate difficulties in getting adequate agreements between groups of judges who are not able to engage in face-to-face communication.

The New Standards Project[1] has addressed this problem through a system of *benchmark tasks* that are used to train scorers and to check their reliability from time to time while scoring is underway. Benchmark tasks are pieces of student work selected by a group of lead teachers as exemplifying a certain score level.[2] The benchmark tasks are presented to candidate scorers along with extended commentary explaining why each warrants a particular score. In training, candidate scorers discuss benchmark papers extensively, and candidates remain "in training" until they meet a criterion of assigning scores identical to the benchmark score to sixteen of twenty successive papers that they have not seen before. By training scorers to match their judgments to the benchmark papers rather than to one another, it is possible to calibrate different groups of scorers to the same standard. New Standards has found

---

[1] The New Standards Project is a partnership of nineteen states and six urban school districts that are developing shared standards and a system of performance and portfolio assessments to instantiate those standards. New Standards partners either will use the New Standards products directly as part of their state or district assessment programs or will participate in a process of linking their own assessment to the standards established by the partnership.

[2] New Standards grades student work at five score levels: 1, 2, 3, 4, and 4 + (candidate for honors). A score of 4 is described as "meeting the standard." A paper marked 4+ will receive special honors jurying.

that by using this form of training-to-benchmark procedure, it is possible to maintain scoring reliability even when scoring is done at multiple, dispersed sites. In principle, there does not seem to be any reason this procedure cannot be spread to an indefinite number of separate scoring sites. This would make it possible to handle scoring of a very large number of performance assessments by simply expanding the number of scoring juries.

The benchmark-papers approach will require some adaptation for portfolios. The important difference is that portfolios will vary from student to student. All students will not have responded to the same question, so there will be no simple way to select a paper that exemplifies a certain level of response. The scorer's job will be not only to judge the quality of a particular piece of work but also to decide whether a collection of portfolio entries, considered as a whole, displays all of the capabilities that are valued. This is a much more sophisticated and demanding judgment task than scoring a single piece of work. Furthermore, for both educational (helping teachers to internalize the standards and providing early feedback to students on how they are doing) and economic reasons, we will probably want a system in which the faculty of a school is charged with the first round of portfolio scoring for its students.

To make this work, we will need a sophisticated set of guidelines and benchmark examples for scoring portfolios. I discuss the nature of these later when considering the question of content and construct validity of assessments. But even with these guidelines and benchmarks available, assuring objective and fair judgments from teachers working in many dispersed sites will require a system in which different groups of judges check one another's scores and are in sufficient communication with one another that via conversation, challenge, and argument, they develop and maintain common standards of judgment. The system I have in mind is not very different from the one developed over decades of practice in Great Britain and other countries with decentralized education traditions that use traditional essay examination systems. In the British *moderation* system, each stage of the examining process—establishing the course syllabus, setting the questions, describing criteria for different grades, grading sample (equivalent to our benchmark) papers, the overall distribution of grades—is cross-checked by an individual or a group from a sister institution. In the least formal form of moderation, moderators look over the grades given by assigned graders and confirm their reasonableness. Knowing what we do about "confirmation bias," we will prefer independent rescoring as a more stringent form of moderation.

We have yet to establish an American version of moderation, suitable to the vast size of this country and responsive, too, to our particular political organization in which states retain constitutional authority for education and in which, in some states, all authority over curriculum—and, hence, the content of any form of assessment that is "taught to"—is further delegated to individual school districts. New Standards envisages a multilayered "auditing" system: initially, scores will be assigned to individual student portfolios by a school faculty—that is, the faculty acting corporately, not as individual teachers. The corporate grading, especially when guided by a set of criteria for portfolios-as-whole and for individual pieces, would act to stabilize scoring and to protect students from the arbitrary judgments of individual teachers.

Next, a selection of every school's portfolios would be sent elsewhere (perhaps to another school, perhaps to a central quality control board) for rescoring. If the rescoring team agreed with the original scores to a sufficient degree, all of the school's scores would be certified, and the faculty grades for all student portfolios would stand. If there were insufficient agreement, a full rescoring might be called for or perhaps only a rescoring of those portfolios on the borderline between "meeting the standard" and not quite meeting it. In New Standards, that would mean rescoring all 3 and 4 portfolios: the former to ensure that students have not been unfairly denied credit for meeting the standard; the latter to control against schools' setting standards that are too lenient.

At the next "layer" of auditing, a state quality board would need to receive reports of the cross-grading and to certify that the school-level auditing is proceeding appropriately, perhaps making some site visits or adding another layer of regrading to do this with confidence. Finally, the New Standards partners want assurance that grading standards are the same from state to state. They are looking to the New Standards Project to add yet another layer of auditing, one that insures that each partner's auditing system is based on equivalent criteria and that it is operating efficiently and equitably.

Many technical and social issues remain to be resolved in this plan, among them the questions of what proportion of portfolios needs to be regraded and what constitutes a sufficient degree of agreement between original scores and audited scores. Answers to these questions will depend, in part, on what is to be done with the scores. If "high stakes" for individual students are attached—for example, if the scores are to play a role in college admissions or gaining employment—tighter levels of agreement are needed than if no major decisions depend on them. Alternatively or in combination, appropriate systems of appeal allowing students who feel that their work has been unfairly judged to call for a rescoring may remove some of the pressure for near-perfect agreement in original scoring and simultaneously create a sense of visible, public fairness in the system.

As this last comment suggests, the appropriate combination of rescoring criteria and appeal processes is not just a technical matter to be resolved by statisticians and decision theorists. It is at least as much a question of social design: finding a system that people—students, teachers, parents, colleges, and employers—are able to believe in and willing to trust.

Beyond the Satchel: The Problem of "Representative Work"

There is more to obtaining a fair judgment of a student than just ensuring that scorers agree with one another. There is also the problem of how to get a fair picture of a student's competence from a few pieces of work. Performance tasks, whether in portfolios or in on-demand assessments, stand for more than just themselves. They are meant to be "representative work" capable of yielding information about the student's competence in a field of accomplishment.

Common sense tells us that a single example of a person's work is not as good an indicator of general competence in a domain as a collection of his or her work. But how many exemplars are needed? And how should they relate to one another?

These are the classic questions of *generalizability* in measurement.

It is an established fact of mental measurements that any two test items are likely to be only weakly correlated. That means it is not safe to generalize from performance on one item to performance on any other. The problem of generalizability is solved in traditional testing by using many short test items. A score is then created by totaling performance on these items. The score based on thirty or fifty items can, if the items have been well selected, generalize well to a different set of items that have been selected according to a similar set of principles. No single test item carries much weight, but the collection as a whole has some generalizability.

The solution of using many different items will not work for performance assessment for the simple, practical reason that performance assessment tasks take a long time to do, and so it is not possible to administer many of them to any single student. Recent work on generalizability in performance assessment is providing estimates of the number of performance tasks needed to stabilize scores. These studies suggest that ten or fifteen performance tasks in a given domain—not thirty to fifty, as previously thought—are needed. But if each task requires about an hour to complete, taking even ten or fifteen is more than we would reasonably ask of an individual student.

Two solutions to this dilemma are typically proposed. The first, available when the score of interest is for a school, a district, or a state but not an individual student, is to use some form of matrix or light sampling. Each student takes only a few of the performance tasks, and the results from many students are pooled to yield a score for the group based on many tasks. Because the group score is based on many tasks, it can be adequately generalizable without undue testing time for individual students. How to choose the tasks for a matrix performance assessment and how to distribute them among students are new problems for assessment theory and practice. Research is required using multiple patterns of task administration to yield data on how performances relate to one another.

A special problem for some forms of performance assessment arises from the fact that the tasks may require some whole-class activities. This is so for many of the New Standards mathematics and English language arts tasks. The whole-class activities are sometimes designed to "level the playing field" for the assessment by providing some common experiences for all students before they take the test. Or, they may be an integral part of what is to be measured, as would occur when class discussion or other teamwork skills were to be assessed. In either case, when whole-class activities are used, it is not possible to give different tasks to different students in the same class; so we cannot derive a classwide group score by matrixing within the classroom.

This in turn may limit the kinds of on-demand testing we can use to derive schoolwide scores. Giving different classes different tasks and then summing across several classes to yield a school score would work in only very large schools. And, even in those schools, there might be interactions between tasks and classes (e.g., because teachers emphasized different aspects of the curriculum, or because of different student ability levels in different classrooms) that would make the matrixing procedure invalid. If research shows that these difficulties do in fact hold, a schoolwide score will be possible only if shorter tasks (so more can be administered) or tasks that do not require full-classroom activity (so different students can do different tasks) are used. These patterns and possibilities, too, will have to be worked out over the next several years as performance assessment comes into wider use.

The most promising long-term solution to the generalizability problem, however, probably lies not in constraining on-demand performances to the requirements of generalizability but in breaking down the distinction between learning events and measurements events, so that most measurement information comes as a natural by-product of worthwhile learning activities in which students engage throughout the school year. That is just what portfolio assessment does. Here, then, is a happy case in which technical measurement demands coincide with desirable pedagogical practice.

Defining the Domain: Questions of Validity

Empirical patterns of association alone cannot provide robust solutions to the generalizability problem. We will also need better ways than we now have of describing the domains over which generalization is expected. We must, in other words, develop

principled ways to answer the question, generalization to what?
A random collection of tasks, no matter how large the number
or how elegant the matrix design, cannot represent an individual's or a group's competence in a field of knowledge or in a
skill. The tasks must be systematically related to a careful definition of the field. This requirement takes us into questions of
content and *construct validity*.

Validity is where performance assessment has its strongest
potential. Indeed, the movement toward performance assessment
has arisen largely in response to a widespread belief that American standardized tests do a poor job of representing the kind of
knowledge and skill that we value. The decomposition of important knowledge and skill into disconnected bits and the decon-
textualization from meaningful situations of use that standardized
tests imposed virtually ensure their inability to validly assess complex
capabilities in which knowledge and skill are combined to produce meaningful intellectual, artistic, or design products. By
contrast, the performance assessments and portfolio projects now
coming into use have won accolades in many quarters for their
capacity to represent the kinds of knowledge and skills most
educators hope will become the dominant focus of teaching and
learning in the future.

Until now, however, these accolades have been based mainly
on inspection of individual performance tasks and portfolio entries. Many of these are elegant and appear to do a fair job of
representing the new forms of academic content that educators
in mathematics, science, English, and other disciplines value. But
how do they represent, as a collection, the range of knowledge
and skill we expect of competent students? To ask this question
is to inquire about the construct validity of an assessment.

There is no way to establish the construct validity of a collection of tasks in the absence of an agreed-upon framework that
describes the knowledge and skill that students are expected to
learn and that should be sampled by the assessment. In the United
States, we actively avoided developing such frameworks until just
a few years ago, for reasons linked to our historical commitment
to local control of education. The absence of such frameworks
has made it essentially impossible to deal sensibly with the problem of content or construct validity in assessment. There has been
no way to establish what the content of assessment tasks *should*

be or how to interpret the collection of tasks as representative of a domain.

A notable exception with respect to content validity is the College Board's Advanced Placement (AP) program, which is a syllabus-based assessment system. Schools that want to prepare their students for the AP exam in any particular year receive a syllabus telling them what the exam will cover. The syllabus guides text selection, teaching, and in-class paper writing and testing. Assuming that students have been in a course that largely follows the syllabus, the exam they take at the end of the year is, by definition, content valid. However, the AP program does not explicitly take on questions of construct validity. A student is assigned a score by summing across the different sections of content, but there is no specification of how to make inferences about what the student knows about the domain as a whole.

The new movement to develop consensus content standards in the major school subject matters represents an important, indeed crucial, step forward in defining content-valid testing. The movement is furthest advanced in the field of mathematics, where the National Council for Teachers of Mathematics (NCTM) *Standards for School Mathematics* has led the way. In attempting to build specifications for the New Standards assessment program in mathematics, we have found that the NCTM *Standards* are helpful in providing criteria for judging whether individual tasks are content valid: that is, whether they reflect knowledge and skills defined in the *Standards*. The *Standards* thus provide a grounding for judgments of content validity, although they are not nearly as precise as the AP syllabi.

It is not an accident that the NCTM *Standards*, as such, do not provide a principled basis for making judgments of construct validity. They are not sufficiently constraining, and they do not specify how the various elements of content are related to one another. By intent, the *Standards* lay out a very broad field of aspiration for mathematics education and do not specify exactly what any school should teach. As a result, schools attempting to use the *Standards* to guide their curriculum redesign have found that they have to make many difficult choices about what to emphasize and what to exclude or to make optional with guidance from the *Standards*. We have had the identical problem in trying to use the *Standards* directly in designing New Standards assessments.

The solution that appears to be workable is to develop what we have come to call a *framework for balance*, which takes up where the broad national consensus standards leave off. The framework dimensionalizes the content standards and specifies which dimensions *must* and which *may* be included in the assessment. These dimensions include strands of specific knowledge (e.g., probability, fractions and decimals, constructive geometry) as well as skills such as displaying data, problem solving, graphing, and manipulating equations. The framework further specifies the broad genres of student work that the assessment program as a whole should sample (e.g., a survey study, a physical experiment). Tasks or extended projects falling within the same genre can be sensibly scored using the same rubric; different genres require different scoring rubrics. Thus, the criteria for excellent work are genre specific.

The framework for balance takes an important step toward the specifications that will be needed for establishing the construct validity of assessments. However, the framework for balance does not—by design—specify the precise performance tasks or portfolio projects that must be included in the assessment. Instead, New Standards is developing a process by which a collection of student work (an individual's work in a portfolio; a group's work in the collection of matrixed performance tasks) can be mapped to the dimensions of the framework to show how the work taken as a whole demonstrates competence in all of the dimensions specified. This should allow us to identify many different specific assessment packages—and thus many different specific curricula—that conform to the framework and allow principled judgments about students' competence in a subject matter.

Conclusions

I opened this chapter with the claim that performance assessment is designed for a different set of social functions than traditional American testing and that it is grounded in a different set of epistemological assumptions. I think it is fair to say that the social design requirements for an assessment system that can set targets for educational effort are today the driving force in assessment research. Because we have decided we need new forms of assessment, many groups are at work developing them. Typically, the time and ingenuity needed to solve the practical problems—of scoring, of educating teachers in the new methods, of generating new assessment tasks, of managing large-scale operations while retaining personalization—absorb most of the resources of assessment development groups. There is not much energy left for reflection on the theoretical aspects of what they are doing.

Yet this practical work is not without theoretical significance. In the spirit of pragmatic epistemology, the efforts to create a new technology of assessment are beginning to point the way toward a new theory. Efforts to define performance standards are producing candidate definitions of fields of accomplishment. The challenge of developing techniques for mapping tasks and performances to frameworks is likely to refine these definitions quickly. And the idea of genres as defining classes of performance situations may be a first step toward a cognitive theory of situations.

One thing that is now clear is that performance assessment cannot develop on solid ground without much more explicit theories of situated cognition than are now available. We need ways of defining situations in terms of their cognitive demands and opportunities so that we can begin to develop a cognitive theory of accomplishment. A cognitive theory of accomplishment would explain how situation and person interact to produce a competent performance, rather than looking for traits that are stable across contexts or, alternatively, contexts that override personal characteristics. Pragmatic philosophy called for this kind of interactionist theory of cognition. Now so too does the practical demand for new forms of assessment.

Suggested Readings

Resnick, D. P., and Resnick, L. B. (in press). Performance assessment and the multiple functions of educational measurement. In R. Mitchell and M. Kane (eds.), *Implementing performance assessment: Promises, problems, and challenges.* Washington, D.C.: Pelavin Associates.

Resnick L. B., and Nolan, K. J. (in press). Standards for education: How are we doing? In *Brookings dialogues on public policy.* Washington, D.C: Brookings Institution.

Resnick, L. B.; Nolan, K. J.; and Resnick, D. P. (in press). Benchmarking education standards. *Educational Evaluation and Policy Analysis.*

Chapter 8

Assessing Student Learning

Robert J. Mislevy

The foundations of educational assessment, as it is usually thought of, extend back a century now, to the quest to "measure intelligence." Just as heights and weights locate people along scales of physical characteristics, numbers were proposed to locate individuals along scales of mental characteristics: first intelligence, then more school-related "traits" such as mathematics achievement or reading level. Technological and statistical machinery have developed over the years to carry out assessments effectively. During the same period, many insights have been gained into how people

I am grateful to Drew Gitomer and Jack Moe for comments on an earlier draft of this paper, and to Lauren Resnick for discussions that helped shape the perspective outlined here—which, of course, should not necessarily be taken as representing theirs. The work was supported in part by the National Center for Research on Evaluation, Standards, and Student Testing (CRESST), Educational Research and Development Program, cooperative agreement number R117G10027 and CFDA catalog number 84.117G, as administered by the Office of Educational Research and Improvement, U.S. Department of Education.

learn and solve problems. How have these advances changed our capability to "measure students' learning"?

- We've learned it can't be done, and
- We've learned to do it better.

This chapter discusses implications of these seemingly para-doxical claims for the further development of educational assess-ment. I begin by reviewing the mental measurement paradigm that underlies familiar assessment practices, noting a certain coherence among its methods, purposes, constraints, and psychology. Develop-ments in each of these factors are then discussed. Some have been used to improve practice within the paradigm, but others cast doubts on the adequacy of its scope. I will argue that the principles of reasoning that underlie standard assessment practice transcend the specifics of those practices, and can serve to ground new assess-ment practices for broader purposes.

Mental Measurement and Educational Assessment

In educational assessment, the "data" are what students say and do—their words, actions, products, and performances. But to evaluate students' progress or to guide further learning, we must reason from what we see and hear, to what it implies about their understandings. These inferences must be framed in some conception of competence and how it is acquired. Such a con-ception generates a "universe of discourse"—the kinds of questions about students one might address through assessment, and the kinds of answers one can obtain. The first part of this chapter shows that questions like, "How many items in this domain would this student answer correctly?" and "What proportion of the population would have scores lower than his?" are directly relevant to the purposes that educational assessment originally addressed. But to help a student extend his understanding, the question might be, "What can this person be thinking so that his actions make sense from his perspective?" And when our role is to communicate the import of a student's project, we will be asked, "What is the nature of the understanding she has demonstrated?"

and "Why should I believe you?" The second half of this chapter addresses these latter questions (see Mislevy, 1994, for a more technical discussion).

Elements of Mental Measurement

The basic elements of the mental measurement paradigm are the kinds of questions one asks (targets of inference), what one can observe to try to answer them (assessment data), and the ways that the weight and coverage of evidence about those questions are established (test theory). The *targets of inference* are aspects of students' learning characterized as numbers on a continuum, upon which evaluations and decisions would be based if the numbers were known with certainty. Under trait psychology, the variable of interest is "a relatively stable characteristic of a person—an attribute, enduring process, or disposition—which is consistently manifested to some degree when relevant, despite considerable variation in the range of settings and circumstances" (Messick, 1989, p. 15). Under behaviorist psychology, the variable of interest is a person's tendency to act in specified ways in specified conditions, both of which are defined from the observer's point of view. Either way, the target of inference is an unobservable variable that characterizes behavior across all the domain of relevant settings; the target of inference is the "true score."

The *data* are "observed scores," which summarize observed behavior in samples from relevant domains of situations (e.g., test items). The "how often" or "how many" of behavior in an actual sample of settings directly reflects the tendency toward such behavior in the similar settings. In classical, or true-score, test theory, the quality of inference from a particular sample to the domain as a whole falls under the term "reliability." Links to "how," "what to do next," or "what would happen in different settings" remain to be established. The quality of inference from a given sample to explanations or to behaviors in different settings falls under the term "validity." Initial work in gathering assessment data was based on sampling theory for homogeneous domains, borrowed in part from astronomical measurement:

Two hundred years ago, Karl Friedrich Gauss studied how to estimate a star's "true position" from multiple observations, each perturbed by the imperfections of the telescope and observer. He found that if each observation is the true value plus a random "measurement error," then the average of the measurements is a good estimate of the true value, and it can be made more precise by averaging over additional observations. The nature of the measuring instrument determines the distribution of the measurement errors. Knowing this, one can determine the accuracy of an estimate based on a given number of observations, or calculate how many observations one needs for a given accuracy.

Large-Scale Assessment for Large-Scale Schooling

This conception suited the mass educational system that also arose in the United States at the turn of the century (Glaser, 1981). Educators attempted to select or place large numbers of students into instructional programs, but could not gather much information about each student, offer many options, or tailor programs to students once a placement decision was made. This decision-making context encouraged building assessment systems around a small number of broadly construed and widely applicable student characteristics, stable over time and informed by data that were easy to gather and summarize. Since "reliability" indicates whether a different sample of similar tasks would order students similarly, thus leading to the same decisions for most of them, it does gauge an important aspect of a test's evidential value for selection and placement decisions along a single dimension.

Despite traditions of oral and written examinations, by the end of the 1930s, most large-scale testing programs had shifted to multiple-choice tests administered under standardized conditions. This was partly from considerations of reliability—greater accuracy for the time and money spent—but also from validity (for the intended purpose), especially when students had to be compared across time or place. Horace Mann recognized by 1850 that the results of oral examinations were subject to the caprice of examiners, and those of written examinations depended heavily on the questions and scorers students happened to be assigned. Using such tests in large-scale assessment, as they could be implemented at that time, would provide weaker evidence and less equitable decisions than using standardized multiple-choice exams, as judged in the context of the time.

Giraffes evolved to thrive in an environmental niche in which they can eat leaves from tall trees. The same long necks would not be beneficial in the tundra successfully occupied by the Arctic hare or in the desert of the coyote. Multiple-choice standardized tests evolved to dominate the niche defined by a particular constellation of purposes, constraints, and societal structures. Their preeminence there suggests likely success in similar constellations, but neither indicates some deeper truth in their premises nor guarantees their value in increasingly different constellations.

Informal Assessment

Inferences about the nature of proficiency and how it develops fall largely outside mental measurement's universe of discourse. High scores on standardized tests can provide efficient predictions for success in further instruction, but standardized test scores neither foster nor provide direct evidence about more sustained and productive capabilities. Low scores can predict lack of success in a given instructional setting, but neither distinguish among such causes as inadequate preparation and poor motivation nor indicate how learning might be improved. Teachers have always relied on a wider array of means to learn about how their students are doing, and to help plan further learning. They use tests and quizzes, to be sure, designed and scored under the mental measurement paradigm. But they also use evidence from projects, work in class, conversations with and among students, and the like—all combined with additional information about the students, the schooling context, and what the students are working on. Teachers call these "informal" assessments, in contrast with the "formal" assessments typified by standardized tests.

The starkness of the contrast between "formal" and "informal" assessment arises because historically, limited conceptual and technical tools have not been able to satisfy, with the same data and analyses, the different purposes of different users of assessment. To guide instruction and monitor its effects, teachers need information intimately connected with what their students are working on, and they interpret this evidence in light of everything else they know about their students and their instruction. The power of informal assessment resides in these connections. Yet precisely because they are individualized, neither the rationale nor the results of the typical informal assessment are easily communicated beyond the classroom. Standardized tests do communicate efficiently across time and place—but by so constraining the content and the timeliness of the message that they often have little utility in the classroom. Today's challenge is to devise assessment systems that by capitalizing on technological and conceptual developments, incorporate strengths of both formal and informal assessments.

Nonmeasurement Functions of the Mental Measurement Paradigm

Thomas Kuhn (1970) notes how shared terminology, tools, and procedures spur the development of scientific communities and enhance the work of their members. Common methods and language allow observations and results to be communicated parsimoniously and rapidly; a scientist does not need to reinvent the conceptual and evidential grounding of another scientist's results if they are cast in familiar terms and procedures.

Although the physical measurement analogue connotes a certain objectivity and detachment, assessment based on the mental measurement model shapes, and is shaped by, social considerations. It structures conversations about learning in several ways:

- *Communication of expectations.* In and of themselves, domains of tasks and modes of testing convey to students, teachers, and the public at large what is important for students to learn and to accomplish.
- *Communication of results.* Once a domain of tasks and conditions of observation have been specified, a score and an accompanying measure of precision give a parsimonious summary of a student's behavior in the prescribed contexts, easily transmitted across time and place.
- *Credibility of results.* Test scores earn credibility beyond the immediate circumstances of the assessment if the data have been verifiably gathered under prescribed conditions.

That traditional assessment procedures serve these purposes is quite independent from the fact that they evolved under the mental measurement paradigm. Any assessment paradigm that might rise in their stead to evaluate and communicate students' learning would, in some way, need to address the same issues.

Progenitors of Change

Educational assessment has been developing in response to changes in its environment, including assessment purposes, possibilities, and constraints. I first consider how by easing constraints, inferential methods and technology have been used to address familiar purposes within the mental measurement paradigm more effectively. I then look at how cognitive psychology provokes more radical change by suggesting new purposes and contexts for assessment, spanning traditional boundaries between formal and informal assessment. I discuss ways that advances in inferential methods and technology can also help address a broader array of assessment purposes.

Advances in Statistical and Evidential Reasoning

The following developments in inferential methods help answer more questions that can be framed in the mental measurement paradigm, or answer them more efficiently.

Extending the Conception of Reliability. While the concept of reliability did suit the intended selection and placement uses, the basic formulas did not apply to many common practices. Generalizability theory ("g-theory") brought about a fuller understanding of the evidential value of observed scores, and expanded the range of inferences about domain proficiency for which the weight of evidence can be determined and efficient assessments designed. G-theory addresses conditions under which the data were obtained (how many items, scored by how many raters, under which design) and how they are used (comparing students to one another, against a fixed criterion, or to their previous status). Further developments in this direction include hierarchical models and structural equations models.

More complex collections of astronomical measurements, varying systematically with observatories, equipment, and observers, for example, are not well explained by a simple "true-value + independent random error" model. More complex statistical models, sometimes formally equivalent to those of g-theory, are needed to sort out the sources of uncertainty in measurements, to estimate star positions from given data, or to design experiments that optimize precision for given resources and costs.

Extending the Conception of Validity. Originally, the validity of placement or selection test scores was characterized mainly by their correlation with scores indicating the outcome of the decision. Factor analysis and structural-equations modeling broadened the study of empirical relationships among test scores, to better characterize the proficiencies that scores betokened. The contemporary view of validity within the mental measurement paradigm is broader still: "Validity is an integrated evaluative judgment of the degree to which empirical evidence and theoretical rationales support the adequacy and appropriateness of inferences and actions based on test scores or other modes of assessment. . . . [W]hat is to be validated is not the test or observation device as such but the inferences derived from test scores or other indicators— inferences about score meaning or interpretation and about the implications for action that the interpretation entails" (Messick, 1989, pp. 13–14). Increasingly, a test's "validity" is seen to encompass not merely predictive efficacy, but grounding in research, relationships with alternative sources of information, and coherence with its context and use.

Extending the Conception of Scores. True-score characterizations of students are bound to specific task domains and observational settings. Inspired by the analogy to physical measurement, item response theory (IRT) originated in the early 1940s as an attempt to characterize examinees' proficiency independently of the tasks they happened to have taken, and to characterize tasks independently of the examinees who happened to have taken them (Hambleton, 1989). IRT still addresses students' behavioral tendencies in a domain of tasks, but it "calibrates" tasks to a posited unobservable examinee proficiency variable from empirical patterns of response.

A domain of pole-vaulting tasks can be defined by a collection of bar settings. Vaulters could be compared in terms of the proportion they would clear—their true score. But some settings are harder and some are easier, in a way calibrated by their height. We can now talk about vaulters' highest jumps and their rates of success at given heights. We need not observe their performances at all settings or a random sample, but just a few in the region near their limits. Note that even though bar settings can be very precise, there is still considerable uncertainty in the measurement system; a vaulter may clear a height on one attempt but fail the next. Note also that this system is satisfactory only if the same calibrations apply to all vaulters.

Here are three examples of how IRT solves problems in the mental measurement paradigm that are hard to handle with classical test theory. First, calibrating tasks to a common proficiency variable makes it possible to design efficient tests, then compare results from students who have taken different test forms. Second, once tasks have been calibrated, the tester can select the tasks one at a time as a student proceeds, in light of previous responses—often cutting test length in half without sacrificing accuracy. Third, IRT provides tools to detect different patterns of response to a task across gender or cultural groups ("differential item functioning," or DIF)—like finding that different-colored bars are differentially hard for different vaulters. DIF techniques serve the objective of using overall scores to summarize performance in a given task domain, across everyone being assessed. In IRT, as in classical test theory, person-by-task interactions are "noise," weakening inference about domain proficiency. We see below that when such interactions are expected as proficiency develops in a learning area, taking them into account rather than averaging over them can serve the objective of inferring the character of proficiency.

Advances in Technology

Familiar forms of assessment were shaped by constraints on how data could be gathered, stored, transmitted, and analyzed. College admissions officers, for example, were in no position to investigate the details of the curricula and the achievements of thousands of applicants. Logistical and economic pressures limited the large-scale use of essays and interviews that required human interpretation, thus favoring objective-response tasks over more constructive and sustained tasks. It was not possible to store or share ephemeral performances in order to develop common standards or to verify that ratings were fair. These constraints are being eased by technological developments, including computers, video- and audio-taping, electronic communication, mass storage, and access to resources. I next describe new assessment possibilities within the mental measurement paradigm.

Computerized Adaptive Testing (CAT). IRT provides the inferential underpinning for adapting tests to students, but early implementations required individual examiners (as with the Stanford-Binet intelligence test) or cumbersome logistics (such as scratching off hidden answers, or testing in stages with scoring breaks). Administering adaptive tests with computers solves this problem, and now appears in large-scale testing programs such as the Graduate Record Examination (GRE).

It turns out that running adaptive testing solely in accordance with the IRT measurement model, as envisioned in the 1960s, often proves unsatisfactory. In paper-and-pencil testing, many considerations that affect results but lie outside the measurement model are handled through test-development traditions, administration conditions, and the socialization of students to the testing environment (e.g., how task content and skill requirements are balanced, and how students learn to allocate their time). Extending CAT to handle these extrameasurement considerations solves the immediate problem. More important, it cautions us that even when a mental measurement model does handle evidentiary concerns satisfactorily, it is not because the model is "true," but because social and logistical conditions have been so arranged that the resulting patterns of behavior are reasonably well summarized in its terms.

New Kinds of Tasks and Scoring. Computers can present students with tasks that are *interactive* (e.g., simulated experiments), *dynamic* (e.g., medical treatment problems in which simulated patients' conditions change over time), *constructive* (e.g., moving elements onto a construction site to meet a client's needs), and *less tightly structured* (e.g., solving a word problem that can be structured in several ways). Some scoring can also be done automatically, including the aforementioned examples. If (1) a domain of such tasks is established, (2) the quality of solutions to each can be scored, and (3) the target of inference is overall proficiency in that domain, then mental measurement test theory can be used to characterize the evidential value of the tasks to that end. The potential benefit is a task domain that better reflects the skills of interest. For example, students taking one computerized architectural exam can access standard building-code books on CD-ROM during testing; they are not expected to recall all the details of the code, but they must show that they have learned its structure, to recognize how it is applied, and to access the code books correctly and efficiently—in short, they will demonstrate that they can use the code the way practicing architects do.

It is important to note that more complex and realistic (and costly!) assessment tasks often provide disappointingly little evidential advantage over paper-and-pencil multiple-choice items for large-scale selection and placement decisions. The greatest gains from "authentic" tasks will *not* come from doing a better job, under the same constraints, of what standardized multiple-choice tests evolved to do.

> *Every patient's temperature is taken when entering the hospital. It is quick and cheap, and it provides a bit of information about health status. Electronic thermometers have supplanted glass mercury thermometers, because they are even quicker and cheaper to use—a gainful application of technology, even though it provides no additional information about health. This is like shifting a standardized test from paper-and-pencil administration to CAT. A fancier thermometer that gives ten-digit precision for $800 would be a waste, because it too adds no information for the job at hand. A magnetic resonance image (MRI) of a knee can be worth $800 when it pinpoints the exact nature and treatment of a problem— but only for the handful of patients, identified through simpler diagnostic tests, whose need it matches. Similarly, complex and realistic assessment tasks have a potential for providing additional information about students' capabilities, but waste time and money unless they are thoughtfully targeted.*

Distributed Testing and Scoring. In the stereotypical standardized test, a large room of silent examinees is paced section by section through the same or similar test forms. Their booklets are gathered when time expires, they are scored centrally, and results are reported back days or weeks later. But we can now capture and electronically transmit students' responses to computerized tasks; we can videotape and audiotape performances; we can scan constructed paper-and-pencil responses and artwork. Students can thus be assessed in remote places and at different times, and raters can evaluate their performances in remote places and at different times. Students now schedule some CAT exams like dental appointments, and raters score scanned facsimiles of some essay tests from their homes. Students in school consortiums share work on a common project, interacting with and receiving feedback from teachers and students across the nation.

Replayability. Besides easing time and location constraints, capturing performances helps us address the reliability problems that troubled Horace Mann: Captured performances can be seen, discussed, and evaluated by as many people, in as many times and places, as desired. Because we are no longer limited to the evaluations of raters present at the original performance, we can reduce biases and improve the accuracy of the scores of individual examinees, and use exemplars to establish shared expectations and standards of evaluation, over time and across distance, among raters, teachers, and students.

Advances in Psychology

The developments sketched above address the same essential target of inference as traditional assessments, namely, an overall behavioral tendency in a specified domain—but with enriched domains, more flexible ways to acquire data, and better communication of standards. I next consider how these same developments can be used in assessments aimed at qualitatively different inferences, first reviewing key developments from cognitive psychology into the ways people acquire and use knowledge and skills.

Mental Models/Schema Theory. A "mental model" or "schema" is a pattern of recurring relationships—anything from what happens at birthday parties, to how to figure out unit prices, to how to carry out conversations—with variables that correspond to particular ways the pattern can occur. Some schemas are informal and intuitive; others we learn in part formally and explicitly. David Rumelhart (1980) claims that schemas "play a central role in all our reasoning processes. . . . Once we can 'understand' the situation by encoding it in terms of a relatively rich set of schemata, the conceptual constraints of the schemata can be brought into play and the problem readily solved" (p. 55). No cognition is purely passive or data-driven; we always construct meaning in terms of knowledge structures. Learning is sometimes adding bits to existing structures; sometimes it involves generalizing or connecting schemas; other times it involves abandoning important parts of schemas, to be replaced by qualitatively different structures. Major restructuring is facilitated by Socratic dialogues and analogies— effective use of which requires account of a learner's current understanding as well as the target understanding.

How Expertise Develops. While experts in a subject generally command more facts and concepts than do novices, the real distinction lies in their ways of viewing phenomena, and representing and approaching problems. Experts learn to work from the "generative principles of the domain," and they automatize recurring procedures (they "compile knowledge") so that they can devote their attention to novel aspects of problems. Increasing "metacognitive skills" also mark expertise: self-awareness of using models, and skill and flexibility in how to construct them, modify them, and adapt them to problems.

Situated Learning. Assessment has focused on aspects of learning that are characterized insofar as possible as properties of individual students. Yet the nature of the knowledge we construct is conditioned and constrained by technologies, information resources, and social situations, as we learn about physical and conceptual tools and how and when to use them. These findings, along with those discussed above, argue that learning is more richly characterized in terms of the student's breadth and configurations of connections across social and substantive contexts than by success in a given domain of tasks—even though such success occurs only by virtue of those connections.

Extending the Conversation

The importance of questions like, "What can this person be thinking so that his actions make sense?" was plainly appreciated long before the advent of cognitive psychology. But cognitive psychology challenges the completeness of an assessment discipline in which these questions play only a tangential role. Such questions can be accommodated in a broader conception of educational assessment, in which principles of learning and principles of inference together help us address them effectively and credibly.

Determining the Target of Inference

Given the multifaceted nature of human knowledge and capabilities, the first step in creating an assessment must be to determine the aspects of knowledge or capabilities we are interested in. There are no "true" or "correct" ways to model students' capabilities, only ways better suited to the job at hand. Sometimes, proficiency in a prespecified domain of tasks suffices; other times, more individuated observations are called for; in other circumstances, mixtures of different kinds of models and tasks prove most appropriate. All doctoral students in a department may be required to take a standardized qualifying examination on the basic principles of their field, but their dissertation topics are assigned neither in common nor at random; each student selects a unique topic. Both kinds of data—from the qualifying exam and the dissertation—provide evidence, in their own ways, about important aspects of learning.

> *Neither the wave model nor the particle model for light is "true," but each captures observable patterns in physical phenomena quite satisfactorily for applied work in certain problems—the particle model for photoelectric effects, for example, and the wave model for radiography. "Scientists are used to having different—even contradictory—theories to explain [different aspects of] reality. . . . Each is useful in certain circumstances" [Nilsson, 1991, p. 45].*

Cognitive psychology challenges the adequacy of the "one size fits all" presumption of standard assessment; that is, defining the target of inference in terms of an assessor-specified domain of tasks that are administered and scored in the same way for all students. One can define and gather data about a *level* of proficiency in this way, and sometimes this characterization suits the job at hand. But there can be better ways to characterize and discover the *architecture* of students' proficiency—observing different students in different situations, interpreting their actions in light of additional information about them, or triangulating across context and situation, as may be required for one's purpose.

Despite technology and efficient statistical models, the objective of characterizing the students' proficiency is poorly met if constrained to "one size fits all" data, limited assessment time, and ignorance of contextual and educational factors. The more examinees differ as to relevant contextual and experiential factors, the more likely it is that each task in a complex and context-rich domain will consume considerable time and costs without providing much information about how students would fare on other tasks—the so-called "low generalizability" problem often associated with performance assessment. Each individual task may provide rich information for some inferences—but not for inferences about the usual target, domain true score. The same complex task can be invaluable in an assessment linked with instruction and grounded in context, yet worthless in a broadly cast survey because it is trivial, unapproachable, or incomprehensible to many students.

Frameworks for Learning

While classroom teachers draw on common instructional resources (notably textbooks) and accompanying assessments, these materials must be fleshed out and tailored to develop a conception of what is to be accomplished—expectations and standards shared with their students. The immediacy and feedback necessary to establish such a community of learning is normally confined to within the classroom walls. Broad, timely, and interactive communication, made possible by technological advances, can simultaneously support individuated learning and foster shared frameworks of meaning across classrooms. Some possibilities can be illustrated with the College Board's Advanced Placement (AP) Studio Art Portfolio program, and the HYDRIVE intelligent tutoring system (ITS) for troubleshooting aircraft hydraulics systems.

AP Studio Art Portfolios. If viewed as assessment alone, the AP Studio Art portfolio program would be nothing short of depressing. Students spend hundreds of hours creating the portfolios they submit for scoring at the end of the year, and the raters (who are art educators and teachers) spend hundreds of hours evaluating the work—all to produce reliability coefficients about the same as those of the SAT Verbal measure, a ninety-minute exam that is scored mechanically for about two cents. But the picture brightens when the program is viewed as a framework for evidence about skills and knowledge, around which high school teachers build art courses with wide latitude for topics, media, and projects. A common understanding of what is valued and how it is evaluated in the central scoring emerges through teacher workshops, talked-through examples with actual portfolios, and continual discussions about how to cast and apply rating rubrics to diverse submissions. (Interactive discussions and sharing work across schools during the year would enhance the process.) This is, at heart, a social phenomenon, not a measurement phenomenon. Measurement models for ratings prove valuable nevertheless to illuminate how raters use evaluative criteria, to characterize uncertainty about students' scores, and to highlight ways to improve the program (Myford and Mislevy, 1995).

HYDRIVE. HYDRIVE is an intelligent tutoring and assessment system that helps Air Force technicians learn to troubleshoot the F-15 aircraft's hydraulics systems. Building on studies of novices and experts, HYDRIVE simulates important cognitive and contextual features of troubleshooting on the flight line. Trainees access video images of aircraft components, act on them, and receive feedback on the results as they work through a problem. The system suggests instruction, or provides it whenever the student desires, in the instructional mode, but not in the assessment mode. HYDRIVE tracks the evolving state of the aircraft system, evaluates the quality of troubleshooting actions in its light, and characterizes student understanding in terms of systems, strategies, and procedures associated with proficient troubleshooting. Summaries of students' status in these aspects of learning are updated as they work though a problem, using extensions of the probability-based reasoning that underlies standard test theory (Mislevy and Gitomer, 1996). Each student's solution path and feedback are highly individuated, but all are cast in a common framework of troubleshooting concepts and targeted mental model for the system. Interestingly, learning is enhanced when students work HYDRIVE problems in pairs, underscoring the social aspect of learning. Having to communicate with each other about the system accelerates their use of the proffered expert models and strategies.

The preceding discussion speaks figuratively of developing a common language for the concepts and phenomena of a learning domain, to be shared by students and teachers, perhaps across classrooms. Unarguably, establishing such a structure constrains learning. The effect is positive to the extent that the framework is genuinely useful and its central tenets can be tailored to local circumstances. Literally learning a language is analogous. We constrain the linguistic possibilities of children when we teach them the language of the culture, but by doing so we make it possible for them to converse with other members of the community.

Mapping to a Common Framework of Evaluation

Can we retain the relevance and connectedness traditionally associated with informal assessment, yet simultaneously serve the communicative and credibility-based functions traditionally associated with formal assessment? The AP Studio Art experience suggests the answer is yes. Learning is individuated, but a shared conception of the nature of intended learning, developed through examples and feedback, makes it possible to interpret work within a common framework. Such a structure appears necessary if assessments with constructive and individuated data, such as portfolios and exhibitions, are to span time and distance.

"Congress shall make no law abridging the freedom of speech." But what do the words of the First Amendment really mean? Can I falsely shout "fire" in a crowded theater? The First Amendment acquires meaning first by the simple examples given by its framers; then, accumulating cases develop additional shades of meaning in new specific situations over time. Law students work through historic precedents and argue moot cases to "learn to think like lawyers"—to internalize the principles and the methods by which unique circumstances are mapped into the legal framework.

Earning Credibility

Common meaning is necessary for credibility, but it is not sufficient. Why should anyone trust an interpreted evaluation of a performance from a distant time and place? Standardized test results gain a measure of credibility from their prescribed procedures; these are established "rules of the game," which, if followed, circumscribe the interpretation of the results. Even though the results do not tell about everything that is important, parents and boards of education can ask questions and verify procedures in order to spot invalidating practices. But the more individuated an assessment is, the more difficult it becomes to establish credibility.

For example, by virtue of their knowledge about context and situation, teachers are in some ways in the best position to evaluate a student's work. Their contextualized evaluations are unquestionably basic for guiding classroom learning. But can their evaluations be used for high-stakes purposes beyond the classroom, in light of their vested interest in their students' success and the typically wide variation in their interpretations of performance? As discussed above, a common framework for interpretation is required first. The validity of mappings of performances into that framework can be addressed by mechanisms such as audits, cross-evaluation across schools, and triangulation of types of evidence (see Resnick's chapter in this book). "Trust, but verify," goes the old Russian maxim. Technology plays an enabling role, through replayability, mass storage, and electronic communication. Statistical modeling plays a quality-assurance role, through the analysis of ratings of multiply-scored work. Both fairness to individuals and opportunities for improving systems can be thus monitored, by detecting anomalous ratings, identifying work that is difficult to evaluate, and studying the nature and degree of variation among raters (Myford and Mislevy, 1995).

When Quetelet studied physical characteristics of human populations in the early 1800s, he viewed the mean of distributions as the "true" or "ideal" value for a given measure, and individuals' departures from this value as "accidental" and devoid of scientific meaning. Anthropologists today study these variations not as "errors" but as individual differences, the scope and nature of which characterize dynamic and evolving groups.

Patterns of ratings of evaluated performances cannot, in and of themselves, define what the standards should be; means are neither "ideal" nor "true"; variations are not simply "noise," but may include reasoned variations in raters' mappings of unique phenomena into a common framework. Now it remains true that even reasoned variation limits what we learn from one rater's evaluations and about how others might evaluate the work; fairness demands we ascertain this before basing any consequential decisions on such evaluations. Measurement models, such as g-theory and IRT models that include raters, help do this. They are additionally useful because patterns that would be interpreted as "bad measurement" in a true measurement context can signal different interpretations of the framework among raters. But rater effects, which reflect both the scope of commonalties and variations in standards, can be changed through discussion and reflection. Attention shifts away from simply reducing variation in ratings, toward deliberating the intended properties of performance. Continual feedback about these patterns to raters, teachers, and students can refresh and refocus their understanding of the evaluative framework, and inform discussions that refine its definition and elucidate its application.

Credibly conveying the import of individuated work across time and distance also requires establishing, and clearly communicating, the conditions under which students are to work. In AP Studio Art, students are to note, in written descriptions that accompany their artwork, support beyond typical classroom levels; raters are then expected to "make appropriate allowances." Their teachers are responsible for monitoring the integrity of the work, an essential element of the credibility of the scores. Highly individualized doctoral dissertations are carried out with the participation, even collaboration, of faculty advisors. The credibility of dissertations rests partly on an understanding of the kinds and levels of faculty participation that are acceptable, and partly on the oral defense—often pro forma, but nonetheless a formal and public opportunity to verify that the candidate "owns" the work represented in the dissertation.

Conclusion

Familiar assessment practices are compiled knowledge—practices that embody sound principles of reasoning from evidence but are commingled with particular concepts of what evidence is meant to be about and what is to be done with it. Opportunities for improving educational assessment include both extending and transcending this framework. Progress in technological and inferential tools can make assessment for familiar purposes more effective, and open new possibilities. Progress in understanding the nature and acquisition of knowledge makes it possible for us to conceive of new possibilities. The greatest opportunities lie not in doing better what large-scale, formal assessments have traditionally done under the traditional constraints, but in supporting and extending purposes that have hitherto been addressed in only local, informal assessment.

References

Glaser, R. (1981). The future of testing: A research agenda for cognitive psychology and psychometrics. *American Psychologist 36*, 923–936.

Hambleton, R. K. (1989). Principles and selected applications of item response theory. In R. L. Linn (ed.), *Educational measurement* (3rd. ed.) (pp. 147–200). New York: American Council on Education/Macmillan.

Kuhn, T. S. (1970). *The structure of scientific revolutions* (2d. ed.). Chicago: University of Chicago Press.

Messick, S. (1989). Validity. In R. L. Linn (ed.), *Educational measurement* (3rd. ed.) (pp. 13–103). New York: American Council on Education/Macmillan.

Mislevy, R. J. (1994). Evidence and inference in educational assessment. *Psychometrika 59*, 439–483.

Mislevy, R. J., and Gitomer, D. H. (1996). The role of probability-based inference in an intelligent tutoring system. *User-Mediated and User-Adapted Interfaces 5*, 253–282.

Myford, C. M., and Mislevy, R. J. (1995). *Monitoring and improving a portfolio assessment system*. Center for Performance Assessment Research Report. Princeton, N.J.: Center for Performance Assessment, Educational Testing Service.

Nilsson, N. J. (1991). Logic and artificial intelligence. *Artificial Intelligence 47*, 31–56.

Rumelhart, D. A. (1980). Schemata: The building blocks of cognition. In R. Spiro, B. Bruce, and W. Brewer (eds.), *Theoretical issues in reading comprehension* (pp. 33–58). Hillsdale, N.J.: Erlbaum.

Part II

Instruction

Chapter 9

Learning Influences

Margaret C. Wang, Geneva D. Haertel, and Herbert J. Walberg

Changes in education should be grounded in a knowledge base derived from research, and such a base is now beginning to take shape. By analyzing the content of 179 handbook chapters and reviews, compiling 91 research syntheses, and surveying 61 educational researchers, we created a knowledge base comprising 11,000 statistical findings that shows reasonable consensus on the most significant influences on learning (Wang, Haertel, and Walberg, 1990; Reynolds, Wang, and Walberg, 1992).[1]

In general, we found that direct influences have a greater impact on learning than do indirect influences. Direct influences in-

[1] This research was supported by the Temple University Center for Research in Human Development and Education and by the Office of Educational Research and Improvement of the U.S. Department of Education. The opinions expressed here do not necessarily reflect the position of the supporting agencies. For complete details on the methods and results of the syntheses, see M. C. Wang, G. D. Haertel, and H. J. Walberg (1993).

clude the amount of time a teacher spends on a topic and the quality of the social interactions teachers have with their students. Indirect influences include policies adopted by a school, district, or state, and organizational features such as site-based management.

Accumulating the Data

We summarized the results of our analysis, using a twenty-eight-category conceptual framework based on models of schooling that posited influences on learning.[2] The earlier models included variables such as student ability, motivation, prior knowledge, and background. Classroom instructional variables such as enthusiasm, clarity, feedback, and correctives were also key elements. Increasingly, models of schooling have been extended to include out-of-school variables, social-psychological influences, instructional delivery systems, program design, and implementation. Table 9-1 lists the twenty-eight categories of the conceptual framework we employed and a representative variable for each category.[3]

By combining the results from the content analysis, the research synthesis, and the survey of experts, we obtained an average score for each of the twenty-eight categories.[4] Figure 9-1 presents the twenty-eight categories of influence from most to least influen-

---

[2] Models reviewed included those by S. N. Bennett, B. S. Bloom, J. S. Bruner, J. B. Carroll, R. Glaser, and A. Harnischfeger and D. E. Wiley. See G. D. Haertel, H. J. Walberg, and T. Weinstein (1983); and M. C. Wang and H. J. Walberg (1985).

[3] The variables listed as part of the conceptual framework were transformed into a 228-item rating form and used to code results from the narrative reviews and research syntheses. Based on the proportions of the confirmatory studies reported, the size of the correlations, or qualitative indicators, we rated the data culled from the narrative reviews and the research syntheses on a three-point scale. A "1" indicated a weak relationship between a given strategy and student learning while a "3" indicated a strong relationship.

[4] To make the results comparable, the data from the three sources were transformed into T scores, standard scores with a mean of 50 and a standard deviation of 10. The relative influences on the variables were calculated by weighing composites of effect sizes and ratings obtained from experts and content analyses of authoritarive literature.

Figure 9-1 **Relative Influences on Learning**

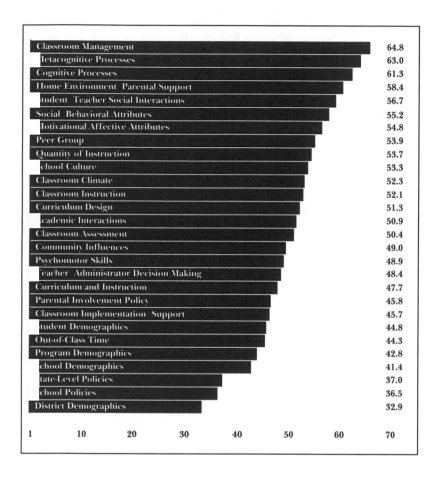

Classroom Management	64.8
Metacognitive Processes	63.0
Cognitive Processes	61.3
Home Environment Parental Support	58.4
Student Teacher Social Interactions	56.7
Social Behavioral Attributes	55.2
Motivational Affective Attributes	54.8
Peer Group	53.9
Quantity of Instruction	53.7
School Culture	53.3
Classroom Climate	52.3
Classroom Instruction	52.1
Curriculum Design	51.3
Academic Interactions	50.9
Classroom Assessment	50.4
Community Influences	49.0
Psychomotor Skills	48.9
Teacher Administrator Decision Making	48.4
Curriculum and Instruction	47.7
Parental Involvement Policy	45.8
Classroom Implementation Support	45.7
Student Demographics	44.8
Out-of-Class Time	44.3
Program Demographics	42.8
School Demographics	41.4
State-Level Policies	37.0
School Policies	36.5
District Demographics	32.9

tial. Classroom management, metacognitive processes, cognitive processes, home environment/parental support, and student and teacher social interactions had the greatest influence on school learning. Program demographics, school demographics, state-level policies, school policies and organization, and district demographics had the least influence on learning.

This method of statistically aggregating the findings of many studies varying in sample size, rigor, and characteristics is called *meta-analysis*. Meta-analysis yields estimates of the effect of all studies that can be found for a given method or condition. Thus, the estimates we obtained represent an average or mean effect.

It should be noted that many of the meta-analyses were based only on standardized tests, essay examinations, and other traditional measures of learning outcomes. Few studies employed portfolio ratings, exhibitions, laboratory exercises, and other newly recommended measures, largely because little research has been done on such measures. Nonetheless, the many scholars who participated in our survey showed a high level of consistency in weighing the possible effects of some of the methods and conditions on the new outcome measures. The collective judgment of these experts then served as one of the indexes of the effectiveness of each method.

To better understand which influences were most important, we grouped the twenty-eight categories into six broad types of influences: student aptitude, classroom instruction and climate, context, program design, school organization, and state and district characteristics (see Table 9-1). Table 9-2 lists the six broad categories and their average rating of influence. These averages again confirmed the significant effect of direct influences.

Student Aptitudes

Our research indicated that student aptitude was the most influential of the six broad types of influences. Among the categories of student aptitude, a student's *metacognitive processes*— that is, a student's capacity to plan, monitor, and, if necessary, replan learning strategies—had the most powerful effect on his or her learning. Research on metacognitive processes has generated new curriculums and new instructional techniques such as reciprocal teaching and cognitive skills instruction.

Cognitive processes were also identified as highly influential. Cognitive processes include not only variables such as general intelligence, but also prior knowledge, competency in reading and mathematics, and verbal knowledge.

Given the social nature of schooling, *social and behavioral attributes* constitute an important category. Children who frequently engage in disruptive behaviors, such as talking out of turn or hitting other children, often perform poorly in school, while children who engage in constructive behaviors are more likely to perform well.

Table 9-1 **Twenty-Eight Categories of Influence
on School Learning**

Categories	Examples of One Variable in Category

Student Aptitude includes academic history; a variety of social, behavioral, motivational, cognitive, affective characteristics; and gender.

Categories	Examples of One Variable in Category
1. Metacognitive Processes	*Comprehension monitoring (planning; monitoring effectiveness of attempted actions and outcomes of actions; testing, revising, and evaluating learning strategies)*
2. Cognitive Processes	*Level of specific academic knowledge in subject area*
3. Social and Behavioral Attributes	*Positive, nondisruptive behavior*
4. Motivational and Affective Attributes	*Attitude toward subject matter instructed*
5. Psychomotor Skills	*Psychomotor skills specific to area instructed*
6. Student Demographics	*Gender and socioeconomic status*

Classroom Instruction and Climate includes classroom routines and practices, characteristics of instruction as delivered, classroom management, monitoring of student progress, quality and quantity of instruction provided, student-teacher interactions, and classroom atmosphere.

Categories	Examples of One Variable in Category
7. Classroom Management	*Group alerting (teacher uses questioning/recitation strategies that maintain active participation by all students)*
8. Student and Teacher Social Interactions	*Positive student response to questions from teacher and other students*
9. Quantity of Instruction	*Active engagement in learning*
10. Classroom Climate	*Cohesiveness (class members share common interests and values and emphasize cooperative goals)*
11. Classroom Instruction	*Clear and organized direct instruction*
12. Academic Interactions	*Frequent calls for substantive oral and written response*
13. Classroom Assessment	*Assessment used as a frequent, integral component of instruction*

continued on page 204

Table 9-1 **Continued**

Categories	Examples of One Variable in Category
14. Classroom Implementation and Support	*Establishing efficient classroom routines and communicating rules and procedures*

Context includes community demographics, peer culture, parental support and involvement, and amount of time students spend out of class on such activities as television viewing, leisure reading, and homework.

15. Home Environment/ Parental Support	*Parental involvement in ensuring completion of homework*
16. Peer Group	*Level of peers' academic aspirations*
17. Community Influences	*Socioeconomic level of community*
18. Out-of-Class Time	*Student participation in clubs and extracurricular school activities*

Program Design refers to the physical and organizational arrangements for instructional delivery and includes strategies specified by the curriculum and characteristics of instructional materials.

19. Curriculum Design	*Instructional materials employ advance organizers*
20. Curriculum and Instruction	*Alignment among goals, content, instructions, students' assignments, and evaluation*
21. Program Demographics	*Size of instructional group (whole class, small group, one-on-one instruction)*

School Organization refers to culture, climate, policies, and practices; includes demographics of the student body, whether the school is public or private, presence of categorical programs, school-level decision-making variables, and school-level policies and practices.

22. School Culture	*Schoolwide emphasis on and recognition of academic achievement*
23. Teacher/Administrator Decision Making	*Principal actively concerned with instructional program*
24. Parental Involvement Policy	*Parental involvement in improvement and operation of instructional program*

25. School Demographics   *Size of school*
26. School Policies   *Explicit schoolwide discipline policy*

State and District Characteristics refers to governance and administration, state and district curriculum and textbook policies, testing and graduation requirements, teacher licensure, provisions in teacher contracts, and district-level administrative and fiscal variables.

27. State-Level Policies   *Teacher licensure requirements*
28. District Demographics   *School district size*

Table 9-2 **Average Influence of Six Categories of Influence on Student Learning**

Types of Influence	Average Influence
Student Aptitude	54.7
Classroom Instruction and Climate	53.3
Context	51.4
Program Design	47.3
School Organization	45.1
State and District Characteristics	35.0

The category *motivational and affective attributes* has received increased attention in the past decade. Student motivation determines effort and perseverance. Long acknowledged as significant by classroom teachers, effort and perseverance are now regarded by educational researchers as key attributes necessary for developing self-controlled, self-regulated learners.

Two remaining influences, *psychomotor skills* and *student demographics* (for example, gender and socioeconomic status) were minimally influential.

Classroom Instruction and Climate

When averaged together, the different kinds of classroom instruction and climate had nearly as much impact on learning as the student aptitude categories. The most influential category, *classroom management*, includes group alerting, learner accountability, smooth transitions, and teacher "with-it-ness."[5] Effective classroom management increases student engagement, decreases disruptive behaviors, and makes good use of instructional time.

Constructive *student and teacher social interactions* also have a documented effect on school learning. The frequency and quality of these interactions contribute to students' sense of self-esteem and foster a sense of membership in the class and school.

The extensive research on *quantity of instruction* indicates that students need to be fully engaged in their academic pursuits and teachers need to make wise use of instructional time. Other things being equal, the more time spent in instruction, the better (within limits, of course).

Classroom climate refers to the socio-psychological dimensions of classroom life, including cooperation among teachers and students, common interests and values, the pursuit of common goals, a clear academic focus, well-organized and well-planned lessons, explicit learning objectives, an appropriate level of task difficulty for students, and an appropriate instructional pace (Haertel, Walberg, and Haertel, 1981).

Classroom instruction includes the techniques for ensuring that students understand both the goals of instruction and the content being presented. One example of these techniques is direct instruction, which emphasizes systematic sequencing of lessons, including the use of review, the presentation of new content and skills, guided student practice, the use of feedback and correctives, and independent student practice.

Both *academic interactions* and *classroom assessment* were moderately influential. Academic interactions include teachers' styles for questions, praise, reinforcement, and use of correctives. Classroom assessment, perhaps more than other methods, depends heavily on the nature and implementation of the assessment for its effectiveness. Many studies indicated that frequent assessment and feedback effectively promoted learning. Some researchers, however, were concerned about national and state assessments and outcome-based education driving educational reform. The mix-

---

[5] The relationship between well-managed classrooms and student achievement is documented in Brophy and Evertson (1976) and in Good (1979). Some of the earliest and most informative research on classroom management resulted in the new terminology described in Kounin (1970).

ture of these good results and grave concerns probably accounted for the moderate rating for assessment.

Classroom implementation and support deals with the delivery of instructional services, and staff development and the adequate training of teachers. This category was the least influential of the classroom instruction and climate categories. As with other categories that have been perceived by educators as important but which showed a weak influence on student learning, this category's weak showing may reflect the lack of implementation of its variables more than its relative influence. Although teachers may receive training on how to implement a particular practice or innovation, they may not be successful at putting these practices into action. This can be due to lack of resources, such as time or materials, or a lack of fit between existing classroom and school routines, instructional goals, and the new innovation.

Even though classroom implementation and support variables did not appear to be strong determinants of student performance in the present knowledge base analysis, they can have large effects if they are well implemented and well aligned with school and district goals. However, implementation not geared toward the targeted student outcomes may do little to enhance student learning.

Context

The four out-of-school contexts influenced school learning to nearly the same degree as student aptitude and classroom instruction and climate. The category *home environment/parental support* was among the most influential of the twenty-eight categories. The benefits of family involvement in improving students' academic performance have been well documented, as have its effects on improving school attendance and on reducing delinquency, pregnancies, and dropping out (Epstein, 1984; Moles, 1982; Peterson, 1989; Walberg, 1984). According to the data reported in the current research, the *peer group* category also had a strong influence on school learning.

The *community influences* category had less effect on school learning than either the home environment/parental support or the peer group categories. Only recently has the influence of the community on school learning been examined through empirical studies, and the evidence is not yet sufficient to suggest strong effects.

Out-of-class time includes student extracurricular activities and social clubs. These activities had considerably less influence on school learning than did the other contextual influences. The lack of measurement of the degree or validity of implementation limits research on student activities. Nevertheless, if well designed and well executed, such activities can contribute much to academic accomplishments. Out-of-class time spent on nonconstructive or nontargeted educationally related activities would not likely yield the expected student outcomes.

Program Design

As a set, the three program design categories had a moderate influence on learning. Well-designed textbooks, appropriate organization of instructional groups, and effective alignment of goals and classroom activities yielded moderate benefits. The degree of program implementation is one likely determinant of the impact of program design variables on student learning.

School Organization

On average, school organization yielded moderate influence. Of its five categories, *school culture* was the most influential. School culture is an ethos conducive to teaching and learning. For example, a school might convey its academic atmosphere through participation in intramural academic competitions or through the use of incentives to reward student scholarship.

The category *teacher/administrator decision making* focuses on the role of the principal as an instructional leader. Although much attention has been paid to the importance of the principal's role, the research showed no strong link between principal leadership and student performance. The influence of an outstanding principal may be mitigated by many factors such as a high teacher turnover rate, an inexperienced team of teachers, or a high concentration of students in at-risk circumstances.

Parental involvement policy refers to parent involvement in the improvement and operation of the instructional program. A school may adopt a parental involvement policy, but successful implementation of a policy closely related to student development has a greater impact on student learning.

The last two categories, *school demographics* and *school policies*, had little influence on school learning compared to the other twenty-eight categories. School demographics include the size of the school, the number of classrooms, and the number of teachers and aides. Examples of school-level policies include assertive discipline and telephoning the home when a child is tardy or absent.

State and District Characteristics

Of the twenty-eight categories we examined, *state-level policies* and *district demographics* were among the least influential in improving student learning. Most of the variables included in these two categories are associated with school governance and administration. Examples of state-level policies include requirements for teacher licensure and evaluation and guidelines for the development and selection of curriculums and textbooks. Examples of district demographics include per-pupil expenditure, contractual limits on class size, and the degree of school district bureaucracy. Given that state and district influences are many steps removed from day-to-day classroom life, their impact on student learning is understandably limited.

Conclusion

Although our three independent sources of evidence generally agreed on the impact of the twenty-eight categories on school learning, discrepancies existed, indicating areas for additional research. We hope that future studies and syntheses will yield greater consistency, but obtaining precise results has limitations. Due to varying circumstances and implementation, educators should not expect results identical to what others have attained. Practices that work well in some settings and with some students may not work well in others (although evidence for such exceptionality is easier to hypothesize than to show consistently).

The estimates obtained on the effectiveness of various educational strategies for improving student learning provide a set of considerations for formulating educational policies and practices as well as a way of identifying school improvement priorities. Overall, our findings support renewed emphasis on psychological, instructional, and contextual influences.

Paradoxically, the state, district, and school policies that have received the most attention recently appear to have the least influence on learning. Fifty years of research contradict educators' current reliance on school restructuring and organizational variables as key components of school reform. Because indirect influences may only slightly affect direct influences, they appear to be weaker and less consistent in their results. For example, implementing a districtwide policy for teacher evaluation does not guarantee that students in any given classroom will have a competent teacher.

Unless reorganization and restructuring strongly affect the direct determinants of learning, they offer little hope of substantial improvement. Changing policies is unlikely to change practices in classrooms and homes, where learning actually takes place. Better alignment of remote policies and direct practices and more direct intervention in the psychological determinants of learning promise the most effective avenues of reform.

References

Brophy, J., and Evertson, C. M. (1976). *Learning, Teaching: A Developmental Perspective*. Boston: Allyn & Bacon.

Epstein, J. (1984). Effects of parent involvement on change in student achievement in reading and math. Paper presented at the annual meeting of the American Educational Research Association, New Orleans, La.

Good, T. (1979). Teacher effectiveness in the elementary school: What we know about it now, *Journal of Teacher Education 30*, 52–64.

Haertel, G. D.; Walberg, H. J.; and Haertel, E. H. (1981). Social-psychological environments and learning: A quantitative synthesis. *British Educational Research Journal 7*, 27–36.

Haertel, G. D.; Walberg, H. J.; and Weinstein, T. (1983). Psychological models of educational performance: A theoretical synthesis of contructs, *Review of Educational Research 53*, 75–91.

Kounin, J. (1970). *Discipline and group management in classrooms.* New York: Holt, Rinehart & Winston.

Moles, O. C. (1982). Syntheses of recent research on parent participation in children's education. *Educational Leadership 40*, 44–47.

Peterson, D. (1989). *Parent involvement in the educational process.* Urbana, Ill.: ERIC Clearinghouse on Educational Management, University of Illinois.

Reynolds, M. C.; Wang, M. C.; and Walberg, H. J. (1992). The knowledge bases for special and general education. *Remedial and Special Education 13*, 6–10, 33.

Walberg, H. J. (1984). Families as partners in educational productivity. *Phi Delta Kappan 65*, 397–400.

Wang, M. C.; Haertel, G. D.; and Walberg, H. J. (1990). 'What influences learning? A content analysis of review literature. *Journal of Educational Research 84*, 30–43.

Wang. M. C., Haertel, G. D.; and Walberg, H. J. (1993). Toward a knowledge base for school learning. *Review of Educational Research 63* (3).

Wang, M. C., and Lindvall, C. M. (1984). Individual differences and school learning environments. In E. W. Gordon (ed.), *Review of research in education, Vol. 11*, p. 161–225. Washington, D.C.: American Educational Research Association.

Wang, M. C., and Walberg, J. (1985) Classroom climate as mediator of educational inputs and outputs. In B. J. Fraser (ed.), *The study of learning environments 1985*, pp. 47–58. Salem, Ore.: Assessment Research.

Chapter 10

Effective Teaching

Jere Brophy

In this chapter I summarize some important findings and implications of research on teaching conducted during the past thirty years. In doing so, I view both teaching and research as means, not ends. Teaching is broadly defined as action taken to help students make progress toward instructional goals. Research is broadly defined as action taken to answer some question. To evaluate either teaching or research, we need to consider both the importance of their goals and the degree to which they get accomplished. Good teaching is good because it succeeds in helping students attain worthwhile learning goals. Good research is good because it succeeds in answering worthwhile questions.

Classroom teaching is difficult to study because it is a multifaceted professional practice that takes place in a complex and evolving interpersonal context. Nevertheless, research on teaching has begun to establish a knowledge base capable of informing teachers' planning and decision making. Some educators are suspicious of this because they believe that attempts to apply an ostensible knowledge base for teaching will place counterproductive pressures on teachers rather than supporting their development as professionals. I have two points to make in response to this important concern.

First, research-based information about teaching should empower teachers by enabling them to act more confidently on the basis of well-established principles. Consider the medical profession. As my colleague, Charles W. (Andy) Anderson points out, if we had the choice of going to our regular physicians or to reincarnations of historically prominent physicians such as Galen or Hippocrates, we would stick with our regular physicians because they give us access to the vital medical knowledge and technology that have been developed since Galen or Hippocrates lived. Far from oppressing modern physicians or turning them into deskilled technicians, the proliferation of the knowledge base that undergirds medical practice has had primarily empowering effects. Modern physicians can do many things that were unknown to medical pioneers, and they can use safe and efficient routines for doing things that formerly were chancy and dangerous. Knowledge advances have brought responsibilities as well (physicians can be sued for malpractice), but their primary effects have been to expand the power of medical practice. Modern medicine demands professional judgments and offers opportunities for artistry and creativity as much as it ever did, but in addition to, rather than in the absence of, systematic application of scientific knowledge and technical skill. We should expect similar developments in the power of educational practice as the knowledge base informing the teaching profession expands.

My second point is an important qualification on the first: The developing research base will have desirable effects only to the extent that it is understood and interpreted accurately. As a researcher who has generated some of this information, I recognize that it can be misinterpreted and misused. Researchers need to summarize their findings accurately and qualify them appropriately. All educators need to appreciate the complexity of good teaching instead of seeking simple formulas. They also need to think in terms of expanding the existing knowledge base, instead of succumbing to the all-too-common "out with the old, in with the new" purview that fosters swings between extremes and leaves practitioners confused and prone to believe that research is not helpful. If interpreted appropriately, research on teaching will be an important resource to teachers, both in validating good practice and in suggesting directions for improvement.

Process–Outcome Research

Especially relevant findings come from studies designed to identify relationships between classroom processes (what the teacher and students do in the classroom) and student outcomes (changes in students' knowledge, skills, values, or dispositions that represent progress toward instructional goals). Two forms of *process-outcome research* that became prominent in the 1970s were school-effects research and teacher-effects research. *School-effects research* (reviewed in Good and Brophy, 1986) identified several characteristics that are observed consistently in schools that elicit good achievement gains from their students: (1) strong academic leadership that produces consensus on goal priorities and commitment to instructional excellence; (2) a safe, orderly school climate; (3) positive teacher attitudes toward students and expectations regarding their abilities to master the curriculum; (4) an emphasis on instruction in the curriculum (not just on filling time or on nonacademic activities) in allocating classroom time and assigning tasks to students; (5) careful monitoring of progress toward goals through student testing and staff evaluation programs; (6) strong parent involvement programs; and (7) consistent emphasis on the importance of academic achievement, including praise and public recognition for students' accomplishments.

Teacher-effects research (reviewed in Brophy and Good, 1986) identified teacher behaviors and patterns of teacher-student interaction associated with student achievement gains. Teacher-effects research initially was limited to correlational studies and focused mostly on basic skills instruction in the early grades. However, eventually it broadened to include a wider range of grade levels and subject-matter areas and to include experimental verification of some of the causal hypotheses suggested by its correlational findings. Some important conclusions established through this research are the following:

1. *Teachers make a difference.* Some teachers reliably elicit greater gains than others, because of differences in how they teach.

2. *Teacher expectations/role definitions/sense of efficacy.* Teachers who elicit strong achievement gains accept responsibility for doing so. They believe that their students are capable of learning and that they (the teachers) are capable of teaching them successfully. If students do not learn something the first time, they teach it again; and if the regular curriculum materials do not do the job, they find or develop others that will.

3. *Exposure to academic content and opportunity to learn.* Teachers who elicit greater achievement gains allocate most of the available time for activities designed to accomplish instructional goals. They do not schedule many activities that serve little or no curricular purpose.

4. *Classroom management and organization.* These teachers are also effective organizers and managers who establish their classrooms as effective learning environments and gain the cooperation of their students. They minimize the time spent getting organized, making transitions, or dealing with behavior problems, and maximize the degree to which students are engaged in ongoing academic activities.

5. *Active teaching.* Teachers who elicit greater achievement gains do not merely maximize "time on task"; in addition, they spend a great deal of time actively instructing their students. Their classrooms feature more time spent in interactive lessons featuring teacher-student discourse and less time spent in independent seatwork. Rather than depend solely on curriculum materials as content sources, these teachers interpret and elaborate the content for students, stimulate them to react to it through questions asked in recitation and discussion activities, and circulate during seatwork times to monitor progress and provide assistance when needed. They are active instructors, not just materials managers and evaluators. It is important to note, however, that most of their instruction occurs during interactive discourse with students rather than during extended lecture-presentations.

6. *A supportive learning environment.* Despite their strong academic focus, these teachers maintain pleasant, friendly

classrooms and are perceived by their students as enthusiastic, supportive instructors.

In addition to these more generic findings, teacher-effects research has contributed knowledge about qualitative aspects of
instructional methods and classroom processes. For example,
research on teachers' lectures and demonstrations has verified
the importance of delivering these presentations with enthusiasm and organizing and sequencing their content so as to maximize their clarity and "learner friendliness." Various studies have
shown the value of pacing, gestures, and other oral communication skills; avoiding vagueness, ambiguity, and discontinuity; beginning with advance organizers or previews that include general
principles, outlines, or questions that establish a learning set;
briefly describing the objectives and alerting students to new or
key concepts; presenting new information with reference to what
students already know about the topic; proceeding in small steps
sequenced in ways that are easy to follow; eliciting student responses regularly to stimulate active learning and ensure that
each step is mastered before moving to the next; finishing with
a review of main points, stressing general integrative concepts;
and following up with questions or assignments that require students to encode the material in their own words and apply or
extend it to new contexts.

Similarly, research on teacher-student interaction processes has
identified some important dimensions of recitations and discussions that need to be adjusted to the instructional goals, the
students, and various context factors. The difficulty of questions
needs to be suited to the students' levels of ability and prior
knowledge. The forms and cognitive levels of the questions need
to be suited to the instructional goals. Primarily closed-ended
and factual questions might be appropriate when teachers are
assessing prior knowledge or reviewing new learning, but accomplishing most significant instructional goals will require more
emphasis on open-ended questions calling for students to apply,
analyze, synthesize, or evaluate what they are learning.

Because questions are intended to engage students in cognitive processing and construction of knowledge about academic
content, it is important for teachers to address them to the class
as a whole rather than to designate an individual respondent in

advance. This encourages all of the students, not just the one who eventually is called on, to listen carefully and respond thoughtfully to each question.

Another important dimension is wait time. After posing a question, teachers need to pause to allow students time to process the question and at least begin to formulate their responses, especially if the question is complicated or high in cognitive level of response demand. Research by many different investigators has shown that teachers often undercut the potential pedagogical value of their questions by calling on students to respond much too quickly (often pausing less than a second after completing the question).

Researchers have also addressed the follow-up options open to teachers who have posed a question and elicited an answer from a student. These include providing immediate feedback about the correctness of the student's answer, asking other students to comment on the answer, redirecting the question to the class, probing to elicit elaboration or in some other way following up with a second question addressed to the original respondent, praising or criticizing the answer, or accepting it and moving on with the activity (preferably in a way that uses or builds on the student's answer). When the initial respondent has answered incorrectly or is unable to respond, the teacher's options include simply repeating the question (or providing negative feedback and inviting the student to try again), providing clues or rephrasing the original question to make it easier for the student to answer, shifting to a lower-level question, giving the answer, or redirecting the question to the class.

Teacher-effects research has not produced findings indicating consistent relationships between these teacher response alternatives and student achievement gain, probably because optimal teacher behavior on these dimensions varies with the nature and goals of the instructional activities. These response options are, however, worth considering in planning recitation and discussion activities, particularly in determining when and why it makes sense to terminate an interaction with the original respondent by giving the answer or calling on someone else and when and why it makes sense to sustain the interaction by repeating or rephrasing the question or giving clues. Sustaining the interaction is often desirable as a way to scaffold thinking and develop confidence, especially in reticent or self-doubting students. However, teachers often feel the need to terminate interactions with students and move on, due to time pressures or growing restlessness among onlooker students.

Teacher-effects researchers have not had much to say about desirable activities and assignments, except for studies relating homework practices to student achievement gains. Findings from these studies have been equivocal for the elementary grades, but junior high and high school studies tend to show positive relationships between assignment of homework and achievement gain. In reviewing these data, however, Cooper (1989) cautioned that attention has been focused too narrowly on quantitative issues (whether or not homework is assigned, or how much is assigned). More attention is needed to qualitative aspects such as the goal relevance and pedagogical value of the assignments, the degree to which they are suited to students' abilities and prior knowledge, whether and how homework performance figures into overall grading, and the degree to which the teacher does not merely assign homework but reviews it promptly, gives feedback, and requires correction of omissions or mistakes.

Research on learning tasks suggests that activities and assignments should be varied and interesting enough to motivate student engagement, new or challenging enough to constitute meaningful learning experiences rather than pointless busy work, and yet easy enough to allow students to achieve high rates of success if they invest reasonable effort. The effectiveness of assignments is enhanced when teachers explain the work and go over practice examples with students before releasing them to work independently, then circulate to monitor progress and provide help when needed.

Brophy and Alleman (1991) suggested several criteria for developing or selecting learning activities. Primary criteria that all activities should meet include relevance to significant instructional goals, feasibility of implementation within expected constraints, and cost-effectiveness (determined by weighing the teacher and student time and trouble needed to complete an activity against its anticipated academic benefits). In selecting from among activities that meet these primary criteria, teachers might consider several secondary criteria: Students are likely to find the activity interesting or enjoyable; it focuses on application of important ideas, not incidental details or interesting but trivial information; it provides opportunities for interaction and reflective discourse rather than just solitary seatwork; if it involves writing, students will compose prose rather than just fill in blanks; and if it involves discourse, students will engage in critical or creative thinking rather than just regurgitate facts and definitions.

Teaching for Understanding and Use of Knowledge

The process-outcome research of the 1970s was important, not only because it contributed the findings summarized above but also because it began to provide education with a knowledge base capable of moving the field beyond testimonials and unsupported claims toward scientific statements based on credible data. However, this research was limited in several aspects. First, it focused on important but very basic aspects of teaching. These aspects differentiate the least effective teachers from other teachers, but they do not include the more subtle fine points that distinguish the most outstanding teachers. Second, most of this research relied on standardized tests as the outcome measure, which meant that it assessed mastery of relatively isolated knowledge items and skill components without assessing the degree to which students had developed understanding of networks of subject-matter content or the ability to use this information in authentic application situations.

During the 1980s, a newer kind of research emerged that emphasized teaching subject matter for understanding and use of knowledge. This research focused on particular curriculum units or even individual lessons, taking into account the teacher's instructional goals and assessing student learning accordingly. The researchers determined what the teacher was trying to accomplish, recorded detailed information about classroom processes as they unfolded during the lesson or unit, and then assessed learning using evaluation measures keyed to the instructional goals. Often these included detailed interviews or portfolio assessments, not just conventional short-answer tests.

Research on teaching for understanding focuses on attempts to teach both the individual elements in a network of related content and the connections between them, to the point that students can explain the information in their own words and can access and use it in appropriate application situations in and out of school. Teachers accomplish this by explaining concepts and principles with clarity and precision and by modeling the strategic application of skills via "think aloud" demonstrations that make overt for students the usually covert strategic thinking that guides the use of the skills for problem solving.

Although it reinforces and builds on findings indicating that teachers play a vital role in stimulating student learning, current research also focuses on the role of the student. It recognizes that students do not merely passively receive or copy input from teachers, but instead actively mediate it by trying to make sense of it and to relate it to what they already know (or think they know) about the topic. Thus, students develop new knowledge through a process of *active construction.* In order to get beyond rote memorization to achieve true understanding, students need to develop and integrate a network of associations linking new input to their own preexisting knowledge and beliefs anchored in concrete experience. Thus, teaching involves inducing *conceptual change* in students, not infusing knowledge into a vacuum. When students' preexisting beliefs about a topic are accurate, this facilitates learning and provides a natural starting place for teaching. When students harbor misconceptions, however, these misconceptions will need to be corrected so that they do not persist and distort the new learning.

To the extent that new learning is complex, the construction of meaning required to develop clear understanding of it will take time and will be facilitated by the interactive *discourse* that occurs during lessons and activities. Clear explanations and modeling from the teacher are important, but so are opportunities to answer questions about the content, discuss or debate its meanings and implications, or apply it in authentic problem-solving or decision-making contexts. These activities allow students to process the content actively and "make it their own" by paraphrasing it into their own words, exploring its relationships to other knowledge and to past experience, appreciating the insights it provides, or identifying its implications for personal decision making or action. Increasingly, research is pointing to thoughtful discussion, and not just teacher lecturing or student recitation, as characteristic of the classroom discourse involved in teaching for understanding.

Researchers have also begun to stress the complementary changes in teacher and student roles that should occur as learning progresses. Early in the process, the teacher assumes most of the responsibility for structuring and managing learning activities and provides students with a great deal of information, explanation, modeling, and cueing. As students develop expertise, however, they can begin regulating their own learning by asking questions and by working on increasingly complex applications with increasing degrees of autonomy. The teacher still provides task simplification, coaching, and other "scaffolding" needed to assist students with challenges that they are not yet ready to handle on their own, but this assistance is gradually reduced in response to gradual increases in student readiness to engage in independent and self-regulated learning.

Research on teaching school subjects for understanding and use of knowledge is still in its infancy, but it has already produced successful experimental programs in most subjects. Even more encouraging, analyses of these programs have identified a set of principles and practices that are common to most if not all of them. These common elements, which might be considered components in a model or theory describing good subject-matter teaching, include the following:

1. The curriculum is designed to equip students with knowledge, skills, values, and dispositions that they will find useful both inside and outside of school.
2. Instructional goals emphasize developing student expertise within an application context and with emphasis on conceptual understanding of content and self-regulated use of skills.
3. The curriculum balances breadth with depth by addressing limited content but developing this content sufficiently to foster conceptual understanding.
4. The content is organized around a limited set of powerful ideas (key understandings and principles).
5. The teacher's role is not just to present information but also to scaffold and respond to students' learning efforts.

6. The students' role is not just to absorb or copy input but also to actively make sense and construct meaning.
7. Students' prior knowledge about the topic is elicited and used as a starting place for instruction, which builds on accurate prior knowledge and stimulates conceptual change if necessary.
8. Activities and assignments feature authentic tasks that call for problem solving or critical thinking, not just memory or reproduction.
9. Higher-order thinking skills are not taught as a separate skills curriculum. Instead, they are developed in the process of teaching subject-matter knowledge within application contexts that call for students to relate what they are learning to their lives outside of school by thinking critically or creatively about it or by using it to solve problems or make decisions.
10. The teacher creates a social environment in the classroom that could be described as a learning community featuring discourse or dialogue designed to promote understanding.

Embedded in this approach to teaching is the notion of "complete" lessons that are carried through to include higher-order applications of content. This implies the need to limit the breadth of content addressed in order to allow for more in-depth teaching of the content that is included. Unfortunately, typical state and district curriculum guidelines feature long lists of knowledge items and subskills to be "covered," and the instructional materials packages supplied by educational publishers usually respond to these guidelines by emphasizing breadth over depth of coverage. This discourages in-depth teaching of *limited* content. Teachers who want to teach for understanding and use of subject-matter knowledge will have to both (1) limit what they try to teach by focusing on the most important content and omitting or skimming over the rest, and (2) structure what they do teach around important ideas and elaborate it considerably beyond what is in the text.

In addition, such teachers will need to structure a great deal of thoughtful discourse by using questions to stimulate students to process and reflect on the content, recognize relationships among and implications of its key ideas, think critically about it, and use it in problem-solving or decision-making applications. Such discourse is not recitation featuring rapid-fire questioning and short answers. Instead, it is sustained examination of a small number of related topics, in which students are invited to develop explanations, make predictions, debate alternative approaches to problems, or otherwise consider the content's implications or applications. Some of the questions admit to a range of defensible answers, and some invite discussion or debate (e.g., concerning the relative merits of alternative suggestions for solving problems). In addition to asking questions and providing feedback, the teacher encourages students to explain or elaborate on their answers or to comment on classmates' answers, and also capitalizes on "teachable moment" opportunities offered by students' comments or questions (by elaborating on the original instruction, addressing misconceptions, or calling attention to implications that have not been appreciated yet).

Skills are taught holistically within the context of applying the knowledge content, rather than being practiced in isolation. Thus, most practice of reading skills is embedded within lessons involving reading and interpreting extended text, most practice of writing skills is embedded within activities calling for authentic writing, and most practice of mathematics skills is embedded within problem-solving applications. Also, skills are taught as strategies adapted to particular purposes and situations, with emphasis on modeling the cognitive and metacognitive components involved and explaining the necessary conditional knowledge (of when and why the skills would be used). Thus, students receive instruction in when and how to apply skills, not just opportunities to use them.

Activities, assignments, and evaluation methods incorporate a much greater range of tasks than do the familiar workbooks and curriculum-embedded tests that focus on recognition and recall of facts, definitions, and fragmented skills. Curriculum strands or units are planned to accomplish gradual transfer of responsibility for managing learning activities from the teacher to the students, in response to students' growing expertise on the topic. Plans for lessons and activities are guided by overall curriculum goals (phrased in terms of student capabilities to be developed), and evaluation efforts concentrate on assessing the progress that has been made toward accomplishing these goals. Subject-specific elaborations of these principles of teaching for understanding are summarized below. For references and more details, see Good and Brophy (1995, 1997).

Reading is taught as a sense-making process of extracting meaning from texts that are read for information or enjoyment, not just for practice. Important skills such as decoding, blending, and noting main ideas are taught and practiced, but primarily within the context of reading for meaning. Activities and assignments feature more reading of extended texts and less time spent with skills worksheets. Students often work cooperatively in pairs or small groups, reading to one another, sharing impressions, or discussing their answers to questions about the meanings or implications of the text. Rather than being restricted to the artificial stories written for basal readers, students often read genuine literature written to provide information or pleasure.

Writing is taught as a way for students to organize and communicate their thinking to particular audiences for particular purposes, using skills taught as strategies for accomplishing these goals. Most skills practice is embedded within writing activities that call for composition and communication of meaningful content. Composition activities emphasize authentic writing intended to be read for meaning and response, not mere copying or exercises focused on displaying skills for the teacher. Thus, composition becomes an exercise in communication and personal craftsmanship calling for developing and revising an outline, developing and revising successive drafts for meaning, and then polishing into final form. The emphasis is on the cognitive and metacognitive aspects of composing, not just on writing mechanics and editing.

Mathematics instruction focuses on developing students' mathematical power—their abilities to explore, conjecture, reason logically, and use a variety of mathematical models to solve nonroutine problems. Instead of working through a postulated linear hierarchy from isolated and lower-level skills to integrated and higher-level skills, and only then attempting application, mathematics is taught within an application context right from the beginning through an emphasis on authentic problem solving. Students spend less time working individually on computation skill sheets and more time participating in teacher-led discourse concerning the meanings and implications of the mathematical concepts and operations under study.

In science, students learn to understand, appreciate, and apply connected sets of powerful ideas that they can use to describe, explain, make predictions about, or gain control over real-world systems or events. Instruction connects with students' experience-based knowledge and beliefs, building on accurate current knowledge but also producing conceptual change by confronting and correcting misconceptions. The teacher models and coaches the students' scientific reasoning through scaffolded tasks and dialogues that engage them in thinking about scientific issues. The students are encouraged to make predictions or develop explanations, then subject them to empirical tests or argue the merits of proposed alternatives.

In social studies, students are challenged to engage in higher-order thinking by interpreting, analyzing, or manipulating information in response to questions or problems that cannot be resolved through routine application of previously learned knowledge. Students focus on networks of connected content structured around powerful ideas rather than on long lists of disconnected facts, and they consider the implications of what they are learning for social and civic decision making. The teacher encourages students to formulate and communicate ideas about the topic, but also presses them to clarify or justify their assertions by citing relevant evidence and arguments.

This kind of teaching demands more from both teachers and students than traditional reading-recitation-seatwork teaching does, but it enables them to get much more out of school. Perhaps teaching for understanding will become more common as researchers articulate its principles more clearly, states and districts make needed adjustments in their curriculum guidelines, publishers make needed adjustments in their textbooks and teachers' manuals, and professional organizations of teachers and teacher educators build on the beginnings that they have made in endorsing the goals of teaching school subjects for understanding, appreciation, and life application and in creating and disseminating position statements, instructional guidelines, videotaped examples, and other resources for preservice and inservice teachers.

Qualifications and Cautions

When interpreted at the level of general principles rather than specific behaviors, the main findings of both the earlier process-outcome research and the more recent research on teaching for understanding suggest a convergence of implications that fit well with one another and replicate across grade levels and subject areas. This bodes well for the prospects of developing an empirically grounded theory of classroom teaching to serve as a basis for teacher education. However, enthusiasm for these recent findings needs to be tempered by some important qualifications and cautions.

First, the research base supporting ideas about teaching for understanding is still quite thin, especially if you look for studies that include both comparison groups and systematic measurement of student outcomes. Several studies in mathematics have shown that treatments based on these principles increased students' attainment of higher-order outcomes without reducing their performance on lower-order outcomes, compared to students taught more traditionally. Also, some work in language arts and science has shown that experimental programs increased attainment of the program's primary goals, although these studies usually did not contain comparison groups or attempts to assess the trade-offs involved in replacing the earlier program with the newer one. However, some of the best known and most widely respected innovations, such as reciprocal teaching, have produced mixed rather than uniformly positive results. Furthermore, the instructional models advocated by many of the intellectual leaders in the subject-matter areas, as well as much of what is included in the position statements published by professional organizations representing these areas, have yet to be tested empirically, let alone to enjoy a rich accumulation of systematic evidence of effects on student outcomes.

I would be less concerned about this paucity of attention to process-outcome relationships if I thought it was just a temporary problem soon to be eliminated through an abundance of data. However, I see little evidence of this. Worse, the current zeitgeist in education features unscientific, and occasionally antiscientific, attitudes. Too often, the effectiveness of advocated practices is merely assumed rather than supported with empirical evidence. Some reform advocates, most notably visible leaders in the whole-language movement, have aggressively pushed policy agendas advocated on the basis of strong theoretical commitments without accepting responsibility for testing their ideas scientifically. Similar advocacy is seen for eliminating tracking and grouping, breaking down subject-matter barriers in order to integrate the curriculum, and various schemes for teaching generic thinking skills, developing multiple intelligences, or matching students' learning styles. These and other ideas need to be assessed scientifically, with emphasis on clarifying their underlying theories and generating appropriate empirical data to assess the trade-offs involved in adopting them.

Recent research points to several such trade-offs. One is the depth versus breadth dilemma. It is clear that we need to cut back on topic coverage and shift from surveys of facts and skills exercises to sustained studies of connected content structured around powerful ideas, but what is the optimal balance? How much do students need to know about a topic, and how long should the teacher persist in efforts to make sure that all students in the class master this network of knowledge? It may take weeks or even months to develop connected understandings of a topic such as photosynthesis, and even then some students will still be vague or confused. Are we ready for middle-school science courses that address only four or five topics across the entire school year? If not, what would be a reasonable compromise between this level of emphasis on depth and the overemphasis on breadth that we have now? Also, how would we decide which topics to retain in the curriculum and which to exclude?

These questions illustrate how even as research on teaching for understanding and use of knowledge has generated increasing consensus around instructional-method issues, it has reopened basic curricular issues: What is worth teaching to K-12 students, and why? Like the process-outcome research that preceded it, this more recent research has finessed these issues rather than addressed them. Process-outcome research did it by using standardized tests as the criteria for learning. More recent research has finessed curricular issues by equating the teaching of K-12 school subjects with socialization into the academic disciplines. Usually this is done only implicitly, although a few investigators have done it explicitly and defended their choice. I believe that this choice leads to problematic curricular decisions.

An academic discipline is a community of inquiry that generates increasingly differentiated and elaborated knowledge about a particular content domain. The discipline focuses on expanding this specialized knowledge base, not on exploring its applications to everyday life or its connections with other forms of knowledge. In contrast, school subjects are collections of knowledge organized for instruction to K-12 students as preparation for everyday living and performance of adult roles in society. Although informed by the academic disciplines, school subjects are mechanisms for accomplishing citizen education, not generating disciplinary knowledge. Therefore, decisions about what ought to be included in the K-12 curriculum should be informed by deliberations about what constitutes basic knowledge that all citizens need to know. This knowledge should be consistent with disciplinary knowledge, but it should be selected, organized, and taught as citizen education, not as induction into an academic discipline.

When I view recent research from this perspective, I often find myself admiring the instructional methods illustrated but at the same time questioning the choice of content. For example, several lessons might be spent engaging students in extended reasoning about what appear to be arcane mathematical questions. From a disciplinary perspective, there is no problem here, because the students are engaged in doing mathematics, and all mathematics is more or less equally acceptable. From a citizen education standpoint, however, I question spending precious curriculum time on content that seems to lack application potential.

Sometimes I question not so much the content itself but the cost-effectiveness of introducing it at a particular grade or seeking to develop it to sophisticated levels. When I read reports on conceptual-change teaching in science, for example, I am impressed with the ingenuity in developing ways to teach complicated topics such as photosynthesis to middle-school students, but I find myself questioning whether it is worth the time and trouble that it takes to do so. Perhaps the topic should be developed less completely, or even withheld until later grades.

As knowledge proliferates, the depth versus breadth dilemma and its underlying curricular issues concerning what content is most worth teaching will become both more important and more difficult to manage. These issues will not be solved by lengthening the school day or school year, or by looking to the disciplines, to assessment data, or to the Japanese for definitive answers. In fact, curricular arguments cannot be resolved through purely empirical methods because they involve value questions. However, they always contain implied assumptions that can be tested empirically, such as readiness assumptions (that students at a given grade level are ready to learn particular content) or transfer assumptions (that mastery of such content will enable them to handle certain life situations effectively). It is important for educational researchers to begin to pay attention to these curricular issues, as well as to press for clarification and testing of the empirical claims embedded in the advocacy of theory-based positions that typifies the public discourse about education. One good place to start is to recognize that the school subjects and the academic disciplines are different entities with different purposes. Particular content does not necessarily belong in the K-12 curriculum just because it is currently of interest to one of the disciplines.

It is also worth noting that different kinds of knowledge are emphasized in different school subjects. The basic-skills subjects emphasize procedural knowledge. They also include propositional knowledge, but this propositional knowledge is limited in scope and is taught in conjunction with procedural knowledge that is tightly linked to it. As my colleague Ralph Putman has noted, it is difficult to consider knowledge about the mean without simultaneously thinking about the mathematical procedures involved in computing the mean. However, it is possible to teach those procedures through isolated skills exercises, and scholars interested in basic-skills subjects complain that all too often, this is exactly what happens. The curriculum becomes a series of fragmented skills exercises in which students use primarily rote-learning methods to practice skills in isolation, without getting sufficient opportunities to use these skills within authentic application contexts or to learn related propositional knowledge that would embed the procedural knowledge within a context of meaning. These concerns have led to calls for more emphasis on comprehension and reader response in teaching reading, on authentic communication in teaching writing, and on problem solving in teaching mathematics.

The situation is different for subjects associated with the sciences, and especially the social sciences and humanities. These subjects feature a great deal of propositional knowledge but not that much subject-specific procedural knowledge. Furthermore, except for a few subareas such as map skills or laboratory procedures, the procedural knowledge taught within these subjects usually is not tightly linked to particular propositional knowledge. Students are not taught about the U.S. Constitution or the human body, for example, to prepare them to perform specific everyday tasks. Instead, they learn about these topics partly as general background knowledge that anyone literate in the current culture would be expected to know and partly as information that could inform thinking and decision making in a broad range of life-application situations (such as deciding how to vote in an election or to maintain one's own nutrition and health). In the humanities, most things (e.g., the works of Shakespeare) are taught without any particular practical life applications in mind but with the intention of improving the learners' quality of life by broadening their purviews, developing their knowledge and appreciation of the human condition as it has evolved through time and exists today across cultures, and exposing them to ideas believed to have enduring heuristic value.

Scholars studying instruction in these subjects that feature a great deal of propositional knowledge are not so much concerned about mindless skills practice as about mindless memorization (followed by forgetting) of disconnected and often trivial information. They want these subjects taught in ways that will help students to appreciate their value and see their applications to life outside of school. They usually recommend developing powerful ideas in depth, which includes focusing questions and activities around these ideas and their applications to students' lives.

These considerations underscore the need for differentiated models of teaching that take into account the different conditions of learning that are presented by different school subjects or instructional situations. In this regard, many of the currently popular models of teaching and learning are badly in need of qualification concerning their spheres of application. For example, models that emphasize strategy instruction, situated learning, or modeling, coaching, and scaffolding appear to be much more suited to teaching basic skills subjects than the sciences, social studies, or humanities.

Social-constructivist notions and conceptual-change notions appear to have broader application potential, although with subject-matter differences in how important they are and how they are manifested in the classroom. These ideas are most applicable when it is possible to engage students in discussion of topics about which they have a great deal of prior knowledge, especially if this knowledge includes personal life experiences that students can reflect on as a basis for reasoning. Social-constructivist and conceptual-change notions are less applicable, however, when students are getting initial exposure to primarily new propositional knowledge, as when fifth-graders are introduced to chronological treatment of U.S. history. In these situations, it is often necessary to first establish a common base of information before attempting to engage students in forms of discourse that implicitly assume understanding of this information. I believe that some social constructivists are being unrealistic, even romantic, in suggesting that teachers should routinely avoid transmitting knowledge and instead function only as discussion facilitators and scaffolders of learning in the zone of proximal development.

Conclusion

The best teaching is adapted to the context, including the instructional purposes and goals, the students, and the subject matter. For example, techniques associated with the terms *active teaching, strategy instruction*, and *situated learning* are most relevant when the context calls for presenting new information, modeling skills, or coaching students as they attempt to implement skills or procedures. In contrast, techniques associated with terms such as *social constructivism* or *teaching for thoughtfulness* are most relevant when one wishes to develop understanding and appreciation of networks of knowledge through shared construction and negotiation of meanings and implications. A principle such as transferring responsibility for managing learning from the teacher to the students applies to all teaching contexts, but figuring out exactly how to apply it (how much modeling, explanation, coaching, and other scaffolding to provide, and how quickly to fade this support) takes experience with the content and the students.

Rather than viewing such qualifications on research findings simply as frustrations or even as evidence that research is not helpful, researchers and teachers need to appreciate them as indications of the complexities involved in adapting instruction to students and contexts. Researchers are making progress in learning about these complexities and their potential implications for instruction, and they will continue to build on this knowledge base. Even so, research-based information can only inform teachers about the trade-offs involved in decision alternatives; it cannot make those decisions for them. It is teachers, working within their state and district guidelines, who must decide what goals to pursue with their students and what combinations of content representations, instructional methods, and learning activities will be most helpful in assisting their students to accomplish the goals.

References

Brophy, J., and Alleman, J. (1991). Activities as instructional tools: A framework for analysis and evaluation. *Educational Researcher, 20*(4), 9–23.

Brophy, J., and Good, T. (1986). Teacher behavior and student achievement. In M. Wittrock (ed.), *Handbook of research on teaching* (3rd ed.) (pp. 328–375). New York: Macmillan.

Cooper, H. (1989). *Homework.* White Plains, N.Y.: Longman.

Good, T., and Brophy, J. (1986). School effects. In M. Wittrock (ed.), *Handbook of research on teaching* (3rd ed.) (pp. 570–602). New York: Macmillan.

Good, T., and Brophy, J. (1995). *Contemporary educational psychology* (5th ed.). New York: Longman.

Good, T., and Brophy, J. (1997). *Looking in classrooms* (7th ed.). New York: Longman.

Chapter 11

Teaching in the Content Areas

Suzanne M. Wilson

A Confession

From the time I was a little girl, I wanted to be a teacher. For a long time I thought I would teach math; after all, I adored problem sets and always got A's. But in college, I fell in love with history and knew that I wanted to help high school students do the same. Begrudgingly, I took all of the education courses I needed for certification as a secondary school social studies teacher. I was impatient with my education instructors. I knew that the best way to learn to teach was to be in a classroom with students (I knew a lot when I was twenty). I knew that my professors had little to teach me, a fact confirmed by their own inability to teach well. My resistance intact and certification in hand, I left college sure I would be a great teacher. If only someone would hire me.

Hire me someone did. Not to teach history, however, but math. I hadn't studied mathematics in college (save one disastrous advanced calculus course), but I was hired by my high school math teacher who knew I had excelled as a high school student. He and I both believed I knew the content of high school mathematics courses. I could review the textbooks to refresh my memory. And I'd taken courses in teaching (never mind the fact that at the time I was to be a social studies teacher). Thus, we also thought I knew about teaching.

It's safe to say that, at the time, my employers and I thought that

teaching = knowing about and using some instructional
            tools, and
content = the main ideas that are covered in textbooks.

Successful teachers, the logic goes, use their knowledge of some generic teaching tools and apply them to the relevant content area. Pretty straightforward.

Like so many things I thought I knew when I was twenty, I was wrong about these self-evident teaching truths. Recent research on teaching in the content areas only highlights how wrong my naive self was. In this chapter, I explain why by examining two questions: "What is teaching and learning *supposed* to be like in the content areas?" and "What do teachers need to know in order to teach in the content areas?"

What We Know

What Is Teaching and Learning Supposed to Be Like in the Content Areas?

One of the problems with my naive assumptions was that I presumed that the questions of "what" and "how" to teach had already been settled. In this view of teaching, content is not an issue, for it has already been determined. The only challenge—really—to teaching is how to manage groups of students and keep them interested. But recent historical studies of educational reform suggest otherwise. Perhaps since schools were started in the United States, but most certainly in the last century, not a decade has passed without debates about not only how to teach but what to teach. It seems the purposes and content of education have never been settled.

The current version of these debates can be seen in both the call for—and the subsequent arguments over—curricular standards. Ever since the National Council of Teachers of Mathematics (1989, 1991) published its standards for curriculum and for teaching, professional organizations have been rushing to produce their own standards. The National Council for Social Studies Education, the National Council of Mathematics Teachers, and the National Council of Teachers of English have all published "standards." So too have the National Board for Professional Teaching Standards, the National Council for Geographic Education and the Association of American Geographers, the National Science Teachers Association, and the American Association for the Advancement of Science. Simultaneously, states have issued their own standards in the form of frameworks, benchmarks, goals, opportunities to learn. In a dizzying array of statements about what students need to learn and how teachers need to teach, every content area has tried to make explicit its answer to the question, "What is teaching and learning supposed to be like in this content area?"

If that wasn't enough, for every argument that is made, a counterargument appears. The Michigan English Language Arts Framework (MELAF) proposes a version of teaching and learning that centers on textual interpretation and the child. Grammar and phonics, worksheets, and the canon seem peripheral if not downright wrong. And recently, Michigan's state school board noticed, insisting that there might be other views: Maybe kids should be taught more didactically and maybe they should read the "classics." Maybe phonics aren't a bad thing, and whatever happened to the basics anyway? Similarly, the California State Department of Education issued frameworks for mathematics and language-arts teaching and learning that emphasized "literature, not basals," "multiculturalism," "mathematical power," and "authentic assessment." And some parents and policymakers objected, worrying that the arithmetic and basic-skills baby has been thrown

out with the bathwater. In a subsequent report, a task force charged
with reviewing the frameworks states:

> The Task Force concluded that the 1987 *English–Language Arts Frame-work* did not present a comprehensive and balanced reading program
> and gave insufficient attention to a systematic skills instruction program . . .
> the Task Force concluded that many language arts programs have shifted
> too far away from direct skills instruction. [California State Department
> of Education, 1995, p. 2]

So where does this debate leave us? Should we be impatient
with those silly educators who can't make up their minds about
what students need to know? Should we be swept away by the
latest rhetoric? Neither seems sensible. If people who care a lot
about education (parents, teachers, administrators, social scientists) continue to argue and disagree, maybe it's because there's
something to argue about. After all, not everyone who participates in the debates can be stupid. But as a former teacher, I'm
also rather cynical about the fads and curricular pendulum swings
that seem the conundrum of teachers everywhere.

David Tyack and Larry Cuban (1995) in perhaps the smallest,
smartest, and most accessible book ever written about educational
reform in the United States characterize this unending effort to
make schools better as a process of "tinkering toward utopia."
They end their analysis with this claim:

> At its best, debate over purpose in public education has been a continu-
> ous process of creating and reshaping a democratic institution that, in
> turn, helped to create a democratic society. To be sure, there were elites
> who wanted to decree rather than debate policy. Some interest groups
> have focused only on their own narrow aims, seeing the politics of edu-
> cation as simply an arena of winners and losers. But to the degree that
> discourse about purpose in public education concerned itself with the
> public good, it can be understood as a kind of *trusteeship*, an effort to
> preserve the best of the past, to make wise choices in the present, and
> to plan in the future. [P. 142]

So what does this have to do with teaching in the content
areas? That's simple. Every teacher, every school, every school
district, every state must understand that the foundation of teaching
in a content area entails making decisions about purpose: What
will I teach children and how might I go about that? Further-

more, the history of debate over what mathematics students should learn, or how children should learn science, or what are the purposes of history, social studies, English, or arts education is bound to continue. Perhaps the best we can do is to "preserve the best of the past" while making "wise choices" about the present and future.

I didn't understand that when I was twenty. I thought the "wise choices" were already made, set in stone, transcribed in my text. They're not. Textbooks are but one resource of ideas about how and what should be taught. But textbooks neither fully nor accurately represent the current or historical debates; they are the products of a political as well as an intellectual process and provide but one view of the central ideas in a content area. Other resources include alternative curricula, professional-development opportunities (workshops, teacher research groups, university coursework, and the like), professional subject-matter organizations, other teachers, historical analyses of what was taught and how, as well as reform documents like standards that suggest "new" ways to think about teaching.

Given all of this, what might we learn from the current debates about teaching in the content areas? The debates suggest that each content area confronts some subject-specific problems. In mathematics, for example, the reforms highlight one such problem: How do we help children "understand" the mathematics they learn. That is, we might have learned a thing or two about how to get children to memorize the times tables, or divide by fractions, or factor inequalities. But even with the very best of students, it appears that we haven't been able to help them understand what they are doing. Consider a simple example:

$$10/0 = ?$$

Many will remember a rule from school: When you divide by zero, the answer is "undefined." Thus, $10/0 =$ undefined. Others will insist that $10/0 = 0$, explaining that anything divided by 0 is 0.

But take a minute and tell me why. What does "undefined" mean anyway? Are you stuck? Most people are. This isn't a fluke, either. Consider another problem:

3/4 divided by 1/2 = ?

Again, most of us learned a rule: When you divide by a fraction, invert the second fraction and multiply. Thus: 3/4 divided by 1/2 = 3/4 x 2/1 = 6/4 or (because you always reduce fractions) one and a half. Have you ever really looked at this answer? How can the answer be *more* than the original numbers? Isn't division supposed to make things *smaller*? What is going on? Can you describe a situation for which 3/4 divided by 1/2 is the appropriate division? When you *do* it, do you suddenly get 3/8 instead of 1 1/2? Why is that?

By now you might be a little annoyed. Just like students in mathematics classes around the country who inevitably ask (out of some combination of frustration and hostility), "But why do I need to learn this? This has nothing to do with my life!" One way to interpret the current mathematics reforms is to think of them as one group's response to the problem underlying these examples: For the most part, those of us who graduate from high school have pretty inflexible, shallow, and irrelevant understandings of mathematics. Returning to the "good old days" won't help. Instead, we need to reinvent our notions of teaching mathematics to include both the old and the new. Students need to master basic skills and facts. They also need to be facile with numbers and the uses of numbers in the world. They might need to be able to use mathematical abstractions in their everyday lives. Furthermore, the perennial and dramatic differences in achievement levels between males and females, between majority and minority poor students, warrant attention as well.

History and social studies teaching and learning seem to suffer from related, but slightly different, problems. Instead of mathematical anxiety, students suffer from historical ennui. Their eyelids drop as teachers launch into yet another lecture. The occasional movie is the only respite for the endless parade of dusty facts. They also learn to treat textbook accounts as authoritative, with little room for bias. The conflict that characterizes much of the past gets erased in the curriculum-development process. Despite a heavy emphasis on memorization, assessments clearly show that students don't know their facts, and they have little knowledge of more recent fields of historical scholarship, say, women's history or African-American history. Their "knowledge" of geography is embarrassing ("Philadelphia is a state near Arizona"), and they know little about economics. And like in mathematics, there isn't an old curriculum out there that will solve these problems. Instead, we need to patch together something new that enables the kind of learning envisioned by the authors of the California History–Social Sciences Framework:

> As educators in the field of history-social science, we want our students to perceive the complexity of social, economic, and political problems. We want them to have the ability to differentiate between what is important and what is not important. We want them to know their rights and responsibilities as American citizens. We want them to understand the meaning of the Constitution as a social contract that defines our democratic government and guarantees our individual rights. We want them to respect the right of others to differ with them. We want them to take an active role as citizens and to know how to work for change in a democratic society. We want them to understand the value, the importance, and the fragility of democratic institutions. We want them to realize that only a small fraction of the world's population (now or in the past) has been fortunate to live under a democratic form of government, and we want them to understand the conditions that encourage democracy to prosper. We want them to develop a keen sense of ethics and citizenship. We want them to care deeply about the quality of life in their community, their nation, and their world. [California State Department of Education, 1988, pp. 2–3]

The woes of English–language arts teaching introduces other problems: Children don't love to read, or see its relevance to their lives. They don't read literature from across cultures, and have little exposure to the lives and values of the diverse populations that constitute the U.S. public. Moreover, they hate to write, viewing it as a technical process of transcription, not a joyful process of learning and self-discovery. New visions of English teaching and learning would address some of these problems, as the authors of one state framework suggest:

> Reading activities, rather than focusing only on identifying words, must help students become fluent in language as they expand their understanding of a text. Writing activities, rather than focusing on legibility or mechanics in isolation, must enable students to plan strategies for communicating their thoughts effectively according to their audience and purpose. Speaking and listening activities, rather than presuming that students are, in the words of Charles Dickens' Mr. Gradgrind, pitchers

"to be filled so full of facts" must involve students actively as they describe their encounters with literature and composition and interactively
as they communicate their understandings and insights to others. [Cali-
fornia State Department of Education, 1987, p. 2]

Science suffers yet other problems. Knowledge about science
and technology is exploding, while teachers and students struggle
to attain some minimum level of scientific literacy. Previously
rigid boundaries among the sciences have to be taken down, so
that students have more opportunity to learn about the connections between earth science and biology, chemistry and physics,
technology and mathematics. Reformers paint the following picture of the purpose and content of science instruction:

> In elementary and secondary schools, the primary reason for teaching
> science knowledge today is the same as it has been in the past—to give
> students an understanding of the natural world and the abilities to rea-
> son and think critically as they explain their world. Students should begin
> early observing and describing the world around them and move to-
> ward progressively more elaborated explanations of phenomena. By the
> end of high school, students should be able to provide comprehensive
> explanations for the most obvious and compelling events that they ex-
> perience, for example, the seasons, day and night, disease, heredity and
> species variation, and dangers of hazardous substances. The curriculum
> should emphasize science as inquiry leading to understanding which
> assesses the students' explanations. Memory of facts, concepts, and prin-
> ciples for their own sakes, unconnected to the kinds of events and phe-
> nomena mentioned here, have little importance either for personal and
> social development or advancing the science enterprise. [DeBoer and
> Bybee, 1995, p. 73]

But these calls for reform (and others I haven't mentioned)
have not sprung from the ground de novo. They are the result
of many forces, among them a growing dissatisfaction across interested parties in American schooling; a history of arguments
about what school is about; and a growing (although still small
and weakly generalizable) stack of research on teaching and learning in the content areas. All of these calls for reform point to
that research to justify their claims, and a careful look at that
research informs the second question I pose in this chapter.

What Kinds of Things Do Teachers Need to Know in Order to Teach in the Content Areas?

I return to my confession. The twenty-year-old me believed that, for the most part, what you needed to know in order to teach was something about the subject matter. I believed this for a number of reasons: I thought that most teachers were born, not bred, and that you either had it or you didn't. So education courses were a waste of time. Nevertheless, I was required to take a few to become certified. Then I *really* knew that all you needed to know was the subject matter, for most of the courses I took were taught by people who could not teach *and* seemed full of pretty mindless activities: How to design a bulletin board and how to write a lesson plan seemed mundane, unnecessary ways to spend my time.

Yet, as Brophy (1986) reflects, research on teaching suggests I was downright wrong:

> Everything that research is discovering about effective teaching in any subject-matter area suggests that good teachers not only know their subject matter but also know their students and their pedagogy. Unfortunately, many mathematicians and scientists do not appreciate these realities, and persist in suggesting that knowledge of the content is the only important prerequisite to instructional effectiveness. Not only is this belief incorrect; it leads to the kind of didactic instruction . . . that produces understanding only in the highest achievers and leaves the rest of the students memorizing facts that they cannot integrate and principles that they do not truly understand. [Pp. 22–23]

Brophy's words ring true. We have all met a teacher, a friend, a mentor, a colleague who was informed and knowledgeable about a particular topic but incapable of explaining it. I remember how frustrating it was for me to take my mathematics homework to my father the physicist who could not, for the life of him, figure out how to help me understand that which he knew well.

Teachers need also to know about the power of certain pedagogical tools, for not all instructional ideas are created equal. I'll use an example from my own teaching of third-grade social studies as an example. One year, I was teaching my students about maps. I had hoped that by the end of the year my students would be able to interpret and use maps in meaningful ways. Rather than show them a map and teach them how to use the scale and key, I decided to start our work on maps by having students construct a map of the classroom. I chose this approach because I knew little about how students make sense of maps and I wanted to see what they knew and could do. I also chose this approach because I guessed that children can learn how to use maps and their scales without understanding much about what those maps represent.

On the first day of our map work, I told the class that we were going to draw maps in our notebooks. The notebooks I had provided them for the year were filled with graph paper, and I began class by asking students how we might use that graph paper in drawing our maps. Several students noticed that the floor of the classroom was made of linoleum tiles and that the graph paper had corresponding squares. As a class, we counted the number of squares from the back wall to the front wall (50) and from the right wall to the left wall (40). Several students suggested that we could count 50 and 40 squares, respectively, on the notebook paper and draw a box for the classroom.

Still in a large group, I asked my students what kinds of objects they would want to include in a map of the classroom. They suggested we include their desks, the flagpole, the teacher's desk, the bookcases, the chalkboards, the rugs, the bathrooms. After we made a list on the board, I let them work on their maps for three days. During that time, I walked around the room and helped students as they worked.

Three days passed. Having looked at what my students were doing in their notebooks, I knew that the maps varied in quality and development. Some students had barely sketched out the location of the bathrooms, others had drawn pictures of individual students, still others had counted the tiles on the floor in an attempt to locate the desks and chairs and rugs. Hugh hadn't done a thing but play with rulers, stick erasers up his nostrils, and hang around Mark.

In an attempt to gauge where the group was in their thinking about maps, I decided to have a class discussion, starting with the question, "What makes drawing a map hard?" Several students talked about trying to locate objects, others talked about not having enough room, many said nothing at all. The discussion fell flat, not surprisingly, since the students who had drawn *pictures* of the classroom or of students—not maps—had not found anything difficult about the making of a map. They had kept quite busy, and many of them liked their products. My question, intended to elicit students' thinking together over the construction of maps, didn't work. I left class feeling distraught. Where was I going with all this map stuff?

After a long discussion with a colleague the next day, I decided to start the next class with another question, "What is the difference between a map and a picture?" In the course of the ensuing lively discussion, my students informed me that maps had keys—instructions for what everything represented—but that pictures didn't have to have them. They also decided that maps helped you find the exact location of objects; pictures weren't required to do so. There was some debate over whether or not pictures were colored and maps were not, but that hypothesis was dropped when someone noticed that the map of the world was colored.

I suggested that we test our definition by considering some of their products. I picked Mary's first, knowing that she had drawn her map with a scale. For each tile on the classroom floor, there was a square on her map. Holding up Mary's drawing, I asked, "Is this a map or a picture?" As is the case with most of our discussions, half of the class yelled "Picture!" The others shouted, "Map!"

"How can we decide?" I asked.

"Let's try to find something!" several students said at once.

"What should we try to find?"

"The rug," Sean suggested.

As a group, we counted the squares on the map and determined that we should be able to find the rug 15 linoleum tiles away from the front wall. Eileen counted the tiles and, sure enough, there was the rug. The class agreed. Mary had drawn a map. Then we considered Melissa's drawing. "Map or picture?" I asked. Again, I selected Melissa's with a purpose—she had drawn hers freehand, and for a key she had drawn a picture of a house key. Melissa is a smart but lazy student who often tested my limits. I chose her picture because I thought that rather than being devastated by criticism, she would pick up the gauntlet and prove that she too could draw a bona fide map.

We tested Melissa's map by trying to locate the bookcase. No luck. We tried to find the bathroom. We couldn't. The class determined that her picture was not a map. With time left for one more discussion, we considered Ned's. Ned's depiction of the classroom was smaller than Mary's but my class was sure that it too was a map because they could find things. However, instead of being 50 by 40 squares, Ned's map was only 25 by 20 squares. "How can this be a map," I asked the class, "when he has 25 squares between the front and the back of the room and there are 50 tiles on the floor?" After a wandering discussion about whether or not Ned's picture was a map, during which half the class seemed engaged and the other half otherwise occupied with rulers, pencils, and notebooks, Katharine stood and stated, "If you divide 50 by 2, you get 25. I think he made every square two tiles instead of one." Ned nodded smugly. I was heartened at this point, for it felt like we were beginning to develop the concept of scale.

I don't offer this example as one of expert teaching, for I was a beginning teacher at the time, but the experience does illustrate a thing or two about what teachers need to know. I knew my subject matter: I knew how to use maps, I knew about the history and various schools of cartography, I even knew how to draw a map of the classroom. What I didn't know was how to help students learn those things. I didn't know that asking them the question, "What makes drawing a map hard?" would be a waste of our time. I didn't know how to help them "invent" the idea of scale. I didn't know whether they would understand scale better if I told them about it or they invented it. I didn't know how much complexity their nine-year-old minds could handle. I would have been a better teacher that year had I known those things.

And there is a growing body of research that substantiates this claim. Again, some of what we are beginning to understand goes across the different content areas, while some of it is subject-specific. Let's consider an example in science. Kathy Roth and her colleagues Andy Anderson and Ed Smith (1987) studied differences in how teachers taught about light and vision and what fifth-graders learned. What nonteachers may not realize is that students bring with them prototypical understandings or misunderstandings of how we see. The four pictures in Figure 11-1 illustrate these different views.

Figure 11–1 **Student Responses to a Question About How People See**

Question: This boy sees the tree.
Draw arrows to show how
the light from the sun
helps him to see the tree.

Description of Response	Illustration of Typical Answer	Percentage of students (N = 123)
Arrows from sun to tree and from tree to boy (correct).		6
Arrows or lines outward from sun only. No arrows between tree and boy (incorrect).		53
Arrows outward from sun and from boy to tree (incorrect).		11
Line between boy and tree, but no indication of direction (ambiguous).		10
Other correct responses.		6
No response or "I don't know."		14

Although the fourth picture leaves us with no clear sense of whether students understand light and reflection, the second and third pictures definitely illustrate that students *mis*understand how light and vision "work." The researchers in this study watched teachers who tried to help students learn about light and vision in a variety of ways, and they found that

> Students will not be able to comprehend science instruction or text-books unless the teacher talks to them in ways that will help them to think hard about why their existing conceptions are incomplete or un-convincing. The teacher must talk to students in ways that will help them change their misconceptions to make their thinking more consistent with scientifically appropriate ways of thinking about the phenomena. To do so, instruction must induce conceptual change in students. The teacher must be actively involved in diagnosing student misconceptions, responding to student misconceptions, presenting content in a way that engages students and makes sense to them, and guiding students to change misconceptions to more scientific views. The teacher must think and talk not only about the scientific content, but also about the students' ideas. [Roth, Anderson, and Smith, 1987, p. 544]

Clearly, then, knowing how light and vision work is not sufficient for quality teaching. Teachers must also know something about how students think about light and vision (especially when their knowledge is incomplete or downright wrong). On top of that, teachers must know something about how to teach in ways that help counteract students' misconceptions. Teaching about light well (that is, reaching the highest percentage of students possible) requires more than just telling them how it works— clearly and slowly. For many students won't get it: Their previous notions about light are too strong, and those ideas act like filters, blocking the development of correct understandings. A teacher who knows nothing more than the subject matter would be at a loss as to what to do next. And like the American tourist who can't speak Italian, saying the English words slower and louder probably won't help. Knowing what kinds of questions to ask, what kinds of experiments to have students conduct, and what kinds of pictures to use to help students change their minds are all important things for teachers to know.

Teachers also need to know something about the interaction of the instructional strategies they use and the messages they send to students. Students are often told that mathematics involves problem formulation as well as problem solving, and that mathematics is messy, that people change their minds, and that some mathematicians even find the work exhilarating and exciting. Yet those same students are typically subjected to practice drills and worksheets. Those methods—drill, fixed problems defined by other people, single-solution paths—are powerful teachers, and students learn from those teachers that mathematics is clear cut, cold, precise, linear. If students are to learn—really learn—that mathematics is as human a field of inquiry as, say, history, teachers need to widen the range of instructional strategies they use to include methods that help develop that message.

It would be impossible—not to mention tedious—to delineate all of the little and big things that research on teaching in the content areas is beginning to surface concerning what teachers need to know in order to teach well. But there is an overarching conclusion to draw here: While there has been much research done on generic principles of teaching (say, for instance, that wait time is a good idea), it has been only in the last ten years or so that researchers have looked more carefully at the subject-specific aspects of teaching in the content areas. And it's clear why: The work requires careful, longitudinal, often microscopic analyses of students' ideas and teaching strategies and the interactions among them. And the researchers need to know the content they are investigating. That is not to say that things are too complicated and too situation-specific for us to know anything for sure. That's simply not true. I am a better third-grade teacher for having learned about what kids know and don't know about scale and maps, and about all of the other topics we covered last year. Like the science teachers that Roth and her colleagues studied, teachers do not have to reinvent the wheel every year with every new group of students. Research into the subject-specific aspects of teaching—what students bring with them, what kinds of teaching strategies typically produce what kinds of learning and understanding, the strengths and limitations of various curricular materials—can inform a growing professional knowledge base.

Conclusion

Our current knowledge concerning teaching in the content areas has some obvious implications for practice and policy. Perhaps most obvious is that teachers need a professional education. They need to know about the history of curricular debates so that they are neither closed to nor swayed by the rhetoric of the latest reform. In fact, I would claim that we all—parents, policymakers, administrators, anyone interested in education— need an education in the history of curriculum, for as Tyack and Cuban (1995) point out:

> To judge from the ahistorical character of most current policy talk about reform, innovators may consider amnesia a virtue. And in those rare occasions when reformers do discuss the history of schooling, they often portray the past in politicized, stylized ways as a golden age to be restored or a dismal legacy to be repudiated. [P. 6]

But teachers need another kind of professional knowledge that is subject-specific—what students believe about light, how their beliefs can act as barriers to new understandings, what teaching strategies work well for some ideas, what questions don't work, when to tell and when to listen.

By no means, however, do I suggest that this fact justifies current teacher education, for most teacher education programs have not been designed to help students learn these kinds of things. And so while one implication might be that individuals with only subject-matter knowledge should not be fully certified teachers, another implication might be that we need a drastic redesign of teacher education that helps prospective and practicing teachers learn the substantive things they need to know.

Yet the nature of subject-specific teaching knowledge—its detail, complexity, and situatedness—makes it clear that no teacher could learn everything that would be helpful to her during a limited teacher-preparation program. Teaching, like medicine, seems a job that demands life-long learning. Doctors are constantly reading journals and receiving videodisks in the mail that teach them about new technology, treatments, research, drugs. Teachers too need such materials, and the commitment to their profession and the time that it takes in order to both conduct one's work and learn new things.

Furthermore, while there is a place for research on teaching and learning in the content areas (every little bit helps), it may be that putting all of our eggs in the research basket may not make much sense, for much significant work on learning to teach in the content areas takes place best in the classroom. So maybe I wasn't so wrongheaded when I started teaching. After all, I was right about a thing or two: You do need to know a lot about the subject matters you teach. And *one* of the best places to learn how to teach is in a classroom with students. However, my youthful egoism and confidence might very well have acted as blinders. It's hard to look at your teaching critically and admit its flaws. That takes both skill and maturity.

So what does the older me know about teaching in the content areas? That we all care passionately about what and how students learn and that those debates are important to understand and participate in. That the professional knowledge needed to teach well is detailed, situational, and subject-specific. (Certainly, "teaching" without such knowledge is possible, but effective and efficient teaching without it might be impossible.) And that we all would do well to find ways to support teachers in generating, testing, and opening up to public scrutiny what it takes to teach content. We all need to tinker toward a more satisfactory educational system—teachers, parents, industry, policymakers, politicians, administrators, and children alike. And we can do so only by learning from the lessons—both past and present—about teaching.

References

Brophy, J. (1986, April). *Teacher effects research and teacher quality.* Paper presented at the annual meeting of the American Educational Research Association, San Francisco, Calif.

California State Department of Education. (1987). *English-language arts framework for California public schools: Kindergarten through grade twelve.* Sacramento, Calif.: Author.

California State Department of Education. (1988). *History-social science framework for California public schools: Kindergarten through grade twelve.* Sacramento, Calif.: Author.

California State Department of Education. (1995). *Every child a reader: The Report of the California Reading Task Force.* Sacramento, Calif.: Author.

DeBoer, G. E., and Bybee, R. W. (1995). The goals of science curriculum. In R. W. Bybee, and J. D. McInerney (eds.), *Redesigning the science curriculum* (pp. 71–74). Colorado Springs: BSCS.

National Council of Teachers of Mathematics. (1989). *Curriculum and evaluation standards for school mathematics.* Reston, Va.: Author.

National Council of Teachers of Mathematics. (1991). *Professional standards for teaching mathematics.* Reston, Va.: Author.

Roth, K. J.; Anderson, C. W.; and Smith, E. L. (1987). Curriculum materials, teacher talk and student learning: Case studies in fifth-grade science teaching. *Journal of Curriculum Studies 19*, 527–548.

Tyack, D., and Cuban, L. (1995). *Tinkering toward utopia: A century of public school reform.* Cambridge, Mass.: Harvard University Press.

Chapter 12

Classroom Management

Carolyn M. Evertson

In the past twenty years, research on effective teaching has pointed to the importance of classroom conditions that depend directly on the ability of teachers to organize and manage their classrooms. Some of these conditions include productive use of time; student involvement in focused, goal-directed learning tasks; opportunities for corrective feedback; and engagement in instructional tasks of an appropriate developmental level.

Classroom management studies have extended our knowledge of what effective classroom managers do and how they do it. They have helped to broaden the definition of classroom management from a focus on controlling deviant behavior to one that refers to the actions teachers take to create, implement, and maintain a classroom environment that supports learning.

The purpose of this chapter is to describe a program of research on classroom management, to describe stable findings, to show how this knowledge has been applied through the development of materials to educate teachers, and to suggest directions for further exploration.

Developing a Research Program

Our program of research on teaching began at the R & D Center for Teacher Education, at the University of Texas, Austin. I will present the development of our research program by describing the findings of studies that formed the background for our efforts, our early descriptive and correlational studies, and the experimental studies that led to the translation of our research findings into recommendations for practice.

Background of the Program

In the 1970s and 1980s, research on teaching yielded a number of important findings that were relevant to classroom teachers. We were influenced in particular by three bodies of work: the work on time and schooling (Fisher et al., 1980), the work on effective group management strategies (Kounin, 1970), and the work on beginning the school year (Tikunoff, Ward, and Dasho, 1978; Moskowitz and Hayman, 1976).

Studies about Time. The work of David Berliner and Charles Fisher in the Beginning Teacher Evaluation Study at Far West Laboratory underscored the importance of time and learning. This work and that of others showed that (1) there is wide variability across schools and classrooms in the amount of time students spend learning the curriculum, (2) even under the best of circumstances, half or less of the school day is used for instruction, and (3) the amount of instructional time spent is often associated with student achievement.

These findings regarding the value of instructional time provided important background and impetus for the study of teachers' classroom management practices. How can teachers maximize meaningful learning time for their students? Furthermore, while the amount of time available imposes outer limits on what can be accomplished in a given classroom, *how* that time is used is really the key issue in what students can learn. Questions about classroom management are fundamentally questions about how time is used. Creation of an orderly social environment directly impacts how much time is available for learning. Effective classroom management conserves instructional time by planning activities and tasks to fit the learning material, by setting and conveying both procedural and academic expectations, and by appropriately sequencing, pacing, monitoring, and providing feedback for student work (Emmer, Evertson, and Anderson, 1980; Evertson and Emmer, 1982).

Group Management Strategies. Central to the approach we eventually took to classroom management were Jacob Kounin's landmark findings from the late 1960s and early 1970s on the management of classroom groups. Kounin (1970) studied how a teacher's handling of misbehavior influences other students who have witnessed it but were not themselves participants. Kounin called this the "ripple effect" and concluded that ways in which teachers handle misbehavior once it has occurred have little effect on student behavior. Rather, it is the means by which teachers *prevent* problems from occurring in the first place that differentiate effective from less effective group managers. Kounin described the more effective group managers as possessing, among other things, "withitness" (the ability to communicate an awareness of student behavior), "smoothness" (the ability to shift in and out of activities without disrupting the flow of events), and "momentum" (the ability to sustain good lesson pace by avoiding sudden starts, stops, or digressions). Effective managers also used "group alerting" to keep their students attentive during lessons. Most often these techniques were designed to keep the rest of the group attentive while one student was reciting (for example, calling on listeners to comment on a response, selecting students randomly, looking around the group before choosing someone to answer). Effective group managers also used techniques for keeping students accountable for paying attention by having them show work, by circulating and checking performance, or by calling on individuals.

Kounin's work was a major influence on those of us who were interested in finding links between how teachers manage to teach and student achievement, pointing us away from desists and toward the planning and teaching decisions that helped teachers to prevent misbehavior from occurring. During the early 1970s, my colleague Jere Brophy and I conducted a two-year research project in which we observed the classrooms of twenty-eight elementary school teachers the first year and forty elementary school teachers the second year. Some of these classrooms were in higher socio-economic schools and some were in lower. All teachers in the observed classrooms had consistent effects on their students' achievement as measured by standardized tests. Some teachers had consistently negative effects on student performance, and some had consistently positive effects. In other words, in some teachers' classes, students scored consistently higher on tests than predicted, but students in other classes scored consistently lower. We were interested in understanding how these teachers differed in their teaching practices. We believed that differences might be due in part to the quality and quantity of questioning, the accuracy and quality of pupil responses, the types of teacher feedback, the teacher-to-student and student-to-teacher private and public contacts, and the teacher sanctions of student behavior.

The data on student behavior yielded information that was relevant to classroom management. Namely, the more effective teachers monitored student behavior closely, intervened to correct inappropriate behavior before it escalated, and made fewer empty threats and warnings when dealing with misbehavior. Other data in this study provided a picture of what these classrooms were like through ratings of teacher and student behaviors and class climate. Some of those scale items were *level of attention*, how well students attended to class lessons; *task-oriented focus*, the degree to which the teacher worked toward content-related substantive goals; *teacher presentation*, the amount of time the teacher provided information that did not require pupil response; *negative affect*, the frequency and intensity of negative, hostile behaviors by students or teacher; *positive affect*, the frequency and intensity of supportive, positive, or reinforcing behaviors; and *enthusiasm*, the degree to which the teacher displayed interest, vitality, and involvement in the subject.

Teachers whose students consistently gained in achievement provided more response opportunities for students, sustained student responses by working with students to arrive at their answers, had fewer but more appropriate behavioral contacts, and monitored students' work more closely. These classrooms were relatively more task-oriented and had higher levels of attention. However, what was intriguing was that we also saw that these teachers organized classrooms that ran smoothly, with a minimum of disruption. The results supported many of Kounin's earlier findings. Teachers in these classrooms also actively taught their students the procedural skills needed to participate in class lessons, such as how to complete assignments, obtain supplies, or get a turn at answering.

Beginning the School Year. Further background for our work was provided by the few studies that had addressed the beginning of the school year. Although educators had long assumed that what happens in a classroom during the first days of the year sets the stage for the entire year, only a few studies of beginning-of-year activities had been conducted. One of these was conducted by Tikunoff, Ward, and Dasho (1978), who reported case studies of three fourth-grade teachers who were observed during the first seven weeks of the school year. These case studies highlighted the importance given to rule-setting, teacher sanctioning of behavior, and the socialization of children to the teacher's system of rules and procedures during these first weeks. Work by Moskowitz and Hayman (1976) in a junior high school confirmed that teachers rated highly by their students used the first class day for orienting and climate-setting, rather than jumping directly into content.

Descriptive and Correlational Studies: What Do Teachers Do?

Our own work in classrooms began with descriptive and correlational studies directed at uncovering teachers' strategies at the beginning of the year, and relating these to student behavior and achievement as the year progressed. Despite the seeming obviousness of the rationale for studying classroom processes at their inception, we found that typically research on teaching had skipped the crucial first days of school, instead obtaining samples of behavior only at some point later in the year. In our work, we believed that the initial phase of the year would be of paramount importance. We had questions about how good managers began the school year and how teachers who had well-run, stimulating, and task-oriented classrooms accomplished this from the first day of school. Therefore, we conducted a series of research studies that addressed the following questions:

1. What principles of management, organization, and group processes were most important for beginning the year?
2. Were these principles related to effective management throughout the year?
3. How did effective managers implement skills and techniques related to good management?

Studies of Elementary School Classrooms. Our research team (Linda Anderson, Edmund Emmer, myself, and others) observed twenty-seven third-grade teachers during the first weeks of school, then periodically for the remainder of the year. We suspected that the important teaching practices might be the routines that teachers established at the beginning of the year, such as setting rules and procedures, handling seatwork, and managing groups of students.

The idea was to describe from the very beginning just how teachers planned for the beginning of school, how they introduced routines and procedures, what kinds of problems they had to deal with, how they managed diverse groups of learners, and generally how they "grooved in" the students. Observers recorded numbers of students engaged and described the sequence of classroom events (e.g., establishing rules, routines, and expectations; using strategies for gaining student cooperation in academic tasks and activities; and controlling student behavior) in narrative form.

The narrative record helped us understand *how* teachers' and students' routines and class activities evolved over time, what effects certain practices had on both students' and teachers' behaviors, and how cycles of both cooperative behavior and misbehavior were fed and reinforced across time. From this information, we could identify teachers who were especially effective at managing their classrooms and those who were less so, based on their effects on student behavior.

Observation ratings also provided a numerical evaluation of various aspects of classroom management and instruction and could be used as indices for selecting case studies from the voluminous narrative records. Several characteristics distinguished the better managers:

1. *Analyzing classroom tasks.* Better managers were able to analyze in precise detail the procedures and expectations required for students to be able to function well in the classroom.
2. *Teaching the going-to-school skills.* Better managers included instruction in rules and procedures as an important part of the curriculum in the first weeks of school and provided opportunities for practice and feedback.
3. *Seeing the classroom through students' eyes.* Better managers could analyze their students' needs for information about how to participate in class activities. This information was signaled in ways that were predictable and consistent.
4. *Monitoring student behavior.* Better managers kept their students in view and dealt with problems quickly.

Studies of Junior High School Classrooms. Because of department-alization in most secondary schools, we believed that the organizational and managerial tasks facing secondary school teachers were likely to be different from those confronting elementary school teachers. Another exploratory study was conducted in junior high school classes. Fifty-one mathematics and English teachers were observed in two of their regularly scheduled classes. We used the same data collection procedures as in the elementary school classes just mentioned. Observations began on the first day of school and continued extensively for the first three weeks, then less often for the rest of the year. Fourteen one-hour observations were conducted in two of each teacher's classes. Effective management at the junior high school level could be distinguished in the following ways:

1. *Explaining rules and procedures.* Better managers had explicit rules, procedures, expectations, and rationales that were developed into a coherent system and communicated to students.
2. *Monitoring student behavior.* Better managers were more consistent in support of their management system. They were aware of and dealt with disruptive behavior and potential threats to their system.
3. *Developing student accountability for work.* Better managers developed a detailed system for keeping track of students' academic work.

4. *Communicating information.* Effective managers could present information clearly, reduced complex tasks to their essential steps, and had a good understanding of students' skill levels.
5. *Organizing instruction.* More effective managers preserved their instructional time and had more students engaged in academic work.

Experimental Studies: How Can We Help Teachers with Classroom Management?

The ultimate purpose of investigating how effective teachers set up their classrooms from the beginning of school was to be able to help new teachers who often struggle to accomplish what more effective managers have learned to do. The previous studies were correlational and descriptive; we learned what practices were *associated* with orderly classroom environments, but we did not know whether our findings could be used to teach teachers to use good management practices and whether these practices in turn would have effects on student behavior and cooperation when compared to a group of teachers who were not so taught.

While early studies provided generic information about class-room characteristics and the teacher actions that related to order and student involvement, it was necessary to take the next step and determine how these findings could be developed into frameworks for assisting teachers. Conceptual frames were needed to help teachers orchestrate these principles in the fast pace of a classroom.

We designed a series of experimental field studies to determine if the findings from the elementary and secondary school corre-lational studies could be developed into materials for teachers. We used the findings from the correlational studies to highlight key elements in organizing and managing classrooms from the first day of school. We were not at all sure that *if* teachers followed these suggestions they would have orderly, productive classrooms, but we wanted to test the proposition. We wanted to know if the relationships found in the correlational studies were causal. In other words, do good managers create productive classrooms? Overall, these field studies strongly supported the necessity of establishing a classroom management system at the beginning of the school year. Teachers trained in classroom management principles not only used effective management strategies and procedures significantly more than comparable untrained groups, but their students exhibited higher task engagement, less inappropriate behavior, and higher academic success (Evertson, Emmer, Sanford, and Clements, 1983; Emmer, Sanford, Clements, and Martin, 1983; Evertson, 1985, 1989, 1995). These findings provide evidence that research results can and do influence teachers' decisions about management practices (Evertson et al., 1983; Evertson, 1985, 1989; Putnam and Barnes, 1984); the following detailed description of the studies clarifies the practices that influenced teacher and student behavior.

Developing Materials for Teachers. Guidelines for effective classroom management were written in manuals and used in a two-day workshop given before the school year began for twenty-three teachers in grades one to six. We also found a group of eighteen teachers who agreed to be in the control group, on the promise that they could participate in the workshop later in the year. The materials for the workshop covered the following areas, along with activities to help teachers think about planning for the start of school: (1) readying the classroom, (2) planning rules and procedures, (3) determining incentives and consequences for appropriate and inappropriate behavior, (4) teaching rules and procedures, (5) planning beginning-of-school activities, (6) developing strategies for potential problems, (7) monitoring student work and behavior, (8) stopping inappropriate behavior, and (9) organizing instruction.

From 1981 to 1994, ten experimental field studies were conducted in classrooms ranging from kindergarten to twelfth grade, including both regular classrooms and special education resource rooms. In all, 362 teachers in eighty schools in four states were involved.

Findings. As in the earlier descriptive/correlational studies, extensive use was made of the narrative record to describe the ongoing events in each classroom. We also made periodic counts of students engaged or not engaged in class activities, rated amounts of inappropriate or disruptive behavior, and interviewed teachers at the end of the study about their planning and management decisions. Table 12-1 describes the key student and teacher variables that were found to be statistically significant in each of the ten studies. (The seven teaching-practice variables presented in the table reflect the nine areas listed above.)

The table shows dramatically consistent findings about the importance of these teaching behaviors and practices. The results indicate that not only can the findings be used for teacher inservice programs, but teachers who use the management suggestions for planning and establishing rules, procedures, and routines have better student engagement, with less off-task, inappropriate, or disruptive behavior. In three studies conducted at both the elementary and middle school levels, students in the trained teachers' classrooms also showed greater growth in reading and mathematics as measured by the school's standardized tests.

Stable Findings: What Works

The culmination of this descriptive/correlational/experimental program of research has been the identification of stable findings that can support recommendations for teachers. The weight of research behind them means that these are recommendations that can be made with confidence, given certain caveats and unexplored areas that I will address in the final section of this chapter.

Readying the Classroom

As teachers already know, there are few "ideal" classrooms with an abundance of space for students, work areas, and storage. For most teachers, the task of planning the physical arrangement of desks and furnishings in the space they are allotted is one of making trade-offs between what they would like to have and what they must work with. How the available physical space is used can have important implications for how students participate in class activities and how they may interact with the teacher and with each other. Studies in elementary and secondary classrooms show that effective teachers plan for the arrangement of furnishings to accommodate different types of activities, to minimize problems

Table 12–1

Indicators of Effective Classroom Management Practices

Key variables from ten observational field experiments
comparing teaching practices and student behavior
in trained versus untrained teachers' classrooms

	Number of studies in which variable was measured*	Number of studies in which variable was significant**	Percentage of studies in which variable was significant
Teaching Practice Variables			
1. Readying the Classroom			
Organizing classroom space and materials	10	8	80
2. Developing Rules and Procedures			
Efficient administrative routines	10	8	80
Appropriate general procedures	10	10	100
Efficient small-group procedures	6	5	83
3. Student Accountability			
Checks for understanding	10	9	90
Routines for checking and giving feedback	10	10	100
Task-oriented focus	10	10	100
4. Managing Student Behavior			
Reinforces good performance	10	9	90
Consistent management of student behavior	10	9	90
5. Monitoring			
Student behavior	10	10	100
Transitions between activities	10	8	80
6. Organizing Instruction			
Attention spans	10	8	80
Good lesson pacing	10	8	80
Lessons related to student interests	6	8	75
7. Instructional clarity			
Describes objectives	10	8	80
Clear directions for academic work	10	6	60
Clear explanations and presentations	10	8	80

continued on page 262

Table 12–1
Continued

	Number of studies in which variable was measured*	Number of studies in which variable was significant**	Percentage of studies in which variable was significant
Student Behavior Variables			
High task engagement	8	7	88
Low amount of inappropriate behavior	10	8	80
Students use time constructively	7	5	71
Students take care of own needs	4	4	100
Student Outcome Variables			
Achievement gain in reading	3	3	100
Achievement gain in mathematics	3	3	100

* The number of studies in which the variable was measured.
** The number of studies in which the variable was measured in which it was statistically significant (or showed an effect size of ⩾.40) in favor of the trained teachers.

of disruptive movement in the classroom, and to facilitate monitoring of student work and behavior.

Provisions for seating students, access to needed storage areas, and locations for posted assignments, equipment, and materials will convey to students how the room will be used and what the teacher's expectations are. Classrooms we studied that functioned in support of instructional goals appeared to have been arranged with the following considerations in mind:

1. *Visibility.* Students were able to see the instructional displays. The teacher had a clear view of instructional areas, students' work areas, and learning centers to facilitate monitoring of students.
2. *Accessibility.* High-traffic areas (areas for group work, pencil sharpener, door to the hall) were kept clear and separated from each other.
3. *Distractibility.* Arrangements that could compete with the teacher for students' attention were minimized.

Planning Classroom Rules and Procedures

The requirements for living in a social world and working in group settings mean that some individual freedoms must necessarily be regulated to accomplish the goals of the group or society at large. Classrooms are no different from other social settings in this regard. Studies focusing on how teachers started the school year indicated that effective managers planned rules and procedures in advance and had clearly in mind the ways that these would function in the classroom.

Effective classroom managers in both elementary and secondary schools had well-developed classroom rules and procedures and spent much of the time at the beginning of the school year teaching these to their students, much as they would teach an academic concept. They also planned time during the year to review the classroom rules and procedures. (Rules differ from classroom procedures in that they define general expectations or standards for behavior. For example, the general rule "Be in your seat and ready to work when the bell rings" defines a set of behaviors that should always be practiced. Classroom procedures, on the other hand, communicate expectations for behavior but are usually directed at accomplishing specific tasks rather than defining general behavior or prohibiting some action: "Put completed assignments in the basket on the teacher's desk.") Specific routines promote smooth and quick transitions between activities and thus add to instructional time. Such routines also reduce disruption that can lead to behavior problems. They help maintain lesson flow, continuity, and student engagement in academic work. A carefully prepared list of classroom procedures can facilitate the establishment of these routines.

Effective managers in our studies developed rules and procedures that were unambiguous, were supported by reasonable rationales, were consistent with school rules and policies, and, in the case of rules, were markedly limited in number: four or five well-planned rules seemed to cover most areas. (Although it is important to keep the number of classroom rules short and manageable, the actual number of rules was not as critical as the development of these rules into a systematic set of expectations that was consistently reinforced and followed.)

Developing Systems for Student Accountability

One of the most persistent features of schooling is that much academic work that students do revolves around the completion of assignments. Effective teachers developed procedures not only to hold students accountable, but also to help them *become* accountable for both academic work and behavior. Five facets of an effective system that supports student accountability are (1) providing clear explanations of overall work requirements; (2) developing procedures for communicating assignments and instructions to students; (3) monitoring the work in progress; (4) establishing routines for turning in work; and (5) providing regular feedback to students regarding their work.

Effective teachers in the classrooms we studied often provided initial "warm-up" activities at the beginning of the class period, as students were entering the room. In math classes, these might be one or two new problems; in English classes, they might be a scrambled sentence or new vocabulary words to define. Students worked on these, and they became part of the daily grade. Warm-ups accomplished several purposes. One was to establish a content focus; another was to use the first few minutes of the class period when the teacher was tending to administrative details; a third was reinforcement of skills and concepts and provision of practice. The fact that "warm-ups" were checked and counted as part of the total grade supported their being taken seriously by students.

Effective managers also made sure that they checked student work regularly, provided feedback and correctives, and rechecked to verify that students were learning concepts correctly. They found ways to accomplish this close monitoring by having students check each other, by continually moving around the room during seatwork and looking over each student's work, or by having students check their own papers and then turn them in. Sometimes, students placed their work in folders that were checked weekly; in other classes, students routinely turned in daily work for informal checking. In secondary school classrooms where teachers often had five separate classes to teach, it was doubly important to find efficient ways to monitor student progress.

Managing Student Behavior

Rules and norms for appropriate behavior must have implicit consequences for compliance or noncompliance in order to function as rules. If teachers fail to make clear to students the consequences of their behavior, students will eventually try to determine the consequences for themselves. One way the effective managers we studied anticipated potential problems was to discuss with students the rules and procedures, their rationales, and the accompanying incentives. These teachers provided evidence that rules and procedures are more likely to be followed if students have a clear idea of the expected behaviors and the consequences for their cooperation or noncooperation. Ultimately, a teacher's goal is to help students develop self-control and manage their own behavior. Students' clear understanding of the consequences of their behavior can be a step toward this end.

When inappropriate behavior occurred, effective managers handled it promptly to avoid its continuance and spreading. Behaviors such as persistent inattention, avoidance of seatwork, and obvious violations of classroom rules and procedures had to be dealt with quickly. Teachers' ways of doing this included redirecting the student's attention to tasks, making eye contact or moving nearer the student, reminding the student of the correct procedure, or directly asking the student to stop.

Inappropriate behaviors that were of short duration and not serious (for example, momentary whispering, brief visual wandering) were ignored, with the assumption that it would be more disruptive to lesson flow to intervene than to allow the behavior to stop on its own. However, more serious misbehavior, such as rudeness or hostility toward others, chronic avoidance of work, or fighting, required both immediate and long-term strategies.

Monitoring Student Behavior

Effective managers regularly surveyed their class or group and watched for signs of student confusion. Teachers are unlikely to be able to deal with student inattention or stop misbehavior before it spreads if they do not see it in the first place. Likewise, teachers can appear inconsistent in reinforcing their classroom rules and procedures if they are not aware of infractions. If some students are consistently out of the teacher's line of sight, it may signal to these students that they are not as accountable as others in the class. All of these things can lead to management problems that can become more severe as time goes on.

Still, the importance of monitoring does not lie only in the detection of potential behavior problems. It also provides teachers with important information about student performance, and the appropriateness of assignments. (Are they too easy? Do students finish them too quickly? Are they too difficult, so that students cannot complete them?) Teachers who make a practice of routinely checking students and attending to nonverbal cues can often catch problems before they continue too long and before errors are practiced and reinforced. Effective managers monitored actively, moving around the room to touch base with all students, rather than focusing on only those who could be seen from the front.

Organizing Instruction

As they planned for and conducted instruction, effective managers were aware of student needs. Activities in these classrooms were paced so that students had enough to do; assignments reflected an awareness of student attention spans and interests; and down time between assignments or activities was minimized.

Instructional Clarity

Teachers in classrooms that ran smoothly scored high on measures of instructional clarity. That is, they described their objectives clearly, gave precise instructions for assignments, and responded to student questions with understandable explanations.

Beginning the School Year

Effective classroom managers appeared to understand the importance of orienting students to the setting and consistently communicating these expectations. Some beginning activities we observed in elementary school classrooms included:

1. *Greeting students.* Teacher provided name tags and designated places to sit and a place for belongings.
2. *Introductions.* Teacher and students told something about themselves.
3. *Describing the room and how to use it.* Teacher pointed out major areas of the room, their use, and any procedures associated with them.
4. *Get-acquainted activities.* Teacher provided ways for students and teacher to know each other better, used sharing activities.
5. *Discussing rules, procedures, and consequences.* Teacher presented these and provided some opportunities for students to practice them. Actively teaching young children the rules and procedures is an important part of instruction during the first day and the first weeks. This includes describing and demonstrating the desired behavior, having students practice, and providing feedback about how well they did.
6. *Teaching a procedure.* Teacher began to instruct students in class procedures that they would need to know, such as heading papers or locating materials and replacing them, using the following steps:
    a. *Described and demonstrated the desired behavior.* Explained precisely what was acceptable and what was not; provided a model. Let students also demonstrate the procedure for the class.
    b. *Rehearsed.* Let students practice the behavior or the correct method. If procedures were complex, broke them down into their components and let students practice each part and then put it all together.
    c. *Provided feedback.* After students had a chance to practice, let them know if they had done it properly. If improvement was needed, repeated practice.
7. *Content activities.* Teacher provided early content activities that students should be able to accomplish. Engaging students in these activities supplied important information about completion rates and skill levels.

In secondary school classrooms, activities for the first day differed in some ways simply because teachers in junior high and high school usually taught a specific content area for several groups of students for shorter periods of time than in elementary classrooms. For students in secondary classrooms, understanding procedures and expectations was more a matter of discerning the norms for a particular class. Also, many of the routines (e.g., taking lunch count, responding to parent correspondence, or organizing materials for student activities) that elementary teachers dealt with were of less concern to secondary teachers.

Materials for Teachers' Professional Development

The areas summarized in the previous section reflect the consistent findings of our observational and experimental studies. The recommendations are well grounded in two decades of research, and have been found to be reliable over time. The uniqueness of each classroom and the variety and complexity of tasks that teachers face make it impossible to prescribe specific techniques for every situation. Instead, these recommendations can be used to provide a framework for thinking about these important areas. Our next goal was to communicate this framework in ways that teachers could use to examine their own classroom management strategies.

In 1989, we further developed the materials described earlier into teacher manuals containing six key areas that reflected the concepts identified in the experimental studies. By this time, we had learned a great deal from conducting workshops across the country and following up on teachers' planning and implementation efforts. The resulting classroom management workshop, called COMP (Classroom Organization and Management Program), received funding from the U.S. Department of Education's National Diffusion Network. The first cycle of funding extended for four years and resulted in several thousand classroom management workshops for both new and experienced teachers across the United States and its territories.

However, this is not enough. Learning to teach is a complex, context-specific enterprise that requires practice in problem solving more than acquisition of rote skills (Brophy, 1988; Evertson, 1987). Teachers need long-term support to extend their teaching repertoires and to learn new practices. Professional development that is embedded within the school culture, that is based on systematic problem identification by those involved, that is specific to the issues and problems teachers face in their classrooms, and that supports change in teachers' thinking as well as in their practice must be present and supported at the system level.

Conclusion

Findings from studies of classroom management provide background and guidance for further exploration in many directions. As research continues, it is essential that earlier findings are used as foundations; to discard them would be to ignore lessons already learned. In this concluding section, I will summarize several principles that must support future researchers and policymakers.

Principles for Research and Policymaking

1. *Focus on preventive rather than reactive approaches.* Research clearly indicates that a comprehensive management system begins from the first day of school, as opposed to a focus on consequences once deviant behavior has occurred (Emmer and Aussiker, 1990). Of course, a carefully planned management system will not, by itself, stop all misbehavior, but teachers can usually handle it unobtrusively with techniques such as eye contact or physical proximity. More serious misbehavior may require more direct intervention. Punishment by itself may control misbehavior temporarily, but as it neither teaches desirable behavior nor instills the desire to behave appropriately, it is at best only a limited response to repeated misbehavior. However, the success of interventions depends on there being agreed-upon norms and expectations in place (Doyle, 1986).

The same holds true of discipline programs such as Teacher Effectiveness Training, Reality Therapy, and Assertive Discipline.

These systems provide methods for dealing with threats to class-room order. However, Emmer and Aussiker (1990), in an analy-sis of thirty-six studies that tested the effects of these programs on outcomes such as student attitudes, self-esteem, and achieve-ment, found that none adequately addresses the complex pre-ventive and supportive functions necessary for effective management and discipline. Their analysis supports the need to establish a comprehensive system of management and organization early in the year.

2. *Supporting teachers' learning.* Teachers can and do make beneficial changes as a result of reflection and intentional inquiry into their own teaching practices. What is more, these changes tend to sustain and provide the basis for other changes. However, reflective practice needs to be understood as an integral part of teachers' work lives.

3. *Management practices are inseparable from good instructional practices.* Good management and organization must focus more on the content and substance of what is being managed and less on the "look of engagement." Whereas good management is necessary for learning, it does not stand alone. Recent research has identified classrooms with high levels of student engagement but meager academic content, which results in low levels of learn-ing (Evertson and Weade, 1991).

4. *Shifts to more learning-centered approaches to instruction mean creating a collaborative climate in which students become resources for each other.* The current climate of school reform clearly calls for teaching problem solving and higher-order thinking skills, integrat-ing learning experiences within and across subject areas, and implementing multiple tasks (Resnick, 1987). Enacting these changes requires methods of organization and management that focus on providing students opportunities to work with peers, to share expertise, to utilize multiple resources both inside and outside the classroom, and to assume a broader range of roles in the classroom.

5. *Developing a classroom management system is not just a matter of enacting a few rules and procedures.* The initiation of any activity or set of activities will necessarily involve planning routines and procedures and establishing norms. Although our discussion has centered around the specific steps teachers can take to develop and establish a management system, these steps should be viewed

as interrelated, cyclical, and dynamic. For example, the introduction of a new unit of work may require that students participate in the classroom in different ways; changes in expectations for participation can mean changes in the classroom arrangement that could require different rules, procedures, and expectations for academic performance and may alter the ways students can demonstrate their knowledge. Each of these shifts in classroom tasks and activities can mean new cycles of planning, establishing, and reestablishing classroom routines and norms. Concluding events also play a part in this cycle. The teacher's task remains one of orchestrating these events in ways that serve curriculum goals and students' needs.

6. *Classroom culture will inevitably be influenced by the school and community context in which students and teachers live.* Although not included in this review, abundant literature documents how school-level disciplinary norms influence classroom management (Moles, 1990). The view presented is that the school and community contexts in which classrooms are embedded affect the values and decisions teachers make in their management systems. In other words, teachers' management decisions that are not supported at the school and community level lose credibility with students.

Past perspectives on classroom management have been limited to concerns about control of student behavior. These views limit our ability to develop classrooms as learning settings in which both teacher and students are active learners. We as educators must make the central distinction between ways of controlling behavior versus enabling students to become self-directed in ways that support learning communities for all participants.

Suggested Readings

Emmer, E. T., and Aussiker, A. (1990). School and classroom discipline programs: How well do they work? In O. C. Moles (ed.), *Student discipline strategies.* Albany: State University of New York Press.

Evertson, C. M. (1987). Managing classrooms: A framework for teachers. In D. Berliner and B. Rosenshine (eds.), *Talks to teachers* (pp. 54–74). New York: Random House.

Randolph, C. H., and Evertson, C. M. (1994). Images of management in a learner-centered classroom. *Action in Teacher Education 16*(1), 55–64.

References

Brophy, J. E. (1988). Educating teachers about managing classrooms and students. *Teaching and Teacher Education* 4, 1–18.

Brophy, J. E., and Evertson, C. M. (1976). *Learning from teaching: A developmental perspective.* Boston: Allyn & Bacon.

Doyle, W. (1986). Classroom organization and management. In M. Wittrock (ed.), *Handbook of Research on Teaching* (3rd ed.). New York: Macmillan.

Emmer, E. T., and Aussiker, A. (1990). School and classroom discipline programs: How well do they work? In O. C. Moles (ed.), *Student discipline strategies.* Albany: State University of New York Press.

Emmer, E. T.; Evertson, C. M.; and Anderson, L. M. (1980). Effective classroom management at the beginning of the school year. *The Elementary School Journal* 80, 219–231.

Emmer, E. T.; Sanford, J. P.; Clements, B. S.; and Martin. J. (1983, March). *Improving junior high classroom management.* Paper presented at the annual meeting of the American Educational Research Association, Montreal (ERIC Document Reproduction Service # ED 234 021).

Evertson, C. M. (1985). Training teachers in classroom management: An experimental study in secondary school classrooms. *Journal of Educational Research* 79(1), 51–57.

Evertson, C. M. (1987). Managing classrooms: A framework for teachers. In D. Berliner and B. Rosenshine (eds.), *Talks to teachers* (pp. 54–74). New York: Random House.

Evertson, C. M. (1989). Improving classroom management: A school-based program for beginning the year. *Journal of Educational Research* 83(2), 82–90.

Evertson, C. M. (1995). *Program revalidation for COMP: Submission to the Program Effectiveness Panel (USDOE),* Nashville: Vanderbilt University.

Evertson, C. M., and Emmer, E. T. (1982). Effective management at the beginning of the school year in junior high classes. *Journal of Educational Psychology* 74, 485–498.

Evertson, C. M.; Emmer, E. T.; Sanford, J. P.; and Clements, B. S. (1983). Improving classroom management: An experiment in elementary school classrooms. *The Elementary School Journal* 84, 173–188.

Fisher, C. W.; Berliner, D. C.; Filby, N. N.; Marliave, R. S.; Cahen, L. S.; and Dishaw, M. M. (1980). Teacher behaviors, academic learning time, and student achievement: An overview. In C. Denham and A. Lieberman (eds.), *Time to learn* (pp. 7–32). Washington, D.C.: National Institute of Education.

Kounin, J. S. (1970). *Discipline and group management in classrooms.* New York: Holt, Rinehart and Winston.

Moles, O. C. (ed.) (1990). *Student discipline strategies: Research and practice.* Albany: State University of New York Press.

Moskowitz, G., and Hayman, J. (1976). Success strategies of inner-city teachers: A year-long study. *Journal of Educational Research* 69, 283–89.

Putnam, J., and Barnes, H. (1984). *Applications of classroom management research findings.* Research Series 154, Institute for Research on Teaching, East Lansing: Michigan State University (ERIC Document Reproduction Service ED 256 752).

Resnick, L. B. (1987). *Education and learning to think.* Washington, D.C.: National Academy Press.

Tikunoff, W.; Ward, B. A.; and Dasho, S. (1978). Volume A: Three case studies. (Report A78–7), San Francisco: Far West Laboratory for Educational Research and Development.

Chapter 13

Learning and Teaching with Educational Technologies

Roy D. Pea

This chapter considers what we have learned about learning and teaching with educational technologies over the past several decades. While there are compelling data and arguments on the positive effects of these tools, there are also well-documented difficulties with implementing such innovations. The social contexts of the uses of technology are crucial to understanding how technology may influence teaching and learning. The classroom influences, in particular the teacher, are seminal. Much more attention needs to be focused on the teacher in research and practice on educational technologies. I provide the metaphor of

Thanks to Christina Allen for her invaluable contributions. I would like to thank the Spencer Foundation and the National Science Foundation (Grant #RED-9454729) for writing support at the Center for Advanced Study in the Behavioral Sciences, Stanford, California. Portions of this chapter were presented to the Panel on Educational Technologies, President's Committee of Advisors on Science and Technology (PCAST), White House Conference Center, October 3, 1995.

an on-line "School Depot," which could serve national needs in support of teaching and learning with educational technologies.

All across America, students and teachers (and increasingly parents) are finding excitement in new technologies for learning and teaching. Stories abound of troubled students who suddenly spring to life as their peers recognize the talents these students express in graphics programming, or in video editing, or in building simulations. Conferences of computer-using educators are abuzz with talk of connectivity to the "information super-highway," of how no school can survive without direct Internet access and TCP/IP, gopher and World Wide Web information servers, and about the relative merits of different computer operating systems or computer chips such as the PowerPC and the Pentium. Schools and parents are buying multimedia computers with CD-ROM players at a rapid pace. Deals among media conglomerates in interactive information services are front-page news virtually every day. What is all this chatter about? What is going on here? And how might it bear on education? Is this just another hyped-up technology infatuation for education, like filmstrips or Skinner machines, which will not really make much of a difference for what or how students learn and teachers teach?

"Educational technologies," in the broad sense of the term, are any resources, including methods, tools, or processes used for handling the activities involved in education. In this sense, the presence of a teacher, written materials such as books or physical materials such as alphabet blocks, the use of display media such as chalkboards or overhead transparencies, the techniques of lectures or hands-on laboratories, or even the use of assessment instruments are all "educational technologies." In practice, though, after World War II the phrase had a more restrictive meaning, referring to technologies such as filmstrips, slide projectors, language learning laboratories using audio tapes, and television. Since the advent of personal computing in the early 1980s, "educational technologies" has come to refer primarily to computer-based learning, to the use of interactive videodiscs and more recently CD-ROMs, and, within the past few years, to learning environments established with computer and communications technologies, such as computer networks. In short, "educational technologies" has commonly been used to refer to the most advanced technologies available for teaching and learning in a particular era.

Given the diversity of educational technologies incorporated in this thumbnail history, it will not be feasible to provide even a cursory review of research on what is known about learning and teaching with them (see CTGV, 1995). I will primarily aim to offer a characterization of *ways of thinking* about the roles of educational technologies in the educational enterprise. For that is the primary purpose of this book—to provide useful guidance for educational policymakers, practitioners, and parents—toward establishing effective conditions for improving learning and settings for learning, such as schools.

I will describe the diversity of ways in which such technologies have been used for learning and teaching, in which their design has been guided by different perspectives on learning, and by which assessments of the "effects" of their use have been made. It is also important to view such considerations against a backdrop of rapidly changing conditions in how accessible computational, software, and networking resources are to schools, and what properties these technologies are coming to have (e.g., greater speed of interactivity, wireless connectivity, more frequent use of graphics, animation, and video).

There is another important reason to consider technologies in education, beyond their potentials for improving the provision of education per se. Over the past fifteen years, computers and their affiliated media and communication technologies have become a fundamental fact of life in this country. They increasingly undergird how citizens and institutions work, learn, and play, and are ubiquitous in our living space. The Secretary's Commission on Achieving Necessary Skills (SCANS) of the U.S. Department of Labor says that "those unable to use . . . [technology] face a lifetime of menial work." Such technologies are thus essential to education for the future, and it is the responsibility of education to find designs for their effective use, or our schools will fall drastically out of step with society.

A recent study from the U.S. Congress's Office of Technology Assessment (OTA, 1995) estimates that in spring 1995 there were

- About 5.8 million computers in United States schools for use in instruction for about 50 million precollege students.
- At least one television and videocassette recorder in every

school, and 41 percent of teachers with a television in their classroom.

- Only one in eight teachers with a telephone in the classroom, and 1 percent of teachers with voice mail.
- Only 3 percent of all instructional rooms connected to the Internet, though 35 percent of public schools have some kind of Internet access.

I believe that such technologies are neither sufficiently nor effectively used in American schools today. On the high end of estimates in the 1995 OTA report, the average K-12 student spends only about two hours a week using a computer, and only one-third of our teachers identify themselves as "computer-using." A large proportion of the school computers (e.g., Apple IIs) are outdated, and cannot handle most software available today.

I begin this chapter by presenting a framework for thinking about the uses of educational technologies. Second, I provide a taxonomy of different uses of computing in education, discussing the theoretical foundations for those uses that define what outcomes the technologies are expected to provide, and under what conditions they have had such outcomes. I then proceed to highlight the fundamental influence of the *social context* of educational technology use in determining any *outcomes* that might result from such uses. Third, with these concerns about social context in mind, I introduce the concept of an on-line "School Depot" to serve educators' appropriation of educational technologies for improving teaching and learning (by analogy to the home-renovation superstore chain, "Home Depot"). What are some of the practical aspects of establishing a culture of improvement in school environments that plan to substantively integrate educational technologies?

A Framework for Educational Technologies

Technology in classrooms provides an extraordinarily complex nexus between institutional and societal change, and presents intricate challenges to the scientific and social analysis of learning. Educational technologies are neither simply a way of automating existing educational practice for efficiency nor a means of innovating and reforming practice through the technologies alone.

It is useful to make an analogy to a basic tool to illustrate a fundamental and often neglected point about educational technologies. Consider a particular type of hammer that was designed to support particular activities—say, nail hammering (with a flat hammer head) and removal (with its claw side). The designer's intentions, as expressed in this tool, do not *guarantee* that the user of the hammer will use the tool in the ways that the designer intended. But the properties of the tool—such as its size, shape, surfaces, weight, and materials—furnish means to use the tool in the intended ways. The user may force this tool into uses ill-matched to its design, such as breaking rocks. The user may also come to invent positive uses of the nail hammer that the designer never intended, such as making the claw end serve to pry up loose boards during house renovation, or to loosen up soil before planting seeds in the spring.

In a like vein, the user of educational technology in the classroom receives *some* guidance from the designer in matching activities using that technology to its properties. But the properties of these educational technologies, just like those of the nail hammer above, do not ensure their use according to the intentions of the designer. And, in like vein again, the users of educational technologies may invent positive, and not only negative, uses of the educational technologies, which were unanticipated by its designers.

In light of this tool analogy, I will now characterize components of a sociocultural framework for thinking about the uses of educational technologies.

Design Ideology

The first component is made up of the primary design influences for the technology. For example, what views of learning, the learner, knowledge, and outcomes, served to guide the design of the technology? On what we may call here the "design side" of the educational technology, the technology-as-artifact comes as a carrier of expectations. The properties it will have are expected by the design ideology to guide its "appropriate use" in educational activities.

Design Properties

The second component involves the properties that are said to be part of the technology itself—its "functions"—which are usually characterized by its designers. What properties of the technology are expected to enable fulfillment of the designer's intentions in the uses of the technology?

Design Interpretation

The third component involves the social, interpretive environment in which this technology is introduced and used. On this "use side" of educational technology, the technology comes into the setting, to the students, teachers, principal, and other administrators, as something that is *interpreted*, like a text—and not with just one meaning, but many. In other words, the intended design of the technology may not be obvious from its properties. How it comes to be talked about, thought about, and used will determine what consequences the technology will have for learning and teaching. A great diversity of influences affects how this object will be conceived of, and what it will be associated with (e.g., vocational education, drill and practice of basic skills, carrier of powerful ideas, or powerful multimedia motivator for the economically disadvantaged). These influences include

1. The promise computers are supposed to hold as harbingers of a new world of education, "attracting," "empowering," "personalizing," and "motivating" youth and "professionalizing" teaching. Teachers and administrators alike may see computers positively or negatively, depending on how the technology may fit with, help evolve, or obstruct the work conditions and power relations in their own institutions.
2. The positive media images of the value of computers as an index of modernization, efficiency, and the likelihood of jobs for those who master their uses; or the negative images of computers as de-skilling workers, reducing face-to-face interactions and hands-on learning, and promoting surveillance.
3. The genres of media-pop culture such as MTV, feature films, broadcast television, and videogames in new multimedia uses of computing.

Some positive aspects of the "use side" of design are that computers may enable teachers to shift their roles in supporting student learning from "sage on the stage" to "guide on the side," and empower their teaching activities. They may allow teachers to model for students educationally desired forms of activity and thinking too constrained by previous classroom tools.

Some negative aspects of the "use side" of design are that teachers are aware of potential threats of "integrated learning systems" (a form of centrally managed, closed network of computer-assisted instruction) to their autonomy in selecting means for meeting student learning objectives. Teachers may be concerned about new kinds of required accountabilities. They may be worried about their teaching becoming dependent on resolving the computer-related technical support issues. Also, with some of the uses of educational technologies I describe below, the new questions students raise for teachers in open-ended learning environments may challenge the limits of the teachers' knowledge and authority in ways they find difficult to handle. Teachers who are undersupported in training and release time and disempowered from using their own judgments about how to appropriately employ computers for augmenting their teaching may feel taken over by these technologies rather than empowered by them.

For students, too, the interpretive frameworks for computers will shape their use. For example, students' identity formation involves their affiliation with specific social groups, which is a process particularly salient in the adolescent years. This will mean that there are signal values of technology acceptance or rejection. Whether or not students react with enthusiasm to these tools will have broad influence over their uses in and out of the classroom.

The Opportunities and Obstacles of Educational Technologies

How have technologies been used for learning and teaching? On one extreme, technologies have been used to "automate," or make "more efficient," traditional methods of instruction, such as by providing drill and practice in basic multiplication facts. On the other extreme, technologies have been used to provide experience with the same productivity tools that are used in work (such as word processors, spreadsheets, and database programs) and in research (such as in the use of microcomputer-based labs for collecting data such as temperature and graphing its changes over time, or in scientific data analysis programs). *The guiding contexts of different uses of technology have thus been very different.* In one context, technology use promotes "business as usual"; in the other, it involves accelerating student access to learning through complex, authentic tasks in order to achieve the higher standards targeted in educational reforms.

I will next present a helpful taxonomy of uses of educational technologies (from Means et al., 1993). Each category of design for technologies has been guided by different theories of learning, or to use the language above, different "design ideologies." Different design properties have emerged from these ideologies, and different interpretations of these categories of technology are found in their uses. Correspondingly, different kinds of assessments have been made of the "effects" of using such educational technologies.

Technologies for Tutorial Learning

Through computer-assisted instruction (CAI), tutors and drill-and-practice programs have been used as "instructional delivery" vehicles for a great diversity of subjects. Common CAI programs teach spelling and basic mathematical skills such as adding, and highlight memorization of facts and theories in subjects such as science and social studies. At the core of this use of technology for education is the traditional model of education as the "transmission" of knowledge from the teacher to the student whose memory will be tested in order to measure achievement. CAI has appealed to educators because of such design properties as brief and branching lessons, well-defined feedback, careful student performance records, and good fit to this traditional pedagogy. Today's CAI programs are often bundled in "integrated learning systems" for managing individualized instruction. They provide for little flexibility in design interpretation—since the very point is a controlled learning experience "delivered" by computer.

Studies of the outcomes of computerized instruction document that on conventional achievement tests, students who receive CAI do as well as or better than students taught with traditional instruction (e.g., students who receive CAI demonstrate increased test item accuracy).

Critiques of this work have emphasized either methodological flaws or misguided educational theory. Critiques that emphasize methodological flaws argue that superior effects from CAI as compared to live instruction are not due to the computer, but to the teaching method embedded in its use (Clark, 1994). Critiques that emphasize misguided theory acknowledge that there is a place for such skill training in K-12 education—but as a broad model for education, the transmission approach is problematic (CTGV, 1995; Means et al., 1993; OTA, 1995). The transmission approach fails to prepare students for a more competitive workplace in which open-ended inquiry, more complex tasks, and collaborative activity are common. Furthermore, it may waste students' time by having them practice skills that are irrelevant due to universal access to computation (e.g., CAI lessons on multiplying fractions instead of an emphasis on calculator use and estimating results from calculations).

Technologies for Exploratory Learning

The use of computers to provide electronic databases, programming languages, simulations, and other kinds of "microworlds" for student-directed explorations has become increasingly common. Interactive video is an increasingly frequent application with videodisc and CD-ROM players in the classroom. Videos often depict rich phenomena and events in such subjects as science, history, and social studies of contemporary life.

A design ideology different from the transmission model guides the design and use of such learning tools. Designers of these tools and the educators who use them seek to provide opportunities for the learner to engage in complex comprehension, reasoning, and authoring tasks that are similar to such tasks in the real world. Learners "construct" new knowledge by engaging their present understanding when thinking about the content provided by these more realistic problems and are motivated to understand a subject by pursuing their own questions about it. Basic skills are learned as larger problems are considered; that is, basic skills become useful rather than decontextualized procedures. Information technologies transform students into discoverers and authors of new information and meaning. Simulation technologies offer students insights into complex systems, including such topics as fractal mathematics, chaos, urban planning, and ecology.

Design properties of such technology that attract educators and learners include rapid electronic access to vast repositories of information (in on-line encyclopedias and databases), and modeling functions that enable learners to frame and test hypotheses about how real-world systems work (e.g., urban planning in SimCity).

Because of the focus on multidisciplinary inquiry, open-ended explorations, and more complex tasks, it is rare for narrow measures of traditional student achievement to be taken when such exploratory learning environments are studied. Instead, assessments of student learning have tended to include "case studies" of students' work (e.g., portfolio outcomes), or have held up the valued learning outcome of the students' use of these systems itself as an index of prima facie importance. As for design interpretation, without substantial support for professional development, teachers might view these exploratory technologies as difficult to connect to the core curriculum for purposes of accountability.

Technologies as Applications

Looking to how computers were used in society, education came to adopt the "tools" provided by computers at work and in other contexts. In the early 1980s, this strategy meant word processing for writing, spreadsheets for mathematical modeling and science, and databases for building up and searching information during research inquiries in many subject domains. Today, it also includes desktop publishing, authoring multimedia documents, CAD (computer-aided design), scientific visualization of complex data, animation, and digital video editing. The design ideology of such tools is to provide "cognitive technologies" that enable more complex activity, with less error and effort, than can be achieved without the technologies. The pedagogy underlying using such applications has been "learning by doing," often associated with John Dewey's work early in this century, but reborn in recent work emphasizing "situated learning" and instructional strategies such as "cognitive apprenticeships." To enable students to learn through participation in complex activities, this educational orientation seeks to harness the power of tools and human supports that characterized learning before schools were even invented. Such tools also lend themselves well to multidisciplinary tasks (e.g., writing and science investigations), and can be "integrated" throughout the subjects of the school curriculum. In one dramatic example, scientific visualization tools allow precollege learners to use the same techniques and data as those used by professional scientists.[1]

The difficulties with this approach often come from this very freedom of design interpretation—it is not a simple matter for teachers to integrate such "flexible" tools into the curriculum. More important, such uses of computers make evident that new technologies should change curriculum, for their use is changing what learners need to know (Pea, 1993). The activity of drill and practice in multiplying and dividing fractions makes very little sense given that calculators are now commonplace. The technologies shift the burden of computation to the computer, and make the human's role one of meaningfully using mathematics to reason about situations. Time in mathematics education is far better spent, according to curriculum experts in the field of mathematics teaching, on helping students achieve facile use and understanding of how the symbol systems of mathematics may be used to model the world and think about it. While this "shifting ground" of learning goals with developments in technology is an important lesson, it is also a ground for controversy. Any time instructional goals are changed or technology is made instrumental to the achievement of learning objectives, there are disputes about the appropriateness of students' using technology to do part of the problem-solving tasks presented in education.

Another difficulty is that the wide range of useful application programs can mean that students and teachers need to learn to use quite a few distinct software programs. In a worst case, some

---

[1] See the World Wide Web server on the Learning through Collaborative Visualization (CoVis) Project at http://www.covis.nwu.edu

schools "teach" students how to operate different word processors, rather than teach them to use a word processor to write better.

We also often find instructional time devoted to teaching students how computers work, because in using computers as tools, fundamental concepts and processes in information technology and sometimes in computer science need to be understood. The 1980s fashion for separate courses in "computer literacy" has now thankfully faded. Many teachers weave in such instruction as students develop proficiency in specific uses of computers. Nonetheless, recent studies document that worldwide a predominant use of computers in education is to teach *about* computers rather than *with* computers. Up to half of the computer use in upper secondary schools is computer education rather than computer use for academic subjects (Becker, 1993). And in U.S. schools, only small proportions of computer access time are devoted to subjects such as mathematics, science, and writing, in which computers are fundamental to adult work.

Furthermore, learning to program a computer for its own sake rather than for particular purposes of modeling or inquiry in science or social studies is viewed as less significant than it was in the 1980s. This shift is in part due to a recognition that programming is unlikely to serve as a general-purpose way of teaching thinking skills, because the considerable knowledge specific to a given programming language or an application area renders the "general" aspects of cognitive skill affiliated with programming rather small.

Appraisals of the tool applications of computers in education have tended to highlight the value of students' learning to use such tools for life outside school. As students use computers for electronic library research, on-line data collection, and writing and preparing desktop publications in collaborative learning groups, they are learning crucial inquiry, analysis, and synthesis skills and are applying these skills to many different subjects.

Technologies for Communication

With the integration of computing and communications has emerged widespread interest in using computer-based communication technologies for education. Perhaps the greatest passion is for students to have connection to the Internet, the huge network of networks that connects computers around the world. The primary design ideology behind telecommunications is to enable and even supersede the capabilities of face-to-face interaction. Initiated in the defense community and its use broadened by university researchers, the Internet is now the backbone of electronic communication, and, increasingly, commerce, for over fifty million computer users.

Design properties of such communication technologies as electronic mail, conferencing systems, file transfer, and World Wide Web standards for multimedia file storage, display, and retrieval enable students and teachers to write and send messages to one another, download information and programs from remote computers, and participate in such exciting educational paradigms as collaborative learning, teleapprenticeships in particular knowledge domains, and telementoring relationships (e.g., with a scientist advisor to work on an investigative project). The ability to go beyond the school walls in order to tap distributed expertise and databases is perhaps the greatest motivation for educators to this use of computing. Network technologies promote local and global collaboration and exchange of information among students, schools, and society.

Educational projects involving such communication technologies have tended to provide textured accounts of their patterns of use by students and other participants, and to highlight students' extensive writing and reading in such electronic exchanges. Of all four categories presented here, telecommunications perhaps represents the greatest flexibility for design interpretation in the educational setting—with the greatest challenges to teachers to make effective use of the technologies.

Synthesis of the Opportunities and Obstacles of Educational Technologies

Across these different guiding perspectives on learning and these varying intervention contexts for uses of educational technology, tremendous potentials for enriching learning experiences and teaching outcomes have been demonstrated. Of particular interest are those uses of educational technologies that are well matched to the higher standards of complex thinking and problem solving sought in today's workplace, even though they are ill matched to the traditional "transmission" model of education common in today's classrooms. Yet persistent problems have emerged when researchers and practitioners seek to implement educational improvements with new technologies on a broad scale. For example:

- Teachers have difficulties linking new technologies to local curricula. And right now, they do not have time to effectively integrate tools into instruction (OTA, 1995).
- There are large differences in how teachers use innovative educational technologies, with corresponding differences in students' learning outcomes. These effects were not so apparent in "teacher-proof" uses of technology to train students in basic skills, because teachers relinquished control to the computer for arranging curriculum and guiding student progress.
- When researchers disappear, classrooms often revert to traditional forms, even when new technologies remain in place. Teachers "close their classroom doors and teach as they were taught" (Smith and O'Day, 1990).

Many of the research studies in educational technology are efforts based on the best learning theory and research findings available. Thanks to the largess of federal funding agencies and private corporations, this research has often included the best available technologies and technological support staff. Under these "design experiment" conditions, it may not be surprising that important improvements in learning were achieved, that students' proficiencies in inquiry improved, and that impressive projects were produced (Hawkins and Collins, forthcoming).

Yet these ideal circumstances for educational "design experiments" will not and cannot be replicated in the large scale. Even with the highest quality equipment, staff, and theoretical underpinnings and the good intentions of all participants, we have learned that it is the *particularities* of individual contexts—the orientations and activities of the different teachers, students, schools, and families in the community—that make the difference between educational gains and no effects whatsoever from the introduction of technological innovations.

Whatever else is "effective," it is *not* educational technologies per se. The social contexts are *all* important. They include not only the technology but its content, the teaching strategies used both "in" the software and "around it" in the classroom, and the classroom environment itself. It is a recurrent finding that the effects of the best software can be neutralized through improper use, and that even poorly designed software can be creatively extended to serve important learning goals.

In this light, consider that the United States has a highly decentralized K-12 school system, with close to three million teachers and fifty million students. There is no national curriculum, but rather state and local control through school districts. Each school system must negotiate state and federal mandates along with the expectations and values of its local community. An effort to set national goals for education in order to prepare American students to compete in the global economy—a program called *Goals 2000*—was recently decimated by Congress. Each school system, each school, and each classroom struggles with its own unique blend of challenges and strengths.

These facts about American education not only create a fundamental tension in efforts for national improvement throughout a decentralized system but must also be faced when implementing improvement efforts that incorporate educational technologies. What educational technology initiatives could have a national impact in the face of such diversity?

Home Improvement and Educational Reform

The success of any educational reform initiative using technologies depends on embracing and utilizing the diversity of American schools and communities. I propose that we address this problem by looking at the services provided by the builder-supply and home-renovator store called "Home Depot." My wife and I owned a fixer-upper in Northern California and became quite dependent upon the store. After four years in Chicago, where there are no Home Depots, we moved back to Palo Alto for a sabbatical. The first time we went to the local Home Depot for supplies, we realized how much we had missed this place.

Home Depot is a vast superstore with virtually every possible component and tool for any home or garden project. But beyond that, there are knowledgeable workers in the aisles: roaming carpenters, contractors, plumbers, electricians, and other home fixer-uppers. We go into Home Depot with a rough sense of what we want to do, a good description of the context of the project, and a sense for a budget, and their job is to help tailor a solution that will meet our needs. Walk in with a problem (our most recent was to build a nine-foot-wide safety gate between two buildings over a brick walkway leading to a pool), and in thirty minutes all of the parts will be in your basket, and step-by-step instructions for building it will be in hand. In addition to support for individual projects, Home Depot holds free seminars on special topics, and their long store hours ensure that there is always support available—even over the telephone—for projects in process.

Home Depot *empowers* us as home builders, not by leaving us to shop alone, or by *taking over* as experts, or by ignoring the local knowledge we have about our home, but by guiding and supporting our creativity and initiative as we seek to improve that home. We emerge not only with a vision for a solution and strategies and tactics to solve our problem, but with a deeper systemic understanding of how the whole house and garden thing "works." This experience provides general expertise that we can utilize the next time a related problem arises, and that we can share with neighbors and friends when their plumbing blows up.

As you can tell, I love Home Depot. It helps us solve our problems and feel great at the same time. I trust Home Depot to make sure I succeed every time. Can you imagine nearly three million school teachers saying such things about a program in support of improving their teaching with technologies? Now consider the outlines of a program, following this analogy, that I will call "School Depot."[2]

---

[2] This chapter is not the place to provide detailed considerations of which aspects of such a program should be provided by the federal government, the states, local school districts, or business and industry. I would argue that such issues as equity of access, coordination across states, telecommunications subsidies, and laws protecting children would be strong candidates for a federal role.

Research experience with "design experiments" involving educational technologies to reorganize processes of education has found that teachers do not like it when technology know-it-alls come into their classrooms with fix-it attitudes that do not utilize their own teaching expertise. Teachers need recognition for their knowledge of local communities, instructional goals, students, curriculum resources, and assessment. Moreover, given the time pressures and classroom stresses faced by teachers, educational technologies, no matter how well crafted or supported, can be a huge burden rather than an opportunity. Without care, approaching educational improvement with technologies risks alienating teachers or yielding minimal outcomes.

The 1995 Congressional Office of Technology Assessment (OTA) report, *Teachers and Technology: Making the Connection*, observes that: "Helping teachers use technologies effectively may be the most important step to assuring that current and future investments in technology are realized" (p. 2). In the past, the focus and funding in schools has largely been devoted to selecting technologies. In the future, teachers should be offered access to successful models and asked what they want to do with educational technologies to improve instruction. Promoting best practice and effective pedagogy is the primary issue. A productive approach will provide adequate training and continuing support to enable teachers to fulfill their objectives with these new tools, as well as guide them to discover new and more demanding objectives, and alternative practices. Teachers need far more support and training than they receive today. They wish for experience with models of the ways that technology can be integrated with curriculum and enhance their teaching. They must have time and administrative support for using these innovations. While on average, school districts devote only 15 percent of their technology budgets to teacher training, the consensus from many states that have experienced implementation efforts (e.g., Florida, Texas, Washington) is that 30 percent would be a more adequate figure (OTA, 1995).

The OTA report notes that support can include *resources*, such as a personal computer with modem and phone line in each teacher's classroom, *release time* for planning and creating applications of computer-based tools (such as databases for history or science explorations, multimedia lessons in English and fine arts, or spreadsheet applications in mathematics), or *professional opportunities*—for identifying cross-curricular applications, team-teaching with their colleagues, or networking with peers from other schools to share experiences and best practices.

In short, educational reforms with technologies must continually help teachers *do their work*, even as they help researchers and policymakers understand what works and what does not. And that is what "School Depot" would do. The aim should be to open up partnerships in which new synergies may grow between the local knowledge of teachers and the knowledge developed by researchers and technology experts outside schools. We can no longer afford technology use just "at the margins" of education (Cohen, 1988), such as in Advanced Placement courses and special education, when it should be fundamental to the entire educational enterprise.

What would need to be done to create "School Depot"?

1. *Give every teacher a computer with a direct connection to the Internet.* Start by getting every teacher and every school wired to the Internet. From any technology platform, a diversity of resources is now accessible through telecommunications, allowing for downloading of information and programs from hundreds of thousands of computers around the globe, as well as electronic mail and teleconferencing interactions with others. In our current studies on network-enhanced science education (see footnote 1), we have found that a level of telecommunications service provision called "basic-rate ISDN" (i.e., connectivity at the rate of 56 kbs) is a minimal standard. Slower dial-up connections through a modem tend to be inadequate. A 56 kbs or faster service is needed for reasonable access to multimedia resources and for real-time communication and collaboration.

2. *Establish a national registry of software technologies useful for education.* Create a national clearinghouse of educational software technologies where everything available is registered and in which reviews are provided by experts as well as by educational users. With the web server technologies available today, this is less difficult than it may sound. Companies and suppliers would be responsible for maintaining up-to-date product information, and simple web-based "forms" could be used over the network by educators and other professionals to submit reviews from the field.

3. *Create a multimedia database of educational technology case studies.*
Design a database that allows teachers to create and to access
case studies like those used by business schools. These case
studies would provide ideas and cautions concerning the
realities of inventing, integrating, and maintaining effective
use of a technology for particular learning purposes. Peabody
College at Vanderbilt University has pioneered such an
approach in teacher professional development (OTA, 1995).
A variety of organizational schemes could point teachers to
cases that most closely match their own situations. These
cases could offer the educator visionary a "pull" into reform-
oriented activities with technologies rather than a technology-
based "push" from either federal or state top-down reforms.
And they could help school districts forge their technology
plans—an effort beginning with goals and integrally involving
teachers.

4. *Establish design forums.* The Internet may be used to replicate
the social network of information and expertise present in
the aisles of each Home Depot, but for improving teaching
and learning. Just as Home Depot holds seminars on such
topics as how to install automatic garden watering systems,
School Depot would hold Internet forums on topics such
as what software is available for teaching introductory physics,
how to assess students' multimedia research projects, how
to develop facility in the use of electronic library resources,
how to identify and train a computer coordinator for your
school. Networked design discussion forums could be
established and populated by teachers and moderated by
teachers, curriculum experts, technology experts, and researchers. These forums would be crucial mediators of broad
reform-oriented appropriations of educational technologies—
for the people who understand local opportunities and
obstacles to technology innovations for learning and teaching
are the educators who live them every day.

In these design forums, participants would help one
another to craft innovative local uses of the learning and
teaching technologies they find in the national registry, and
identify appropriate assessment techniques for the learning
targeted by such activities. Kids and parents could also link
into these forums to share what they find useful, compelling,
or problematic. The role of an initiative such as School

Depot should be to facilitate teachers' creativity in curriculum integration of technology—on an ongoing basis—not just to "train" teachers in brief workshops on the mechanics of computer operations, which is the typical in-service "support" that teachers receive today. Some states, such as Texas, have pioneered the use of regional technology resource centers and on-line forums for teachers' continuing professional development.

5. *Provide "just-in-time" support to teachers in effective uses of technologies.* Go to the schools when teachers need help. One thing Home Depot does not do is come to your house to see how your project is going. In business, such guidance in reform-oriented activities is called "change management." Most schools do not have an on-site person devoted to facilitating uses of technology. While this function is probably best handled at the state and local levels, it would be nice if federal support of a School Depot could provide standards for a coordinated framework of support and analysis across states. "Virtual visits" to the classroom can use the telecommunications technology itself to provide just-in-time support to the teacher seeking to effectively integrate new technologies.

6. *Establish educational telecommunications subsidies.* Unpredictable usage fees on a business model have proven to be a deterrent to many schools considering Internet access. As specified in the Telecommunications Act of 1996, the federal government has the power to support School Depot by providing telecommunications hookup and connection time subsidies to schools. And state governments, such as in Texas, have successfully negotiated very advantageous telecommunications installation and access rates for their schools.

7. *Provide links to teacher preparation.* Use School Depot to make sure that teacher education is tuned to the realities of educational technologies in actual schools. Unfortunately, preservice teacher education today rarely provides experiences in either coursework or internship placement with computer or communications technologies (OTA, 1995). Yet as a resource for teaching, technologies may help teachers do their work in more effective and satisfying ways, enable them to establish different arrangements of learning environments, or provide access to critical information for improving their teaching practices.

Conclusion

As I have noted, use of computer technologies in society and in schools often leads to redefining what learners need to know, and to changing the nature of instruction and assessment. We know that educational computing has demonstrable benefits. But the studies commonly illustrating these benefits rest on a CAI model of technology use that is no longer adequate to guide design and implementation of educational computing. The CAI model commonly emphasizes teaching the same things more rapidly, and ignores higher educational goals, new learning objectives, and new instructional strategies for teachers to use that were impossible (or cumbersome) without the technology. Such a CAI model is not consonant with emphases on active learning, authentic and challenging learning tasks, and performance-based assessment in educational reform-oriented uses of computers. CAI studies usually restricted their outcome measures to multiple-choice tests that do not tap the communication skills, teamwork, and whole-task reasoning that higher standards for K-12 education demand. Such CAI studies have also insufficiently recognized the diverse social contexts of technology use in classrooms.

A new generation of empirical studies of innovations in educational technology use is underway (e.g., Hawkins and Collins, forthcoming). These action-oriented "design experiments" taking place throughout educational computing research are embedded in the complexities of real educational settings rather than in controlled laboratory studies. They are likely to have greater utility for improving educational processes and outcomes than did CAI research. The primary reasons are that the design experiment approach embraces the qualitative transformations that technology makes possible in what students need to know, and in how their activities can be structured for learning with such technologies (e.g., in distributed collaborative groups). Education needs many more such design experiments. Design experiments involve ongoing partnerships of design, intervention, and evaluation that engage researchers with school systems in realistic conditions over time as technology-based educational innovations are brought into the classroom and researchers seek to establish patterns for the effective use of these innovations. A primary aim of such work has been to provide guidance regarding what works and does not, at a sufficient level of detail so that other schools can "scale" up the model provided in the design experiment.

But educators who take an overly cautious approach to educational technology planning and implementation by awaiting "definitive research" will miss crucial opportunities to learn how to improve the educational experiences in their schools through ongoing testing, monitoring, and refinement at their school sites. It is noteworthy that double standards are often placed on research on learning with educational computing: We insist on research results to warrant investments that are rarely insisted upon for other teaching and learning resources.

In this chapter, I have provided a high-level characterization of an imagined support service for education, which I called "School Depot." It would have the aim of guiding educators' appropriation of educational technologies for improving teaching and learning. This focus has emerged from extensive research on the social context of information technology use, particularly the classroom context, as providing major determinants of the effectiveness of such educational tools. Comprehensive resources, including information, technologies, and ongoing involvement with human expertise, are needed by educators, as well as learners, to achieve effective results with such tools. An initiative like School Depot is needed to coordinate and motivate the creative use of these resources for improving education. It should link teachers, parents, students, developers, and researchers in substantive and sustainable ways. It is realistic: There are already many commercial and free software products that begin to provide the necessary technical functionality. Furthermore, since much of the content is provided by participants, simply "starting it up" would begin the process of providing valuable content and facilitating synergistic partnerships.

Since in their uses of computer tools teachers and students continue the process of design by virtue of inventing and ignoring aspects of their intended designs, it is unproductive to consider these folks to be "problems" for the breakthrough possibilities of educational computing. Instead, their perspectives must be acknowledged, respected, and nurtured. During the post-Sputnik curriculum reforms, "teacher proofing" of instructional materials was a mistaken objective. It still is. Teachers *must* be partners in design in order for new technologies to work in education. New design methods recognizing the contributions of teachers and students to educational computing should be developed, assessed, and broadly disseminated through such a mechanism as School Depot if the promises of computers for learning and teaching are to be broadly fulfilled.

Comprehensive References

CTGV (Cognition and Technology Group at Vanderbilt). (1995). Looking at technology in context: A framework for understanding technology and education research. In D. C. Berliner and R. C. Calfee (Eds.), *The handbook of educational psychology*. New York: Macmillan Publishing.

Means, B., Blando, J., Olson, K., Middleton, T., Morocco, C. C., Remz, A. R., and Zorfass, J. (1993, September). *Using technology to support education reform*. Washington, D.C.: U.S. Government Printing Office.

OTA (U.S. Congress, Office of Technology Assessment). (1995, April). *Teachers and technology: Making the connection*. OTA-EHR-616. Washington, DC: U.S. Government Printing Office.

Other Citations

Becker, H. J. (1993, May). Teaching *with* and *about* computers in secondary schools. *Communications of the ACM 36*(5), 69–72.

Clark, R. E. (1994). Media will never influence learning. *Educational Technology Research and Development 42*(2), 21–29.

Cohen, D. K. (1988). Educational technology and school organization. In R. S. Nickerson & P. P. Zodhiates (eds.), *Technology in education: Looking toward 2020* (pp. 231–264). Hillsdale, N.J.: Lawrence Erlbaum Associates.

Hawkins, J., and Collins, A. (forthcoming). *Design experiments in educational technology*. New York: Cambridge University Press.

Pea, R. D. (1993). Practices of distributed intelligence and designs for education. In G. Salomon (ed.). *Distributed cognitions* (pp. 47–87). New York: Cambridge University Press.

Smith, M. S., and O'Day, J. (1990). Systemic school reform. In *Politics of Education Association Yearbook* (pp. 233–267). London: Taylor & Francis.

Chapter 14

Teacher Beliefs

Greta Morine-Dershimer
and
Stephanie Corrigan

Mandating change in curriculum, instruction, and assessment is a timeworn procedure for prompting change in teacher practice. Although state and federal policy changes have influenced practice only weakly, or for brief periods of time, policymakers continue to try to improve education by mandating change. One recent set of case studies reveals the barriers that teacher beliefs erect as teachers begin to implement new policy.

In 1985, state policymakers in California announced a new set of curriculum guidelines in their *Mathematics Curriculum Framework*. To help insure successful change, they pressed publishers to develop textbooks conforming to the new framework, and they began developing new tests to assess the goals articulated therein. These goals, consistent with the recent research on learning and instruction, stated that pupils should be able to reason mathematically, apply mathematics to everyday situations, understand the conceptual basis of mathematical procedures, and evaluate mathematical arguments. To accomplish these goals, teachers should use manipulative materials, encourage pupil discussion of alternative ways of framing and solving problems, and explore with pupils their reasoning about why their solutions make sense. These goals and instructional processes are in conflict with many teachers' traditional beliefs about teaching, learning, and mathematical content, but they are in accord with respected research on learning and instruction.

During the second year of statewide implementation of the new California mathematics framework, researchers from Michigan State University observed and interviewed twenty-three elementary teachers in six schools to identify the ways in which they were using the new framework in their teaching. In each of five reported case studies, the teachers had adapted the new concepts and procedures to conform to their own belief systems and techniques of practice, drastically transforming the mandated curriculum in the process.

For example, one teacher, Joe S., saw the recommended procedure for pictorial representation of mathematics problems as an added "tool" to help his fifth-graders arrive at the right answer more rapidly. Another, Mark B., followed the new textbook with his fifth-grade class, but skipped the lessons that did not fit his belief that pupils should be learning mathematical rules and procedures step by step by step. He also adapted lessons that required manipulatives so that he could teach them without the recommended materials, because he saw himself as untrained in these procedures. Cathy S. conceived of manipulatives as a way to make number facts more concrete, so that her second-graders could memorize the facts faster. Mrs. O. had been converted several years earlier to the use of manipulatives to promote mathematical understanding with her second-graders, but she accepted right answers, rejected wrong answers, and never asked how pupils had arrived at the answers they gave. Carol T. adapted the recommended technique of having students explain how they got an answer, but her second-graders' explanations, to be considered correct, had to follow precisely the steps and phrases she had taught them.

These teachers willingly modified their practice as a result of the new curriculum policy, but the modifications were limited and shaped by the teachers' beliefs, knowledge, and experience.

The result in each case was a strange amalgamation of traditional and innovative mathematics instruction. The outer trappings of the new framework were evident in their lessons; the central intentions were elusive. These case studies illustrate one of the rarely acknowledged problems associated with trying to improve teaching by mandating change in practice: Teacher beliefs strongly influence teacher perceptions and behavior, and teacher beliefs are difficult to change.

Characteristics of Teacher Beliefs

Why are teacher beliefs so difficult to change, and why do they have such an impact on behavior? The critical features of teacher beliefs help to explain the problem.

- Beliefs about teaching are formed during early school experiences, long before students enter teacher-preparation programs.
- Beliefs are deeply personal, and have a strong emotional component.
- Beliefs serve as a filter or screen, influencing teachers' interpretations of events, and they may distort information processing.
- The longer a belief is held, the more difficult it is to change.
- Beliefs about teaching are initially formed from the perspective of a pupil, and thus fail to account for the full complexity of classroom interactions.
- Constellations of beliefs form a belief system, with some beliefs being more central than others. Educational beliefs are connected to other beliefs in the system.

Prior Beliefs as Constraints on Change

Beliefs formed early tend to persevere, despite contrary evidence that may be encountered through education or experience. A complicating factor is that many beliefs are tacit, difficult to bring to conscious awareness, and not readily available for verbalization or analysis. Explicit presentations of information, such as lectures in college classes, rarely impact prior beliefs.

Beliefs about Teaching and Learning

Many prospective teachers were pupils who felt happy and competent in their childhood school environment. Since their experiences with school were largely positive, their beliefs support maintenance of traditional educational processes. As one prospective teacher noted, "I always wanted to be a teacher, ever since I was a little kid. I used to teach all my animals on a chalkboard I had hanging in my room. I would line them up and pass out stickers and tests." When newer instructional techniques are demonstrated in college courses, prospective teachers with similar memories may dismiss these as inappropriate, unnecessary, or unmanageable. Alternatively, they may seem to accept a newer technique, but their prior beliefs lead them to misinterpret the underlying intent, and thus misuse it.

Personal relationships loom large in prospective teachers' beliefs about teaching. They often recount experiences with particular teachers who played a crucial role, either positive or negative, in their own development. Former teachers are seen as models, and serve to shape prospective teachers' perceptions of their own future roles. Those planning to become secondary teachers tend to conceive of teaching as careful organization and management, with an emphasis on transmission of subject matter through interesting lectures. Those planning to become elementary teachers tend to conceive of teaching as promoting pupils' self-esteem and personal development. The ideal teacher is generally seen as caring, creative, and enthusiastic. Since personal characteristics are major factors in these definitions of the ideal, prospective teachers emphasize their own personal characteristics as crucial to their expectations of becoming good teachers. In the words of another prospective teacher, "I, like those who taught me, want to take on the challenge of teaching students. I feel that I have the talents to have an impact on the students as a few teachers had on me." Beliefs like this contribute to a false sense of competency in novice teachers, who consistently express the view that they will be better-than-average teachers. This reliance on personal characteristics prompts many to discount the importance of their professional preparation courses.

Prior beliefs about pupils stem from prospective teachers' own experiences as successful pupils, and reinforce their views that personal characteristics are crucial for successful teaching. They view most pupils as basically capable of learning, if motivated. They consider that good teachers can motivate pupils by stimulating their interest. And they think that interested pupils will learn by actively listening to a teacher's presentation of information. This comment of a prospective teacher is illustrative: "I was inspired by a former teacher who I respect and admire. She encouraged me, motivated me, and made the class fun. This is what I hope to do someday. When I become a teacher, I hope I am not dull and boring. I want my students to enjoy school." These types of interlocking beliefs support a lecture-style of teaching, and a knowledge-transmission approach to learning. Research in cognitive psychology shows that such methods produce little depth of understanding. The personal concepts developed independently by students through their everyday experiences conflict with information presented in these forms, and hinder understanding. The traditional view is in sharp contrast to our current understanding of learning as a process of individual and social construction of knowledge.

Teachers consistently rate student teaching and the initial years of classroom practice as the most important components of learning to teach. Since the settings for these experiences frequently reflect traditional educational processes, teachers' initial classroom practice often supports their prior beliefs about teaching and learning. Even in settings where more innovative procedures are promoted, these practical experiences may be interpreted in terms of prior beliefs and thus be seen as providing confirming evidence for the beliefs, making them stronger and harder to change.

Beliefs about Content

Both prospective and experienced teachers harbor implicit beliefs about content areas that have been formed primarily through their own experiences with that content in school. History has often been taught as a large collection of dates, names, and sequences of events, rather than as a system for determining facts by exploring alternative perceptions of events through careful analysis of various records. Science has frequently been introduced as a set body of knowledge about the world around us, rather than as a method for developing and testing competing explanations for the phenomena we observe. Mathematics has traditionally been presented as a set of procedures and rules to be learned by rote to the point of automaticity, rather than as a process for solving logical and real-world problems through deductive reasoning. Reading has traditionally been approached as a process of using decoding skills to discern an author's intent, failing to take into consideration the experiences the reader brings to the comprehension process.

Such traditional views of content tend to replicate themselves— teachers reproduce the same type of instruction they experienced as students. It is difficult for teachers to explain concepts they have never really understood or experienced themselves. To teach for understanding requires a depth of content knowledge that many teachers lack because of their traditional educational experiences. Content knowledge and beliefs about how knowledge is developed are closely intertwined and difficult to tease apart. These beliefs have an important impact on *what* is taught, as well as *how* it is taught.

Beliefs about Management

Beliefs about the role of the teacher as manager are formed early and reinforced often through experiences in school, media messages, and the expectations of parents and administrators. As media messages and the play of children indicate, teachers are seen as the "boss" in addition to being the provider of information or knowledge. This deep belief or image is difficult for most teachers to change.

Control is an issue about which teachers have definite beliefs. Many people begin teacher preparation with the aim of promoting pupil independence. To quote one prospective teacher, "My motives for becoming a teacher lie in the fact that I really want to facilitate young people's natural desire to become self-confident, independent, and knowledgeable." However, classroom practice, particularly during student teaching and the first years of teaching experience, makes novices more custodial and controlling in their beliefs and actions. Teacher beliefs in the need to control may move beyond ensuring appropriate pupil behavior to keeping tight reins on pupil information processing as well. As one student teacher put it, "I go through the lesson, putting the information on the board one step at a time, so that they have to keep up with me."

Beliefs about management as control are not surprising, since the structure and organization of schools and classrooms force consideration of the issue of control over pupils. Administrators and parents hold teachers accountable for acceptable pupil behavior. Teachers are legally liable for inappropriate or harmful behavior that occurs in their classrooms. These conditions promote novice teachers' beliefs in the need to control pupils' behavior and learning, and conflict with ideas introduced in teacher preparation programs about freedom, responsibility, and experimentation in learning.

Impact on Innovation

Teachers' prior beliefs help to explain why change in classroom practice is so difficult to achieve and sustain. Much of the research detailing the early demise of many promising educational innovations lays the blame at other doorsteps, but teacher beliefs are a critical deterrent to teacher adoption of new instructional techniques and new curriculum content. One experienced teacher of our acquaintance, confronted with a new state-mandated textbook for a revised curriculum, held the text aloft and declared defiantly to her student teacher, "Sometime this year someone from the central office will come into my room and ask me whether I've been using this book regularly. And I will be able to tell them honestly, yes, I've been using it. Because I'm using it right here on my desk as a paperweight. And later this year I plan to use it as a doorstop. Meanwhile I'm going to teach my kids some content they can understand, not all this new nonsense!"

The Influence of Beliefs on Practice

Teacher beliefs influence the instructional plans that teachers make and the types of activities they select to engage their pupils in learning. Their beliefs also impact what teachers observe in their interactions with pupils, as well as how they interpret and react to what they observe. All of these elements of instruction affect what pupils may learn.

Consider, for example, some lessons taught by two different groups of student teachers. The first group of teachers (Anne, Anita, and Amy) displayed beliefs about the importance of knowing the background and characteristics of pupils they would teach, and of drawing on principles of effective practice in planning their lessons. The second group (Chip, Candace, and Clay) placed no particular importance on pupil characteristics or principles of practice. Instead their beliefs about teaching and learning emphasized the importance of evaluation and assessment of pupils at the close of a lesson.

Anne planned a lesson for twelfth-grade English pupils that engaged them in working in pairs to analyze different poems. They then shared their analyses and criticisms of the poems with classmates. Anita planned a lesson for tenth-grade biology pupils that involved them in working in cooperative learning teams, where classmates who had become "experts" on particular types of organisms guided their teams through teacher-designed exercises, using videotapes and slides to illustrate characteristics of the organisms. Amy worked with a low-ability eighth-grade class reading "The Hound of the Baskervilles." Her lesson led pupils to compare the various suspects' motives and availability, to predict the identity of the murderer before reading Sherlock Holmes' solution. All these lessons encouraged pupils to work together in developing an understanding of subject-matter content.

These student teachers commented on their lessons as they reviewed videotapes of their teaching. Their comments reveal their beliefs in pupils' ability to learn:

- "If you point out, or lead them a little bit, they're real sharp."
- "He's my fastest student; he has lots of lightbulbs going on."
- "I try to give them a little space and see what they can do on their own before I jump in."

Other comments reveal beliefs about content and classroom management:

- "We talked earlier about how authors of stories convey through language what they're trying to say. Now I want them to see how poets convey ideas."
- "I can see how this unit is going to be really useful down the road. I'm trying to help them make connections between the groups of organisms they're studying now and the broad topics like evolution."
- "When students have a question, especially if it's something we've just gone over, instead of my repeating it, I'll have one of their peers restate it. It kind of reaffirms them as students, and their responsibility in the classroom."

These beliefs are consistent with research in cognitive psychology that shows the importance of pupils' taking responsibility for their own learning, and becoming dynamic participants in student-centered instructional activities.

The videotapes of these three lessons showed pupils actively engaged in meaningful discussion with their classmates and teachers. At the end of each lesson, pupils were asked to write down a "key idea" of the lesson and two things that they heard anybody saying during the lesson. Key idea statements showed the pupils' awareness of learning both content and procedures for becoming independent self-directed learners. For example, "There are many, many different views that can be taken from poems. Who knows what the author really means? You must think for yourself and get your own ideas. It helps to discuss the poem with a few other people."

Pupils' reports of what they heard being said showed that their attention in these lessons was focused on comments their classmates made about the subject-matter content of the lesson; for example: "Sam said that there are three types of worms—segmented, round, and flat." Pupils in these lessons were aware of learning from their own efforts, from the contributions of their peers, and from information provided by their teachers.

The lessons taught by the second group of student teachers provided a sharp contrast. Chip planned a lesson for eleventh-grade algebra pupils in which he gave a lecture-demonstration on how to use graphs to solve mathematical word problems.

Candace conducted a lesson in tenth-grade social studies in which she presented the range of political positions from reactionary to radical, noting contemporary and historical figures who could be placed in each category. Clay taught an eleventh-grade pre-calculus class by demonstrating procedures for solving interest-rate problems. All of these lessons required pupils to learn by listening to information provided by the teacher. There was little or no opportunity for pupils to offer or test their own ideas.

These three student teachers also commented on their lessons as they reviewed videotapes of their teaching. Although all three teachers described their pupils as bright and academically able, their comments reveal beliefs that pupils could not independently learn or contribute to the content being presented:

- "I felt like they would be lost as to my intent."
- "None of them gave the answers I was looking for, so I decided to pretty much ignore them."
- "They weren't really grasping any of the stuff I was talking about."

Other comments reveal beliefs about procedures teachers use that might help pupils learn content:

- "You want to use a precise language—to convey what you want to say, right to the T."
- "Sometimes I write things on the board that aren't exactly what I'm looking for. If there's a similar concept given by a pupil, I write that down and then underneath I'll write down the answer I originally had in mind."
- "I do try to get them involved, just to keep them on their toes somewhat."
- "I give them odd-numbered problems to do for homework, then the answer is in the back of the book. I want them to check their answers before they come to class so they can troubleshoot a little bit of their own problems, but that rarely happens. If they get it wrong in the back of the book, they just give up on that problem."

These beliefs are consistent with traditional approaches to teaching, portraying teachers and textbooks as the authoritative sources of information, and pupil motivation as a critical factor for learning.

The videotapes of these three lessons showed pupils who were withdrawn and bored, or who were carrying on side conversations with their peers on topics unrelated to lesson content. Their statements of key ideas in the lessons tended to be very general references to the main content, or rather sarcastic comments about the value of learning that content. For example:

- "Graphs can be used to find maximum and minimum values."
- "We learned the definitions of those terms that will help us better understand people and political issues."
- "There is more than one way to solve a system of equations."
- "The whole lesson was important, considering it's going to be on the test."
- "Our political system has too many definitions."
- "Solving systems using matrices, which will help me in my next life, after I die."

Pupils' reports of what they heard being said in the lessons showed that too much of their attention was focused on the side conversations that occurred:

- "What a great party this weekend!"
- "I like your hair."
- "Cathryn said something to the effect of, 'This sucks.'"

Pupils in these lessons were uninvolved, showed minimal interest in learning the content being presented, and displayed no sense of responsibility for their own learning or for that of their classmates.

The comments of pupils and student teachers about these lessons serve to illustrate the critical impact that teacher beliefs can have on the instructional processes selected for use and on learning. Both groups of student teachers were equally well-qualified academically and equally committed to promoting pupil learning. The pupils taught by Chip, Candace, and Clay were no less adept than those taught by Anne, Anita, and Amy. What prompted the very different procedures and outcomes observed in these two sets of lessons were the different sets of beliefs about teaching and learning held by the two groups of teachers. The most recent research on learning and instruction supports the type of beliefs exhibited by Anne, Anita, and Amy.

Procedures to Promote Change in Beliefs

The strength of traditional prior beliefs, reinforced by experiences as students and teachers, makes real change extremely difficult. Teachers implementing mandated changes interpret those mandates through the screen of their prior beliefs, modifying and adulterating the desired reform strategies. New practices require new beliefs.

Changing beliefs involves cognitive stress, discomfort, and ambiguity. In changing beliefs, individuals must reconcile or realign other related beliefs to resolve conflicts and contradictions, and come to terms with what actions guided by previous beliefs meant. Such cognitive reorganization is not easily or quickly accomplished. It can often be accompanied by realizations of error and feelings of failure or guilt. Most people avoid such situations.

Changing beliefs also requires resources that are often scarce in schools. Time for discussion, reflection, and experimentation is necessary to make implicit beliefs explicit and then work through changes or realignments in beliefs. Because changing beliefs and practices is disconcerting and uncomfortable, personal support and encouragement from supervisors and colleagues is often necessary. This requires supportive and trusting relationships between supervisors and colleagues in order for individuals to take risks that make them vulnerable, such as the intense self-analysis involved in changing beliefs. Such relationships are often missing in the hierarchical or isolated relationships found at all levels in education.

Studies show that effective change occurs slowly over time, with uneven progress. Some research indicates that purposeful changes in practice can lead to changes in beliefs, while other studies indicate that changes in beliefs lead to changes in practice. Which comes first is a chicken-and-egg question. It is clear, however, that the two types of change are closely interconnected. One does not occur without the other.

Changing Images

One recommended process for promoting change in teacher beliefs is the exploration of images or metaphors for teaching. Several studies have shown that changes in teachers' images of teaching are related to changes in their own behavior and associated changes in their pupils' participation in lessons.

In one study, Robert Bullough, a teacher educator at the University of Utah, worked with twenty-two secondary school teacher candidates over a full year, encouraging them to generate and periodically reconsider their metaphors for teaching. Images reported by these students included teacher as guide, coach, parent, artisan, problem fixer, manager, and policewoman. The most prevalent image was teacher as expert, an image consistent with the typical prior beliefs of prospective teachers. Over time, students in this study modified this view, deciding that there is much more to teaching than being the primary source of knowledge.

Another study by Kenneth Tobin at Florida State University followed "Sarah," a high school science teacher having great difficulty with classroom disruptions. Sarah had taught science at the college level for several years, but found that materials and activities she had used successfully with college students were hard to manage with high school students. She reverted to lectures, worksheets, and poorly controlled discussions. Students reacted by becoming increasingly wild, and she retaliated by sending them to the principal's office for increasingly minor infractions.

A team of researchers and four teacher colleagues worked with Sarah over the academic year to establish a classroom climate conducive to learning. A central feature of their work involved an exploration of her beliefs about teaching. Sarah's initial beliefs were expressed in several different images of the teacher, associated with different critical teaching tasks. She saw her tasks of planning and organizing for instruction in terms of teacher as "effort miser," budgeting her time and energy to provide for a life outside the classroom. Her principal metaphor for classroom management was that of teacher as "comedian," using humor to charm pupils into cooperating with her. Her ideas about the role of teacher as assessor of pupil learning were expressed by the metaphor of teacher as "fair judge," punishing or rewarding pupils according to their effort and performance.

Together with the research team, Sarah began to explore new ideas about learning as a social construction of knowledge. She was encouraged by her colleagues and the research team to develop new metaphors for teaching, consistent with the constructivist view of learning, which accords more responsibility to students. Sarah first decided to change her metaphor for management to teacher as "social director," issuing invitations to pupils to come to the "learning party." Classroom disruptions diminished considerably, but some pupils remained uncooperative. The research team then suggested that Sarah try viewing her role as assessor in terms of a "window into the student's mind." To Sarah this meant using assessment to learn what pupils knew, rather than as a means to motivate them to study through threats of failure. This additional change in perceptions led her to implement more innovative assessment procedures, and contributed to further improvement in the learning environment.

By the end of the school year, Sarah, her principal, her teacher colleagues, her pupils, and the research team all agreed that she had made significant improvement in her teaching. Sarah identified some of her important new beliefs:

- Students can be given the responsibility for their own learning.
- Students can learn from one another.
- The "party" that works for one set of students or one individual might not work for others.
- Students are more likely to "attend" or engage in a learning event that they have had a hand in creating.
- At a good party, the host becomes invisible. When learning is working, the teacher becomes a resource often in the background.
- When kids fail to learn, my job is to find out why and if needed, reinvite them to a more appropriate "party."

Exploration of new metaphors assisted Sarah to adopt new beliefs about teaching and learning that were consistent with new knowledge from psychological research, but the change was not quick or easy. It required an extended period of time, a great deal of reflective thought, and substantial assistance from her colleagues and school administrators.

Confronting Contradiction

Another recommended procedure for promoting change in beliefs involves confronting teachers with experiences that contradict their preconceptions of appropriate teaching. Several different studies have explored the effects of different sources of contradictory or discrepant views of teaching.

In one study by Sandra Hollingsworth at the University of California at Berkeley, fourteen prospective teachers participated in a year-long exploration of changes in beliefs. Most began their preparation program believing that learning was accomplished by teachers providing information to pupils. They thought that good teachers managed classrooms fairly loosely, and related to pupils as equals. They saw the teaching of reading as heavily based on use of the textbook. The teacher education program sought to move these beliefs toward views more consistent with recent research on learning and instruction: learning is accomplished by pupil participation in the guided construction of new knowledge; good management requires teacher direction and the development of structured routines; and the teaching of reading requires teacher assessment of individual reading difficulties and use of literary materials beyond the basal textbook.

College coursework promoted the desired change in prospective teacher beliefs, but other program components were critical in determining the degree of change that occurred. During the nine-month preparation program, only five of the fourteen participants modified their beliefs enough to establish teaching processes consistent with program goals. Critical contributors to their change in beliefs were a dissonance or disequilibrium created by differences between their beliefs and those of the cooperating teachers with whom they did their practice teaching; an opportunity to try their own ideas in teaching groups of pupils with differing backgrounds and abilities; and the provision of supportive and content-specific feedback from cooperating teachers and college supervisors. This study demonstrated the difficulty of changing prior beliefs as well as the importance of careful selection of settings for early classroom practice.

In another interesting study done by G. Williamson McDiarmid at Michigan State University, prospective teachers were confronted with a contradictory view of teaching and learning in an introductory education course. Through a series of experiences focused on the teaching of elementary mathematics, these students were pushed to reconsider their beliefs. First, students had to solve a simple problem involving subtraction of negative numbers: $-8 - (-2) = $? While they easily solved the problem (answer $= -6$), almost none could explain why their answer was correct. They realized that they knew rules to follow in math, but did not understand the concepts underlying those rules. (Why *is* subtracting a negative number the same as adding a positive number?)

Next, students observed a series of lessons on addition and subtraction of positive and negative numbers taught to a class of third-graders by Deborah Ball, another Michigan State faculty member. After each lesson they questioned her about her instructional procedures. Ball's class worked as a "learning community," with some pupils posing solutions to problems while other pupils raised questions or challenged their reasoning. Pupils' alternative solutions were often supported or illustrated by mathematical representations (number lines, bundles of sticks, diagrams). Pupils could revise their proposed solutions without penalty after listening to classmates' challenges or alternative solutions. Together, the class developed an agreed-upon understanding of the problem. Ball's role was to present the problem and guide the discussion. She rarely told pupils whether a given solution or representation was wrong or right; instead, she probed for pupils' reasoning. The prospective teachers were surprised to note that the third-grade pupils seemed to understand the subtraction of negative numbers better than they themselves had, and could offer rather sophisticated mathematical arguments to support their proposed solutions.

Finally, the prospective teachers were required to teach someone else subtraction with negative numbers. Some found they did not understand the "simple" mathematics well enough to teach the concept. Others wrestled with their compulsion to simply tell the rule, rather than encourage their "students" to develop their own explanations. Those who resisted the compulsion reported a strong sense of accomplishment when their students figured out the problem for themselves.

In reflecting on these experiences, participants confronted their prior beliefs about teaching and learning, the nature of mathematics, and the intellectual abilities of young children. Many modified their beliefs enough to make sound criticisms of a more traditional mathematics lesson observed at a later date. But several clearly resisted the evidence inherent in their observations of Ball's lessons. McDiarmid warns readers of his study that even students who do reexamine and modify their beliefs may not transfer their new conceptions of teaching to subject areas other than mathematics. He likens teacher beliefs to a giant spider web, with each individual strand or belief being both strong and resilient. Severing one strand will not weaken the total web.

Addressing Cases

A third approach to promoting change in beliefs involves the use of case methods. Problem solving using realistic cases has been part of the professional preparation of lawyers, doctors, and business administrators for many years. Teacher educators began using cases in teacher preparation only about ten years ago, at the instigation of Lee Shulman, of Stanford University. Shulman sees cases as analogous to the manipulative materials widely used in teaching young children mathematics, in that they provide concrete representations of classroom events. By representing the complex reality of the classroom, cases provide the potential for prospective teachers to learn vicariously.

In presenting specific types of realistic practical problems that defy simple solutions, cases can prompt prospective teachers to identify and reflect on their prior beliefs. Through case discussions, students are guided to consider the perspectives of the various participants in the problem situation, generate alternative solutions, and predict the possible consequences of each alternative. Inevitably, the values inherent in the proposed alternatives spark divergent views. Students generate varied interpretations of the same case, encouraging explication and exploration of the beliefs that underlie these interpretations.

Cases come in various forms. They can be slices of classroom interaction on videotape or in interactive multimedia materials. They can be written "short stories." They can highlight various types of classroom problems. Deborah Ball, at Michigan State University, has produced videocases focused on the teaching of mathematics. Judith Kleinfeld, at the University of Alaska, has published interesting written cases that raise issues related to multicultural education. Judy Shulman, at the Far West Laboratory for Educational Research and Development in San Francisco, has encouraged classroom teachers to write their own cases, as a way of reconstructing or reinterpreting their practical experience.

In a course for prospective teachers at the University of Virginia, we use a videocase of a student teacher from another university teaching an English lesson. "Lisa" is teaching a class of low-achieving multiethnic ninth-graders in a Northeastern urban high school. To introduce a play whose theme addresses questions about the meaning of success and failure, she has organized pupils into small groups and asked them to generate their own ideas or illustrations of success and failure. When the pupils report their ideas to their classmates, they begin to name each other as examples of failure.

> "Pusher, alcoholic, Cheech," says Connie, while her peers giggle, and Cheech frowns.
>
> "No education, failure, no pride, poor, divorce, loser, anger, no confidence, Zak, drunk," reports Derek, to the tune of more giggles and snickers. Zak stares down at his desk.
>
> Lisa smiles, "Thank you, Derek."
>
> Anthony protests, "No names. No names."
>
> Lisa, in sudden realization, repeats Anthony's admonition. "No names. That's not very nice."

When prospective teachers view the videocase on Lisa's lesson, their interpretations of the events differ, revealing their different beliefs. Sample comments are:

- "She shouldn't have let that student (Derek) go on, she shouldn't have thanked him, she should have stopped him immediately."
- "In my high school classes there was always stuff like that going on. If you think a student can handle it, you might let it go. If you think a student would be really bothered by it, I don't know that the appropriate thing would be to make a big deal of it in class."
- "I don't think she even heard it. I don't think she was re-

ally listening to them. Sometimes you're so busy thinking about your next question, you're not really tuned in to what students are saying."

- "I thought maybe she was just trying to ignore the behavior, but I thought *that* behavior shouldn't be ignored."

After discussing and comparing their own reactions to the events in Lisa's lesson, students read the reactions of the actual participants in the lesson. Lisa, after reviewing her videotaped lesson, said, "I hadn't expected them to come up with some of those examples for failure. But I think overall they came up with some very thoughtful responses. I think they got the idea of success versus failure. There was a little bit of a control problem with the group work, but I thought they did well with it—this is only the second time they've done group work."

The experienced teacher who had principal responsibility for this class was more bothered than Lisa. Upon viewing the videotaped lesson, she remarked, "They started to name each other as failures. I would have jumped on that real fast. But it was the students who initiated the idea that that was not nice, not acceptable. The students brought up a lot of things that I would have liked to talk about. A lot of their values clearly showed in their words, their choices."

As students review these perspectives, they begin to see the multiple possible lessons to be learned within one brief class period. Pupils could engage in social learning (being considerate of classmates' feelings), academic learning (relating a dramatic theme to their own experience), or behavioral learning (practicing appropriate conduct for productive independent group work). Which was the most important lesson to be learned, they wonder. Lisa was most concerned about the academic learning, and her secondary focus was on the behavioral learning. The cooperating teacher was most concerned about the social learning. Pupil's reports of what they heard anybody saying in the lesson indicated that their attention was directed toward negative social learning:

- "Steve's cheating."
- "Tina, you're a stoner." (Zak)
- "Zak telling Derek to shut up."

- "Cheech was yelling at someone who wrote his name down."
- "Steve said that Danielle is on drugs."

As they analyze cases like this, prospective teachers can see that different teacher beliefs lead to different decisions about what is the most important thing for a particular group of pupils to be learning at a given point in time. They realize that the beliefs that teachers hold about teaching and learning have an important impact on what they teach, how they teach, how they interact with pupils, and what their pupils may eventually learn. They begin to understand the importance of exploring their own beliefs about teaching.

While there is limited research available as yet to demonstrate the effects of case-based teaching, the research that has been done is promising. Evidence is slowly accumulating to demonstrate that the vicarious experience provided by case analysis can encourage teachers to view problems of practice from an expanded perspective. Cases appear to assist teachers to reveal and reconsider their beliefs.

Conclusion

The research described here amply demonstrates that change in instructional practice will not readily result merely from telling teachers that change is desirable, or even required. Deep-seated beliefs based on long experience in traditional educational settings shape teachers' interpretations of curriculum content and classroom interaction. These beliefs exert a pervasive influence on perceptions and actions. They should not be ignored by anyone intent on improving educational outcomes. Change in teacher beliefs must accompany and support change in practice if any desired reform is to be enacted and expected to endure.

Four conditions are essential for change in beliefs to occur. These necessary conditions are time, dialogue, practice, and support.

Time

An extended period of time is required for teachers to raise tacit beliefs to conscious levels, critically appraise them in the light of new evidence or experience, revise or adapt them as appropriate, and relocate the reframed beliefs within the total belief system, making necessary adjustments in adjacent or associated beliefs. Prospective teachers will never accomplish this difficult task in any six-week alternative certification program. It is doubtful that many will achieve such a change in a full academic year of teacher preparation. When experienced teachers' beliefs have been reinforced by classroom experience, change will require even more time.

Dialogue

Discourse with mentors, colleagues, and peers is essential in promoting change in beliefs. Dialogue with nonjudgmental others can encourage reflection on experience. Discussion with those who hold discrepant views can promote awareness of alternative possibilities. Teacher educators who merely lecture to prospective teachers will neither elicit nor influence their students' prior beliefs about teaching, learning, or subject-matter content. To stimulate change in beliefs of experienced teachers, inservice workshops must promote interaction among participants rather than rely on presentations by acclaimed experts, however engaging those presentations might be.

Practice

Since most teachers formed their initial beliefs through personal experience, it is in personal teaching performance that new beliefs are created. Actual use of new procedures is necessary for realistic understanding of what an innovation entails, and what it may achieve. Some depth of understanding must be acquired before beliefs can change to accommodate new procedures. Observation of another teacher's skilled performance is not enough to enable either prospective or experienced teachers to gain such understanding. Clearly, reading about a new technique in a college textbook or a teacher's guide will not suffice.

Support

Relationships with others are as important in changing beliefs as they are in initially forming them. Because beliefs have a strong emotional component, change in beliefs involves personal risk. A close and trusting relationship with someone who is familiar with the instructional setting can facilitate the honest self-evaluation that is so indispensable for adoption of new procedures. Formal, highly evaluative supervision of prospective or experienced teachers is not conducive to change in beliefs.

Coordination of Conditions

Change in beliefs is most likely when these four conditions occur together. The element of extended time permits development of dialogue, prolonged practice, and sustained support. Dialogue contributes to the formation of a support network, enabling teachers to observe and comment on their own and each other's performance. Practice of new procedures produces classroom events that can serve as examples to fuel professional discussion and enhance understanding of an innovation.

Interacting together, these conditions can help to foster the changes in teacher beliefs that are essential for real reform in classroom practice. Policymakers who truly wish to improve teaching and learning must ensure that these conditions are provided for in the planning and implementation of any innovation. Teacher educators who seek to equip professionals for successful practice must incorporate these conditions in their preparation programs.

References

Educational Evaluation and Policy Analysis 12(3), Fall 1990. (Special issue on instructional policy and practice.)

Hollingsworth, S. (1989). Prior beliefs and cognitive change in learning to teach. *American Educational Research Journal* 26(2), 160–189.

McDiarmid, G. W. (1990). Challenging prospective teachers' beliefs during early field experience: A quixotic undertaking? *Journal of Teacher Education*, 12–20.

Morine-Dershimer, G. (1996). What's in a case—and what comes out? In J. Colbert, P. Desberg, and K. Trimble (eds.), *The Case for Education: Contemporary approaches for using case methodology.* Needham Heights, Mass.: Allyn & Bacon.

Morine-Dershimer, G., and Reeve, P. T. (1994). Studying teachers' thinking about instruction: Issues related to analysis of metaphoric language. In I. Carlgren, G. Handal, and S. Vaage (eds.), *Teachers' Minds and actions: Research on teachers' thinking and practice.* London: Falmer Press.

Tobin, K. (1990). Changing metaphors and beliefs: A master switch for teaching? *Theory into Practice* 29(2), 122–127.

Part III

Environments and Programs

Chapter 15

Classroom Environments

Barry J. Fraser

A classroom's climate or environment not only is important in its own right, but also influences student learning. Policymakers need to know the impact of a new curriculum or teaching method on the classroom environment, and teachers need simple and convenient methods to assess the climates of their own classrooms and to change these environments. Another interesting question is whether teachers and their students perceive the same classroom environments similarly. Although classroom environment is a subtle concept, this chapter describes the considerable progress that has been made over the last thirty years in conceptualizing, assessing, and researching it (Fraser, 1986, 1994; Fraser and Walberg, 1991).

Although systematic classroom observation and qualitative case studies are common approaches in studying classroom environment, the main approach focused on in this chapter involves questionnaires that assess students' perceptions of their classroom climate. These paper-and-pencil perceptual measures are economical, are based on students' experiences over many classes, and involve the pooled judgments of all students in a class. Also,

students' perceptions of classroom environment explain the variation in student learning. The main topics considered in this chapter
are instruments for assessing classroom environment, research
using classroom environment instruments, and techniques for
improving classroom environments.

Instruments for Assessing Classroom Environment

This section considers the following instruments used in prior
research to assess perceptions of classroom learning environment:
the *Learning Environment Inventory, Classroom Environment Scale,
Individualized Classroom Environment Questionnaire, My Class Inventory, Science Laboratory Environment Inventory, Constructivist Learning Environment Survey*, and the *Questionnaire on Teacher Interaction*.
Each instrument is suitable for convenient group administration,
can be scored either by hand or by computer, and has been
described in detail in Fraser (1994).

Table 15-1 shows the name of each scale contained in each
instrument, the level (elementary, secondary, higher education)
for which each instrument is suited, the number of items contained in each scale, and the classification of each scale according to Moos's scheme for classifying human environments (see
Fraser, 1986). Moos's three basic types of dimension are "relationship dimensions" (which identify the nature and intensity of
personal relationships within the environment and assess the extent
to which people are involved in the environment and support
and help each other), "personal development dimensions" (which
assess basic directions along which personal growth and self-
enhancement tend to occur), and "system maintenance and system change dimensions" (which involve the extent to which the
environment is orderly, clear in expectations, controlled, and
responsive to change).

Learning Environment Inventory (LEI)

Over a quarter of a century ago, the *Learning Environment Inventory* was used as part of the research and evaluation activities

Table 15–1
Overview of Scales Contained in Seven Classroom Environment
Instruments
(LEI, CES, ICEQ, MCI, SLEI, CLES, and QTI)

Instrument	Level	Items per scale	Scales Classified According to Moos's Scheme		
			Relationship dimensions	Personal development dimensions	System maintenance and change dimensions
Learning Environment Inventory (LEI)	Secondary	7	Cohesiveness Friction Favoritism Cliqueness Satisfaction Apathy	Speed Difficulty Competitiveness	Diversity Formality Material Environment Goal Direction Disorganization Democracy
Classroom Environment Scale (CES)	Secondary	10	Involvement Affiliation Teacher Support	Task Orientation Competition	Order and Organization Rule Clarity Teacher Control Innovation
Individualized Classroom Environment Questionnaire (ICEQ)	Secondary	10	Personalization Participation	Independence Investigation	Differentiation
My Class Inventory (MCI)	Elementary	6–9	Cohesiveness Friction Satisfaction	Difficulty Competitiveness	
Science Laboratory Environment Inventory (SLEI)	Upper secondary/ Higher education	7	Student Cohesiveness	Ope-Endedness Integration	Rule Clarity Material Environment
Constructivist Learning Environment Survey (CLES)	Secondary	7	Personal Relevance Scientific Uncertainty	Critical Voice Shared Control	Student Negotiation
Questionnaire on Teacher Interaction (QTI)	Secondary/ Elementary	8–10	Helpful/Friendly Understanding Dissatisfied Admonishing		Leadership Student Responsibility and Freedom Uncertain Strict

of Harvard Project Physics. In selecting the fifteen climate dimensions, an attempt was made to include as scales only concepts previously identified as good predictors of learning, concepts considered relevant to social-psychological theory and research, concepts similar to those found useful in theory and research in education, or concepts intuitively judged relevant to the social psychology of the classroom. The final version of the LEI contains a total of 105 statements (or seven per scale) descriptive of typical school classes. The respondent expresses his or her degree of agreement or disagreement with each statement on a four-point scale, with response alternatives of "strongly disagree," "disagree," "agree," and "strongly agree." The scoring direction (or polarity) is reversed for some items. A typical item contained in the Cohesiveness scale is "All students know each other very well." An item from the Speed scale is "The pace of the class is rushed."

Classroom Environment Scale (CES)

The CES was developed by Rudolf Moos at Stanford University and grew out of a comprehensive program of research involving perceptual measures of a variety of human environments including psychiatric hospitals, prisons, university residences, and work milieus. The final published version of the CES contains nine scales, each with ten items requiring a response of "true or false." Published materials include a test manual, a questionnaire, an answer sheet, and a transparent handscoring key. Typical items in the CES are "The teacher takes a personal interest in the students" (Teacher Support) and "There is a clear set of rules for students to follow" (Rule Clarity).

Individualized Classroom Environment Questionnaire (ICEQ)

The ICEQ differs from other classroom environment scales in that it assesses those dimensions (e.g., Personalization, Participation) that distinguish individualized classrooms from conventional ones. The initial development of the long form ICEQ was guided by several criteria: dimensions chosen characterized the classroom learning environment described in the literature of individualized and open education; extensive interviewing of teachers and secondary school students ensured that the ICEQ's dimensions and individual items were considered salient by teachers and students; items were written and subsequently modified after receiving reactions from selected experts, teachers, and junior high school students; and data collected during field testing were subjected to item analyses in order to identify items whose removal would enhance scale statistics. The final published version of the ICEQ contains fifty items altogether, with an equal number of items belonging to each of the five scales. Each item is responded to on a five-point scale with the alternatives of "almost never," "seldom," "sometimes," "often," and "very often." The scoring direction is reversed for many of the items. Typical items are "The teacher considers students' feelings" (Personalization) and "Different students use different books, equipment, and materials" (Differentiation). The published form of the ICEQ consists of a handbook and test master sets from which unlimited numbers of copies of the questionnaires and response sheets may be made.

My Class Inventory (MCI)

The LEI has been simplified to form the MCI, which is suitable for children in the eight-to-twelve years age range. Although the MCI was developed originally for use at the elementary school level, it also has been found to be very useful with students in junior high school, especially those who might have difficulty reading the LEI. The MCI differs from the LEI in four important ways. First, in order to minimize fatigue among younger children, the MCI contains only five of the LEI's original fifteen scales. Second, item wording has been simplified to enhance readability. Third, the LEI's four-point response format has been reduced to a two-point ("yes or no") response format. Fourth, students answer on the questionnaire itself instead of on a separate response sheet, which avoids errors in transferring responses from one place to another. The final form of the MCI contains thirty-eight items altogether. Typical items are "Children are always fighting with each other" (Friction) and "Children seem to like the class" (Satisfaction). The reading level of these MCI items is well suited to students at the elementary school level.

Science Laboratory Environment Inventory (SLEI)

Because of the critical importance and uniqueness of laboratory settings in science education, an instrument specifically suited to assessing the environment of science laboratory classes at the senior high school or higher education levels was developed (Fraser, Giddings, and McRobbie, 1995). This new questionnaire, the SLEI, has five scales, and the response alternatives for each item are "almost never," "seldom," "sometimes," "often," and "very often." Typical items include "We know the results that we are supposed to get before we commence a laboratory activity" (Open-Endedness) and "The laboratory work is unrelated to the topics that we are studying in our science classes" (Integration). The Open-Endedness scale was included because of the importance of open-ended laboratory activities claimed in the literature. A noteworthy feature of the validation procedures was that the SLEI was field-tested simultaneously in six countries (the United States, Canada, England, Israel, Australia, and Nigeria) with a sample of 5,477 students in over 269 classes in order to furnish comprehensive information about the instrument's cross-national validity and usefulness.

Constructivist Learning Environment Survey (CLES)

Traditionally, teachers have conceived their roles to be concerned with revealing or transmitting the logical structures of their knowledge, and directing students through rational inquiry toward discovering predetermined truths expressed in the form of laws, principles, rules, and algorithms. Recently, developments in history, philosophy, and sociology have provided educators with a better understanding of how knowledge develops. Meaningful learning is a cognitive process in which an individual makes sense of the world in relation to the knowledge he or she has already constructed. This sense-making process involves active negotiation and consensus building.

The CLES (Taylor, Dawson, and Fraser, 1995) was developed to assist researchers and teachers to assess the degree to which a particular classroom's environment is consistent with a constructivist epistemology, and to assist teachers to reflect on their epistemological assumptions and reshape their teaching practice. To help ensure that the CLES empowers teachers to overcome constraints to the development of constructivist learning environments, a critical theory perspective was incorporated into the instrument. The scales in the CLES are Personal Relevance (the relevance of classroom experience to out-of-school experiences), Student Negotiation (emphasis on creating opportunities for students to explain and justify their ideas, and to test the viability of their own and others' ideas), Uncertainty (provision of opportunities for students to experience knowledge as arising from inquiry, involving human experience and values, evolving and insecure, and culturally and socially determined), Shared Control (emphasis on students' negotiating and sharing control for learning activities, assessment, and social norms), and Critical Voice (emphasis on developing a critical awareness of the prevailing curriculum and assessment policy).

Researchers could make use of the CLES in monitoring the effectiveness of preservice and inservice attempts to change teaching and learning styles to a more constructivistic approach; evaluating the impact of constructivistic teaching approaches on student outcomes; guiding teacher-researchers' attempts to reflect on and improve classroom environments; reducing the amount of classroom observation needed in studies of constructivist teaching and learning (by collecting information from students via the CLES); complementing qualitative information in constructing richer case studies that also include quantitative information based on student perceptions obtained with the CLES; and investigating the relationship between teacher cognition and teaching practice.

Table 15-2 is a complete copy of the CLES's "actual" form (see the next section for a clarification of the distinction between "actual" and "preferred" forms). Items with their item numbers underlined are scored 1, 2, 3, 4, and 5, respectively, for the responses "almost always," "often," "sometimes," "seldom," and "almost never." Underlined items are scored in the reverse manner. Omitted or invalidly answered items are scored 3 (or, alternatively, assigned the mean of the other items in the same scale).

Table 15-2
Constructivist Learning Environment Survey (CLES)

This questionnaire asks you to describe important aspects of the science classroom which you are in right now. There are no right or wrong answers. This is not a test and your answers will not affect your assessment. Your opinion is what is wanted. Your answers will enable us to improve future science classes.

Below you will find 30 sentences. For each sentence, circle *only one* number corresponding to your answer. For example:

- If you think this teacher *almost always* asks you questions, circle the 5.
- If you think this teacher *almost never* asks you questions, circle the 1.
- Or you can choose the number 2, 3, or 4 if one of these seems like a more accurate answer.

If you want to change your answer, *cross it out* and circle a new number.

Learning about the world	Almost Always	Often	Sometimes	Seldom	Almost Never
In this class ...					
1. I learn about the world outside of school.	5	4	3	2	1
2. My new learning starts with problems about the world outside of school.	5	4	3	2	1
3. I learn how science can be part of my out-of-school life.	5	4	3	2	1
4. I get a better understanding of the world outside of school.	5	4	3	2	1
5. I learn interesting things about the world outside of school.	5	4	3	2	1
6. What I learn has *nothing* to do with my out-of-school life.	5	4	3	2	1

Learning about science	Almost Always	Often	Sometimes	Seldom	Almost Never
In this class ...					
7. I learn that science *cannot* provide perfect answers to problems.	5	4	3	2	1
8. I learn that science has changed over time.	5	4	3	2	1
9. I learn that science is influenced by people's values and opinions.	5	4	3	2	1
10. I learn about the different sciences used by people in other cultures.	5	4	3	2	1
11. I learn that modern science is different from the science of long ago	5	4	3	2	1
12. I learn that science is about *inventing* theories.	5	4	3	2	1

Learning to speak out	Almost Always	Often	Sometimes	Seldom	Almost Never
In this class . . .					
13. It's OK for me to ask the teacher, "Why do I have to learn this?"	5	4	3	2	1
14. It's OK for me to question the way I'm being taught.	5	4	3	2	1
15. It's OK for me to complain about activities that are confusing.	5	4	3	2	1
16. It's OK for me to complain about anything that prevents me from learning.	5	4	3	2	1
17. It's OK for me to express my opinion.	5	4	3	2	1
18. It's OK for me to speak up for my rights.	5	4	3	2	1

Learning to learn	Almost Always	Often	Sometimes	Seldom	Almost Never
In this class . . .					
19. I help the teacher to plan what I'm going to learn	5	4	3	2	1
20. I help the teacher to decide how well I am learning.	5	4	3	2	1
21. I help the teacher to decide which activities are best for me.	5	4	3	2	1
22. I help the teacher to decide how much time I spend on activities.	5	4	3	2	1
23. I help the teacher to decide which activities I do.	5	4	3	2	1
24. I help the teacher to assess my learning.	5	4	3	2	1

Learning to communicate	Almost Always	Often	Sometimes	Seldom	Almost Never
In this class . . .					
25. I get the chance to talk to other students.	5	4	3	2	1
26. I talk with other students about how to solve problems.	5	4	3	2	1
27. I explain my ideas to other students.	5	4	3	2	1
28. I ask other students to explain their ideas.	5	4	3	2	1
29. Other students ask me to explain my ideas.	5	4	3	2	1
30. Other students explain their ideas to me.	5	4	3	2	1

Scale allocation: The successive blocks of six items assess, respectively, Personal Relevance, Uncertainty, Critical Voice, Shared Control, and Student Negotiation.

Scoring: The circled number represents the score for an item, except for Item 6, which is scored in the reverse manner. Omitted or invalid responses are scored 3.

Questionnaire on Teacher Interaction (QTI)

In research that originated in The Netherlands, a learning environment questionnaire was developed to enable teacher educators to give preservice and inservice teachers advice about the nature and quality of the interaction between teachers and students (Wubbels and Levy, 1993). Drawing on a theoretical model of proximity (Cooperation-Opposition) and influence (Dominance-Submission), the QTI was developed to assess student perceptions of eight behavioral aspects: Leadership, Helpful/Friendly, Understanding, Student Responsibility and Freedom, Uncertain, Dissatisfied, Admonishing, and Strict. The original version of the QTI has seventy-seven items altogether (approximately ten per scale), although now there is also a more economical forty-eight-item version.

Each item is responded to on a five-point scale ranging from "never" to "always." Typical items are "S/he gives us a lot of free time" (Student Responsibility and Freedom behavior) and "S/he gets angry" (Admonishing behavior). The QTI has been found to be valid and reliable in studies of secondary school students in The Netherlands, the United States, and Australia.

Preferred Forms of Scales

A distinctive feature of most of the instruments in Table 15-1 is that, in addition to a form that measures perceptions of *actual* or *experienced* classroom environment, there is another form to measure perceptions of *preferred* or *ideal* classroom environment. The preferred forms are concerned with goals and value orientations and measure perceptions of the classroom environment ideally liked or preferred. Although item wording is identical or similar for actual and preferred forms, different instructions for answering each are used. Having different actual and preferred forms has enabled these instruments to be used in the range of research applications discussed later in this chapter.

Validity and Reliability

Each of the instruments described above has been field-tested extensively and found to be valid and reliable for applications involving either the individual student's score or the class mean score as the unit of analysis (Fraser, 1994). In order to optimize the validity of these questionnaires when used in a new class (e.g., at the beginning of a school year), they should not be administered until the class and its teacher have been meeting together for at least three weeks.

Research Using Classroom Environment Instruments

Associations Between Student Outcomes and Classroom Environment

The strongest tradition in past classroom environment research has involved investigation of associations between students' cognitive and affective learning outcomes and their perceptions of their classroom environments. Student perceptions account for appreciable amounts of variance in learning outcomes, often beyond that attributable to student characteristics. The practical implication from this research is that student outcomes can be improved by creating classroom environments with a greater emphasis on those dimensions found to be positively related to learning. I have tabulated the results from forty past studies of the effects of classroom environment on student outcomes (Fraser, 1994). These studies involved a variety of cognitive and affective outcome measures, a variety of classroom environment instruments, and a variety of samples (ranging across numerous countries and grade levels). Learning environment was found to be consistently and strongly associated with cognitive and affective learning outcomes, with better achievement on a variety of outcome measures occurring in classes perceived as having greater Cohesiveness, Satisfaction, and Goal Direction, and less Disorganization and Friction. In research specifically in science laboratory classroom environments (Fraser, Giddings, and McRobbie,

1995), both cognitive and affective outcomes were superior in situations in which Integration (i.e., the link between the work covered in laboratory classes and theory classes) was greater.

Curriculum Evaluation

One promising but neglected application of classroom environment instruments is to provide process criteria in evaluating innovations and new curricula. For example, a study involving an evaluation of the Australian Science Education Project (ASEP) revealed that, in comparison with students in a control group, students in ASEP classes perceived their classrooms as being more satisfying and individualized and having a better material environment (Fraser, 1986). The significance of this evaluation is that classroom environment variables differentiated revealingly between curricula, even when various outcome measures showed negligible differences between ASEP students and those in the control group.

Differences Between Students' and Teachers' Perceptions of Actual and Preferred Classroom Environment

The fact that some classroom environment instruments have different actual and preferred forms that can be used with either teachers or students permits investigation of differences between students' and teachers' perceptions of the same actual classroom environment and of differences between the perceived actual environment and that preferred by students or teachers. This research reveals that, first, students prefer a more positive classroom environment than they perceived to be present and, second, teachers perceive a more positive classroom environment than did their students in the same classrooms. These interesting results replicate patterns in other studies in school classrooms in the United States, Israel, and Australia (see Fraser, 1994). These studies inform educators that students and teachers are likely to differ in the way in which they perceive the actual environment of the same classrooms, and that the environment preferred by students commonly differs from that perceived to be present in classrooms.

In a study involving the use of the QTI in The Netherlands, Wubbels and Levy (1993) also found that a high proportion of teachers (70 percent) viewed the learning environment more favorably than did their students. However, the perceptions of the remaining teachers (30 percent) were more negative than those of their students. Overall, this study suggested that teacher perceptions of the learning environment are shaped partly by their ideals of what the learning environment should be (i.e., teachers' ideals can distort their perceptions of the actual learning environment). The mismatch between teachers' and students' perceptions was, on average, larger for teachers who showed less behavior that promoted positive student cognitive and affective outcomes than did teachers who showed a lot of those behaviors.

It is important that discussions between university staff and preservice teachers about their teaching practice are not based merely on teachers' perceptions. Feedback gathered through classroom observations or students' perceptions also are desirable. Similarly, because teachers' perceptions can depend on their beliefs, it is important that evaluations of teacher-preparation and staff-development programs do not rely heavily on the teachers' self-reports.

Do Students Achieve Better in Classrooms Similar to Their Preferred Environment?

Whereas much past research has concentrated on investigations of associations between student outcomes and the nature of the actual classroom environment, actual and preferred forms of classroom environment instruments can be used together in exploring whether students achieve better when there is a higher similarity between the actual classroom environment that students perceive and the environment that students prefer. A person-environment interaction framework was used to explore whether or not student outcomes depend not only on the nature of the classroom environment, but also on the match between students' preferences and the environment. I have described a study that involved the prediction of achievement from the five actual individualization variables measured by the ICEQ and the five variables indicating the interaction between the actual and the preferred environments (Fraser, 1986). The similarity between perceptions of the actual and the preferred environments was as important as individualization per se in predicting student achievement of important affective and cognitive aims. This research has interesting practical implications—in any classroom, students' achievement of certain outcomes can be enhanced by attempting to change the actual classroom environment in ways that make it more congruent with the environment the students prefer.

School Psychology

The study of the psychosocial environment of the classroom can furnish a number of ideas, techniques, and research findings that could be valuable in school psychology. Traditionally, school psychologists have tended to concentrate heavily and sometimes exclusively on their roles in assessing and enhancing academic achievement and other valued learning outcomes. Research findings on the classroom environment can inform school psychologists and teachers about the subtle but important aspects of classroom life. For example, classroom environment instruments have been used in helping British teachers to change how they interact with students and to guide improvements in their classrooms by pointing out discrepancies between students' perceptions of their actual and their preferred environments.

Incorporating Learning Environment Ideas into Teacher Education

The improvement of preservice and inservice education programs for teachers requires new ideas that will help teachers become more reflective and retrospective about their teaching. Although research on the psychosocial learning environment has furnished a number of ideas and techniques that are potentially valuable for inclusion in teacher education programs, surprisingly little progress has been made in incorporating these ideas into teacher education. However, I (Fraser, 1994) reported some case studies of how classroom and school environment work has been used within preservice and inservice teacher education to (1) sensitize teachers to subtle but important aspects of classroom life, (2) illustrate the usefulness of including classroom and school environment assessments as part of a teacher's overall evaluation and monitoring activities, (3) show how assessment of classroom and school environment can be used to facilitate practical improvements in classrooms and schools, and (4) provide a valuable source of feedback about teaching performance for the formative and summative evaluation of student teaching. It appears that information on student perceptions of the classroom learning environment during preservice teachers' field experience adds usefully to the information obtained from university supervisors, school-based cooperating teachers, and student teachers' self-evaluation.

Practical Attempts to Improve Classroom Environments

Information on student perceptions has been employed in discussions about classroom environments and in systematic attempts to improve those environments (Fraser, 1986). The following example of an attempt to improve a classroom environment made use of the short twenty-four-item version of the *Classroom Environment Scale* (CES) discussed previously. The class involved in the study consisted of twenty-two Grade 9 boys and girls of mixed ability studying science at a government school in Australia (Fraser, 1986). The procedure incorporated the following five fundamental steps:

1. *Assessment.* The CES was administered to all students in the class. The preferred form was answered first, and the actual form was administered in the same time slot one week later.
2. *Feedback.* The teacher was provided with information derived from student responses in the form of the profiles shown in Figure 15-1 representing the class item means for students' actual and preferred environment scores. For each scale, Figure 15-1 provides the mean item score obtained (i.e., the mean total scale score divided by the number of

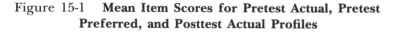

Figure 15-1   **Mean Item Scores for Pretest Actual, Pretest
Preferred, and Posttest Actual Profiles**

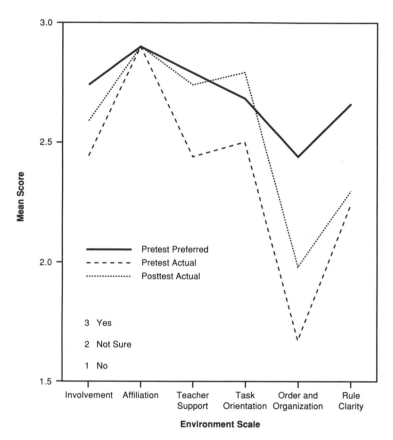

items in that scale), rather than the mean total scale score, because this allows better comparability between different scales that contain different numbers of items. These profiles permitted ready identification of the changes in classroom environment needed to reduce major differences between the nature of the actual environment as perceived by students and the students' preferred environment. Figure 15-1 shows that the interpretation of the larger differences was that students would prefer more of all dimensions except Affiliation.

3. *Reflection and discussion.* The teacher engaged in private reflection and informal discussion about the profiles in order

to decide whether to attempt to change the environment along some of the CES's dimensions. The teacher decided to introduce an intervention aimed at increasing the levels of Teacher Support and Order and Organization in the class.

4. *Intervention.* The teacher introduced an intervention of approximately two months' duration in an attempt to change the classroom environment. This intervention consisted of a variety of strategies, some of which originated during discussions between teachers, and others of which were suggested by examining ideas contained in individual CES items. For example, strategies used to enhance Teacher Support involved the teacher moving around the class more to mix with students, providing assistance to students, and talking with them more than previously. Strategies used to increase Order and Organization involved taking considerable care with distribution and collection of materials during activities and ensuring that students worked more quietly.

5. *Reassessment.* The student actual form of the scales was readministered at the end of the intervention to see whether students were perceiving their classroom environments differently from before.

The results are summarized graphically in Figure 15-1, which includes a dotted line to indicate the class mean score for students' perceptions of actual environment on each of the CES's five scales at the time of posttesting. Figure 15-1 clearly shows that some change in student perceptions of actual environment occurred during the time of the intervention. Pretest-posttest differences were statistically significant only for Teacher Support, Task Orientation, and Order and Organization. These findings are noteworthy because two of the dimensions on which appreciable changes were recorded were those on which the teacher had attempted to promote change. (Note also that there appears to be a side effect in that the intervention could have resulted in the classroom becoming more task oriented than the students would have preferred.) Overall, the above case study, in conjunction with other previous studies, suggests the potential usefulness of teachers' employing classroom environment instruments to gain meaningful information about their classrooms to guide improvements in classroom environments.

Conclusion

Over the last thirty years, classroom environment instruments have been increasingly and more widely used and cross-validated in various countries, preferred forms have been developed to augment the original actual or experienced forms, short and hand-scorable forms have been designed for the convenience of teachers, and new instruments have been developed to fill gaps (e.g., for use in science laboratory classes). Currently, instruments are being translated and adapted for use in different countries, to develop new instruments for settings that existing questionnaires do not address well (e.g., computer-assisted instruction, preschool classrooms, constructivist classrooms), and to use the instruments in settings in which they have not been used previously (e.g., special education classes). The topic of classroom environment is beginning to become included in preservice and inservice courses for teachers around the world, and is gaining attention among school psychologists.

The research discussed in this chapter provides the following practical implications for policymakers and practitioners:

- Learning environment assessments should be used in addition to student learning outcome measures to provide information about subtle but important aspects of classroom life.
- Because teachers and students have systematically different perceptions of the same classrooms, student feedback about classrooms should also be collected.
- Teachers should strive to create "productive" classroom learning environments as identified by research (e.g., classroom environments with greater organization, cohesiveness, and goal direction and less friction).
- In order to improve student outcomes, classroom environments should be changed to make them more similar to those preferred by the students.
- The evaluation of innovations and new curricula should include classroom environment instruments to provide process measures of effectiveness.
- Teachers should use assessments of their students' perceptions of the actual and the preferred classroom environments to monitor and guide attempts to improve classrooms.

- Learning environment assessments should be used by school psychologists in helping teachers change their styles of interacting with students and improve their classroom environments.

References

Fraser, B. J. (1986). *Classroom environment.* London, England: Croom Helm.

Fraser, B. J. (1994). Research on classroom and school climate. In D. Gabel (ed.), *Handbook of research on science teaching and learning* (pp. 493–541). New York: Macmillan.

Fraser, B. J.; Giddings, G. J.; and McRobbie, C. J. (1995). Evolution and validation of a personal form of an instrument for assessing science laboratory classroom environments. *Journal of Research in Science Teaching 32,* 399–422.

Fraser, B. J., and Walberg, H. J. (eds.) (1991). *Educational environments: Evaluation, antecedents and consequences.* Oxford, England: Pergamon Press.

Taylor, P.; Dawson, V.; and Fraser, B. (1995, April). *Classroom learning environments under transformation: A constructivist perspective.* Paper presented at the annual meeting of the American Educational Research Association, San Francisco, Calif.

Wubbels, T., and Levy, J. (eds.) (1993). *Do you know what you look like?: Interpersonal relationships in education.* London, England: Falmer Press.

Chapter 16

School Cultures

Avi Kaplan and Martin L. Maehr

More than a decade has passed since "A Nation at Risk" was published. Many observers of education today see the "rising tide of mediocrity" continuing to rise. Not for want of trying to stem the tide, it may be noted. A multiplicity of reform efforts have been and continue to be initiated. Few of these programs, however, have proven effects on the bottom line for education: the motivation and learning of students. And so, the need to reform remains. With an increasing number of others (e.g., Sarason, 1990), we believe that clear and lasting changes in student motivation and learning will occur only if and as fundamental aspects of school life—specifically, "school culture"—are changed.

In this chapter, we examine how, when, and in what ways school culture is basic to student motivation and learning. We begin by describing the nature of school culture, focusing especially on those facets most closely associated with student motivation and learning. Second, we summarize studies that demonstrate the role that school culture plays in student motivation. Third, we propose changes that can and need to be made in order to enhance the role that school cultures can play in encouraging student motivation and learning. And finally, we briefly summarize our own experiences regarding how these changes can be brought about.

School Culture

The topic of school culture has hardly been ignored, especially in the last decade or so. However, the meaning of the term and the topics covered under that label have varied considerably. School culture has served as a wide umbrella under which management practices, administration policies, innovations, and attitudes and actions of staff and students have all been discussed—and in a variety of ways. Common to the very different uses of the term is the observation that individual schools really do seem to have their own character. Someone visiting different schools, even in the same city, will encounter many differences immediately and directly. Physically, building structures differ among schools, and when structures are similar, they are often used in quite dissimilar ways. Walls may contain examples of student art and official pronouncements—or graffiti. Floors may be clean or dirty, cluttered with the signs of "work in progress"—or clean and a bit too sanitary. On a behavioral dimension, one can hear differences in the way that students address teachers—and teachers, students. Join a meeting in progress and you learn something about issues and concerns, values and objectives—all of which differ from school to school. Join the staff for informal coffee and you will often get a real earful. A Catholic school in rural Ohio is likely to have a different code of dress for students and teachers than a school in the inner city of San Francisco. And these two schools are different in this respect, as in many other ways, from a suburban school in New Jersey.

These are the obvious differences—things we can immediately see or hear or readily come to understand. They are not unimportant. They may rightly be included as part of the school culture. But they are probably not the most fundamental part of school culture so far as student motivation and learning are concerned. Most who have tried to understand or change schools have come to understand that underlying much of the behavior that they have observed are certain more hidden assumptions about how life is to be lived in this place called school (Deal and Peterson, 1990). Teachers have certain beliefs about students and hold to theories regarding how they can be taught. Students in turn operate with their own assumptions of why they are doing what they are doing and what it's worth, and hold some not-so-hidden notions about teachers, the assignments they receive, and the discipline that teachers and administration exercise. This gets closer to what we feel is the heart of school culture—but not close enough.

The Purpose of Schooling

Recent research on student motivation and learning has paid special attention to the role that purposes and goals play in framing and guiding student motivation and learning. There are, of course, a variety of purposes that students may and do hold vis à vis schooling. But two in particular seem to play an especially important role in determining motivation and learning. Each purpose represents a contrasting definition of schooling. And these different definitions lead to profound differences in the way students act, feel, and think as they attend classes, do their homework, walk the halls, relate to peers and teachers—or just hang out. So, these purposes, or "goals," are not really specific objectives to be reached or standards to be met. Rather, they are more like theories that deal with the means and ends of schooling as well as its worth—theories that are closely tied to who one is in school and what one is able to do.

Two Critical and Contrasting Goals

The first such goal we label "task." In this case, the focus is learning: progress, growth in acquiring a skill, solving a problem, or gaining knowledge. To a considerable degree, it is accepted that the academic task is worthy in its own right and can and should be interesting and enjoyable. We call the second goal "ability," for the focus is on demonstrating that one is able and competent—actually, more competent than others. Those who hold ability goals view schooling and school tasks as essentially a competitive game in which some lose. School is a contest to establish various hierarchies of achievement, competence, and often, at least by implication, worth and acceptance. A rather significant body of information shows that these two goals—task and ability—are widely held by students at virtually all levels of schooling. Students commonly adopt one of the two goals as the primary guide for their behavior in school. There are individual differences in the saliency of the two goals: We all know students who are very "grade conscious" and students who seem to really like the process of learning. But especially interesting is that most students also vary in the degree to which they follow these goals in the performance of any given task. We will return to that point later. First, it is important to emphasize that these goals play a very important role in how students approach schooling. More specifically, they are associated with different patterns of action, feelings, and thoughts.

Actions, Feelings, and Learning

There is a large body of information from research that has examined how individuals act, feel, and learn when they hold primarily one or the other of these two theories about schooling. Generally, students who hold task goals are qualitatively different students from those who hold ability goals. This is apparent in the way they engage in academic tasks, the attitudes they have toward school, and the emotions they experience in school.

When students hold task goals, they exhibit an interest in learning, are stimulated by challenge, and are more likely to use efficient and productive metacognitive strategies. They plan and monitor their learning and manage their time to meet their learning objectives. They may use a "rehearsal" strategy when appropriate, but do not limit their studying to only this strategy. Rather, they are likely also to employ "deep-processing" strategies, such as relating information learned in one sphere to that learned elsewhere. In short, they act on the material to organize it in a way that is meaningful to them and that helps them to retrieve it and use it effectively. Moreover, these students are likely to believe that effort can improve skills and knowledge. Therefore, they learn from mistakes and are not deterred by an occasional failure. They feel successful when they master a skill or when they learn something new and interesting, and the opportunities they perceive for success depend on the tasks and resources provided by the school and the freedom they have to pursue their interests. These characteristics are found among students who hold task goals regardless of their achievement level.

In contrast, students who hold ability goals focus on their ability and self-worth. They are interested in learning activities when these activities show that they are smart. They try to avoid challenging and difficult tasks when these pose a threat to their ability, and rather than use "deep" learning strategies, they are much more likely to use "surface" strategies, such as rote memorization and rehearsal. These students are likely to believe that if one puts much effort into a task, then one is not smart or able. Therefore, they are less likely to engage in tasks for a long time, and in the face of a possible mistake or failure, they tend to engage in "self-handicapping strategies." These strategies provide these students plausible excuses for failure that are different from low ability and thus do not undermine their self-esteem (Covington, 1992). When students hold ability goals, they feel successful when they do better than other students and when they can do their schoolwork quickly and without difficulty. Since only a few students can be the "best," the opportunities these students perceive for success are limited. Those students who are unable to be the best are likely to engage in other nonadaptive strategies, such as devaluing learning and school.

Students who hold task goals are much more likely to have positive attitudes toward school and learning than are students who hold ability goals. They report that they enjoy being in school, are less bored, have less anxiety, and have a better sense of well-being. Students who hold ability goals are more likely to report negative attitudes and emotions. Interestingly, this is true also for those students who are objectively viewed as doing well in school but who happen to hold ability goals. More broadly, a growing body of research shows that goals are associated not only with positive attitudes toward learning and schooling, but with adaptive behavior more generally. In contrast, ability goals are associated with disruptive behavior, alienation, and lowered self-esteem. The reasons for this are apparent. Ability goals put the focus on self, and often how badly one fares in school. When school is a competitive game that some, perhaps even a substantial number, cannot expect to win, there are bound to be effects on self-esteem and feelings of belonging.

In summary, there is strong reason to argue that task goals are associated with being good students as well as good school citizens. Few would question that the qualitatively different types of behavior that have been differentially associated with holding task (as opposed to ability) goals are preferred. Not only do we want students to love learning, we want them to acquire necessary knowledge in the most efficient ways. We also want them to feel good about themselves as students and persons. If, as seems the case, task goals are more likely to bring this about than are ability goals, it follows that schools ought to have an interest in how they can encourage students to adopt task goals and avoid the all-too-common obsession with ability goals. That is where recent research on school cultures makes an interesting and, we believe, important contribution.

School Cultures and Student Goals

Recent research (Maehr, Midgley, et al., 1996) indicates that individual classrooms and schools as a whole differ not only in some of the obvious features of decorum and dress, but also in how they define learning and schooling. More specifically, individual schools and classrooms stress task and ability goals to different degrees—or at least their students see them as doing this. And so far as student motivation and learning is concerned, students' perception is what counts.

Two initial studies on school, family, and peer factors associated with student motivation and learning provide a basis for this assertion. A first finding of one study was that students very definitely recognize the existence of goal stresses in their schools. Second, and equally important, the perceived stress on a task goal emerged as an important correlate of motivation as well as achievement. Interesting also was that goal stresses were likely to be most critical for children of lower socioeconomic and minority background. This was really one of the earliest indications that in the minds of children, schools as a whole define their purposes differently—and thereby possibly influence the degree of children's investment in learning.

However, another study, by Carole Ames and Jennifer Archer (1988), carved out the place for context and culture in framing the quality of students' motivation and learning in school. In their study, the context was the classroom and the specific focus was on students' perception of classrooms' relative stress on task and ability goals. Students not only clearly recognized these different classroom emphases, but appeared to be influenced by them. That is, students framed their own definitions and approaches to learning accordingly. When students saw classrooms as stressing task goals, they tended to use "deeper" learning strategies, to choose challenging tasks, and to have more positive attitudes toward the class.

Since then, several studies have found that school and classroom stress on task and ability goals is a very recognizable part of the school context. While we cannot see goal stresses as we can see the posters on the walls or the books and technology used, we can recognize them when they are reliably indexed using readily administerable, standardized instruments. Most certainly, the indices reflect distinguishing features of learning contexts. And arguably, the indices obtained reflect an important feature of what could be called the "subjective culture" of motivation and learning—for the perceptions of what school and classrooms were stressing turned out to be associated with the task and ability goals that children had employed in the course of their learning (e.g., Anderman and Young, 1994).

Sources and Resources for School Culture Change

The study of differences in context stresses and the variations in the saliency of goals from classroom to classroom and school to school leads ineluctably to the conclusion that goal stress is a contextual variable. And if goal stress is a variable, what are the sources for this variation and how can they be controlled, manipulated, and managed? As already stated, most of us prefer that students hold task rather than ability goals. Can school context be designed and managed to work toward this preference?

It is relatively easy to criticize schools for what they are. And it would be easy to stop at this point and simply exhort those who are teachers and administrators to do something about their school's goal stresses. The thought of school reform, of course, not only is scary for practitioners, but is something that researchers seldom dare risking their reputations on. And besides, what is there about schools that really brings about these differential stresses? Researchers should be able to point to something there—and they can.

As this work on goals and school contexts was beginning, a number of researchers had begun pulling together the disparate literature on the contextual sources of student motivation (e.g., Ames, 1992; Epstein, 1989) and made it clear that certain types of school policies and practices probably influenced students to adopt task and ability goals. Three areas of school policy and practice seem to be especially important in this regard.

The Nature of the "Learning Task"

Blumenfeld and others (e.g., Blumenfeld, Puro, and Mergendoller, 1992) have pointed to the necessity of considering what the student is asked to do. How do educators construct and define learning tasks? First, some tasks are simply more likely to be meaningful and interesting. As a result, students are more readily drawn to them for their inherent value. And given that, a task goal orientation becomes more likely. The potential for task-oriented environments is created by school policies and instructional methods—decisions that educators make in designing instruction. There are several interrelated ways in which schools and classrooms impact the meaning of the task. First, they affect the inherent value of tasks by making the tasks moderately challenging and complex for the students who are asked to do the task. Second, they give students an optimum degree of choice over what to do and how to do it. And finally, they assist the students in tying tasks to more general meanings, making learning "relevant" (cf. Lepper and Cordova, 1992). Assisting the student in constructing meaning in what she is doing is among the most important of educational tasks. Too often, however, school practices and policy actually work against this goal. For example, scheduling classes into forty- to fifty-minute time blocks tends to reduce the choices allowed students and the opportunities for hands-on experiences—and thus the opportunities to engage deeply in knowledge construction. Encouraging interdisciplinary team teaching to address such time constraints can serve to broaden the meaning of making a particular mathematical calculation or reading a poem.

In sum, the encouragement of the adoption of a task goal begins with the nature of the task that the student is asked to do. The framing of these tasks is heavily controlled not only by teacher beliefs and choice of "learning materials" but also by accepted assumptions about how schools and schooling should be organized and managed.

Evaluation and Recognition Systems

Most obviously important, perhaps, in reflecting, communicating, and shaping theories of school are evaluation and recognition practices. It is in the way that we assess learning that we not only define what it is but specify its value. The recognition that can be associated with this process serves to publicize and promote what may be presented more subtly in the assessment and evaluation process.

Many examples could serve to make this point. We single out one as especially illustrative. Assessment and evaluation of student learning is often oriented around comparative performance levels that take little or no account of entering levels of competence, skill, previous experience, and the social and cultural world of the student. When making the top score on a test becomes the prime objective of students and the essence of a school endeavor, a number of things happen—most of them bad. Students tend to forget that growth and learning are the purpose of schooling. Those who are in a position to win the academic sweepstakes will at times avoid the venture of thinking new thoughts in order to imbed the "right" answer into their consciousness and thereby avoid the risk of "looking stupid." Equally bad, the student who does not compete well will have little chance of experiencing the joys of learning that he can and should have.

In short, when the demonstration of ability vis à vis competition with others becomes the name of the school game, then learning is subverted. Perhaps a not-so-subtle form of class warfare is encouraged. Perhaps those with "talent" will be taught to avoid errors rather than learn from them. Certainly, those from "disadvantaged backgrounds" are likely to feel incompetent and perhaps experience a loss of self-esteem—or to protect the latter, write off school as irrelevant.

Distribution of Authority

Finally, it is well to emphasize an obvious fact: students learn. As is increasingly clear from a number of different research programs, children do this best as they are in deed, as well as in theory, major players in the learning process. For some time, motivational research has emphasized that providing an optimal degree of choice is critical to eliciting the investment of students. Recently, researchers have stressed how students' participation in the learning process is critical to their quality of learning. That is, students are most likely to develop appropriate metacognitive skills as well as engage in deep processing if and only if they are not treated as passive vessels into which wisdom is poured. Knowledge is constructed by learners—it is an active process stemming significantly from the initiative of the learner in an enriching social environment.

Having stressed that fundamental point, it must be added that examples abound that school policy and practice often stand as a stern example of how a fundamental point can be forgotten. Order and safety are needed to have an effective school, of course. But equally critical is an environment in which the learner is not just controlled but increasingly becomes a controller—first of her own learning and then of her own destiny. Schools and school cultures vary significantly on this dimension, and this variance is crucial. Among the results to be considered in this regard is that the reduced choice in turn reduces the likelihood of holding a task-goal theory of learning and schooling.

The Process of Culture Change

Of course, knowing what to change does not complete the circle of knowledge needed. Schools struggle to make school change of any type, and policy changes of the type that we call for will not be easy either. One cannot simply call for school change. One has to consider seriously whether it is within a school's power to do what is called for. Our answer is that indeed it is, but it is by no means easy.

Experiences with School Change

In order to determine the feasibility of making the kind of policy changes that are called for, Maehr and Midgley and their colleagues (1996) initiated two comprehensive school-change experiments. To date, these experiments have yielded several very critical findings regarding school culture change.

School Control over Policy and Practice. A first conclusion reached was that schools indeed have considerable jurisdiction over the policy and practice areas designated above—sufficient to make significant changes in this regard if they so choose. In many elementary schools, for example, it is possible to initiate new ways of evaluation and assessment, including different grading practices. Even in cases where district policy sets rigid guidelines, teachers and administrators still have a remarkable amount of freedom regarding how they implement these policies. Teachers give A's and B's if they have to, but they give them for a variety of reasons. And most important, they interpret what these grades should mean to students. Schools have considerable freedom in the way in which they choose to recognize "desirable" performance and behavior. They can emphasize academics more than athletics, of course. They can also make a point of stressing learning and progress and not limit themselves to recognizing those who happen to get the highest scores on tests. They can recognize novelty and creativity—or conformity. They can also recognize altruism and good citizenship. And it is clear also that students see schools as doing or not doing these things.

Schools cannot change their culture without effort and per-haps some pain. And they are likely to do it successfully only if certain other conditions are met. One of these conditions is having a clear and workable vision of what schooling, teaching, and learning are to be.

Having a Vision for School. School change involves both a recognized need and a projected goal. A vision for school provides both. By a vision for school, we mean a theory for school that embraces a view of purpose as well as strategies for achieving that purpose. Here we have presented our vision of school that is based on current research as well as on our own experience in changing schools. That vision is not perfect; it is an emergent vision at best. However, it does provide an example of what we have in mind when we, as others, argue that a vision is necessary for school change—or for the school to function well and effectively (cf., Roueche, Baker, and Rose, 1989).

First, our vision clearly states what we want for students: learning. Students are the ultimate focus and learning the ultimate product. Our goal is not a clean building, a safe house, a social or socializing agency, a club, or a workplace. It may have a bit of all of these, of course. But in the final analysis, the school must be a place of learning for all students. Further, we argue that being as specific as we can about what we want from school is necessary to obtain the allegiance not only of staff members and school boards, but also of the most important clients: students. Early on in our research, we found that when the students perceived that the school had a sense of what it was about, especially when the school stood for learning, they were more likely to invest in the learning process.

A mission, a clear and viable sense of purpose, is an important first step toward achieving effectiveness. However, not every school mission is equally good. Our hypothesis, undergirded by considerable research, indicates that a mission associated with promoting task goals is likely to have quite different personal and learning effects than one that concentrates on ability goals. For most if not all conditions, a task-focused culture is clearly preferred.

A Shared Vision. It is not enough for the vision to be in the eyes of one school community member, such as the principal. It must be shared by administration, staff, parents, and students, and the process of realizing it is in the fullest sense a group process. Communication, cohesiveness, good social relationships do not by themselves insure that good things will happen in a school. But good things are not very likely to happen if the school is not a reasonably cohesive, socially supportive place. Culture change involves effective communication, working together toward a certain end, and trust among members.

Leadership. But someone has to stick her neck out if the critical steps on the road to change are to be made. To an important degree, all involved have to risk something, but usually it is also someone like the principal who will have to say at some crucial point of uncertainty, "OK, we'll do it." And not only "take the heat" for this decision but also defend, promote, and support it. As we reflect on our own experiences with school-culture change, we see that many had to be involved in the process, but there were always those moments when work would have stopped had not someone in the position to lead stepped out and said, "Let's do it." Indeed, the leader's dedication to the change, belief in the vision, and willingness to take risks and encourage others to take risks is the main force that holds the change process together and moves it forward.

Conclusion

In recent years, communities, the states, and the nation have spent considerable resources on school reform. Much of this has been spent on training and retraining teachers, putting new materials in their hands, and sometimes giving them a little technology to use. Amidst all this, precious little thought has been given to the design of school, especially to creating visions of what it is supposed to be. Yet, such a vision is surely one of the most important of concerns. In the final analysis, that is what the examination of school culture is about. We have presented what we believe to be not only a worthy vision but a workable one. We have also reported evidence that when put in place, a vision that promotes task goals will yield results in students' investment in and love for learning. Putting it in place, of course, is more than half the problem. As a result, our experiences in effecting school culture change may be useful. We hope they will serve not as a heuristic in thinking about change but as a stimulant and guide for effecting change. We trust our suggestion or two will, at a bare minimum, enhance the concern to try.

Reference

Ames, C. (1992). Classrooms: Goals, structures, and student moviation. *Journal of Educational Psychology 84*, 261–271.

Ames, C., and Archer, J. (1988). Achievement goals in the classroom: Student learning strategies and motivation processes. *Journal of Educational Psychology 80*, 260–267.

Anderman, E., and Young, A. (1994). Motivation and strategy use in science: Individual differences and classroom effects. *Journal of Research in Science Teaching 31*, 811–831.

Blumenfeld, P. C.; Puro, P.; and Mergendoller, J. R. (1992). Translating motivation into thoughtfulness. In H. H. Marshall (ed.), *Redefining student learning* (pp. 207–239). Norwood, N. J.: Ablex Publishing Corp.

Covington, M. V. (1992). *Making the grade: A self-worth perspective on motivation and school reform.* New York: Cambridge University Press.

Deal, T. E., and Peterson, K. D. (1990). *The principal's role in shaping school culture.* Washington, D.C.: U.S. Printing Office.

Epstein, J. L. (1989). Family structures and student motivation: A developmental perspective. In C. Ames and R. Ames (eds.), *Research on motivation in education, Vol. 3* (pp. 259–295). San Diego: Academic Press.

Lepper, M. R., and Cordova, D. I. (1992). A desire to be taught: Instructional consequences of intrinsic motivation. *Motivation and Emotion 16*, 187–208.

Maehr, M. L.; Midgley, C.; et al. (1996). *Transforming school cultures.* Boulder, Colo.: Westview Press (Harper/Collins).

Roueche, J. E.; Baker, G. A.; and Rose, R. R. (1989). *Shared vision: Transformational leadership in American community colleges.* Washington, D.C.: The Community College Press.

Sarason, S. B. (1990). *The predictable failure of educational reform.* San Francisco: Jossey-Bass.

Chapter 17

Home Environments for Learning

Herbert J. Walberg and Susan J. Paik

The home environment greatly influences learning within and outside school. In this chapter, we summarize research on the home environment that has looked at home-based reinforcement, home instruction, and homework, among other educational and psychological activities in the home. This work suggests that some features of the home environment may be changed to increase children's academic learning. First, we will look at how children's use of time and changing family demographics affect learning.

Time for Learning

Parents and educators tell children that time is valuable and must not be wasted, and various authorities recommend increasing the amount and quality of school time. However, estimates of the actual value of children's time spent in school are unavailable; researchers and policymakers rarely even account for the amount, let alone the value, of the time that children spend in school and at home.

A look at how children spend their waking time reveals the educative potential of efficient time use. The typical child in the United States spends 175 to 180 days in school each year, which is equivalent to twenty-seven full-time, forty-hour weeks—or roughly half of an adult's work year. This amount compares unfavorably with the average of about three hours per day that students watch television.

Not all time in school, moreover, is learning time. Lost school time attributable to tardiness, absence, early dismissal, interruptions, and inattentiveness takes away from nominal hours. Children's individual differences might also lead to wasted time. Some students already have knowledge of what is presented; others are yet incapable of learning it. Depending on our assumptions, as little as 270 hours per year or about seven 40-hour weeks may remain for suitable instruction.

Considering that only a small amount of in-school time is actually educative, it may be less than surprising that corporate and military programs that require "total immersion" produce relatively impressive results. Efficient second-language programs for adults can produce near-native competence in non-Western languages in as little as 1,300 hours—the equivalent of eight months of forty-hour weeks of study. In contrast, many American schoolchildren, despite years of formal study, lack mastery of English to meet reasonable standards.

Investment Value of Time

Assessing students' time productivity and budgeting it well may help us raise students' levels of academic learning as well as their proficiency in nonacademic fields. Not only does educational productivity have value in itself, but it is required for accomplishments of excellence in fields in which performance can be measured and ranked. Doubling and even redoubling educational time and its efficiency may go a long way toward raising students' potential.

An hour a day of concentrated instruction, effort, and practice may be enough to achieve excellence in mathematics, chess, and other competitively ranked pursuits. World-class performance in such endeavors may require four to twelve hours a day over one to twenty years (Walberg, 1983). Knowledge of the time and means required to attain excellence is likely to help educators, parents, and students in making better informed decisions about time allocations among curricular, extracurricular, and nonschool activities. The "Matthew effect" of the academically rich getting richer from formal education may be at least partly accounted for by large differences in parental investments in support of their children's knowledge and skill acquisition during the school years (Walberg, 1983).

Through the formative years until the end of high school, parents influence directly or indirectly 87 percent of the student's waking time that is spent outside of school, including choosing their children's neighborhood and influencing peer group choices and other activities. This is by far the largest fraction of the student's life, and it strongly influences the productivity of the time spent in school. During this remaining 87 percent of waking time, some parents give up to five times more attention to their children than do other parents (Hill and Stafford, 1974).

Demographic and Family Trends

Because of vast changes in the age structure of the U.S. population, parents' effectiveness in developing their children's abilities may be more important today than it was in past decades. Seven million fewer young people will be reaching working age in the 1990s than in the 1970s. If present fertility rates continue, in about twenty-five years, only two members of the baby-bust generation will be actively employed in partial support of each retired person of the baby-boom generation—in contrast to the ratio of sixteen to one in 1950. Even if adults today lack altruism for the young generation, they might want to think about its competence and willingness to pay for their pensions and Social Security.

While parents and educators are raising a smaller generation of children than had previous generations, the demand for a large, sophisticated workforce may continue to rise; for example, it is suggestive that the percentage of all U. S. workers in the "knowledge industries"—those that produce, process, and distribute information goods and services—rose from 5 percent in 1860 to about 50 percent in 1980 and is undoubtedly higher today. The growth sectors of the economy, moreover, may require even greater verbal, quantitative, scientific, social, and other abilities if the United States is to remain internationally competitive (Walberg, 1983).

Family trends, however, may not bode well for children's learning. During the century from 1860 to 1960, the divorce rate in the United States held between thirty to thirty-five per thousand marriages. Fertility declined after 1960, nonmarital cohabiting relationships rose dramatically, and divorces increased to unprecedented levels. At current rates, about one-third of all American children will witness the dissolution of their parents' marriage. The percentage of working mothers, moreover, rose from 32 percent in 1960 to 56 percent in 1981 (Cherlin, 1983). Whatever one's opinion of the value of these changes for adults, it is important to consider how they may affect children's learning at home and in school.

For these demographic and sociological reasons, educational psychologists today must be concerned about how children's home life affects their learning. Thus, next we will consider what parents and educators can do to foster learning outside school.

Classroom and Home Teaching

Time, opportunity, and concentrated effort appear to be the chief determinants of learning, and it is hard to find substitutes for them. Psychological studies of ordinary as well as distinguished accomplishments of children, adolescents, and adults show that experience, in whatever institution it takes place, is the pervasive determinant of achievement.

Ideas and findings about home and classroom learning, moreover, appear to be converging on the fundamental learning processes. These fundamental processes may be thought of as the amount and appropriate quality of the following:

1. *Stimulation*—or motivation, cues, and other information presented to the child by the teacher, parent, medium of instruction, and general experiences.
2. *Engagement*—or the child's mental processing of new and stored information and experience.
3. *Reinforcement*—or feedback and other signaling of the correctness, desirability, and short- and long-term value of the child's spontaneous or elicited responses.

Classroom Teaching

Nineteen major reviews of research on teaching covered thirty-five teaching tactics that can be classified as stimulation, engagement, or reinforcement. These reviews of research suggest consensus that these tactics promote student learning (Waxman and Walberg, 1982).

About a decade ago, Ann Brown and Annmarie Palincsar showed that carefully delegating to students some control over learning goals and monitoring their progress in achieving the goals yields substantial learning gains. That is, students can be taught to take increasing responsibility for allocating their time to these activities. Many studies have corroborated Brown and Palincsar's findings (Haller, Child, and Walberg, 1988).

To impart such "metacognitive" skills, teachers may employ modeling to exhibit the desired behavior, guided practice with their help, and application in which students act independently of them. A successful program of "reciprocal teaching" fosters reading comprehension by having students take turns in leading dialogues on pertinent features of texts. By assuming the roles of planning and monitoring ordinarily exercised by teachers, students learn self-management. Perhaps that is why tutors learn from teaching, and why we say that to learn something well, teach it.

Teaching for comprehension encourages readers to measure their progress toward explicit goals. If necessary, they can reallocate time for different activities. In this way, self-awareness, personal control, and positive self-evaluation can be enlarged.

Home Teaching

Laosa (1981) identified tactics of maternal teaching that promote young children's development. They are similar to the classroom teaching practices described above.

Mothers stimulate their children as follows:

1. *Informing*—imparting information about the task.
2. *Motivating*—eliciting the child's interest and cooperation by suggesting that the task would be a rewarding experience or by promising external rewards.
3. *Orienting*—developing an expectation in the child's mind for the task to follow. ("I'm going to show you how to put these blocks in the right place.")

Mothers reinforce their children's learning as follows:

1. *Seeking physical feedback*—getting the child to sort or group the blocks or complete other tasks.
2. *Seeking verbal feedback*—asking the child to identify attributes of the blocks, explain sorting principles, or otherwise verbally respond.
3. *Giving positive reinforcement*—confirming correct responses by the child.
4. *Giving negative reinforcement*—noting incorrect responses with remarks like "No, that's wrong."
5. *Requiring discrimination*—requiring the child to perceive and see differences among the relevant attributes of the blocks.

Although the fundamental processes of school and home learning may be similar, they differ markedly in manifestation. Children's home learning may extend throughout the first two decades of their lives with the same parents. School learning, in contrast, usually involves a new teacher in each grade of elementary school and multiple teachers starting in middle or high school. Home learning usually involves a smaller and more stable group of peers (siblings), although their ages vary more than do school classmates' ages.

Home teaching, moreover, is more concrete, extensive, and happenstance; school teaching is usually more abstract, intensive, and intentional. Parents more often concentrate on character, morals, and socialization; teachers, on academic subjects and other educational goals.

Perhaps even more striking than these differences are the large inequalities in the number of adults and children in different homes, compared to differences among schools. For example, one to six children and one or two adults are common in homes, but school class size is usually between fifteen and forty students with one teacher. Thus the child-to-adult ratios in homes may vary by a factor of six or twelve between the largest families and the smallest, while the child-to-adult ratio in classes varies by a factor of only 2.67 from the largest class to the smallest.

Similarly, the wealth and income of some families is twenty times greater than other families, and the cost of childrearing is five times more in upper-socioeconomic-status families than in poorer families (Hill and Stafford, 1974). In sharp contrast, school districts' investment and operating expenditures per student rarely vary by more than a ratio of four to one, within a given state. Surprisingly, however, these inequalities in family size and wealth are only weakly linked to the achievement of children in school when compared to the quality of parental stimulation in the home.

Family Characteristics

About a dozen models have guided inquiry about the relations of learning to family and home characteristics (Walberg and Marjoribanks, 1976). Research shows that influences of parental education, occupation, and income indexes of socioeconomic status (SES) on academic achievement is surprisingly weak. Social ascendancy through education may also be far less constrained by social class than many have believed. A compilation of results from about 1,500 studies, however, concluded that the number of children in a family has a weak negative influence on achievement and socialization. More powerful negative influences are divorce, separation, and family strife.

Family Environment

Although socioeconomic status is a popular construct and easy to measure, it is not the only home factor that fosters ability and achievement. Detailed assessments of parental practices provide far better predictions of children's achievement. For example, study of homes in England showed that the quality of maternal discipline, even though statistically controlled for SES, predicts ability, and that children in intellectually demanding homes where rewards depend on achievement tend to score higher than others on ability.

Although several thousand studies that assess the effects of the number of children in a home SES and *sibsize studies* have been published, a search of educational, psychological, and sociological literature (Iverson and Walberg, 1982) turned up only eighteen noninterventional, parent-interview studies of the association between home-environment constructs and learning in samples of about five thousand students in eight countries. Correlations (the units of analysis) of students' intelligence, motivation, and achievement with indexes of parental stimulation of the students were substantial. These learning correlates are considerably higher than those involving SES. The magnitudes of the correlations do not depend on the student's sex, SES, age, or nationality, or on the type of learning measured.

Intervention Research

It is dangerous to rely on mere correlations to assess the effects of the home environment on learning. Intervention studies in which investigators alter conditions in experimental groups that are then contrasted with control groups give a better assessment of the effects of changes suggested by case and correlational studies.

Home Reinforcement

Barth (1979) found twenty-four studies of home-based reinforcement of school motivation, behavior, and learning. His review begins with the sentence, "It has been demonstrated frequently and incontrovertibly that classroom behavior can be controlled by teachers who are trained in the use of differential reinforcement and token economies" (p. 436). He might have ended that the same apparently applies to the effects on students of trained parents cooperating in school-based programs.

The studies in the Barth review are rigorously experimental in the Skinnerian tradition. Start-up periods of daily or weekly teacher notes or checklists on classroom behavior and no reinforcements are followed by a period of home-administered consumable reinforcers, earned privileges, verbal praise, or penalties geared to the reports of classroom performance. Reinforcement is phased in and out; and behavior appears to be consistently controlled.

Such programs are impressive in their impacts on normal as well as delinquent and disturbed children, and they have remedied a wide variety of problem behaviors and academic deficiencies at small costs to teachers, counselors, and parents. Permanent or long- term changes in character, intrinsic motivation, and other psychological traits, however, appear to be more difficult to demonstrate.

Homework

Another obvious, but neglected, home ingredient in learning is homework—the amount, standards, and usefulness of which is jointly determined by educators, parents, and students. Empirical studies of homework show that assigning and grading or commenting on it produces a huge effect on learning—about three times that of computer-assisted instruction or family socioeconomic status. Homework appears to produce uniformly positive effects on factual, conceptual, critical, attitudinal, and other aspects of learning.

Analysis of the data from a study called "High School and Beyond," however, shows that American high school students average 4.5 hours of homework and 30 hours of television per week. The television is watched for more hours than what is optimal for learning (Williams et al., 1982); and educators, families, and students might do well to ensure that more of this discretionary time is spent on academic study and other active and constructive pursuits.

Home Environment

In addition to more narrow reinforcement approaches, broad academic conditions in the home correlate moderately with learning. As Iverson and Walberg's (1982) quantitative synthesis indicates, what might be called "the curriculum of the home" accounts for three times more learning variance than does family socioeconomic status. This general curriculum refers to informed parent-child conversations about everyday events, encouragement and discussion of leisure reading, monitoring and joint analysis of television viewing and peer activities, deferral of immediate gratifications to accomplish long-term goals, expressions of affection, and interest in the child's academic progress and progress as a person.

Moreover, deliberate, cooperative intervention efforts by parents and educators to modify academic conditions in the home have an outstanding record of success in promoting achievement (Graue, Weinstein, and Walberg, 1983). In twenty-nine controlled studies, 91 percent of the comparisons favored children in such programs over those in nonparticipant groups. Because few of the programs lasted more than a semester, the potential for programs sustained over the years of schooling is great, since the programs appear to benefit older as well as younger students.

These home-enrichment programs are less precisely defined than home-based reinforcement programs; but, like effective classroom instruction, they generally include efforts to improve stimulation, engagement, and reinforcement as well as efficient management of the child's time. That is, the parent adopts the broader roles of teacher, co-teacher, or assistant teacher rather than only executing the amount of reinforcement corresponding to the degree called for in reports by the school teacher.

Because of the convergence of research on time, school-teaching effects, home environment, home reinforcement, and home-coordinate teaching, there seems little doubt that parents can directly and indirectly exert strong, consistent causal influences on academic and other learning. Programs that expand and systematize these influences might contribute much to the expansion of learning and to the further development of talent.

Home-School Partnerships

Although parent-teacher interventions targeted on achievement goals may show the greatest learning effects, Williams (1983) at the Southwest Education Development Laboratory in Austin, Texas, described other constructive roles for parents in school programs. These roles include the following: audience for the child's work; home tutor; co-learner with the child; school-program supporter; advocate before school board members and other officials; school committee member; and paid school-staff worker. Although parents view their participation in some of these roles more favorably than do teachers and principals, all parties agree that there should be more parent involvement than now exists.

An Exemplary Program

Chicago educators and parents developed an exemplary parent-education program for grades 1 to 6 and asked one of us to evaluate it. "Operation Higher Achievement," at the Grant School in Chicago's severely depressed Westside area, illustrates what educators can do in inner-city public schools with parent partners (Walberg, Bole, and Waxman, 1980).

A joint steering committee of school staff and parents at Grant initially formulated seven program goals such as "increasing parents' awareness of the reading process" and "improving parent-school-community relations." Seven 10-member staff and parent committees met periodically to plan and guide the accomplishment of each goal. The goals were based on a survey that showed that parents wanted closer school-parent cooperation, stricter school discipline, and more educational activities conducted in the school and community for their children.

The committees wrote staff-parent-child agreements to be followed during the school year. The district superintendent, the principal, and the teachers signed contracts for educational services to be provided to each child. The parents pledged such things as providing a quiet, well-lit place for study each day; informing themselves about and encouraging the child's progress; and co-operating with teachers on matters of schoolwork, discipline, and attendance. The children also signed improvement pledges. Small-business merchants in the community raised funds to provide book-exchange fairs and other school activities.

Evaluation of this program, along with other research, shows that inner-city children can make as much progress in achievement as do suburban middle-class children. To help them, educators need to sustain active cooperation with parents on joint goals.

Conclusion

Educational and psychological research in ordinary schools shows that improving the amount and quality of instruction can result in vastly more effective and efficient academic learning. But educators can do even more by enlisting families as partners and engaging them directly and indirectly in their efforts.

Those concerned with human resources find surprisingly large differences in families' time investments in their children. As discussed above, even before school age, children differ by as much as five to one in the value of time mothers have invested in them. Such vast differences may go a long way in accounting for children's varying capacities to profit from schooling and other educative experiences.

As noted, the effects of home environment interventions on learning are plausible, robust, and moderate to large in size. Research also suggests that the effects might even be larger if home-intervention programs were to be more sustained and systematic. Thus, while continuing local evaluation and further research are in order, there seems little reason to hesitate in more widely and comprehensively implementing extensions of the kinds of programs described here.

References

Barth, R. (1979). Home-based reinforcement of school behavior. *Review of Educational Research 49*, 436–458.

Cherlin (1983). A changing family and household. In Ralph H. Turner and James F. Short (eds.), *Annual Review of Sociology: Volume 9*. Palo Alto, Calif.: Annual Reviews.

Graue, M. Elizabeth; Weinstein, Thomas; and Walberg, Herbert J. (1983). School-based home instruction and learning: A quantitative synthesis. Paper presented at the annual meeting of the American Educational Research Association, Montreal.

Haller, E.; Child, D.; and Walberg, H. J. (December 1988). Can comprehension be taught? A quantitative synthesis, *Educational Researcher 17* (9), 5–8.

Hill, R. C., and Stafford, F. P. (1974). The allocation of time to preschool children and educational opportunity. *Journal of Human Resources 9*, 323–341.

Iverson, B. K., and Walberg, H. J. (1982). Home environment and learning: A quantitative synthesis. *Journal of Experimental Education 50*, 144–151.

Laosa, L. M. (1981) Maternal behavior: Sociocultural diversity in modes of family interaction. In R. W. Henderson (ed.), *Parent-child interaction*. New York: Academic Press.

Palincsar, A. M., and Brown, A. (1984). Reciprocal teaching of comprehension fostering and comprehension monitoring activities. *Cognition and Instruction, 1*, 117–176.

Walberg, H. J. (1983). Scientific literacy and economic productivity in international perspective. *Daedalus 112* (2), 1–28.

Walberg, H. J.; Bole, R. E.; and Waxman, H. C. (1980) School-based family socialization and achievement in the inner city. *Psychology in the Schools 17*, 509–514.

Walberg, H. J., and Marjoribanks, K. (1976). Family environment and cognitive development. *Review of Educational Research 45*, 527–51.

Waxman, H. C., and Walberg, H. J. (1982). The relation of teaching and learning: A review of reviews of the process-product paradigm. *Contemporary Education 1*, 103–120.

Williams, D. L. (1983). Parent perspectives regarding parent involvement at the elementary school level. Paper presented at the meetings of the American Educational Research Association, Montreal.

Williams, P.; Haertel, G. D.; Haertel, E. H; and Walberg, H. J. (1982). Leisure-time television and school learning: A quantitative synthesis. *American Educational Research Journal 19*, 19–50.

Chapter 18

Education of Gifted Students

Gary A. Davis

Let's capsulize the case for gifted education with two rhetorical questions. First, precisely *where*—at this moment—are tomorrow's leaders in business, politics, the arts, medicine, and engineering and science? In today's schools, of course. Second, should these children be forced to suffer through a system that deprives them of an education that fits their needs, abilities, and interests— that makes them work at a fraction of their capacity; bores them with material they knew two years earlier; ignores their energetic need to innovate and create; fosters poor study habits because they never need to work; and causes endless frustration and feelings that they are different, alone, perhaps "weird," and must hide their gifts from cynical schoolmates? Of course not.

Variations of these simple arguments led in the early 1970s to a resurgence of interest in identifying and providing special educational services to children with gifts and talents. The movement mushroomed across America and Canada. Presently, almost every state has passed legislation on behalf of gifted and talented students. While some milquetoast directives simply acknowledge that such children exist and should receive special services, legislation in other states defines what is meant by "gifted and talented," recommends identification criteria and educational services, and provides funding and leadership. The movement has become worldwide, with gifted programs in place from Alaska to South Africa, from the two Chinas to Brazil.

Space will permit only a small sample of highlights and developments. In the following sections we will look briefly at (1) current difficulties, with a glance at the 1993 *National Excellence* report, (2) methods and challenges in identification, (3) acceleration and enrichment strategies, grouping, program models, and curricula concerns, (4) counseling considerations, and (5) legal issues.

Current Difficulties

Some trends are damaging and even terminating many programs for gifted students. There always have been persons, perhaps preoccupied with egalitarianism and democracy, who focus only on the need to help below-average and at-risk students become more equal. In regard to the gifted, some standard arguments are, "These kids will make it on their own," "Their needs can be accommodated in the regular classroom," and "Let's help the kids who really need it." Gifted education is perceived by such critics as elitist and undemocratic because it appears to offer special opportunities to middle-class kids who already bask in advantages.

Gallagher (1997) and others have noted America's "love-hate" relationship with giftedness. We applaud the individual who rises from a humble background to high educational and career success, yet as Americans we are committed to equality. Labeling some children *gifted* threatens the self-esteem of both other children and adults. The pendulum swings between a zeal for *equity* and an enthusiasm for *excellence.* Beginning in the late 1980s, equity has become the more forceful concern. Richert (1997) used James Madison's term "tyranny of the majority" to describe the gifted-bashing national wave of school reform.

Detracking

The *detracking movement* went straight for the throat of motivated, high-achieving students. Movement leader Jeannie Oakes (1985) argued to democratic-minded Americans that separating students into slow-, average-, and fast-track classes deprives slower learners of educational opportunities and damages their self-esteem. Worse, tracking was called *racist* because disproportionate numbers of minority students often appear in slow-track classes. Tracking programs have been trashed wholesale. Unfortunately, many educators and others have not separated *tracking* from *gifted education*, and gifted programs have been scrapped as well. Bright students are losing not only fast-track classes, but also the acceleration and enrichment opportunities of gifted programs. Logically, tracking plans can be ended while preserving gifted programs.

Cooperative Learning

Imagine for a moment that the gifted program—along with tracking—has been terminated, and bright students are back in heterogeneous-ability classrooms. In addition to waiting for slow learners to catch up, what are they doing? *Cooperative learning.* Cooperative learning is a fast-growing teaching strategy, literally a reform movement, and for good reason. When small groups of children work cooperatively to solve a problem, complete a worksheet, or reach conclusions for a class presentation, on average they realize these benefits: Achievement runs higher; motivation improves from the mutual encouragement; thinking skills are stimulated by discussions and conflict resolution; social, interpersonal, and leadership skills improve; school attitudes and school climate improve; and even self-confidence and self-esteem show gains. Splendid. The difficulty is that gifted students too often find themselves a "junior teacher." Further, they often become frustrated and feel like "suckers" because of the injustice of carrying the work load for disinterested "free riders" (Robinson, 1997). Gifted students also miss opportunities for accelerated work, self-selected independent projects, and group work with other gifted students, all of which would better match their abilities, needs, and self-concepts.

Problems Beyond Detracking and Cooperative Learning

There are other problems beyond the detracking and coop-erative-learning movements. Funding, of course, is an eternal difficulty that can terminate any type of program perceived as a "frill" or as otherwise expendable. But other problems arise when accelerated and enriched programs are created for special subgroups of students.

Under the heading of "The Death of Gifted Programs," Davis and Rimm (1994) collated these factors, drawn from several sources, that contribute to the passing of services for gifted students:

- The program may appear to be a fun-and-games waste of time.
- Regular teachers sometimes resent the gifted teacher's easy-to-teach, motivated students—as well as the field trips and other benefits—while they struggle with slow learners, at-risk students, and children with learning disabilities.
- Regular teachers may dislike the disruption of class routines caused when gifted students must leave the class for several hours per week in "pull-out" programs.
- Parents of regular students may resent the presumed superiority of students labeled "gifted" and the special activities offered to upper-crust kids. All parents want the best teachers and best opportunities for their children.
- Providing gifted students with expensive equipment and plenty of field trips provides strong evidence to support charges of elitism.
- Program participants sometimes become snobbish and arrogant.
- Students not selected for the gifted program may become resentful, acquire poor self-concepts, or both.
- If gifted students are moved to special classes or special schools, their contributions to the regular class are lost, for example, modeling "good student" behavior and assisting other students.
- Accelerating the curriculum for gifted students can create problems of continuity in higher grades.

- Competition, pressure, and stress in the gifted program/class may become unhealthy.
- Gifted students may acquire unhealthy levels of perfectionism, caused by the flattery and high expectations of parents, teachers, and others. Perfectionism becomes unhealthy when students are overly precise; worry themselves sick trying to maintain straight "A" grades; stay up all night working on papers because they must be "perfect"; have sweaty palms and accelerated heart rates the morning of tests; procrastinate, because each new project threatens failure; avoid new experiences, which include the possibility of making mistakes; and feel dissatisfied or even guilty about their good work.
- Many students "level off" after entering a gifted program.
- The program can appear to be a reward—a prize, plum, status symbol—for polite, cooperative, high-achieving children with good attitudes.
- Activities in the gifted program appear to be good for all children, not just those labeled *gifted.*
- Many teachers believe the needs of the gifted can be handled within the regular class structure, for example, with cooperative learning or by using technology to individualize learning.

These are a sample of problems and criticisms that plague gifted programs and that provide ammunition for those who would eliminate programs and ignore the educational needs of gifted students. The predicament is that many of these problems are absolutely true. Program coordinators and teachers of the gifted must be prepared to cope with or correct them.

Generally, critics of gifted education are quick *not* to think about the fairness of a suitable education for all students, nor the professional and artistic services that gifted students eventually will provide the country and world. The U.S. government position on gifted education, however, seems more attuned to both fair play and democracy, on the one hand, as well as to fostering the capabilities of talented students, on the other. As described by Patricia O'Connell Ross, author of *National Excellence: A Case for Developing America's Talent* (Ross, 1993), the federal view has evolved from the post-Sputnik Cold War stress on cultivating math and science talent to the current position of improving expectations for and education of all students—including those with gifts and talents (Ross, 1997).

The National Excellence Report on America's "Quiet Crisis"

The 1993 publication of the U.S. Department of Education document *National Excellence: A Case for Developing America's Talent* was a response to antigifted feelings and actions. The title of Part I is "A Quiet Crisis in Educating Talented Students." The "quiet crisis" oxymoron is fitting indeed.

A few highlights of the report are these:

- The United States is squandering one of its most precious resources—the gifts, talents, and high interests of many of its students.
- The problem is especially severe among economically disadvantaged and minority students.
- Compared with students in other industrialized countries, American students perform poorly on international tests, are offered a less rigorous curriculum, read fewer demanding books, do less homework, and enter the work force or postsecondary education less prepared.
- Americans have shown ambivalence about high academic and artistic performance and interest. We praise creativity and academic success. . . . But some also pin negative names [*nerd*, *dweeb*] on students who excel academically.[1]
- The message (e.g., in minimum standards) that society often sends to students is to aim for academic *adequacy*, not *excellence*.
- Only two cents of every $100 spent on K-12 education in the U.S. in 1990 supported special opportunities for talented students.

The report did not stop with an elaboration of the quiet crisis. Proactive recommendations are to

- Set challenging curriculum standards.
- Provide more challenging opportunities to learn.

---

[1] High-achieving minority students sometimes are accused of "acting white."

- Increase access to high-quality early childhood education, especially for poor and minority children.
- Increase learning opportunities for disadvantaged and minority children with outstanding talents.
- Broaden the definition of *giftedness* to encompass newer categories of intelligence as well as ability in creative, artistic, leadership, or specific academic areas.
- Improve teacher training for teaching high-level curricula.

Consistent with the *National Excellence* report, many leaders in "gifted education" are recommending that the terms *gifted* and *gifted education* be replaced by *talent development*. This approach stresses developing the varied and unique talents of *all* students— including bright ones. Also, identification must be broader and more imaginative than using only IQ and achievement scores, for example, by profiling students' capabilities. Further, programming should be more varied to accommodate individual characteristics and needs. Finally, the talent development concept eliminates the awkwardness of the word "gifted" and—for everyone else—"not gifted."

It remains to be seen whether the *National Excellence* report will remain revered only in gifted/talent development circles, or if it will impact educators and the general public by causing a second, longer look at the needs of tomorrow's creators and leaders.

Identification

On the surface, selecting students for a gifted and talented (G/T) program may seem simple: Students who are bright and motivated surely could be identified via IQ scores, grades, and teacher recommendations. In fact, identification is a can of worms.

IQ and related academic criteria will discriminate against poor and minority children: African-American, Hispanic, and Native American students currently are underrepresented in G/T programs by 30 to 70 percent (Richert, 1997). If math and science scores are weighted heavily, females will be underrepresented. Students with disabilities often are ignored, although most disabilities do not preclude giftedness—Einstein, Edison, Nelson

Rockefeller, and Picasso all were dyslexic. If grades and teacher recommendations are weighted heavily, underachieving gifted students will be missed—and these are students who may thrive in a flexible and challenging gifted program. Perhaps the majority of creative students—children and youth with great potential for social contributions—will be missed if IQ and grade criteria are applied inflexibly.

Consider also the "teacher pleaser" phenomenon: Many teachers will favor students who are cooperative and anxious to please, who do their work well, neatly, and on time, and who never talk back. In contrast, some extremely bright or creative students may think oddly, dress oddly, ignore rules and conventions, ask too many questions, do poor work when not interested, and be stubborn, egotistical, rebellious, and/or hyperactive. Such students probably are not the teachers' favorites, but they may be the smartest or most creative.

Some additional identification issues are these. First, most scholars in gifted education agree that *both* objective data (test and rating scores) and subjective data (largely parent and teacher nominations, sometimes peer or self nominations) must be used. Meanwhile, many screening committees continue to use "defensible" ability and achievement scores for selection. A sample difficulty is that a student with an IQ score of 115 may show greater giftedness in the sense of originality, critical thinking, problem solving, motivation, and thought-provoking ideas than a student with an IQ score of 140—who will be selected automatically. Or if an IQ cutoff score is set firmly at 125, a creative and energetic student with a score of 124 might be excluded; 125 is "gifted," 124 is "not gifted."

Second, regarding program structure, does the screening committee select a restrictive 3 to 5 percent of the school for participation? Or does it select a more generous 15 to 20 percent for participation in a talent-pool plan? Two benefits of the talent-pool approach described later are that more students are served, and fewer persons in the community will complain of exclusiveness and elitism.

Third, multiple criteria sometimes are combined in unsound ways. For example, points might be assigned based on fifteen or twenty sets of test scores, ratings, grades, and the like, and students above a total-score cutoff will be selected. The difficulty is that a student outstanding in just one area—for example, creativity—will not accumulate a large total point score and will not be selected. Using multiple selection criteria is widely recommended; but the best use of multiple criteria is in an "either/or" fashion. For example, a student might be selected based on high IQ or high achievement or high creativity, or be strongly recommended by teachers (or others).

Fourth, one remarkably common-but-peculiar practice is to formally adopt the U.S. Department of Education definition of giftedness (which includes general intellectual ability, specific academic talent, creativity, leadership, or gifts in the visual and performing arts), but then aim identification instruments and procedures at identifying only academically achieving students.

I have never seen two programs use identical selection procedures, which supports the argument that the ideal identification system is yet to be created. One method that comes close, however, was proposed by Renzulli and Reis (e.g., 1991). Their identification procedure stems from a talent-pool approach—selecting 15 to 20 percent of a school for participation in, for example, Renzulli's *Schools for Talent Development* model, which revolves around his *Enrichment Triad* model.

The five-step strategy is comprehensive and inclusive:

1. *Test-score nominations.* Students who score above the 92nd percentile on standardized intelligence or achievement tests are admitted without further evaluation, thus identifying traditionally bright youngsters.
2. *Teacher nominations.* Excluding students already nominated via Step 1, teachers nominate students who display such worthy characteristics as high creativity, high motivation, unusual interests or talents, or special areas of superior performance or potential.
3. *Alternate pathways.* This procedure includes such other identification strategies as self, parent, or peer nominations, creativity test results, or virtually any other information that might lead to consideration by a screening committee.
4. *Special nominations.* To avoid biases of current teachers, lists are circulated to all teachers in the school (and students' previous schools), which permits other teachers to make recommendations.

5. *Action Information nominations.* The *Schools for Talent Development* model, like previous models, includes Action Information Messages. These typically are filled out by a teacher or talent-pool student to describe the student's high interest in pursuing an independent project in the resource room. Action Information also may be used to nominate non-talent-pool students for projects, and thus for inclusion in the talent pool.

Overall, the Renzulli and Reis identification strategy seems the least likely to overlook and exclude motivated, bright, and creative students.

Program Features

Acceleration and Enrichment

Acceleration and *enrichment* are virtually self-defining. Acceleration means moving the student faster through the system at a pace commensurate with the student's ability. Acceleration may take the form of early admission to kindergarten, first grade, high school, or college; grade skipping (full acceleration); subject acceleration (partial acceleration); credit by examination; college courses while in high school, including Advanced Placement and correspondence courses; telescoped programs, such as condensing three years of algebra into two or collapsing four years of high school into three; residential high schools (the handful of existing ones focus primarily on math and science); and International Baccalaureate Programs (also scarce).

Enrichment is adding breadth and depth. Enrichment goals typically include

- Maximum achievement in basic skills.
- Content and resources beyond the prescribed curriculum.
- Exposure to a variety of fields of study.
- Student-selected content, including in-depth studies.
- High content complexity—theories, generalizations, applications.

- Creative thinking, problem solving, critical thinking, and other thinking skills.
- Library and research skills.
- Affective development, including self-understanding.
- Development of academic motivation, self-direction, independent study skills, communication skills, and high career aspirations.

Some delivery systems for reaching these objectives include various combinations of independent study and projects (e.g., library research, scientific research, art, drama, creative writing); commercial or teacher-made learning centers; field trips; Saturday and summer enrichment programs; mentorships; Future Problem Solving, Odyssey of the Mind, and Junior Great Books programs; and in high school, special honors seminars or Academic Decathlon or other competitions (see Davis and Rimm, 1994).

Grouping

The topic of *grouping* overlaps the topics of acceleration and enrichment, since students will be grouped together for many of the options. Full-time grouping can take the form of special elementary classes; a cluster group of a half-dozen gifted students within a regular class; special schools, including magnet schools and private schools; and the school-within-a-school option, in which gifted students from around the district attend a school that separates them for special academic classes, but they mix with regular students in, for example, physical education, manual arts, and home economics classes.

There also are part-time grouping options, as in the popular-but-criticized pull-out plan in which students are "pulled out" of the regular class for a few hours, usually once per week, for example, for development of creativity and thinking skills, research skills, library and information-retrieval skills, and independent projects. Two criticisms are, first, that such plans are expensive because they require a resource teacher, who typically visits a different school each weekday; and, second, they do not truly meet the needs of students who are gifted all day every day, not just on Wednesday afternoon. Other part-time options are districtwide pull-out plans (often called resource programs), part-time special classes in a school, and special-interest groups and clubs (e.g., after-school French, chess, or computer clubs).

Program Models

Program models guide and structure enrichment activities. Perhaps the best-known model is Renzulli's (1977) *Enrichment Triad* model, which is incorporated in his broader-scope model mentioned above. The Triad model guides, for example, pull-out-program activities by beginning with Type I enrichment, General Exploratory Activities, in which field trips, visiting speakers, and a well-stocked instructional materials center provide academic breadth and help students find topics for research (Type III enrichment). Type II enrichment, Group Training Activities, aims at cognitive and affective growth—for example, creativity and other thinking skills, self-understanding, and communication skills, along with special skills (e.g., operating a video camera or microscope) that will be needed for Type III enrichment, the students' independent or small group projects. Renzulli's most recent programming model, the *Schools for Talent Development* model, outlines how to use Types I and II enrichment in the regular classroom—for all students—while limiting Type III projects to talent-pool students.

Renzulli's approach to programming, as mentioned earlier, avoids charges of elitism by opening the program (talent pool) to a full 15 to 20 percent of the school population. Further, it does not close the door at any time to other motivated and creative students who wish to participate. Also, the approach responds to the criticism, "Wouldn't that be good for all students?" by bringing Types I and II enrichment into the regular classroom for all students. Renzulli's approach seems thoughtful, humanistic, and effective, and it is widely endorsed.

Betts's (1985) Autonomous Learner model resembles Renzulli's models in being a total programming guide. Five components include Orientation (e.g., self-understanding, understanding the program), Individual Development (e.g., learning skills, career involvement), Enrichment Activities, Seminars (with a required presentation), and In-Depth Study. Other models build enrichment activities around, for example, the U.S. Department of Education definition of giftedness (general intellectual ability, specific academic talent, creativity, leadership, and visual and performing arts talent), or the Taylor multiple-talent totem pole categories of academics, productive thinking (creativity), forecasting, communication, planning, and decision making (e.g., Schlichter, 1997).

One never-ending issue is whether acceleration is somehow superior to enrichment, or vice versa. A second issue is whether or not the first issue is getting tiresome. A solid gifted program should have both acceleration and enrichment options available, depending on students' individual needs.

Scope and Sequence

Some authors have noted that too many goals and activities in gifted programs are trivial. VanTassel-Baska (1994), for example, argued that enrichment activities tend to be too product-oriented; instead, they should focus on important issues and themes and develop high-level thinking processes. Gifted students learn faster, are good problem solvers, and can manipulate abstract ideas and make connections. Curriculum design should take advantage of these capabilities, as well as focus on content that is important and worthy of the time to be expended (to use VanTassel-Baska's example, consumer economics is more important than a study of designer jeans or the history of teddy bears); sufficiently conceptually complex, as well as interesting; and relevant to how the world works (e.g., law and languages are more relevant than movies of the 1940s). Her *Integrated Curriculum Model* (ICM) synthesizes the three dimensions of Advanced Content, Process-Product, and Issues/Themes to provide a "coherent curriculum that is responsive to diverse needs of gifted students and yet provides rich challenges for optimal learning." VanTassal-Baska translated ICM concepts into units for both a National Language Arts Curriculum Project and a National Science Curriculum Project for High-Ability Learners.

Counseling the Gifted

Over the past decade or so, the counseling needs of gifted students have become better understood and increasingly emphasized. The customary goal is to help gifted students understand themselves and help counselors, teachers, and parents understand the gifted students. Space will not permit a review of all relevant concepts and recommendations, but the following are some representative highlights.

Terman (1925) is noted for his conclusion that gifted kids are psychologically and socially better adjusted than the average—which led decades of gifted teachers and program planners to ignore problems among gifted students that are both common and damaging, for example, suicide. Leta Hollingworth (1942) was an early pioneer who recognized the emotional needs and vulnerabilities of the gifted. She noted, for example, that moderately gifted students (IQ scores between 120 and 145) do indeed adjust well socially, but students above this level do not; and the greater the gift, the greater the social/psychological problems. Some recurrent predicaments are these:

- Difficult social relationships; isolation.
- Conformity pressures that cause gifted students to hide their talents.
- Anxiety, depression, feelings of stress.
- Lack of challenge in school work; refusal to do routine, repetitious assignments.
- Poor study habits, due to lack of challenge.
- Difficulty finalizing a career goal due to multipotentiality.
- Neurotic levels of perfectionism.

One fascinating syndrome common among high-IQ persons has been called *emotional sensitivity, overexcitability,* or *emotional giftedness.* The five-part syndrome includes (1) near-hyperactive *psychomotor* activity, including high energy, enthusiasm, restlessness, and compulsive and rapid speech; (2) *intellectual* characteristics, such as questioning, metathinking, sustained concentration, high curiosity, searching for truth, and preoccupation with certain problems; (3) *imaginational* traits of lively fantasy and creativeness, magical (paranormal) thinking, and animistic thinking; (4) *sensual* traits of high pleasure from the usual senses, plus perhaps overeating, buying sprees, and sex; and (5) the *emotional* area, which includes soaring highs (waves of joy, feelings of fantastic aliveness and energy), dark lows, a strong sense of right and wrong, and high concern for injustice and others' feelings.

Therapy for gifted students includes many options. For example, personal essay writing (e.g., addressing "Who am I?") and bibliotherapy help students understand their social and emotional difficulties. Stress-management tactics, such as making the student aware of irrational beliefs (e.g., I must be perfect in all things; everyone must like me; I must not disappoint anyone; it is important for me to worry continually), help reduce anxiety. The single most highly recommended therapy is simply bringing gifted students together for sharing problems and solutions, for friendship, and for general social support.

Legal and Ethical Issues

Legal matters, which typically originate with disgruntled parents of gifted children, have haunted gifted programs for many years. Only recently, however, have legal problems and recommended actions coalesced into a coherent topic, thanks to the efforts of Frances Karnes and Ronald Marquardt at the University of Southern Mississippi, where in 1994 they created the Legal Issues Network (see Karnes and Marquardt, 1997).

Legal difficulties, some more common than others, evolve around these categories of problems: early admission to school; the provision of programs or appropriate instruction; racial balance in gifted programs; awarding high school credits toward graduation (Carnegie units) to students who take advanced courses prior to high school; transferring students to districts that offer more suitable programs; the legal status of certification in gifted education (e.g., when applying for a G/T teaching job or when staff positions are cut); transportation to sites that provide appropriate instruction; tort liability (e.g., for injury on a field trip); fraud and misrepresentation (e.g., by a private school claiming to accommodate the gifted); and home schooling (e.g., whether home-schooled children are entitled to participate in public school gifted programs).

Karnes and Marquardt offer the following advice to anyone considering legal action. Conflicts can be settled at any level, from informal discussions to Supreme Court decisions. The best solution, however, is to resolve the problem at the lowest level possible, because as the complainant proceeds up the ladder, costs and delays expand exponentially.

The authors identify five major levels. First, within *negotiation*, one begins resolving an issue at the source. For example, if the issue is admission to a program, one talks to the person in charge of selection; if the issue is the particular program in which the student was placed, one talks to the person responsible for placement and/or programming. Second, *mediation* is a process for resolving problems that also is relatively informal and requires a minimum of time and stress. Twelve states have a formal mediation process, which involves a mediator who hears both sides and then writes a mediation agreement. Third, if mediation is unavailable or unsuccessful, more expensive and adversarial *due process* procedures may be available through special education provisions or through general due process procedures for all students. An open or closed meeting is held, with the student, attorneys, and expert witnesses (on both sides) present. After the meeting, a hearing officer makes a decision and prepares a report, based on his or her interpretation of the evidence as related to local, state, and federal laws. The next step is *state court* or, if federal laws or constitutional provisions are involved, *federal court*. At these levels, parents or other complainants are looking at attorney's fees, court costs, and probably years of litigation.

This newcomer topic of legal issues is an intriguing and needed addition to the field of gifted education.

Conclusion

This chapter has presented an overview of some practices and related issues in some central topics of gifted education and talent development, such as identification, programming, and counseling. In addition, the chapter mentions some current trends and topics, namely, the high-profile and seemingly antigifted detracking and cooperative learning movements, the progifted response in the form of the *National Excellence* report, and the newly formulated topic of legal issues.

The needs of gifted students are real and pressing. While such students are indeed a minority, their preparation for becoming tomorrow's leaders must not be ignored.

References

Betts, G. T. (1985). *Autonomous learner model: For the gifted and talented.* Greeley, Colo.: Autonomous Learning Publications and Specialists.

Davis, G. A., and Rimm, S. B. (1994). *Education of the gifted and talented* (3rd ed.). Boston: Allyn & Bacon.

Gallagher, J. J. (1997). Issues in the education of gifted students. In N. Colangelo and G. A. Davis (eds.), *Handbook of gifted education* (2nd ed.; pp. 10–23). Boston: Allyn & Bacon.

Hollingworth, L. S. (1942). *Children above 180 IQ Stanford-Binet: Origin and development.* New York: World Book.

Karnes, F. A., and Marquardt, R. G. (1997). Legal issues in gifted education. In N. Colangelo and G. A. Davis (eds.), *Handbook of gifted education* (2nd ed.; pp. 536–546). Boston: Allyn & Bacon.

Oakes, J. (1985). *Keeping track.* New Haven, Conn.: Yale University Press.

Renzulli, J. S. (1977). *Enrichment triad model.* Mansfield Center, Conn.: Creative Learning Press.

Renzulli, J. S., and Reis, S. M. (1991). The Schoolwide Enrichment Model: A comprehensive plan for the development of creative productivity. In N. Colangelo and G. A. Davis (eds.), *Handbook of gifted education* (pp. 111–141). Boston: Allyn & Bacon.

Richert, E. S. (1997). Excellence with equity in identification and programming. In N. Colangelo and G. A. Davis (eds.), *Handbook of gifted education* (2nd ed.; pp. 75–88). Boston: Allyn & Bacon.

Robinson, A. (1997). Cooperative learning for talented students: Emergent issues and implications. In N. Colangelo and G. A. Davis (eds.), *Handbook of gifted education* (2nd ed.; pp. 243–252). Boston: Allyn & Bacon.

Ross, P. O. (1993). *National excellence: A case for developing America's talent.* Washington, D.C.: U.S. Department of Education.

Ross, P. O. (1997). Federal policy on gifted and talented education. In N. Colangelo and G. A. Davis (eds.), *Handbook of gifted education* (2nd ed.; pp. 553–559). Boston: Allyn & Bacon.

Schlichter, C. (1997). Talents unlimited model in programs for gifted students. In N. Colangelo and G. A. Davis (eds.), *Handbook of gifted education* (2nd ed.; pp. 318–327). Boston: Allyn & Bacon.

Terman, L. M. (1925). *Genetic studies of genius: Vol. 1. Mental and physical traits of a thousand gifted children*. Stanford, Calif.: Stanford University Press.

VanTassel-Baska, J. (1994). *Comprehensive curriculum for gifted learners* (2nd ed.). Boston: Allyn & Bacon.

Chapter 19

Linguistically Diverse Students

Tomás Galguera and Kenji Hakuta

More Than a Question of Language Instruction

The language characteristics of students attending public schools in this country have undergone a dramatic change in recent years. According to one national study, the number of limited-English-proficient (L.E.P.)[1] students in grades K-12 increased by almost one million between 1984 and 1991, to an estimated 2.3 million (Development Associates, 1993). This is a conservative estimate representing an intensification of a trend that began in 1979—

---

[1] We are aware of the numerous objections raised against using L.E.P. to identify students who are in the process of learning English. Specifically, critics have alluded to its pejorative connotations. Nevertheless, we chose to use L.E.P. because of the familiarity among educators with the meaning of the acronym and its legal definition. Please note that we have included periods to suggest that it should be read as three separate letters and not as the unfortunately common "lep."

from 1979 to 1989, the number of speakers of languages other than English who reported speaking English less than "very well" grew from 10.2 million to 13.9 million (McArthur, 1993). American schools face a great challenge in dealing with these changes, especially since this trend is likely to continue well into the future (Fix and Zimmermann, 1993).

A distinction should be made between issues of linguistic diversity—those concerning the education of L.E.P. students—and issues of ethnic diversity. Although we recognize that English proficiency, ethnicity, and linguistic background are complementary, we choose to center our discussion around linguistic diversity. The reason for our choice lies in the history of legislation, litigation, and policies that have addressed issues of diversity in education as a civil rights problem. From this perspective, limited English proficiency is seen as both a barrier to education and a valid criterion for special treatment. Yet, research has shown that the effectiveness of programs spurred by legislation and litigation has been limited in closing the achievement gap between L.E.P. and non-L.E.P. students, even though promising programs have been documented (see Crawford, 1995; Garcia, 1994).

Studies have also shown that the L.E.P. student population is predominantly poor, Hispanic, educationally disadvantaged, and present in over 42 percent of all school districts nationwide (Abt Associates, in press; Development Associates, 1993). Although the concentration of language groups and total numbers of L.E.P. students fluctuate greatly between districts and between schools, it is clear that the challenge has come to present itself to a substantial proportion of educators and is no longer a problem confined to specific regions of the country.

As is frequently the case with social-intervention programs, the proposed solutions to linguistic diversity in American schools have been the result of rather simplistic interpretations of the problem. As we will argue, linguistic diversity is a complicated phenomenon that requires educators to reconsider the role of all factors that contribute to the situation, not just English proficiency. Also, given the significant numbers of language-minority students present in today's schools and the projected increases in their numbers, the challenge of linguistic diversity in the classroom should no longer be the exclusive purview of teachers with specialist credentials, but a responsibility for all educators.

Who Are Linguistically Diverse Students and Who Teaches Them?

What do we mean by limited English proficient? According to the 1995 reauthorization of the Bilingual Education Act, an L.E.P. student meets one or more of three conditions: (1) the student was born outside of the United States or the student's native language is not English; (2) the student comes from an environment where a language other than English is dominant; or (3) the student is American Indian or Alaskan Native and comes from an environment where a language other than English has had a significant impact on the student's level of English proficiency. In addition, the student experiences sufficient difficulty speaking, reading, writing, or understanding the English language to deny him or her the opportunity to learn successfully in English-only classrooms.

Sixty percent of students meeting these criteria are born in the U.S. (Development Associates, 1993) and concentrated in the West (over 50 percent of them are in California) and the South (20 percent) (McArthur, 1993), with some of the most dramatic recent increases reported in states not traditionally associated with language-minority populations, such as North Carolina (32 percent increase) and Tennessee (80 percent) (U.S. Department of Education, 1991).

Increases in the proportion of L.E.P. students in states such as these are evidence that the phenomenon is not restricted to certain regions of the country. Still, the concentration of L.E.P. students varies considerably from district to district. Total district populations range from several districts with only one L.E.P. student to the case of the Los Angeles Unified School District with over 242,000 L.E.P. students. Still, a majority of districts (67 percent) report serving less than one hundred L.E.P. students (Development Associates, 1993). All these figures translate to classrooms with students at various stages of English proficiency, regardless of their ethnic or linguistic backgrounds.

Substantial increases in the numbers of L.E.P. students are but one indication that issues of limited English proficiency deserve serious consideration in discussions of student diversity. In addition to a need for redefining student diversity around issues

of language diversity, the sheer magnitude of the problem requires a new vision and shared responsibility among all teachers.
One striking finding is that 15 percent of all public school teachers
have at least one L.E.P. student in their classroom who is not
fluent enough in English to complete most of the assigned work
(Development Associates, 1993).

How prepared are the teachers assigned to teach L.E.P. students
present in numerous classrooms? In 1992, only 10 percent of all
teachers of L.E.P. students were certified in bilingual education
and 8 percent, in ESL. Regardless of training, only 42 percent
of all teachers of L.E.P. students reported sharing a non-English
language with their students (Development Associates, 1993). These
findings speak of a need to make training in the teaching of language-minority and L.E.P. students a regular component of most
teacher education programs, especially in states with large numbers of such students. The agreement reached by the Los Angeles Unified School District with the California State Department
of Education requiring all its teachers to undergo staff development in ways to teach L.E.P. students underscores the need to
adjust our perception of language as a factor in student diversity.

Finally, the ethnolinguistic background and socioeconomic status
of teachers and their L.E.P. students are quite different. Most
teachers of L.E.P. students are from an English-speaking background and middle class. In contrast, L.E.P. students tend to be
mostly from Spanish-speaking backgrounds and poor. Only 18
percent of teachers describe themselves as being Hispanic, whereas
73 percent of all L.E.P. students fall in this category (Development Associates, 1993). Regarding socioeconomic status, Abt
Associates (in press) found that in a nationally representative
sample of first- and third-grade students "*more than one-half of
L.E.P. students in both grade cohorts are in families with incomes under
$15,000*" (p. 12; authors' emphasis). These findings have important
implications, not only for policy, but also for classroom practice.

Inherent Tensions in Legislation and Litigation

From the late 1950s through the 1960s, a national preoccupation with civil rights reached public schools. Beginning with the

1954 landmark ruling in *Brown v. Board of Education*, schools were asked to follow mandates that guaranteed equal access to education for all students. The ruling set the tone for subsequent cases where plaintiffs demanded educational equality regardless of student characteristics.

Almost a decade later, Title VII of the Elementary and Secondary Education Act (ESEA) of 1965 aimed to help children of limited-English-speaking ability, especially poor students, to achieve full English literacy. The political atmosphere at the time prompted several politicians to sponsor a series of bilingual education[2] bills. Nevertheless, funding for these bills did not match the rhetoric. This would prove to be indicative of future trends. Federal expenditures on Title VII programs remain relatively low to this day, especially when compared with other compensatory programs. Title VII funding, adjusted for inflation, has been consistently between 30 percent and 40 percent below the 1980 level and only reached the $200 million mark in 1993. In comparison, funding for Chapter 1, a program for economically disadvantaged students, totaled $5.94 billion in 1993 (Fix and Zimmermann, 1993).

Title VII legislation functions primarily as an incentive for districts and local education agencies in the form of grants funding programs for L.E.P. students. In addition, states have adopted statutes mandating special education programs for L.E.P. students, although the severity of these laws varies from state to state. Only nine of the twenty-nine state bilingual laws currently in effect mandate bilingual education programs under specified conditions. Notoriously missing among these states is California, where more than one-half of all L.E.P. students reside (Development Associates, 1993). The absence is the more significant given that California's bilingual law at one time was considered "a virtual bill of rights for language-minority children" (Crawford, 1995; p. 152). California's bilingual law was allowed to expire in 1987 and has not been reauthorized since, a fact that underscores the political nature of the debate surrounding bilingual education.

The passage of the 1968 Title VII amendment to ESEA provided

---

[2] Bilingual education includes programs in which academic instruction is given in languages other than English. The extent of native language instruction varies greatly across and within programs.

funding for several experimental bilingual education programs throughout the country. Additional muscle behind the legislation was provided by a ruling by the U.S. Supreme Court and a series of legal suits in the spirit of the then recently passed Civil Rights Act of 1964 (Crawford, 1995). Up to that time, a number of cases had been making their way through the courts, arguing that schools were violating the civil rights of L.E.P. students by not providing them with meaningful education in a language they could understand. *Lau v. Nichols* became the landmark case that significantly influenced the definition of, and proposed solutions to, linguistic diversity as a civil rights problem.

The ruling in *Lau* reflected the concern for equal access to education first present in the *Brown* decision. Also, and in agreement with prior rulings on issues related to education, the Supreme Court left the solution up to the local school boards. The ruling suggested that schools either instruct students in their native language or teach English to students, but the court was explicit in stating that neither approach was required and that other approaches might be tried (Crawford, 1995; Hakuta, 1986).

To this day, Title VII grants and the court system continue to function as "carrots" and "sticks" for schools serving L.E.P. students. The prevalence of one incentive over the other has been due more to political ideology and actions from school officials and parents than to their relative effectiveness. Similarly, political ideology tends to influence whether schools' effectiveness in dealing with L.E.P. students is measured in terms of inputs or outcomes. On the one hand, people have argued that comparisons between programs and schools are meaningless unless all students enjoy equal opportunities to learn. On the other hand, it is believed that the most effective way to ensure accountability on the part of schools is to assess the skills and knowledge that every student needs. In reality, both conditions are necessary in order to guarantee that all students receive adequate instruction.

However, if the goal is equality in educating L.E.P. students, we face what Martha Minow (1990) calls a "dilemma of difference." In reference to specific programs for diverse students, Minow describes the quandary as follows:

> With both bilingual and special education, schools struggle to deal with children defined as 'different' without stigmatizing them. Both programs

raise the same question: when does treating people differently emphasize their differences and stigmatize or hinder them on that basis? and
when does treating people the same become insensitive to their differences and likely to stigmatize them on *that* basis? [P. 20; Minow's emphasis]

In *Brown*, racial separation was proven indefensible, and schools
were ordered to move toward integration. In contrast, the ruling in *Lau* confirmed the rights of L.E.P. students to equal educational opportunities, while simultaneously validating English
proficiency as a "different" characteristic in students.

Few would argue against the need for students to be proficient in the language of instruction in order to fully participate
in and benefit from education. Yet, attention to English proficiency as a valid criterion of classification has also resulted in a
view of limited English proficiency as a deficit rather than as a
potential for bilingualism. Such a way of thinking is evidenced
by the restricted choice of courses available to most L.E.P. students, especially at the middle and high school levels (see Minicucci
and Olsen, 1992).

An emphasis on English proficiency has also polarized the classification of students into either proficient or limited proficient.
These two broad categories ignore the complex and long-term
nature of the language acquisition process. Rather than perceiving students as complex individuals with numerous strengths and
weaknesses, there is a tendency to separate them into those who
are proficient in English and those who are not. This classification distracts educators from appreciating each student's academic
needs and abilities. Furthermore, proficiency in a language develops continuously over time and in more dimensions than simply
"proficient" or "not proficient." As we will see, programs have
been created for students at intermediate stages of proficiency
in order to address this very aspect of the problem.

Attention to English proficiency has also resulted in policies
and legislation that fail to address other important characteristics of L.E.P. students. For instance, the proportion of L.E.P.
students served by Chapter 1 (now called "Title I") programs
does not match the poverty levels in this student sector. This
problem is due in part to wording in the law itself and in part
to widespread tendencies among school officials and educators
to classify students as either L.E.P. or non-L.E.P. (Fix and

Zimmermann, 1993). The latest reauthorization of Chapter 1 is clearly intended for poor students, regardless of ethnolinguistic background. It remains to be seen whether widespread beliefs will change accordingly.

Finally, framing the problem in terms of civil rights has drawn attention away from schools and onto L.E.P. students. Following the mandates of the *Lau* decision, numerous programs have been developed to assist L.E.P. students in becoming proficient in English and transitioning into mainstream classrooms as soon as possible. Fewer programs, however, have questioned social perceptions and the overall design of schools as institutions intolerant of diversity. At one end of the spectrum, we find programs that make English-language instruction their sole concern. At the other end, we find programs that begin to question assumptions about the nature of teaching and schools and attempt to develop academic skills and knowledge in all students, regardless of the language of instruction.

Truly innovative approaches in dealing with linguistically diverse students also offer an opportunity to move away from a remedial mentality and enrich the instruction of L.E.P. and non-L.E.P. students alike. The tensions inherent in many of these approaches stem from perceived threats to American culture. It is precisely this perception of threat to American customs and institutions that tends to infuse politics into the quest for effective ways to educate L.E.P. students.

Making Teaching Accessible to L.E.P. Students

Assessment

Aspects of tensions associated with positive and negative incentives, criteria of selection, and input versus output measures can be found in the linguistic and academic assessment of L.E.P. students. Although most programs consist of variations or combinations of the two approaches suggested in the *Lau* decision (bilingual education and ESL), considerable variety exists in the methods and techniques used and in the emphasis of language or academic content. In contrast, little effort has been devoted to developing appropriate assessment for the identification and evaluation of L.E.P. students.

Few would argue against the need to assess L.E.P. students in order to determine the best way to serve them. However, objections have been raised about the procedures and instruments used (see August, Hakuta, and Pompa, 1994). Most states mandating services of some kind for L.E.P. students also require assessment of the students' English proficiency before placement in a program. Similar requirements exist for federally funded programs.

A recent study of first- and third-grade L.E.P. students found that a majority of schools (about 78 percent) assess the ability of students to understand and speak their home language and English in order to decide whether or not the student should be in a bilingual or ESL program (Abt Associates, in press). Despite findings such as these suggesting that schools are not using arbitrary selection criteria, a lack of consistent and widely accepted instruments and techniques for the selection and classification of L.E.P. students persists. Just as important, a lack of adequate assessment instruments poses problems in monitoring the accountability of programs.

Lack of consistency is also reflected in the large variation among students who are eligible for special services and in tendencies by some districts to determine student eligibility based on local needs and pressures from the community. A lack of adequate assessment instruments also contributes to obscure the nature of diversity in students. It is indeed very difficult for the average teacher to determine whether difficulties experienced by an L.E.P. student are due to the student's troubles with English or her lack of subject knowledge.

Although successful programs have made language proficiency the key criterion for grouping students (Crawford, 1995, p. 126), L.E.P. status is but one of several factors considered when grouping students. Typically, the composition of linguistically diverse classrooms ranges from only one or a few to all L.E.P. students with varying levels of English proficiency, regardless of whether students are from similar or different ethnic groups.

Finally, recent trends in education toward the development and use of performance-based assessment pose particular problems for L.E.P. students. Greater demands on language associated with authentic assessment tasks make it difficult both for students to demonstrate their skills and for teachers to assign a fair grade.

The issue of assessment and its relation to linguistic diversity remains unresolved, and a thorough discussion on the subject demands more space than is available in this chapter. In any case, teachers of L.E.P. students will have to confront equity issues with regards to assessment and make decisions that will have a profound impact on the academic future of their students. (For further reading, see August, Hakuta, and Pompa, 1994.)

Bilingual Education

The advantages of receiving instruction in a language one can understand should be obvious. Still, the issue of native-language instruction remains a contentious one among people interested in the education of L.E.P. students. A typical argument used by opponents of native-language instruction is that L.E.P. students learn English faster when "immersed" in English-only environments. Furthermore, they claim that the use of native language in school conveys "the wrong message" to students. Supporters argue that by making English proficiency a prerequisite for regular instruction, L.E.P. students are unable to maintain an equal pace with English speakers. They argue that since it takes from five to seven years to become proficient in a language, English-proficiency prerequisites tend to have profound and lasting effects on L.E.P. students' educational and professional futures. (See Minicucci and Olsen, 1992, for an assessment of differences in course offerings.)

In trying to inform the debate, researchers have had to deal not only with political interests, but also with the many factors involved in bilingual education. Most of the evidence regarding the nature and effectiveness of bilingual programs comes from two large studies funded by Title VII. Both studies—a 1989 longitudinal study by Burkheimer and associates evaluating services for L.E.P. students and a 1991 study by Ramirez and associates comparing immersion with early- and late-exit bilingual programs—were in turn reviewed by the National Academy of Sciences in 1992. In this chapter, we are unable to review the numerous methodological objections contained in the National Academy of Science report (Meyer and Fienberg, 1992). Nevertheless, we recommend the report to readers interested in exploring the nature of research in this field.

Due to the problems mentioned above, we chose only two findings that are both valid and relevant for our discussion. First, language of instruction did not seem to matter as much as people on both sides of the debate had hoped, although slight advantages were detected for approaches that used native language over English immersion. Second, regardless of program type, instruction consisted mostly of tasks and routines involving passive learning and low- rather than high-order thinking skills. These findings add support to our claim that problems associated with the education of linguistically diverse students are more than just linguistic.

A recently released technical report by Development Associates (1993) reports that almost all districts (92 percent) provided special services of some kind to L.E.P. students. Over 76 percent of all the districts that reported offering special services to students taught English as a second language. In contrast, 39 percent of these districts taught language arts in the students' native language. A more interesting finding for the purposes of our discussion is that 28 percent of all L.E.P. students in elementary grades did not receive any instruction in their native language. This percentage is even higher for students in junior/middle school (42 percent) and high school (46 percent).

The extent of native language instruction in these programs varied, although a majority (61 percent) were what the researchers called "intensive" services. These services consisted of either extensive ESL instruction (at least ten hours) combined with regular content instruction, or content instruction specifically for L.E.P. students, without any ESL instruction. All together, about one third (34 percent) of all L.E.P. students were in intensive programs that made "significant"[3] use of native-language instruction. Researchers found that the proportion and national origin of L.E.P. students were important factors associated with the type

---

[3] Programs with "significant" use of native language were those where 50 percent or more of the class time is in the students' native language in at least one academic content area other than language arts, or 25 percent or more time in math, sciences, and social studies combined.

of services offered (Development Associates, 1993). Thus, the fact that L.E.P. students are mostly Hispanic should figure prominently in efforts to develop programs and policy.

As this evidence suggests, most school districts report having made efforts to meet the linguistic needs of L.E.P. students. The findings also suggest that variations and combinations of the two approaches recommended in *Lau*, bilingual education and ESL, continue to be used predominantly. Similarly, programs continue to favor English transition over native-language maintenance, a consequence of the deficit mentality that dominates litigation and legislation.

Missing from the research findings mentioned above is an evaluation of particular bilingual education techniques at the classroom level. We know that providing immediate translations in the students' native language tends to minimize opportunities and incentives to learn English (Crawford, 1995). Nevertheless, "concurrent translation," as this technique is known, is sometimes the only way to ensure that students understand critical instructions. Also, translation may help teachers point out similarities across languages, so as to expand on the student's proficiency.

A recommended alternative to concurrent translation consists of teaching each day or class period predominantly in either English or the students' native language. This technique is especially effective when combined with another technique known as "preview-review." In preview-review, the teacher precedes the lesson with a preview in the other language, which provides students either with an organizer for the material to follow or with vocabulary for future use. The two techniques combined can also minimize status differences between languages.

Another set of techniques used by teachers of L.E.P. students are those involving some variation of cooperative instruction. Simply seating students in groups has the effect of increasing opportunities for oral interaction, which is effective for language acquisition, especially among young people. Seating arrangements are also a central feature of several methods and approaches in bilingual education and language instruction, especially when the latter has a communicative emphasis. Cooperative techniques are also an integral component of most constructivistic approaches to education and, as we will see, offer teachers a way to deal with heterogeneous classes (Cohen, 1994).

On the negative side, groups may contribute to the creation and maintenance of patterns of behavior and attitudes among students that are particularly detrimental to L.E.P. students. It is of little benefit for L.E.P. students to be exposed to native English language when the only words they hear are commands, put downs, and mockery. As we will see, certain pedagogical approaches rely on the power of cooperative groups to change students' attitudes and behavior.

The emphasis in legislation and litigation on equal access has resulted in programs that are evaluated primarily on their efficacy to teach English to L.E.P. students (The Stanford Working Group, 1993). A predominance of language over content is understandable given that, with the exception of English proficiency, most instructional issues surrounding the schooling of L.E.P. students are applicable to all students.

English as a Second Language

The history of language instruction can be thought of as a succession of methods, each influenced by contemporary popular beliefs, theories, and research. Our review of language teaching methods is not intended to be exhaustive, but rather a sampling of techniques and approaches available to ESL teachers. Readers interested in greater detail and deeper analyses are encouraged to read David Nunan's (1991) *Language Teaching Methodology.* Our discussion in this section borrows heavily from this source.

Most language teaching methods have emerged predominantly from the tradition of foreign-language instruction and applied linguistics. These teaching methods include Audiolingualism, Cognitive Code Learning, Community Language Learning, the Silent Way, and Suggestopedia. Although the creators of these and other methods commonly attribute enormous success to their way of teaching language, empirical evidence of their effectiveness tends to be mixed at best (see Bialystok and Hakuta, 1994). We should also note that these methods have been used principally to teach foreign languages to relatively successful students, not English to L.E.P. students. Significant differences exist between a foreign-language student and most ESL students, particularly in terms of motivation and objectives.

A method familiar to numerous teachers of L.E.P. students in American schools is Stephen Krashen and Stacey Terrell's Natural Approach. This method is based mostly on Krashen's Monitor Model, one of the most ambitious theories of second language acquisition. Starting from the assumption that first- and second-language acquisition are essentially the same, Krashen has developed a set of principles and concepts that have become part of ESL jargon. Krashen's ideas have received more than their fair share of criticism, especially from researchers who object to the difficulty of testing the many "slippery" concepts included in the theory.

From a more practical perspective, Nunan (1991) joins in the criticism of Krashen and Terrell's method by stating that "like most other methods, the Natural Approach contains activities which, in themselves, are generally unexceptional. It is only when they are elevated to the status of a movement, and when they are fed to learners as an unvarying diet, that they pose a problem to pedagogy" (pp. 243–244). Nunan's admonition regarding language teaching methodology is worth heeding, particularly since, despite the optimistic claims of their proponents, almost all methods are somewhat effective when teaching foreign languages to well-schooled students.

Learning a second language is not the same for everyone. Obviously, a foreign investment banker interested in attracting American investors and a tenth-grade L.E.P. student interested in passing an English proficiency test in order to take a mainstream algebra course do not share the same motivations, concerns, and resources. Although both want to be proficient in English, the needs of each learner are different.

The movement of English for Specific Purposes (ESP) was born out of the realization that the communicative needs of language learners depend on the context in which the language will be used. In our example, the investment banker would be interested in learning the jargon and appropriate sequence of utterances typical in most business transactions. In contrast, the student would be mostly interested in learning reading and writing skills. By basing their instruction on the students' needs, proponents of ESP have blurred the separation between foreign- and second-language instruction.

ESP curricula are typically organized around a communicative syllabus that specifies different functions realized by native-language speakers, such as "Greetings and Salutations" or "Asking Questions." In response to critics who saw little difference between a syllabus organized in this manner and one organized around pronouns and verb tenses, three new organizational topics have been proposed: tasks, projects, and processes. As the terms imply, each one of the three variations consists of assigning rather specific contexts to linguistic functions.

Courses organized around tasks are based on the premise that the nature of the task dictates the linguistic needs. Also, in trying to complete a task, students are required to apply higher-order thinking skills in solving particular linguistic demands associated with the task. Closely related to task-based instruction, project-based language instruction aims at having students produce an actual final product. This requires curricula designed around units that are longer in duration than are tasks. Ideally, the finished project should have a direct relevance to the students' future needs. The last version is process-based instruction, in which the final project is the course syllabus. Although the risk exists that in the hands of an inexperienced teacher instruction might become chaotic, the main advantage of process-based instruction lies in its flexibility.

Most communicative approaches, especially ESP, require that teachers have a clear understanding of their students' needs. This is perhaps the greatest weakness of ESP as far as ESL teachers are concerned. It is difficult to imagine the future linguistic needs of students who themselves are not sure of their own futures, let alone convince them of learning a dialect of English that is useful only in school.

Factors Related to Linguistic Diversity in Schools

The relevance of dialects in education became clear in a 1979 landmark case in the U.S. District Court from the East District in Detroit, Michigan. In what later would become known as the Ann Arbor Decision, Judge Joiner ruled in favor of the plaintiffs, a group of parents suing the Ann Arbor School Board. The court sided with the parents in stating that Afro-American students did not enjoy equal access to educational opportunities as specified in Title 20 of the Equal Educational Opportunities Act (the same as that used in linguistic-diversity cases) (Vaughn-Cooke, 1980). After extensive testimony by linguists and educators, Judge Joiner ordered the Ann Arbor School Board to submit to his court a plan to train teachers in identifying students who spoke Vernacular Black English (VBE) and in teaching such students how to read "standard English."

The court ruling in Ann Arbor rested on notions of linguistic deficit common to most Title VII legislation and related litigation. Similarly, the solution mandated by the court favored a transitional approach. In this case, however, the target was literacy in "standard English."

The Ann Arbor case is evidence of the specialized nature of the language needed to succeed in American schools. As most teachers of L.E.P. students will assert, oral proficiency in playground English does not necessarily translate to proficiency in reading or language arts. This observation could be extended to include other aspects of schooling, so that we might think of schooling as involving very specific behavior that reflects societal values and norms.

The problem of linguistic diversity for educators is not restricted to language and academic skills. Intertwined with these two groups of skills are social aspects of the problem that tend to surface in status differences among students. As it soon became evident, race-related problems did not disappear instantaneously with school integration. Moreover, integration appeared to exacerbate interracial differences under certain circumstances. These observations led Elliot Aronson, a social psychologist, to develop the Jigsaw Method of cooperative learning.

Students in a Jigsaw activity are each accountable for making a necessary contribution toward a final product. The idea behind this method is that by making the contributions of each and every member necessary for the final outcome, attitudes toward all members improve, especially attitudes toward minority students.

Elizabeth Cohen (1994) has expanded on Aronson's ideas and designed what she calls "status expectation treatments" for students. A status treatment consists of carefully training low-status minority students to become experts in a high-profile, academic task. Once the student becomes an expert, he or she teaches fellow students the task. Cohen's evaluations of the treatment support its effectiveness. Cohen is careful to point out, however, that teachers must be trained to carry out expectation treatments. Unless the teacher carefully prepares the low-status student to minimize his chances of failure, negative attitudes about the student's ability may be reinforced by any lack of success.

Status treatment is but one component of several in Complex Instruction. According to Cohen (1994), Complex Instruction offers teachers a way to deal with academic heterogeneity, a feature common to linguistically diverse classrooms. Complex Instruction, as with most group work, requires that students learn to cooperate with each other. To the extent that cooperation may or may not be an accepted and valued form of behavior among certain groups, the institution of cooperative norms in the classroom is likely to favor some groups over others. The problem for teachers is in deciding which norms other than cooperative norms to include and which to exclude, given the multiple cultures at work in their classrooms.

Effective Programs for L.E.P. Students

As a research strategy, it makes sense to determine what makes a program for L.E.P. students effective. After all, most of the loudest objections regarding bilingual education come from its apparent failure to produce expected student outcomes. Several researchers have attempted to determine the effect of bilingual programs on L.E.P. students' English proficiency and academic performance and have concluded that these programs are not effective. Studies such as these have been severely criticized for assuming that individual bilingual programs are comparable simply because of their funding source. In reality, no standard model exists. (For a review of research, see Hakuta, 1986.)

Effective schooling of L.E.P. students includes both classroom and schoolwide characteristics. At the classroom level, and in addition to some of the techniques reviewed in the previous section, effective schools are characterized by teachers who do not simply challenge their students with tasks requiring high-order thinking and language processing, but also do this in a non-threatening environment. Also, clear and explicit instruction is

especially helpful for L.E.P. students who may not only have difficulty understanding English, but also come from cultures where
school behavior differs greatly from that of students in most
American schools.

Finally, effective teachers of L.E.P. students tend to draw from
their students' background in planning and teaching lessons. This
practice has several advantages, including enhancing the students'
ability to relate new material to previous information, thereby
improving recall. Given the importance of culture in the education of linguistically diverse students, the integration of the students' culture into classroom and school norms offers a way for
educators of linguistically diverse students to begin addressing
the more difficult aspects of the problem.

Prominent among the schoolwide characteristics is the presence of a school culture that favors linguistic and ethnic diversity and appreciates the resources within this diversity (Minicucci
and Olsen, 1992). Also, school districts must contend with linguistically diverse student populations who are not only at various levels of English proficiency, but also from diverse language
backgrounds. Thus, effective schools must be sensitive to context
in their design and implementation of programs and curricula.
In other words, there is no "formula for effectiveness" to be applied
everywhere. Instead, each school's mission and cultural norms
must emerge from the meeting between the concerns and interests of the entire school community.

Eugene Garcia (1994), in his review of the literature on effective schools for L.E.P. students, includes studies that rely on different ways to assess school effectiveness. Some studies have relied
on conventional measures of effectiveness such as proficiency tests.
We have discussed many of the difficulties in assessing L.E.P.
students that make this task especially difficult. As a way around
this obstacle, other researchers have asked teachers, staff members, students, and parents to nominate "effective" schools. Although the majority of studies reviewed by Garcia were conducted
at schools with a majority of Mexican-American students, Garcia's
conclusions help us understand the intricacies associated with
teaching linguistically diverse students.

Effective schools in these studies are characterized by classrooms that, among other things, promote functional communication in all media and favor collaboration in an informal, "almost

familial" social setting. Instruction in these schools included tasks and activities that required students to think and use language in abstract, academic ways.

Most effective schools displayed a trend toward English instruction in the upper grades. Students are allowed to progress in reading and writing from their native language to English. Garcia also reports that effective schools have both attributes that have been found to be effective in schools generally and attributes that are specifically appropriate for linguistically diverse classrooms. Thus, to the frequently heard opinion that effective teaching for diverse students is nothing more than good teaching, Garcia's work suggests the following answer: "Yes, and more."

Conclusion

The relevance in effective programs of a school culture reflecting the values and concerns of the school community speaks of a need for inclusion in the creation of this culture. However, in order for all members of the school community to participate in the creation of a positive school culture, we must abandon the current deficit mentality that dominates discussions and policy. Minow (1990) proposes questioning the validity and usefulness of existing norms as part of the solution to the "dilemma of difference." American schools stand to gain in questioning their current beliefs and practices and creating cultures that contain the best characteristics of those sectors of the population they serve.

Just as we argued for the need among teachers to share in the responsibility and the discussion regarding L.E.P. students, a similar movement is necessary in the funding of special services for educationally disadvantaged students. The high poverty levels among L.E.P. students make it necessary to redefine the problem as involving more than simply limited English proficiency. In doing so, we should be careful not to adopt a "one size fits all" approach to the problem (Reyes, 1992), but instead evaluate the effect on educational outcomes of each and all relevant factors.

We would like to be optimistic and believe that in moving away from a categorical approach to student diversity problems, educators as a whole have an opportunity to contribute to the solution. We realize that, given the very nature of the problem, decisions regarding programs and levels of funding are likely to eventually take place in political circles. Nevertheless, it behooves teachers to participate in the discussion, especially since they will be asked to actually implement the policies in their daily practice.

As is frequently the case with educational problems, linguistic diversity has turned out to be more complex than first thought. Undoubtedly, language proficiency is an important factor. However, as studies have demonstrated time and again, other factors seem to be contributing to L.E.P. students' poor academic performance and low graduation rates. Crucial among these other factors are L.E.P. students' socioeconomic level and particular ethnolinguistic background. Research findings suggest that the solution to the problem involves more than simply finding the "right" language teaching method or the best combination of native-language and English instruction.

References

Abt Associates (in press). *Prospects: The congressionally mandated study of educational growth and opportunity.* Cambridge, Mass.: Author.

August, D.; Hakuta, K; and Pompa, D. (1994). *For all students; Limited-English-proficient students and Goals 2000.* Washington, D.C.: National Clearinghouse of Bilingual Education.

Bialystok, H., and Hakuta, K. (1994). *In other words: The science and psychology of second language acquisition.* New York, N.Y.: Basic Books.

Cohen, E. (1994). *Designing group work* (2nd ed.). New York, N.Y.: Teachers College Press.

Crawford, J. (1995). *Bilingual education: History, politics, theory, and practice* (3rd ed.). Los Angeles: Bilingual Educational Services.

Development Associates (1993). *Descriptive study of services to limited English proficient students* (Vol. 1). Arlington, Va.: Author.

Fix, M., and Zimmermann, W. (1993). *Educating immigrant children: Chapter 1 in the changing city.* Washington, D.C.: Urban Institute Press.

Garcia, E. E. (1994). Attributes of effective schools for language minority students. In E. R. Hollins, J. E. King, & W. C. Hayman (eds.), *Teaching diverse populations: Formulating a knowledge base* (pp. 93–103). Albany: State University of New York Press.

Hakuta, K. (1986). *Mirror of language.* New York, N.Y.: Basic Books.

McArthur, E. K. (1993). *Language characteristics and schooling in the United States, a changing picture: 1979 and 1989.* Washington, D.C.: National Center for Education Statistics; USDE-NCES93-699

Meyer, M. M., and Fienberg, S. E. (eds.). (1992). *Assessing evaluation studies; The case of bilingual education strategies.* Washington, D.C.: National Academy Press.

Minicucci, C., and Olsen, L. (1992). *Programs for secondary limited English proficient students: A California study.* Washington, D.C.: National Clearinghouse for Bilingual Education.

Minow, M. (1990). *Making all the difference: Inclusion, exclusion, and American law.* Ithaca, N.Y.: Cornell University Press.

Nunan, D. (1991). *Language teaching methodology: A textbook for teachers.* Hertfordshire, U.K.: Prentice Hall International.

Reyes, M. (1992). Challenging venerable assumptions: Literacy instruction for linguistically different students. *Harvard Educational Review* 62, pp. 427–446.

The Stanford Working Group. (1993). *Federal education programs for limited-English-proficient students: A blueprint for the second generation.* Stanford, Calif.: Author.

U.S. Department of Education (1991). *The condition of bilingual education in the nation: A report to the Congress and the President.* Office of the Secretary. Washington, D.C.: Author.

Vaughn-Cooke, F. B. (1980). Evaluating the language of Black English speakers: Implications of the Ann Arbor decision. In M. F. Whiteman (ed.) *Reactions to Ann Arbor: Vernacular Black English and education* (pp. 24–54). Arlington, Va.: Center for Applied Linguistics.

Chapter 20

Categorical Programs

Maynard C. Reynolds, Margaret C. Wang, and Herbert J. Walberg

All children and youth are expected to be in school these days, at least through high school graduation. The drive for universal enrollment has brought about increased diversity in characteristics of students, which in turn has led to changes in the schools to accommodate differences as well as producing strains all around. Clearly, "bowling alley" school programs—just sending instruction "down the middle"—do not suffice today. This chapter tells about students at the margins, those most likely to be neglected unless quite extraordinary efforts are made.

A common method of dealing with diversity is to create categorical programs that "set aside" to the margins students who stretch existing school programs. Some of the categorizing is dimensional, that is, it is based on cutoff points along a continuum of differences among students. For example, millions of children have been placed in special classes because their IQs are below 70 or 75. As tests of "g" (general mental ability) came into common use, it was but a small step to categorize those with low IQs as mentally retarded and then set them aside. Serious doubts are being raised today about such classification and grouping procedures, especially those that involve formal testing. According to Glaser and Silver (1994, p. 397), "Tests are frequently used to sort students into instructional tracks that provide differential opportunities and differential expectations. . . . The general failure of this process to increase educational outcomes has been amply demonstrated." More acceptable are cutoff points that occur quite naturally in connection with curricular progress. For example, enrollments in third-year Spanish are limited to students who completed second-year Spanish successfully, and enrollments in geometry are limited to those who completed the preceding class in algebra.

Other categorical programs are typological rather than dimensional. The program in braille, for example, involves a distinct mode of instruction in reading for students who have extremely limited vision. This may or may not involve a segregated class or school; the braille instructor may come to the regular classroom to offer instruction and related supports. Instruction for students who are deaf necessarily circumvents aural modes of communication and involves distinct methods invented for this purpose. School programs for students showing severe and profound limits in mental ability also require distinct curricular elements. Programs for these three groups (blind, deaf, and severely retarded) were the first to be developed in special education, and they remain the clearest instances of distinct categories of special education. The field of speech correction also has a number of distinct methods for treating specific conditions, such as cleft palate, and so may be regarded as mainly typological. In these several instances, the special education categories meet the ATI (aptitude-treatment-interaction) test, that is, there are distinct treatments (or instructional alternatives) and ways of assessing individuals such that differential allocations to treatment can be made with validity.

A special panel created by the National Academy of Science (NAS) to study placement practices in special education proposed the following approach to student classifications: "It is the responsibility of a placement team that labels and places a child in a special program to demonstrate that any differential label used is related to a distinctive prescription for educational practices . . . that lead to improved outcomes" (Heller, Holtzman, and Messick, 1982, pp. 101–102). This recommendation implies two standards for categorical school placement: first, that there be a distinctive aspect of the instruction prescribed for those in the category; and, second, that there be evidence that the special program "works" to enhance the life and learning of the students given the special placement. Only a limited number of categorical school programs, such as those designed for meeting the needs of children who are blind, deaf, or severely retarded, meet those standards. For at least three-fourths of special education students, mainly those with mild disabilities and those enrolled in early versions of the Chapter 1 program, current practices do not meet the NAS standards. (*Note*: Chapter 1 was recently reauthorized as Title I, and will hereafter be referred to as such.) This does not mean that such students do not have significant learning problems; rather, it is the validity of partitioning practices, the forming of student groups *by category*, that has become doubtful.

Background of Programs

The U.S. Department of Education lists a number of categories of special education that are not linked to distinctive interventions that lead to improved learning outcomes. Table 20-1 lists these categories and several others used by federal education authorities. Many states have added still more categorical programs. The Title I program for economically disadvantaged students, for example, is the largest federal educational program in terms of dollars spent, distributing about $6 billion per year. But that figure is only marginally larger than the amount of money (more than $5 billion per year) spent on categorical education programs in just one state (California). A variety of special programs are operated for children whose primary language is other than English. Some states, such as California, Texas, and Florida, provide large numbers of language-related special programs, mainly because immigration to the United States in recent years has been higher than ever before in terms of raw numbers.

The situation of categorical programs becomes complicated when there are multiple sources of funding and control. A recent report tells of forty-four federal sources of funding for early intervention programs in the schools, and of twenty-five laws and programs addressing the same target population. Without doubt, the myriad categorical programs and countless sources of support for them contribute to the fractionation of school organizations, especially those in inner-city schools and others that serve many students with special needs.

Table 20–1

Categorical Programs as Designated by Federal Authorities

	Estimated Number of Students in the United States
Specific learning disabilities	2,369,385
Speech or language impairments	1,000,154
Mental retardation	533,715
Serious emotional disturbance	402,668
Multiple disabilities	103,215
Hearing impairments	60,896
Orthopedic impairments	52,921
Other health impairments	66,054
Visual impairments	23,811
Autism	15,527
Deafness-blindness	1,425
Traumatic brain injury*	3,903
Chapter 1 (economically disadvantaged**)	5,000,000
Gifted and talented	——
Bilingual (Low-English-proficiency students)	3,000,000
Migrant	——
Homeless	——
"At risk"	——

 * All of the above categories and data are from U.S. Department of Education (1994).
** The data for Chapter 1 programs have limited applicability because of the growing practice of whole school interventions.

Problems and Issues

Some degree of classification of students is, of course, inevitable. Students are not assembled randomly. The most common approach is based on chronological age. The age-grade system is applied universally and is not highly controversial, but other approaches are applied selectively and create problems. Clearly, classification is both a scientific matter and a social act. But often the processes involve too little science and doubtful social benefits. Following is a brief discussion of some of the problems and issues of classification.

Taxons versus Classes

It is sometimes assumed that the categories of students as established in the schools are basic or taxonic, that is, "carving nature at its joints." The assumption is that the categories would exist whether or not the schools recognized them, but this is often untrue. Some years ago a presidential advisory group published a report on the "six-hour retarded child," implying that some children are retarded only in school. It is appropriate to see most school-related categories as classes of convenience rather than taxons. Who may be regarded as mentally retarded, is decided somewhat inconsistently, although not in a totally arbitrary way, over time by committees of professionals. Before a child is classified in the largest special education category, learning disabled, there must be evidence of a discrepancy between the child's expected achievement and actual achievement. Such discrepancies could be said to reflect an overprediction (and expectation), thus putting the onus on the psychologist who makes the prediction rather than on the child. In any case, the category is not taxonic; even if it were, there might be no related and distinct treatments available for application.

Categories Beyond the Schools

Increasingly, schools are linking their work with that of social and health agencies. But each agency has its own categories, often based in law or on the standards of the particular professionals they employ. Mental health clinics, for example, may require classification of patients in accord with the diagnostic manual of the American Psychiatric Association. Educators were surprised by a recent edition of such a manual in which the number of childhood mental disorders had tripled since the preceding edition; the manual included "mental disorders" relating to specific academic deficiencies such as in reading. The problem is that the mental health committees, for example, may arrive at different formulations than do the school-related committees. None of the diagnostic categories may be taxonic or useful in cross-professional work. These are problems that will need to be settled as schools and other agencies seek to collaborate in providing services to children and families.

Reliability

Classifications of students, especially those who show only "mild" disabilities, are quite unreliable. It has been estimated that 80 percent of all students could be classified as learning disabled (LD) according to one or more of the more than a dozen LD assessment procedures used in various school districts. In the early 1970s, the numbers of students labeled mentally retarded declined by hundreds of thousands nationwide after a challenging and persuasive court case. In the same period, the numbers of students labeled "learning disabled" increased sharply, showing how sensitive classification procedures are to the social climate and how unreliable they often are when considered only in their technical aspects.

Stigma

Some student classifications result in labels for particular students that become public and stigmatic. "Mental retardation" and "emotionally disturbed" tend to be especially stigmatic and are often resisted and resented by parents. Unfortunately, rates of stigmatic labeling often correlate with racial differences, as do so many other negatives about schooling, such as suspension and expulsion, school dropouts, poor attendance, and low achievement. This adds complex tensions and issues.

The Political Context

Categorical programs usually get started through political action by groups of parents and other advocates. Much of the early energies for categorical programs came from the National Association for Retarded Children (NARC). The earliest work of NARC focused on the federal courts; later attention turned to legislation. NARC pointed to neglect of retarded children in the schools and then made a claim for legislation supporting new and expanded programs. The political action was based only minimally on research evidence. Virtually no data showed that efficient treatments were available. As in the NARC case, schools often are pressured to organize programs that have no clear foundation in a knowledge base. Equally, the process often results in distinctions among programs that relate to social issues but that have no related and valid distinctions in instructional practices. This is the case, many observers believe, in the distinctions between Title I and learning disability programs. In both cases, teachers are mostly engaged in teaching reading using a common knowledge base, but the two programs often operate separately.

In the case of the NARC advocates, most were relatively privileged middle-class people, but the consequences engendered by their work included the massive development of special classes in neighborhoods serving poor, minority families. The parents of these children do not always welcome the labels given to their children, and the special classes do not seem to enhance their children's learning. These findings tend to lead to complex court proceedings that stall, and sometimes reverse, program development.

There is growing interest in the concept of *consequential validity*, in which "the uses and interpretations of the results of an assessment . . . are validated rather than the assessment itself" (Linn, 1994, p. 6). In the case of special classes for mildly retarded children, the assessment processes related to placement usually involve a construct of intelligence that has validity in a limited sense, but the processes lack validity in terms of *consequences*. The emerging consensus on the importance of consequential validity requires that school psychologists give careful attention to the validity of programs as well as to the constructs represented by the assessment tools they use.

Once categorical programs are established and money is flowing in support of them, there appears to be a hardening of the categories. That is, it becomes harder to undo them, regardless of the evidence concerning their value. However, at this time categorical programs are coming under close scrutiny, perhaps mainly because of their high and growing costs. Many school administrators and political leaders feel that funding for categorical programs, often protected by rules and regulations, is causing retrenchments in regular school programs.

Organizational Arrangements

The Continuum

Figure 20-1 is typical of a schematic used in special education to represent the organization of programs and the major policy. At the base is the regular or general education classroom that is expected to serve many exceptional students. According to a recent report by the U.S. Department of Education (1994), 34.9 percent of students identified as disabled were served mainly in regular classrooms. This method might involve consultation with the regular teacher by special education teachers, the school psychologist, or others, or it might involve co-teaching in a common environment by the regular and special education teachers. At a second level is the resource room, usually used only for part-time placements, for individual or small-group instruction. The recent federal report shows that 36.3 percent of disabled students received their special education mainly in resource rooms. Use of resource rooms entails much movement by students between regular classes and resource rooms, often on a prescribed schedule, which can cause disruptions of routines in both settings. Figure 20-1 shows other organizational elements, the order of which depicts their degree of separation from ordinary school arrangements; the schematic also notes the rates of enrollment at each level. As one moves up the continuum, management and instruction come increasingly under the control of specialists, students are increasingly isolated from nondisabled students, and programs become more expensive.

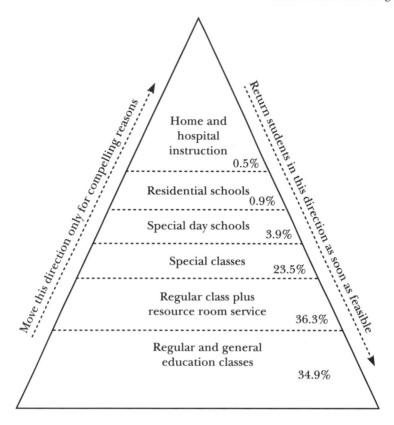

Figure 20–1   **The Continuum of Special Education Organizational Arrangements**

In the most thorough of cost studies (Moore, Strang, Schwartz, and Braddock, 1988), it was estimated that average annual expenditure per pupil for special education in resource rooms was $1,325; in special classes, $4,233; and in residential programs, $28,324. Overall, the per-pupil costs for special education were found to be about 2.3 times the cost for nondisabled pupils.

In the 1990–91 school year, the estimated "regular" per-pupil expenditure for K-12 education across the nation was $5,266; the estimated excess cost for special education was $6,845.80— yielding a total per-pupil expenditure for special education of $12,111.80. Multiplying that cost by the 4.8 million students enrolled in special education in the same year yields a total expenditure for special education students of about $58 billion.

Along the sides of Figure 20-1 are notes expressing the least restrictive environment (LRE) principle. That policy is expressed in law, but is qualified and made arguable by another principle that requires education to be individualized and *appropriate*. The LRE idea is a familiar one in other fields, such as mental health, suggesting that as a public agent enters the life situation of an individual, it must do so in the least intrusive way feasible. Similarly, a first duty of educators is to try to make appropriate arrangements for exceptional students in the regular class environment and to use other elements of the continuum only for compelling reasons and in time-limited ways. Following the LRE principle through time, it should be expected that more students and programs would move down the continuum, thereby concentrating more special education in regular classes and schools. Although that is occurring, many argue about how far and how fast the movement toward full inclusion in the mainstream should proceed. The main focus of disagreements is on severely disabled students. Should they be placed in regular classes? If so, what are the consequences for the nondisabled students?

Program Outcomes

Outcomes of categorical programs may be considered at three different levels: (1) for each individual; (2) for each program at the local level; and (3) for each set of programs at some broader level, such as for an entire state or the nation. In the case of special education, it is required that each student have an individualized plan for instruction and related services and that a review of progress under the plan be conducted periodically. That is a valuable feature of special education operations, but it is not a focus of the present statement.

Even if broad evidence about a set of programs is positive, the local situation may be deficient. Or, a particular local teacher may be especially competent and conduct a program of great value. Thus, it is important that those who make decisions about placements of children be aware of the quality of local programs.

This is an aspect of the consequential validity concept; ultimately, all program validity is local.

It is useful to have outcome data at the third or broadest level, however, to help inform judgments about the general validity of each of the categorical programs and the policies that support them. Achieving broad and valid evaluation studies is very difficult. Experimental designs are preferable, but it is difficult to achieve random assignments of students to experimental and control conditions, all with the informed consent of parents. Another difficulty concerns separation of focus on programs from focus on administrative arrangements. Very often, only the administrative arrangement is examined. One might, for example, conduct a braille program at any one of the levels represented in the continuum (see Figure 20-1). Or, an LD program might be conducted in a resource room or by co-teaching approaches in a regular classroom. The inclusiveness of the organizational arrangement is one matter; the distinctiveness of the instructional program is something else.

Early meta-analytic studies of outcomes in special education, which focused mainly on classes for students with mental retardation, were extremely crude and do not merit review here. A study of higher credibility, covering eleven special education studies reported from 1975 to 1984, produced an effect size of 0.44 for academic effects and 0.11 for social effects, both favoring inclusive organizational arrangements. That is, regular class outcomes were superior to outcomes in special placements. Several categories of special education, representing mild disabilities, were included. A similar meta-analysis covering a set of thirteen studies from 1983 to 1992 showed effect sizes of 0.08 and 0.28 for academic and social effects, respectively (Baker, Wang, and Walberg, 1995). These results suggest small advantages for serving exceptional students in regular classes rather than in separately organized arrangements. There is much debate about these matters, but no evidence of dramatic advantages either way. Therefore, one might invoke the LRE principle and recommend, to the extent possible, retention of disabled students in regular classes.

But no placement can be judged satisfactory unless and until highly effective instruction that meets individual needs is provided. Many regular teachers do not tailor instruction to meet individual differences. In such circumstances, learners who have fallen behind tend to become passive or inactive learners, interacting with teachers at relatively low rates. Gifted students may languish in boredom. All of that will need to change. By shifting some of the resources associated with separate categorical programs to the regular classrooms, perhaps the broader tailoring of instruction can be accelerated. That is the idea advanced by advocates of the much-debated regular education initiative (REI).

Numerous evaluation studies of Title I programs have been conducted, many showing small positive short-term achievement effects. Most such studies were of programs in which selected students were served in pullout programs that emphasize reading. In early longitudinal studies, the early gains of Title I students often declined once students were returned to full-time instruction in regular classes. Therefore, programs should be continually enriched in order to avoid the "washout" of earlier positive effects. The most recent studies have shown modest evidence of long-term positive achievement effects but nothing like a true closing of gaps with more advantaged students.

There has been rising concern that the Title I programs have been framed too narrowly, often emphasizing decontextualized skills training. One study group called for a transformation of the program "to one dedicated to spurring the kinds of educational change that would result in children born into poverty acquiring high-level knowledge and skills"; the call was for "deep change in the way whole school systems operate" (Commission on Chapter 1, 1992, pp. v–vi). Recent revisions in law are in accord with that schoolwide orientation and provide for more program flexibility at the local level. Programs of the future will be concentrated increasingly in schools serving many students who experience poverty, but they will be less categorical—that is, requiring less special within-school identification of students by category. Title I programs may now be coordinated fully with other categorical programs and with regular education. When required to teach low-achieving and economically poor students, regular educators will less often be able to say, "That's not my job"; instead, we hope, they will accept the challenge and the extra resources now available to effectively teach children of the poor within the regular school framework. It is intended, also, that management concerns will move from system compliance to program improvement.

A similar shift is occurring in programs for language-minority students. In the case of bilingual education, the evidence on programs is mixed. The situation is very complex, involving varieties of approaches to instruction and factors other than language. When instruction takes into account cultural differences as well as language differences, there appear to be better academic outcomes. But conducting programs within a whole-school framework is gaining in preference over noninclusive arrangements (Garcia, 1995).

An Agenda for Action

This section summarizes actions that can be suggested on the basis of evidence to help accommodate school programs to the wide diversity of student characteristics. The suggestions are presented in two broad sets: those that involve organizational arrangements and those that concern instruction. In no instance is the suggestion fully or absolutely confirmed by research; rather, the suggestions represent ideas and practices that are indicated in view of present knowledge. Thus, continuing research and evaluation are important in all of the domains discussed. Literature concerning each suggestion is quite readily available, providing both conceptual details and implementation approaches that have been tried and tested.

Organizational Arrangements

Inclusion. There is not sufficient evidence to justify removal of mildly disabled students by category from regular education schools and classes. Strong efforts should be made to be as inclusive as possible in regular school settings. Even severely disabled students can usually be included in regular schools, although full inclusion in regular classes may often be doubtful as a practice.

Early Education. Evidence suggests that high-quality early education programs that include children who are placed at risk by a variety of circumstances result in reductions in later referrals to special education. Such programs tend to establish positive school-parent relations and to avoid the stigmatic labeling of children.

Intensive Early Preventive Programs. Intensive instructional programs for students who show limited progress in early primary education (for example, in reading at the first-grade level) tend to prevent many later learning disabilities. Making an early start in offering very intensive help to children who lag in the early phases of academic learning is exceedingly important.

Prereferral Interventions. Teachers who become greatly concerned about pupil behavior and/or learning should be provided help in arranging prereferral interventions. For example, a school psychologist, a special education teacher, or some other staff member should enter into a consulting relationship with the teacher. One result is a reduced need for referral to special education, which can result in substantial savings.

Parents. A positive approach is to seek strong working relationships with parents, emphasizing mutual trust and commitments to healthy supports in the life of each child. Through time, increased student involvement should be sought in school planning and in preparing for the transition to post-school life.

Cross-Category Programs. Another arrangement involves the creation of broadly framed mixes of categorical programs rather than narrowly framed programs. For example, many schools now combine programs for so-called learning disabled, mildly retarded, and emotionally disturbed children, with Title I programs. Labels for students are dropped. Such programs can be conducted within regular classrooms through co-teaching arrangements between special and regular teachers.

Mini-Schools. Evidence favors formation of small schools or schools within schools, in which clusters of teachers and pupils remain together for more than one school year. This fosters deeper and improved relationships between teachers and students and enhanced accountability (to one another) among teachers. Such mini-schools should serve heterogenous groups of students. The procedure is consistent with important findings on childhood resilience.

Teacher Assistance Teams. Small teams of regular teachers can be used to assist particular teachers at times of stress and uncertainty about the behavior of pupils or about instructional planning. This approach builds on the idea of coordinated consultation, that is, using people whose situation is like yours in arranging help. Not all help must come from specialists. Ongoing teams of teachers can also offer leadership and support in working through change processes in their schools.

Intensive Special Education. If resource rooms or other forms of special education that involve separate placements are used, they should be restricted to time-limited periods and offer very intensive help on particular topics or skills. Speech-correction programs frequently operate in this way.

Funding. Funds to support categorical programs for mildly disabled students and those whose circumstances place them at risk should be distributed to individual schools that then pay for the special programs they use. If the special program involves sending a student to a center beyond the local school, the costs could be quite extraordinary. The idea is to create incentives for serving all students, even those with exceptional needs, in the schools they would ordinarily attend. It might be necessary to arrange exceptions to this site-based funding system in the case of programs that meet the ATI test (i.e., for students who are deaf, blind, speech impaired, or severely/profoundly disabled). In these instances, some districtwide arrangement might be made for operations and funding. The distribution of funds to schools should be based on the number of students at each school who have special needs, with bonuses paid on evidence that the school program is successful in preventing and solving the problems of special-needs students.

Coalitions of Agencies. Schools should seek coalitions with social, health, and corrections agencies; with churches and other elements of the community; and with families as a means of meeting the special needs of students and families in cohesive and efficient ways. The orientation should not be just "clinical," that is, to serve individual needs; the coordinating body should help serve the general needs of the community as it affects the life and learning of children and youth.

Waiver for Performance. Schools should be enabled and encouraged to seek waivers from existing rules and regulations when they are barriers to trials and testing of new modes of operation. The waivers should include provisions for melded use of categorical funds when, in fact, programs represent a melding of previously separated programs. Waivered programs should always require strong evaluative components, that is, evidence of outcomes or "performance."

Demissions. Today's schools require strong efforts to reduce all forms of demission: dropouts, suspensions, expulsions, exclusion, and excuses. Work on school climate, broadly framed judiciaries to deal with conflicts and unacceptable behavior, clear statements of expectations for student behavior, rewards for progress in "civilized behavior," strategic involvement of parents and community agencies, and more, are involved. What is clear is that solid efforts do pay off in this domain.

Instruction

Several factors concerning instruction must be considered as attempts are made to bring categorical programs into more cohesive relations with regular education. First, it is clear that the same principles apply to instruction in all programs (Reynolds, Wang, and Walberg, 1992). Thus, it is not necessary—at basic levels—to separate teachers according to category for most of their initial preparation or continuing education. There has been too much separation and narrowness in higher education in ways that correlate with separations in the schools. This separation needs to be repaired. Second, it is clear that the state of practice in schools falls far short of the state of the art in instruction. There is a substantial knowledge base about effective instruction that should serve as an organizer for efforts to improve schools and to bring programs into a cohesive form.

A massive metareview of the research literature on effective instruction was completed recently by Wang, Haertel, and Walberg (1993). Discussed below are a very small sample of topics that emerged in that study. For each topic, stated here in declarative terms, it is essential to make transformations to practical procedures (presumably of many kinds) that can be used effectively in teacher preparation and in student learning. The examples should not be seen as bits of technical knowledge to be inserted in simple fashion in teaching-learning situations. Rather, they are domains of knowledge to be considered by teachers, parents, and others as they perform their functions within the particular contexts where they meet with children and youth. The topics considered below are important and reasonably well-confirmed elements of knowledge, worthy of awareness and reflection by all who share in the teaching of children.

Time. Perhaps the clearest and most ubiquitous factor shown to be important in learning is time. Active, conscious, and deliberate commitment to learning is, of course, of key importance. But even if learning activities are well designed, *time* has an added independent importance. Indeed, greater knowledge of how children use their time would likely yield solid predictions of what they are learning. But here there is great failure for many children, especially for those who watch low-grade TV for four to six hours per day or who languish on unsafe streets. There is much talk these days about lengthening the school day and year, each of them potentially positive in effects. But carefully using the time already allocated to schools and to home life is essential. We need efforts in every school and, in cooperation with parents, in every home to monitor the use of time by children and to improve its use. The emerging coalitions of community agencies can come together to influence the available opportunities and the rates at which children use time constructively. There is very little that is reassuring about how students use time now or about how communities make provisions for the controlled use of time. This is prime territory for improvements.

Metacognition. No topic has emerged more forcefully in recent years than that of helping students become more aware of their own learning and become self-managers in their education. It may be easier for teachers to lay out all plans and to manage classes in detail, leaving compliance as the duty of the students. But the evidence is clear that students who become reflective about their own learning and who gradually assume more of the management of it show the most advances. Such management involves thinking, planning, judgment, and accountability. Teachers who reveal openly their own thinking processes, who help students learn to keep track of their own learning, and who share with students the planning of learning activities are those who help most. Having students help one another in learning provides another step in becoming aware of essential elements in learning and self-management. All of these observations apply to students who are mildly disabled or whose circumstances place them at risk of educational failure.

Cooperative Grouping/Student Interdependence. Evidence relating to students helping one another in classroom work has advanced rapidly in recent years. The estimated effect size of cooperative grouping on learning outcomes is too high to be ignored by any teacher. These arrangements engage students in awareness about individual differences and cultural diversity, but in ways that encourage appreciation rather than depreciation. It is but a small step from cooperative grouping to procedures for teaching methods of nonviolent conflict resolution. When students are expected to be interdependent, that is, to be useful and helpful to one another, schools become far different places than they were in decades past.

Frequent Feedback. Students need frequent information on how their knowledge and skills are advancing in the various domains of the curriculum. The realm of feedback is where the expertise of the teacher, coach, counselor, and parent can be helpful. But students also can learn to chart their own progress. Common sense and research agree that information about learning progress can be reinforcing.

Social Skills. One of the most common reasons for suspending students from school or for referring them to special education is that their social behavior is unacceptable. This unacceptable behavior can occur because students do not know what is acceptable. Training in social skills is an area of rapid development to meet this need. Although much evaluative work remains to be done, progress thus far is impressive. School psychologists have taken a lead in this area.

Much more could be added about the possibilities for instructional improvement. A more complete delineation of evidence on effective instruction is available quite readily (viz., Wang, Haertel, and Walberg, 1993).

Conclusion

To meet the challenge of the growing diversity in student characteristics, schools have created a variety of categorical programs. Most school systems now have a dozen or more such programs. Typically they have come about through socio-political processes with but little reference to research findings. The segregation of many categorical programs probably has caused a neglect, or at least a delay, of efforts to expand the powers of general education programs to deal with individual differences among students. Due to the disjointedness that categorical programs create within schools and the extremely high dollar cost of separate categorical programs, the situation is changing. As efforts now go forward to create broadly systemic and inclusive schools that serve all students, it is suggested that the designs begin with consideration of the evidence now at hand concerning organizational arrangements and effective instruction. In the main, students at the margins, those now so often set aside in categorical programs, need not receive a different kind of instruction, but only more intensive and effective instruction in inclusive settings.

References

Baker, E. T.; Wang, M. C.; and Walberg, H. J. (1995). The effects of inclusion on learning. *Educational Leadership, 52*(4), 33–35. See this entire issue of *Educational Leadership* for a variety of reports of evaluation of special education programs.

Commission on Chapter I (1992). *Making schools work for children in poverty: A new framework prepared by the Commission on Chapter I.* Washington, D.C.: American Association for Higher Education (One Dupont Circle N.W., Suite 360, Washington D.C. 20036).

Garcia, E. E. (1995). The impact of linguistic and cultural diversity on America's Schools: A need for new policy. In M. C. Wang and M. C. Reynolds (eds.), *Making a difference for students at risk: Trends and alternatives* (pp. 156–180). Thousand Oaks, Calif.: Corwin Press, Inc.

Glaser, R., and Silver, E. (1994). Assessment, testing and instruction: Retrospect and prospect. *Review of Research in Education 20,* 393–419.

Heller, K. A.; Holtzman, W. H.; and Messick, S. (eds.). (1982). *Placing children in special education: A strategy for equity.* Washington, D.C.: National Academy Press.

Linn, R. L. (1994). Performance assessment: Policy promises and technical measurement standards. *Educational Researcher 23*(9), 4–14.

Moore, M. T.; Strang, E. W.; Schwartz, M.; and Braddock, M. (1988). *Patterns in special education delivery and cost.* Washington, D.C.: Decision Resources Corporation.

Reynolds, M. C.; Wang, M. C.; and Walberg, H. J. (1992). The knowledge bases for special and general education. *Remedial and Special Education 13*(5), 6–10.

U. S. Department of Education (1994). *Sixteenth Annual Report to Congress on the Implementation of the Individuals with Disabilities Education Act.* Washington, D.C.: Author.

Wang, M. C.; Haertel, G. D.; and Walberg, H. J. (1993). Toward a knowledge base for school learning. *Review of Educational Research 63*(3), 249–294.

Conclusion

Herbert J. Walberg and Geneva D. Haertel

Despite American psychology's centennial (Walberg and Haertel, 1992), educational policymakers and professionals have paid insufficient attention to psychological research with implications for improving learning—the major purpose of education. In an effort to reduce the gap between psychological inquiry and educational practice, the foregoing chapters summarize findings about learners, teaching, and educational environments and programs—concentrating on findings that have implications for educational practice.

Our conclusion identifies what we take to be sixteen major themes of the book. Each theme appears in at least two chapters and each can be viewed as a solid research finding with practical implications for educational practice, policy, and reform. We state each theme as a topic in two or three words, then summarize it in a single declarative sentence, and finally briefly explain the theme (with references to chapters from which it was derived).

This treatment of the sixteen themes serves three purposes: summarizing and explaining key points that cut across the chapters, indexing the findings to the chapters, and juxtaposing the findings so that they may be compared and contrasted. The summary findings are hardly a substitute for a close reading of the foregoing chapters. They may, nonetheless, serve as a selective review of the corpus of the book, and provide helpful starting points for further study or for choosing among courses of action.

Part One: Students

Student Diversity

> Diversity in students' intelligences, knowledge, skills, morals, values, preferences, and cultural backgrounds should be reflected in the design of curriculum, instructional materials, instruction, classroom organization, and assessment.

Seven of the eight chapters in Part One show that responsive educational environments adapt to diversity among learners (Sternberg, Hatch and Kornhaber, Brown, Blumenfeld and Marx, Ford, Nucci, Resnick, Mislevy). The authors propose ways to offer content, instruction, and assessment aligned with diverse students' needs. Rising numbers of students from culturally, linguistically, and economically diverse backgrounds mean that such accommodations will be increasingly important if all students are to learn well.

Socially Situated Learning

> Students learn in social situations that both enrich and constrain their competence.

Learning in social situations is stressed in Part One. In each chapter, students' learning and motivation are shown to be related to the social processes that surround them. Children and youth learn in socially complex environments: home, classroom, museum, and athletic field—all these involve many individuals with their own goals, interpretations of situations, and local values. In classrooms, social processes include the presentation of content, questions asked, hands-on experiences, and group learning activities. The groups in these learning environments influence the knowledge, skills, beliefs, and behaviors that individuals acquire. Collaboratively, learners produce new understandings that reflect the resources and limitations of the social setting.

Learning for Understanding

> Learning for understanding is fostered by sustained rigorous intellectual activities with intrinsic value.

Reminiscent of John Dewey's "authentic activities," learning for understanding engages students in rigorous intellectual activities and reasoning required for meaningful applications of knowledge and skills. Hatch and Kornhaber, Brown, Blumenfeld and Marx, Ford, Resnick, and Mislevy show the importance of these types of activities that steer away from the mastery of isolated facts and skills and embrace culturally relevant, project-based activities that require coordination of information, skills, and diverse resources. Students find the skills acquired can be applied in the world, which increases their motivation and practical learning.

Self-Regulated Learning

> Students who employ self-regulated learning are more successful at complex learning tasks.

In the past decade, evidence has accumulated on how students acquire mastery of their own learning and enhance their likelihood of school success. Five of the chapters recognize the role of self-regulated learning on students' school performances (Hatch and Kornhaber, Ford, Brown, Blumenfeld and Marx, Nucci). Self-regulated learning can be defined as the way individuals allocate and control their intellectual resources. Setting goals, record keeping, and seeking help are examples of self-regulated learning tasks that are used during such diverse activities as critical moral reflection, acquiring new knowledge, and reading comprehension. Students who believe that they can accomplish goals are likely to engage in planning and other strategies that facilitate successful outcomes.

New Assessments

New forms of assessment hold promise for describing student performances on complex, meaningful tasks that have importance within and beyond the school setting.

Increasingly, educators are using curriculum and instructional activities that promote understanding, advanced skills, and reasoning. Determining whether students learn this content requires assessments that match the content, can be consistently scored, and are sound and fair. Five of the chapters in Part 1 (Sternberg, Hatch and Kornhaber, Brown, Resnick, Mislevy) look to new forms of assessment to fill these needs. In the past, the best information to assess learning came from classroom quizzes, class projects, and teachers' own interactions with students. Such assessments, however, are informal, cover limited content, and rarely can be used in other classrooms. New forms of assessment are being designed to try to combine the relevance of classroom assessments with the rigor of traditional standardized tests.

Part Two: Instruction

Centrality of Teachers

Along with students, teachers hold direct responsibility for learning and strongly influence its effectiveness.

Five chapters in Part Two make this important point (Brophy, Evertson, Wilson, Pea, Morine-Dershimer and Corrigan). Though policies, governance, and school organization affect learning, their influences are attenuated and mediated by teachers. Such forces within and outside the school are interpreted by teachers who bring them to bear in the classroom along with their own ideals

and methods. A long line of authority extends from state legislatures, state departments of education, school districts, and principals, but teachers enact their policies to varying degrees.

Diverse Influences

> Aside from teachers and teaching, other agents and processes affect what
> students learn.

Teaching occurs in a context that is in part determined by
teachers. Though not teaching itself, classroom management sets
the stage for teaching and limits or expands its efficacy (Evertson).
Plans, preparation, curricular materials, educational technologies,
and organizations similarly enhance or detract from what
teachers can accomplish (Wang, Haertel, and Walberg, Brophy,
Evertson, Pea).

Productive Organization

> Efficient arrangements of curriculum, teaching, and technology lend
> efficacy to teaching.

With respect to curriculum, it is wasteful to teach things that
students already know or that they are yet incapable of learning.
Brilliant acts of teaching may count for little if they are ill-
sequenced or wrongly triggered. On the other hand, good sequencing of teachers' acts and presentations of instructional
materials raise learning rates. Teachers, moreover, may need to
keep silent at certain strategic moments to elicit independent
student insights. Thus, instructional organization can be as decisive as the quality of component acts and materials (Wang, Haertel,
and Walberg; Brophy; Evertson; Morine-Dershimer and Corrigan).

Subject Matter

> The subject matters: Some instructional methods appear to have generic
> efficacy while some subjects and units of study require special instruc-
> tional methods.

Science may require some direct experience in the laboratory; computers may remove computational burdens from statistics exercises; summarizing may facilitate reading comprehension; firm memorization and understanding may inspire confidence in drama. Yet time spent in guided practice may enhance all these and other experiences. Thus, teachers will benefit from knowledge of general learning principles as well as mastery of both the specific subject matter and how it is best taught (Brophy, Wilson).

Instructional Technologies

Under certain conditions, computers, the Internet, CD-ROMS, adaptive instruction and other media and methods can supplement and even supplant conventional instruction.

The present has been called "the information age" and "the age of the computer." As we write, a computer has just beaten the best of human competitors in a round or two of top cerebral activity—chess. Though new educational media and technological methods are hardly panaceas, they are opening up new possibilities for learning (Wang, Haertel, and Walberg, Pea). For several decades, computer-assisted instruction has shown favorable results in the teaching of delimited topics and skills. We now see the possibilities of electronic links to helpful experts and millions of other learners around the world, and the potential of recording a library and all a student's previous writings, sketches, and records on a one-ounce disk.

Part Three: Environments and Programs

Student Diversity

Student diversity, including students' talents, special needs, goals, values, preferences and cultural backgrounds, influences schools' learning environments.

Four chapters address this theme (Davis, Galguera and Hakuta, Reynolds, Wang, and Walberg, Kaplan and Maehr). Some types of diversity, such as deafness or giftedness, may require greater-than-usual instructional support to provide students with a quality education. Historically, categorical programs were used to educate diverse student groups. Increasingly, however, categorical approaches are perceived as providing an inferior education, socially segregating participating students, and placing the responsibility for instruction in the hands of specialists. For these reasons, inclusive practices are eclipsing categorical programs. Diversity in students' goals, preferences, and values also influences school culture. Goals and values affect students' engagement in learning activities, their judgments about the relevance of content, and attitudes toward school, subject areas, and learning.

Program Adaptation, Inclusion, and Integration

> Instructional programs, classrooms, and schools can be designed to accommodate the academic, psychological, or physical needs and preferences of students.

Four chapters in Part Three conclude that features of schools, classrooms, and programs can be adapted to better meet the needs and preferences of students (Galguera and Hakuta, Reynolds, Wang, and Walberg, Davis, Fraser). Increasingly, these adaptations are made within regular classrooms by blending curriculum, instruction, and social support tailored to students' needs. Many of these adaptations accommodate the academic, psychological, or physical needs of special children. Classroom environments can also be adapted to students' preferences for classroom life—a desire for more frequent academic interactions with teachers, more diverse curricula, or a faster instructional pace (Fraser). Students' orientation toward learning can be shaped by the learning activities presented, school organization, distribution of authority, and relevance of curricula and instructional activities to local community values (Kaplan and Maehr).

Challenging Environments

Challenging learning environments provide rigorous content and instructional opportunities for students in a context that promotes learning.

Reform advocates of the 1980s and 1990s warned against a remediation mentality and proposed rigorous learning for all students. Challenging activities provide advanced content while linking students' lives to curriculum content, academic principles to extramural activities, and past to current events. Each chapter in Part Three identifies practices that create enriched learning environments (Galguera and Hakuta, Reynolds, Wang, and Walberg, Davis, Walberg and Paik, Fraser, Maehr and Kaplan), including high academic standards; nontrivial, culturally relevant curricula; ample opportunities to learn advanced content; the design of learning environments based on students' needs and preferences; and a task-oriented school culture.

Communities of Learners

Instructional practices that involve communities of learners provide intellectual and social benefits for students.

Cooperative learning groups and reciprocal teaching are contemporary instructional techniques that enhance learning and motivation and increase opportunities for students to develop communication, social, and leadership skills. Two chapters in Part Three describe this approach (Galguera and Hakuta, Davis). While cooperative approaches are not advocated as a mainstay of instruction for gifted and talented students (Davis), they can play a key role in subject areas and programs (e.g., bilingual) that emphasize communicative experiences (Galguera and Hakuta).

Parents and Home Environment

Parent involvement programs enhance student learning and engagement in school, and contribute to a school culture that reflects community values.

Parents can be part of the everyday life of schools. They can amplify the beneficial values, opportunities, and learning activities children experience at school and in the local community. In Part Three, two of the chapters address the role of parents and the home (Walberg and Paik, Galguera and Hakuta). Parental involvement practices, such as parenting-skills classes, membership on school governance teams, and literacy training can connect schools to communities and foster student success (Walberg and Paik). Effective bilingual programs are likely to incorporate linguistic and ethnic diversity in their schools' culture and create an informal, familial atmosphere (Galguera and Hakuta). Family involvement provides teachers with background about the community's cultural experiences. These experiences can be related to curriculum content and students' prior knowledge and, ultimately, make children's learning easier.

Local Communities

> Incorporating the values and concerns of local communities contributes to positive school cultures that reflect the interests and values of their students and families.

Two of the chapters (Kaplan and Maehr, Galguera and Hakuta) show how local communities influence school cultures. As some communities become more culturally, linguistically, and economically diverse, schools will be educating children with vastly different prior experiences. Empowering students requires familiarity with their strengths, interests, values, and cultural experiences. The creation of optimal school, program, and classroom learning environments may require integrating the culture, experiences, and values of the local community.

References

Walberg, H. J., and Haertel, G. D. (1992). Educational psychology's first century. *Journal of Educational Psychology.* *84* (1), 1–14.

Contributors' Biographies

Phyllis C. Blumenfeld received her Ph.D. from the University of California, Los Angeles, and is Professor of Education at the University of Michigan. She teaches in the Combined Program in Education and Psychology. Dr. Blumenfeld's research focuses on how teacher behavior and classroom tasks influence student motivation. She has written about how classrooms affect student perceptions of ability, responsibility, and goals. Currently, she is working on how project-based instruction affects student knowledge, thought, and motivation.

Jere Brophy received his Ph.D. from the University of Chicago, and then for eight years was a faculty member in the College of Education at the University of Texas at Austin. For the last twenty years, he has been in the College of Education at Michigan State University, where he has served as Co-director of the Institute for Research on Teaching and currently is University Distinguished Professor of Teacher Education. He has authored, co-authored, or edited more than twenty books and more than 250 articles, chapters, and technical reports on teacher expectations and the dynamics of teacher-student interaction, classroom management, teacher effects, motivating students to learn, teaching school subjects for understanding and use of knowledge, and teaching and learning in social studies.

Ann L. Brown received her Ph.D. in psychology at the University of London, England. She has been a faculty member of the University of Sussex, England, the University of Illinois, and the School of Education at the University of California, Berkeley. An expert in cognitive science, she has published widely on such topics as memory strategies, reading comprehension, analogical thinking, self-regulated learning, metacognition, and reciprocal teaching. Presently her research focuses on students as researchers and teachers within a wider community of learners. She has received many honors and awards for distinguished contributions to educational research, including a Guggenheim Fellowship, a Spencer Senior Fellowship, the Lifetime Achievement Award from AERA, APA Distinguished Scientific Award for the Applications of Psychology (1995) and membership in the National Academy of Education. She served as President of the American Educational Research Association in 1993-1994.

Stephanie Zweig Corrigan received her initial teaching certification from the University of Tennessee in elementary education. After five years teaching in the middle grades, she returned to graduate school. She received a master's degree in curriculum and instruction from Peabody College at Vanderbilt University and a doctorate in curriculum and instruction from the University of Virginia. She is currently on the faculty at Mississippi State University. Her area of research interest is prospective teachers' beliefs about management and instruction in classrooms with diverse pupil populations.

Gary A. Davis is Professor Emeritus of Educational Psychology at the University of Wisconsin, Madison. He is author of many articles in the areas of creativity, gifted education, values education, and effective schooling, and of many books, including *Education of the Gifted and Talented* (with Sylvia Rimm), *Handbook of Gifted Education* (with Nicholas Colangelo), *Creativity Is Forever, Teaching Values, Values Are Forever, Educational Psychology,* and *Effective Schools and Effective Teachers.* He is a reviewing editor for *Journal of Creative Behavior, Creativity Research Journal, Roeper Review,* and *Gifted Child Quarterly.*

Carolyn M. Evertson received her Ph.D. from the University of Texas at Austin and is Professor of Education and Chair of the Department of Teaching and Learning, Peabody College, Vanderbilt University. She was named Harvie Branscomb Distinguished Professor for Vanderbilt University in 1992. She has published numerous books, handbook chapters, and articles about teacher education, learning to teach, creating and managing learning environments, and the culture of the classroom, including two books: *Learning from Teaching* and *Student Characteristics and Teaching,* with Jere Brophy. Her texts for preservice teachers, *Classroom Management for Elementary Teachers* and *Classroom Management for Secondary Teachers* (co-authored with Edmund Emmer, Barbara Clements, and Murray Worsham) are soon to be published in their fourth editions.

Martin E. Ford is Professor of Education and Associate Dean at George Mason University's Graduate School of Education. He earned his Ph.D. in 1980 from the University of Minnesota's Institute of Child Development, and has received Early Career Contribution awards from two American Psychological Association divisions (7 and 15). His current work addresses the motivational foundations of personality, intelligence, and competence development. He is the creator of Motivational Systems Theory (*Motivating Humans: Goals, Emotions, and Personal Agency Beliefs,* Sage Publications 1992) and author of over fifty articles, books, and book chapters. He is also co-editor with his father, Donald Ford, of a volume designed to illustrate the utility of a living systems approach for human development researchers and professionals (*Humans as Self-Constructing Living Systems: Putting the Framework to Work,* Erlbaum 1987).

Barry J. Fraser is Professor of Education and Director of the federally funded Key Centre for School Science and Mathematics at Curtin University of Technology in Perth, Australia. He was President of the National Association for Research Science Teaching in the U.S.A. during 1995-1996 and is Executive Director of the International Academy of Education. He received his Ph.D. from Monash University. He has written hundreds of books, articles, and conference papers on topics including learning environments, science education, and curriculum evaluation. His recent books include *International Handbook of Science Education, Improving Science Education, Gender, Science and Mathematics* and *Improving Teaching and Learning in Science and Mathematics.*

Tomás Galguera is a Bilingual Research and Teaching Fellow at the Stanford Teacher Education Program, where he coordinates and teaches courses in Cross-cultural Language and Academic Development credential emphasis. Dr. Galguera received his Ph.D. from Stanford University and has published articles in *Language Learning* and the *NABE Newsletter.* His current research interests include the study of student attitudes toward teachers' bilinguality, ethnicity, and gender.

Geneva D. Haertel is Senior Research Associate at Temple University's Center for Research in Human Development and Education, where she conducts research syntheses on the achievement of children at risk of school failure. Dr. Haertel received her Ph.D. from Kent State University. She has published over forty-five articles in educational and psychological journals and books. In 1990, she co-edited *The International Encyclopedia of Educational Evaluation* with Herbert Walberg. Her recent publications include a research synthesis, "Toward a Knowledge Base of School Learning," which she co-authored with Margaret Wang and Herbert Walberg, and an article reviewing the history of educational psychology, "Educational Psychology's First Century," with Herbert Walberg.

Kenji Hakuta is Professor of Education at Stanford University, where he teaches in the Language, Literacy, and Culture and the Psychological Studies in Education programs. He received his Ph.D. in Experimental Psychology from Harvard University in 1979. His books include *Mirror of Language: The Debate on Bilingualism* (1986) and *In Other Words: The Science and Psychology of Second Language Acquisition* (1994). He is a member of the National Educational Research Policy and Priorities Board for the U.S. Department of Education.

Thomas Hatch is Research Associate at Harvard Project Zero. Currently, he is the Director of the ATLAS Seminar, in which members of the Coalition of Essential Schools, the School Development Program, the Education Development Center, and Project Zero share their research and experiences in school reform efforts around the country. Formerly, he was the Director of the Mather Afterschool Program. His research includes studies of the ways children display and develop their intelligences and interests in early education settings.

Avi Kaplan is a doctoral student in the Combined Program in Education and Psychology at the University of Michigan. He is a former high school teacher and has extensive experience in formal as well as nonformal educational settings. His research interests lie in the influence of educational environments on students' achievement, motivation, and well-being.

Mindy Kornhaber is a researcher at Harvard Project Zero. She is particularly interested in how institutions enhance or impede individual potential. This interest has led her into numerous investigations of the theory of multiple intelligences and how it is applied in various settings. She is co-author with Howard Gardner and Warren Wake of *Intelligence: Multiple Perspectives* (Harcourt Brace College Publishers, 1996).

Martin L. Maehr is Professor of Education and Psychology at the University of Michigan, Ann Arbor, where he is affiliated with the Combined Program in Education and Psychology. He was formerly Professor of Educational Psychology and Director of the Institute of Human Development at the University of Illinois, Urbana-Champaign. He is a fellow of the American Psychological Association and the American Psychological Society and the author of approximately one hundred articles and research reports. His most recent book (with Carol Midgely) is entitled *Transforming School Cultures*. Together with Paul Pintrich he edits a series of scholarly books entitled "Advances in Motivation and Achievement."

Ronald W. Marx is Professor of Education and Chair of the Educational Studies Program at the University of Michigan. He has conducted classroom-based experimental and observational research focusing on how classrooms can be sites for learning that is motivating and cognitively engaging. In the late 1980s, he conducted policy research in British Columbia that led to substantial reform of the province's schools. Recently, he has been working with computer scientists, science educators, and educational psychologists to enhance science education and to develop teacher professional development models to sustain long-term change in science education.

Robert J. Mislevy is Principal Research Scientist in the Model-Based Measurement Group at Educational Testing Service. He earned his Ph.D. at the University of Chicago. Dr. Mislevy's research interests center on applying developments in statistical methodology and cognitive research to practical problems in educational and psychological testing, and he has published over fifty articles and chapters and has edited volumes on these topics. He twice received the National Council of Measurement in Education's Triennial Award for Technical Contributions to Educational Measurement, the first for the multiple imputation methodology used in the National Assessment of Educational Progress. He was President of the Psychometric Society in 1993-1994.

Greta Morine-Dershimer is Professor of Curriculum and Instruction in the Curry School of Education, University of Virginia, having also served there as Director of Teacher Education and Senior Researcher in the Commonwealth Center for the Education of Teachers. She is a past Vice-president of the American Educational Research Association, Division K (Teaching and Teacher Education). Her research focuses on teacher and pupil cognitions. She is author of six books, twenty book chapters, and numerous articles and technical research reports, and serves on the editorial boards of two international journals.

Larry P. Nucci is Professor of Education and Psychology at the University of Illinois at Chicago, where he also serves as Director of the Office for Studies in Moral Development and Character Formation. Dr. Nucci received his Ph.D. in Psychology from the University of California, Santa Cruz. He was a Fulbright Fellow in Brazil, and a Visiting Professor at Fribourg University, Switzerland. He has published extensively in the area of moral and social development, and has served on the Board of the Association of Moral Education. He is the editor of *Moral Development and Character Education: A Dialogue,* published by McCutchan Publishing, 1989.

Susan J. Paik is a doctoral student in educational psychology, educational consultant, and former Program Coordinator of Early Outreach at the University of Illinois at Chicago, where she coordinated academic enrichment for underserved students. She has spoken on motivation in about fifty Chicago schools and founded a program for inner-city youth to improve their life chances. Interested in evaluation and international program development, she has worked in eleemosynary projects in China, Honduras, Hong Kong, Korea, and Macau. She is also interested in cross-cultural family dynamics as they affect learning and development. Her current projects include value-added assessment in education and automated content analysis on world education goals.

Roy D. Pea is the Director of the Center for Technology in Learning and Principal Scientist at SRI International in Menlo Park, California. From 1991-1996, he was John Evans Professor of Education and the Learning Sciences at Northwestern University, and from 1993-1996, served as Dean of its School of Education and Social Policy. He works as a cognitive scientist to integrate theory, research, and the design of effective learning environments using advanced technologies, with particular focus on science, mathematics, and technology. Dr. Pea has published one book and over eighty articles. He was formerly Senior Research Scientist at the Institute for Research on Learning, and Associate

Director of the Center for Children and Technology, Bank Street College of Education. His awards include a Rhodes Scholarship, Schumann Fellowship (Harvard University), and Fellow, Center for Advanced Study in the Behavioral Sciences. He is also a Fellow of the American Psychological Society.

Lauren Resnick is Professor of Psychology and Director of the Learning Research and Development Center at the University of Pittsburgh. She specializes in the cognitive science of learning and instruction. She is also Co-director of New Standards, a consortium of states and school districts setting shared performance standards and building examinations that will yield an internationally benchmarked system of standards and authentic assessments for American students. Professor Resnick serves on the Board of Directors of the National Center on Education and the Economy, the Harvard University Board of Overseers, and the Smithsonian Council. She was the founding editor of *Cognition and Instruction* and author of a widely circulated monograph commissioned by the National Academy of Sciences, *Education and Learning to Think.*

Maynard C. Reynolds is Professor Emeritus (Education Psychology), University of Minnesota and Senior Research Associate, Center for Research on Human Development and Education, Temple University. He is a past president of the Council for Exceptional Children and received that organization's highest honor, the Wallin Award. He has written and edited forty books and numerous articles, mainly on exceptional children. In 1989, he edited the book entitled *Knowledge Base for Beginning Teachers* for the American Association of Colleges for Teacher Education.

Robert J. Sternberg is IBM Professor of Psychology and Education at Yale University. He has won numerous awards, including the Outstanding Book, Research Review, and Scribner Awards of AERA. He is a past President of Division 15 (Educational Psychology) of the American Psychological Association, and is editor of the Educational Psychology series with Erlbaum publishers. As past editor of the *Psychological Bulletin*, Dr. Sternberg has written about six hundred books and articles. His research on education is supported by the OERI of the U.S. Department of Education.

Herbert J. Walberg is Research Professor of Education and Psychology at the University of Illinois at Chicago, and has served on the National Assessment Governing Board, which is referred to as the "national school board" due to its mission to set education standards. Dr. Walberg holds a Ph.D. from the University of Chicago and was Assistant Professor at Harvard University. He has edited more than fifty books and written articles on such topics as educational productivity and exceptional human accomplishments. A fellow of four academic organizations, Dr. Walberg has won a number of awards and prizes for his scholarship and is one of three U.S. members of the International Academy of Education.

Margaret C. Wang is Professor of Educational Psychology, founder and Director of the Center for Research in Human Development and Education (CRHDE) at Temple University, and Director of both the National Center on Education in the Inner Cities (CEIC) and the Mid-Atlantic Laboratory for Student Success. Dr. Wang has published fourteen books and over one hundred articles; she is recognized for her research on student diversity and urban school politics, which has positioned her in leadership and policy-development roles at the national and international levels.

Suzanne M. Wilson is a Professor in the Department of Teacher Education at Michigan State University, and she received a Ph.D. in Educational Psychology from Stanford University. She has been a high school mathematics and social studies teacher, an elementary school teacher, a teacher educator, and a researcher. Her research interests include the professional knowledge base of teaching, the role of subject matter in teaching, and the relationship between curricular policies and teaching practices. She is currently completing a book on ten years of mathematics education reform efforts in California.

Index

DATE DUE

JE-1 '99			
JUL - 2 6 1999			
JE 25 W			
OC 25 00			
NOV 3 0 2001			
ILL			
569058			
11/14/02			